THE PREACHING OF
JONATHAN EDWARDS

THE PREACHING OF
JONATHAN
EDWARDS

John Carrick

THE BANNER OF TRUTH TRUST

THE BANNER OF TRUTH TRUST
3 Murrayfield Road, Edinburgh EH12 6EL, UK
P.O. Box 621, Carlisle, PA 17013, USA

*

© John Carrick 2008

*

ISBN-13: 978 0 85151 983 8

*

Typeset in 10.5/13.5 Adobe Caslon Pro at
The Banner of Truth Trust, Edinburgh

Printed in the U.S.A. by
Versa Press, Inc.,
East Peoria, IL

To
LINDA

Contents

PREFACE

In 1977, when I was still working as a schoolmaster in Somerset, England, I travelled up to London to consult Dr Martyn Lloyd-Jones with regard to entering the ministry. In the course of our conversation at his home in Ealing, I asked him if he would give me some advice on the matter of reading. Without any hesitation he replied, 'Read Jonathan Edwards!' I had, in fact, already acquired a copy of the two-volume Banner of Truth edition of Edwards' Works and had begun to read them; but Dr Lloyd-Jones' advice spurred me on to read Edwards more, and I began to read his sermons and treatises with greater vigour. Thus began my interest in and love for the great American preacher-philosopher-theologian—an interest and a love that have lasted more than thirty years.

Some ten years later, when I was ministering in Cheltenham, England, I had the privilege of engaging in research, under Paul Helm of Liverpool University, on the concept of divine immediacy in the thought of Edwards. Every few months I would travel up to Liverpool and discuss, over lunch, in what was, in effect, a tutorial, various related aspects of Edwards' thought. My contact with Professor Helm introduced me to the ever-expanding field of Edwards scholarship and opened my eyes to the sheer depth and riches of Edwards' thought.

In 2002, by which time I was teaching Homiletics at Greenville Presbyterian Theological Seminary, in South Carolina, U.S.A.,

I received an invitation to give two lectures on the preaching of Jonathan Edwards at the Banner of Truth Conference to be held the following year in Grantham, Pennsylvania. It was thus that I turned my attention again to Edwards' sermons. In preparing for these lectures I realized that my research had potentially laid a foundation for a book on Edwards' preaching; and when I returned from the conference in May 2003, I began to write. Five years later this book is, by God's grace, the result.

I would like to take this opportunity to express my appreciation to Dr Joseph A. Pipa, Jr., the President of Greenville Seminary, for the support and encouragement which he has, from the beginning, afforded me in this project. I want to thank Dr Wilson H. Kimnach, Presidential Professor in the Humanities at the University of Bridgeport, for his kindly making his pre-publication manuscript of volume 25 in the Yale series available to me. I wish to thank Dr Kenneth P. Minkema, the Executive Director of the Jonathan Edwards Center at Yale University, for his kind helpfulness in sharing his knowledge and in graciously answering a number of questions in matters Edwardsean. I would also like to thank Dr George M. Marsden, the Francis A. McAnaney Professor of History at the University of Notre Dame, who kindly reviewed a number of chapters and who made some very helpful suggestions. I wish also to record a special word of gratitude to Professor Paul Helm, Teaching Fellow at Regent College, Vancouver, who graciously reviewed my entire manuscript and who made some invaluable recommendations. Professor Helm has been a kind mentor and friend to me, and I owe him an incalculable debt.

As one that 'hunts and pecks' his way across the laptop, I would like to take this opportunity to thank my friends at Greenville Seminary who have, over the years, helped me out of many a technological scrape! I would also like to thank my mother-in-law, Mrs Thelma Rutland, who, on our visits to her home, patiently allowed me to sit for many hours each day on my 'perch' (as I called it) at her kitchen table, where many pages of this book were written. Last, but not least, I would like to thank my wife, Linda, for her patience, support, and encouragement over the last five or six years as I have pored over Edwards' sermons and treatises. It is to her that I devote this book.

JOHN CARRICK
Greenville Presbyterian Theological Seminary
April 2008

I

The Edwards Legacy

'O what a legacy my husband, and your father, has left us!'[1] It was thus that Sarah Edwards wrote from Stockbridge to her daughter, Esther Edwards Burr, on April 3, 1758, just twelve days after the death of Jonathan Edwards as a result of complications from a smallpox vaccination. On February 16 Edwards had been officially installed as President of the College of New Jersey (Nassau Hall) in Princeton, and thus entered what would have been, after Northampton and Stockbridge, the third major phase of his ministerial career. One week later he was inoculated against the smallpox that was rampant in the area. At first all went well; but before long he contracted the disease itself on the roof of his mouth and in his throat. Soon he was unable to swallow, and after weeks of fever and inevitable starvation, he fell asleep in Christ on the afternoon of March 22.[2]

Edwards' own death occurred in the midst of a remarkable cluster of deaths within his extended family. On September 24 of the previous year he had lost his son-in-law, Aaron Burr (1716-1757), at the age of 41. On January 27, 1758, he had lost his father, Timothy Edwards (1669-1758), in his eighty-ninth year. Esther Burr was never to receive the letter sent to her by her mother, for she died of a fever on April 7, leaving two orphaned children. Sarah Edwards, who had faced the responsibility of moving the family to Princeton to join her husband, now faced the responsibility of taking care of her two orphaned grandchildren, one of whom was Aaron Burr, Jr., the future vice-president.

[1] *Works* (Hickman), 1:clxxix.
[2] See George M. Marsden, *Jonathan Edwards: A Life* (New Haven and London: Yale University Press, 2003), p. 493. I am indebted to Marsden's fine biography for a number of these details.

Thus in September she travelled *via* Princeton to Philadelphia to pick up the children, but was seized with dysentery and died on October 2 at the age of forty-eight. She was buried next to her husband in Princeton. Thus the Edwards family had lost five very significant members within twelve months. Elizabeth D. Dodds has remarked that the Edwards narrative ends like 'a Shakespearean tragedy where bodies strew a stage'.[3] It is a striking testimony to that truth of life's uncertainty and man's frailty which Edwards himself had so emphatically, consistently, and faithfully preached throughout a ministry that spanned over thirty-five years.

But the legacy remains, and it is a colossal legacy. 'This towering edifice',[4] as Perry Miller described it in 1957, is, in fact, remarkably multifaceted. It includes a *theological* legacy, a *philosophical* legacy, and a *homiletical* legacy, any one of which would, in its own right, unquestionably have earned for its author a very significant place in either ecclesiastical or intellectual history. On the ecclesiastical front, for instance, it is incontrovertible that his influence upon the British Isles has been colossal. David W. Bebbington describes him as 'the American theologian who stands at the headwaters of [British] evangelicalism.'[5] Ironically, one of the earliest channels of Edwards' influence was that of John Wesley. Wesley showed particular interest in his writings on revival and spiritual experience – works such as *A Faithful Narrative, The Distinguishing Marks of a Work of the Spirit of God, Some Thoughts on the Revival, The Life of David Brainerd,* and *Religious Affections.* Wesley had these works published in England. It is important to note, however, that, as D. Bruce Hindmarsh explains, Wesley's editions of Edwards' works in this area 'did much to *popularize* a certain version of Edwards for large numbers of English evangelicals ... But they ... popularized an Edwards who was shorn of his Calvinism.'[6] Wesley's somewhat

---

[3] Cited ibid., p. 598 n. 23.

[4] *Works,* 1:vii.

[5] Cited David W. Kling and Douglas A. Sweeney, 'Introduction', in *Jonathan Edwards at Home and Abroad: Historical Memories, Cultural Movements, Global Horizons,* David W. Kling and Douglas A. Sweeney, eds. (Columbia: University of South Carolina Press, 2003), p. xiv.

[6] D. Bruce Hindmarsh, 'The Reception of Jonathan Edwards by Early Evangelicals in England', in *Jonathan Edwards at Home and Abroad,* p. 204.

high-handed anti-Calvinistic pen simply expurgated all Calvinistic elements that offended.

Edwards' influence amongst the Particular (or Calvinistic) Baptists in England in the latter decades of the eighteenth century was powerful and salutary. It was, notes Hindmarsh, in the 1760's and especially in the 1770's that Andrew Fuller and others 'began to read Edwards carefully for themselves and to see the revolutionary implications of his writings'.[7] For a number of decades the Particular Baptists, who had succumbed to a 'high Calvinism' or 'Hyper-Calvinism', had been wrestling with the question of 'duty faith', that is, the question as to whether it is properly the duty of the unconverted to believe the gospel, and the corollary of this question, whether it is the duty of the preacher to command the unconverted to repent and believe. Edwards' *Freedom of the Will* (1754) constituted a colossal theological counterblast, not only to Arminianism, but also to this prevalent Hyper-Calvinism, and Fuller, who read this treatise in the late 1770's, was persuaded by it to espouse a more evangelical Calvinism. Indeed, Fuller described it as 'a book which has been justly said to go further toward settling the main points in controversy between the Calvinists and the Arminians, than any thing that has been wrote.'[8] In 1785 Fuller published his *Gospel Worthy of all Acceptation*. A new spirit of optimism and expectancy arose in Baptist circles in the 1780's and 1790's, and the tendency towards stagnation produced by the Hyper-Calvinism of earlier decades gave way to an evangelical Calvinism that placed great emphasis upon means, activity, evangelism, missionary enterprise, and prayer. In 1792 the Baptist Missionary Society was founded which sent William Carey to India, and when Carey left the shores of England he took with him a copy of Edwards' *Life of Brainerd*, which he regarded as "'almost a second Bible"'.[9]

---

[7] Ibid., p. 208.

[8] Cited Mark Noll, 'Jonathan Edwards's Freedom of the Will Abroad', in *Jonathan Edwards at 300: Essays on the Tercentenary of His Birth*, Harry S. Stout, Kenneth P. Minkema, and Caleb J. D. Maskell, eds. (Lanham: University Press of America, Inc., 2005), p. 104.

[9] Cited David W. Bebbington, 'Remembered around the World: The International Scope of Edwards's Legacy', in *Jonathan Edwards at Home and Abroad*, p. 186.

Thus towards the end of the eighteenth century there emerged in Baptist circles (and elsewhere) what Hindmarsh describes as 'a revised Calvinistic framework that would accommodate higher views of human agency and mission activity'.[10] Roger Hayden summarizes Edwards' influence thus:

> Jonathan Edwards's impact on eighteenth-century Baptists in Britain is almost incapable of exaggeration. Out of his experience of revival and through his theological and narrative writing he produced evidence for a vital evangelical Calvinism which could stand side by side with the vitality of the Wesleyan movement. He produced theological keys which unlocked the closed doors of hyper-Calvinism with absolutely no concessions to Arminianism or antinomianism. He fired the English Particular Baptist imagination with his own involvement with revival and his description of the remarkable missionary endeavours of David Brainerd among the American Indians. What English Baptists yearned for, as the Association letters testify so often, Edwards was able to demonstrate as the true heart of the old Puritan Gospel – an evangelical Calvinism which could legitimately reach out into all the world with the gospel of Christ.[11]

It was in Presbyterian Scotland, however, that Edwards' influence was, perhaps, greatest. It was *via* a transatlantic network of correspondence that 'the Edwards-Scotland connection',[12] as Christopher W. Mitchell terms it, was established. At the centre of this network were four of the most prominent evangelical ministers of the Church of Scotland: John MacLaurin of Glasgow, William McCulloch of Cambuslang, James Robe of Kilsyth, and John Erskine of Edinburgh. Erskine was to become Edwards' chief publicist in Scotland. The context and the catalyst for this connection was that of the revivals in New England. Edwards' *A Faithful Narrative* was first published in London in 1737; it was reprinted in Edinburgh in the same year and in the following

[10] Hindmarsh, p. 212.

[11] Cited ibid., p. 211.

[12] Christopher W. Mitchell, 'Jonathan Edwards's Scottish Connection', in *Jonathan Edwards at Home and Abroad*, p. 222. I am indebted to Mitchell for a number of details in this paragraph.

year. 'Edwards' astonishing narrative created an immediate stir', notes Marsden. 'It served as an inspiration for revivals in both Scotland and England.'[13] Indeed, Mitchell contends that, in the 1730's and 1740's Edwards produced 'the most enlightened, most articulate and influential presentation and defense of revivalism and evangelical Calvinism published in the eighteenth century. It is not at all surprising, therefore, to find that these Scottish ministers initiated the relationship, actively promoted his work, sought his counsel, and enlisted his help. In fact, due to their efforts, Edwards became one of the chief advocates of Scottish evangelical Calvinism in the eighteenth century without ever crossing the Atlantic.'[14] Mitchell goes on to make this assertion:

> In the end, his efforts helped his Scottish friends redefine Scottish evangelical Calvinism by adapting it from its old didactic/catechizing function within a godly commonwealth, to a more mission-oriented role where the faith of the individual became prominent and the pursuit of sanctification, not salvation, defined the Christian's life. One of the most far-reaching results of this shift was the growth of Scottish missions.[15]

But it was not merely his writings on revival and conversion that attracted Scottish evangelical Calvinists; it was also his most profound theological and philosophical works. Marsden observes that '*Freedom of the Will* had an immense influence for at least a century, especially in Scotland and America.'[16] Thomas Chalmers, the virtual leader of the Free Church of Scotland at the time of the Disruption in 1843, stated his position thus at the end of his life: 'My theology is that of Jonathan Edwards.'[17]

On the intellectual front it is equally incontrovertible that Edwards holds a position of the highest rank. The tributes which his legacy has elicited in the last two hundred and fifty years demonstrate this fact. Dugald Stewart (1753-1828), who occupied the Chair of Moral Phil-

---

[13] Marsden, *Edwards*, pp. 172-173.
[14] Mitchell, pp. 222-223.
[15] Ibid., p. 223.
[16] Marsden, *Edwards*, p. 446.
[17] Cited Bebbington, p. 185.

osophy at Edinburgh University from 1785 to 1810, having examined the systems of Locke, Leibnitz, Berkeley, and Condillac, made this observation: 'There is, however, *one* metaphysician, of whom America has to boast, who, in logical acuteness and subtilty, does not yield to any disputant bred in the universities of Europe. I need not say that I allude to Jonathan Edwards.'[18] Perry Miller (1905-1963), Cabot Professor of American Literature at Harvard University, gave this assessment of *Freedom of the Will:* 'Beyond all peradventure, the *Freedom of the Will* is the cornerstone of Edwards' fame; it is his most sustained intellectual achievement, the most powerful piece of sheer forensic argumentation in American literature. It . . . is considered by logicians one of the few proofs in which the conclusion follows inescapably and infallibly from the premises.'[19] The Yale editor, Paul Ramsey, describes *Freedom of the Will* as 'a superdreadnaught which Edwards sent forth to combat contingency and self-determination'.[20] "'Edwards on the Will'", observes Allen C. Guelzo, '—no single title in American literature has ever had quite the ring of finality, of unquestioned settlement of dispute, as this.'[21] 'Its power, it can be argued', contends Marsden, 'was a significant factor in the intellectual resilience and influence of Calvinism in America well into the nineteenth century.'[22] Marsden further notes that 'for about half a century from 1800 to 1850, Edwards was the polestar of the most formidable and influential American theology.'[23]

---

[18] *Works* (Hickman), 1:clxxxviii.

[19] Perry Miller, *Jonathan Edwards* (New York: W. Sloane Associates, 1949; reprint, Amherst: The University of Massachusetts Press, 1981), p. 251.

[20] *Works,* 1:2.

[21] Allen C. Guelzo, *Edwards on the Will: A Century of American Theological Debate* (Middletown, Connecticut: Wesleyan University Press, 1989), p. 1.

[22] Marsden, *Edwards,* p. 446.

[23] Ibid., p. 499. Marsden echoes here the view of B. B. Warfield: 'The movement against Calvinism which was overspreading the land was in a great measure checked, and the elimination of Calvinism as a determining factor in the thought of New England, which seemed to be imminent as he wrote, was postponed for more than a hundred years.' B. B. Warfield, 'Edwards and the New England Theology', in *The Works of Benjamin B. Warfield,* vol. 9 (New York: Oxford University Press, 1932; reprint, Grand Rapids, Michigan: Baker Book House, 1981), p. 532.

It is important to note, however, that from the mid-nineteenth century onwards the Edwardsean legacy in America underwent a significant period of eclipse. Marsden explains that this eclipse was the inevitable corollary of the collapse of New England Calvinism itself:

> By the late nineteenth century, however, rigorous Calvinist theology was in full retreat in most American cultural centers, and Edwards' reputation suffered accordingly. All but a dwindling group of ardent followers jettisoned the particulars of his Calvinist teachings. Oliver Wendell Holmes Sr. entertained his contemporaries with 'The Deacon's Masterpiece, or The Wonderful "One-Hoss Shay"' (1858), which lampooned the dramatic collapse of New England Calvinism. The heirs of Charles Chauncy had finally won a long-standing battle for cultural supremacy . . .
>
> By the early decades of the twentieth century . . . Puritan bashing had become widely acceptable as a way for progressive Americans to free themselves from Victorian moralism. Edwards was an easy target. This was the era of the invention of American literature as a field of study and the canonization of Holmes' 'One-Hoss Shay' and of *Sinners in the Hands of an Angry God*. The latter fixed Edwards in the public mind as simply a hell-fire preacher.[24]

It is an interesting and significant fact that, at the time of the Edwards bicentennial in 1903, the Edwards manuscripts were stored in a vault in the bowels of Sterling Library at Yale.[25] The legacy of one of Yale's greatest sons – indeed, perhaps her greatest son – lay neglected and unvalued by his own *alma mater*. 'He must be counted obscure and little known', contends John F. Wilson, 'except perhaps as a negative reference point, from the mid-nineteenth century at least until after the First World War.'[26]

In a cogent, incisive article entitled 'Jonathan Edwards and His Detractors' Clyde A. Holbrook noted that, historically, there have been two broad lines of criticism with regard to President Edwards. The first

---

[24] Marsden, *Edwards*, pp. 500-501.

[25] I am indebted to Stephen D. Crocco, 'Perry Miller and the Early Years of the Yale Edition of "The Works of Jonathan Edwards"', TMs, Princeton Theological Seminary, July 1999, p. 4, for this fact.

[26] *Works*, 9:84-85.

of these lines is one that might be described as that of *an almost hysterical denunciation:*

> With the passing of time two general directions of criticism have been developing. The first of these lines of thought centers upon the almost completely negative thesis that Edwards as a man and as a thinker was an evil force, a kind of blunder in the plans of the Almighty, whose influence was destructive of human hopes and freedom and whose horrendous conception of God set back the American religious consciousness to the dark ages . . . Indeed for his own day and ours, original sin, infant damnation, and divine sovereignty had become too strong a dose for those whose personal security rested in the ordered amiability of the natural world, the innate virtue of men, and the tender rational benevolence of a loving heavenly Father. The Northampton pastor and theologian played traitor to the emerging American dream of self-sufficiency, self-reliance, and that peculiar utilitarianism which conceives God as a convenient tool for the self-perfection of Western man.[27]

The second of these two lines of criticism noted by Holbrook is one that might be described as that of *an admiring pity:*

> A second general type of appraisal deals more gently with Edwards. The favorite word found among these scholars is 'tragic.' Edwards here appears as a genius or near-genius who for one reason or another missed the way to the highest fulfillment of his remarkable powers. A sad shake of the head rather than the denunciatory finger is in order. One typical expression of this is found in T. H.

[27] Clyde A. Holbrook, 'Jonathan Edwards and His Detractors', *Theology Today* 10 (1953): 386. Michael J. McClymond, *Encounters with God: An Approach to the Theology of Jonathan Edwards* (New York: Oxford University Press, 1998), p. 114, makes this observation: 'During the late nineteenth and early twentieth centuries, Edwards evoked a rich literature of denigration.' Mark A. Noll, 'Jonathan Edwards and Nineteenth-Century Theology', in *Jonathan Edwards and the American Experience,* Nathan O. Hatch and Harry S. Stout, eds. (New York: Oxford University Press, 1988), p. 279, notes that it was JE's wounding of nineteenth-century sensitivities that lay at the heart of this denigration: 'Over and over in the nineteenth century, the attack on Edwards returned to his inadequacy with respect to modern sensitivities. His system, to cite just one of the many expressions of this complaint, was simply "contrary to the common consciousness and experiences of mankind". No one expressed this opinion with greater force than Oliver Wendell Holmes, a Unitarian who also spoke for those more theologically conservative than himself.'

Johnson's comment. 'One of the greatest of the many tragedies in Edwards's life is strikingly seen in his refusal or failure to use with any breadth of application the full power of a mind that had the rarely coupled talent for keen observation and philosophical synthesis ... One cannot refrain ... from pondering what this intellectual arm might have accomplished had it not been so tightly bound by theological dogma.' This statement touches upon several of the counts which place Edwards in the 'tragic' category. The reference to the many tragedies of his life, his uncommon talents left fallow, the implication that what he did accomplish was of transitory value compared to what might have been, and the inevitable reference to theological dogma as the throttling factor of his abilities, are all discovered in these lines.[28]

But when Holbrook penned these words in 1953, the tide had already begun to turn in Edwards' favour; indeed, Holbrook's own article itself reflects that turning of the tide. The sources of the remarkable revival of interest in Edwards' legacy since the 1930's are as surprising as they are diverse.

The first source is, interestingly, that of *neo-orthodoxy*. The 'crisis theology' of neo-orthodoxy emerged in Europe in the context of the catastrophe of the First World War (1914-1918). Karl Barth had, as a student, sat at the feet of the doyen of liberal theology, Adolph von Harnack. As a pastor in Safenwil, Switzerland, in 1914, however, Barth could actually hear 'the guns of August' in Alsace. Disillusioned by the palpable bankruptcy of liberalism, Barth rejected, during the course of the War, the naïve, easy-going optimism of Harnack's theology, and in 1919 published his famous *Römerbrief* – it 'fell like a bombshell on the playground of the theologians.'[29] David E. Wells gives this assessment of the impact of world events upon liberal theology on either side of the Atlantic:

---

[28] Ibid., pp. 388-389. Ola Elizabeth Winslow's Pulitzer Prize-winning *Jonathan Edwards 1703-1758: A Biography* (New York: The Macmillan Company, 1940) belongs to this category. See ibid., pp. 325-330.

[29] I am indebted here to Alec R. Vidler, *20th Century Defenders of the Faith: Some Theological Fashions Considered* in the *Robertson Lectures* for 1964 (London: SCM Press Ltd., 1965), pp. 84-86.

European theology reached one of its dramatic turning points shortly after the First World War. In North America it came a decade later. On both sides of the Atlantic the kingdom of God had been equated with social progress by the Protestant liberals; on both sides this equation was shattered, in the one case by war and in the other by the Great Depression. The familiar propositions of man's innate goodness and God's untroubled benevolence could no longer be squared with reality. Not only were cities and lives destroyed but so was the naïve theology of the liberals.[30]

Marsden observes that in the 1930's and 1940's 'a new Edwards – best characterized as the neo-orthodox Edwards – was emerging. This new trend was signaled in 1932 by the publication of theologian A. C. McGiffert's sympathetic biography and the more explicitly neo-orthodox Joseph Haroutunian's *Piety versus Moralism: The Passing of the New England Theology* ... H. Richard Niebuhr in a number of influential publications from the 1930's through the 1950's also celebrated what he saw as the essence of Edwards' theology, even while moving far from most of its particulars.'[31] McGiffert had attacked the 'saccharine sentimentality about the fatherhood of God'[32] by which modern religious liberalism was characterized; and in 1937 Niebuhr (1894-1962), in *The Kingdom of God in America,* had attacked the naïve optimism of liberal theology in America with this incisive analysis: 'A God without wrath brought men without sin into a kingdom without judgment through the ministrations of a Christ without a cross.'[33] Holbrook demonstrates that the rise of neo-orthodoxy involved a revival of interest in the doctrine of man's innate corruption:

In the middle decades of the twentieth century (*circa* 1930-1960) with the appearance of Neoorthodox theology, a vigorous dispute broke out over the doctrine of original sin. Not since Jonathan

[30] David E. Wells, *The Search for Salvation* (Eugene, OR: Wipf and Stock Publishers, 2000), p. 53.

[31] Marsden, *Edwards,* p. 501.

[32] Arthur Cushman McGiffert, Jr., *Jonathan Edwards* (New York and London: Harper and Brothers Publishers, 1932), p. 173.

[33] H. Richard Niebuhr, *The Kingdom of God in America* (Hamden, Connecticut: The Shoe String Press, 1956), p. 193.

Edwards attempted to repair the fortunes of that unpalatable doctrine had there been such a stir over a matter that sophisticated minds had long since consigned to the theological rubbish heap . . . The theological temper of the late nineteenth and early twentieth centuries virtually disposed of the doctrine or had so interpreted it that it lost whatever relevance it had once had to the theological agenda. Then the Neoorthodox theology resurrected the category of original sin, to the acute discomfiture of moral philosophers and Protestant liberal theologians.[34]

Thus the theology of Karl Barth both reflected and fostered a climate that was now much more sympathetic to the theology of the New England divine. Conrad Cherry observes that 'whatever quarrel one may have with specific features of the theologies' of the neo-orthodox, they had 'reclaimed Augustinian and Calvinist categories in order to prick the contemporary conscience, wean man from religious sentimentality, and throw him up against the hard reality of a God who judges as well as forgives.'[35] The grim realities of life both in Europe and in America in the first half of the twentieth century had forced a reconsideration of the theology of the New England preacher-theologian who had lived two hundred years earlier.

The second source is, remarkably, that of *atheism*. Marsden notes the close historical connection between neo-orthodox interest and atheistic interest in Edwards: 'At the same time, and closely related, was the emergence of the scholar's Edwards. Miller contributed immeasurably to this trend with the publication of his intellectual biography in 1949, characterizing Edwards as America's greatest genius and as a profound modern philosopher who happened to use Calvinistic categories. Miller thereby created the possibility of 'atheists for Edwards.' At the same time he enlisted scholars from a wide spectrum of theological or nontheological views to launch the publication of Edwards' *Works*. Since Miller's time Edwards has been a major scholarly

---

[34] Clyde A. Holbrook, 'Jonathan Edwards Addresses Some "Modern Critics" of Original Sin', *The Journal of Religion* 63 (July 1983): 211.

[35] Conrad Cherry, *The Theology of Jonathan Edwards: A Reappraisal* (New York: Anchor Books, 1966), p. 6.

industry.'[36] Indeed, but for the persistent agitation for and promotion of the republication of Edwards' manuscripts by the Harvard scholar, they might well have continued to lie in shameful neglect. 'My main effort', wrote Miller in 1948, 'is to get Yale excited about its own.'[37] 'He is unique, an aboriginal and monolithic power.'[38]

'In time', observes M. X. Lesser, 'the eighteenth-century pastor came to dominate the twentieth-century intellectual historian, and, in time, Miller's labors came to dominate the labors of others.'[39] Ramsey, the editor enlisted by Miller in the republication of *Freedom of the Will*, made this observation: 'Its publication is a consequence of the growing interest during recent years in the study of American intellectual history in general and of Edwards in particular . . . Not for the past hundred years has serious work been done on Edwards' texts, nor has there been much concern to keep his writings readily available to the republic of readers. In comparison with the frequent publication of Edwards' writings during the first hundred years, we have been exceedingly improvident of our heritage.'[40] There can be no doubt but that Miller has played a colossal role in the mid-twentieth century in the recovery of that heritage and in the rehabilitation of the philosopher-theologian-preacher. Miller clearly shared with the neo-orthodox the conviction that the catastrophic events of world history in the first half of the twentieth century constituted a very significant catalyst in the disillusionment with the naïve *shibboleths* of liberal theology and thus in the revival of interest in the New England divine. Writing in his capacity as general editor of the definitive Yale edition of Edwards' *Works* in 1957, Miller made this observation:

> The very existence of the project is itself testimony to the deepening appreciation in the mid-twentieth century of the importance of Edwards to the intellectual as well as to the religious history of America. A generation or so ago, outside a restricted circle of professional theologians, he was popularly known only as one who

---

[36] Marsden, *Edwards*, pp. 501-502.

[37] Cited Crocco, p. 5.

[38] Miller, *Edwards*, p. xxxii.

[39] M. X. Lesser, *Jonathan Edwards* (Boston: Twayne Publishers, 1988), p. 125.

[40] *Works*, 1:119.

had preached a distasteful and happily outmoded brand of hell-fire and brimstone. There was, in fact, a general disposition to pass him over as an anachronism, as retrograde. Recent events in world history have no doubt stimulated drastic re-examination of such complacent assumptions.[41]

Thus the events that unfolded on the stage of world history between the Edwards bicentennial in 1903 and the Edwards tercentenary in 2003 have been such that they have provided colossal empirical support for the anthropology of the New England divine. More precisely, it was the catalyst of two catastrophic world wars which, on conservative estimates, cost the lives of at least 50 million people that stimulated the 'drastic re-examination of such complacent assumptions'. Indeed, the events of the first half of the twentieth century have provided massive corroboration of the truth of Edwards' position in *Original Sin* (1758) with regard to the sheer, unparalleled destructiveness of the human race:

> Here, to strengthen the argument, if there were any need of it, I might observe, not only the *extent* and *generality* of the prevalence of wickedness in the world, but the *height* to which it has risen, and the *degree* in which it has reigned. Among innumerable things which confirm this, I shall now only observe, The degree in which mankind have from age to age been *hurtful* one to another. Many kinds of brute animals are esteemed very noxious and destructive, many of them very fierce, voracious, and many very poisonous, and the destroying of them has always been looked upon as a public benefit: but have not mankind been a thousand times as hurtful and destructive as any one of them, yea, as all the noxious beasts, birds, fishes, and reptiles in the earth, air, and water, put together, at least of all kinds of animals that are visible? And no creature can be found any where so destructive of its own kind as man is. All others, for the most part, are harmless and peaceable, with regard to their own species. Where one wolf is destroyed by another wolf, one viper by another, probably a thousand men are destroyed by those of their own species. Well therefore might our blessed Lord

[41] Ibid., pp. vii-viii.

say, when sending forth his disciples into the world, (Matt. x. 16, 17.) 'Behold, I send you forth as sheep in the midst of wolves; – *but beware of men.*' Why do I say wolves? I send you forth into the wide world of men, that are far more hurtful and pernicious, and of whom you had much more need to beware, than of wolves.[42]

The twentieth century has been described by J. A. S. Grenville as 'history's bloodiest century'.[43] Thus, if, in the mid-eighteenth century, the New England theologian was justified in contending that 'where one wolf is destroyed by another wolf, one viper by another, probably a thousand men are destroyed by those of their own species', would he have been guilty of exaggeration if, in the light of the appalling events of the first half of the twentieth century which so palpably demonstrated 'man's inhumanity to man', he had raised the ratio from a *thousand to one* to a *million to one?* Marsden makes this observation: 'No Christian teaching has had more empirical verification during the past century than the doctrine of innate human depravity.'[44] Thus the history of the twentieth century has very significantly vindicated Edwards' essentially pessimistic, tragic view of man and the world without God; it has very significantly vindicated his biblical, Calvinistic realism and thus demonstrated the great relevance of his works. In 1953 Holbrook had predicted that 'another age may return to find in this man an interpretation of humanity and God which the liberalism of the post-Edwardean era falsified by its extravagant optimism about man and its sentimentality about God.'[45] But that age was, in fact, already dawning. In an address delivered in 1958 in Northampton, on the bicentennial of Edwards' death, Niebuhr made this significant statement: 'We have changed our minds about the truth of the many things he said. No rather, our minds have been changed by what has happened to us in our history. We have seen evil somewhat as he saw it, not because we desired to see it, but because it thrust itself upon us.'[46]

[42] *Works* (Hickman), 1:162.

[43] J. A. S. Grenville, *A History of the World in the Twentieth Century* (Cambridge, Massachusetts: The Belknap Press of Harvard University Press, 2000), p. 959.

[44] Marsden, *Edwards*, p. 458.

[45] Holbrook, *Jonathan Edwards and His Detractors*, p. 395.

[46] H. Richard Niebuhr, 'The Anachronism of Jonathan Edwards', in *H. Richard Nie-*

'By the mid-twentieth century', observes John F. Wilson, 'Edwards had emerged from a long period of scholarly neglect.'[47] The old caricatures and the old stereotypes of him as 'the misanthropic author of "Sinners in the Hands of an Angry God"'[48] and as 'a wreck on the remote sands of time'[49] were by now fading fast. Indeed, the decision by Yale University Press to publish a definitive edition of Edwards' works, commenced in 1957, reflects what C. Samuel Storms has described as 'a monumental reversal'[50] in scholarly opinion concerning the significance of the New England divine. In that same year Miller described Edwards as 'the greatest philosopher-theologian yet to grace the American scene'.[51] In 1958 Niebuhr described the Northampton pastor as 'our greatest American theologian'.[52] In 1963 Edmund S. Morgan expressed the view that 'Edwards possessed the most powerful theological mind of the eighteenth century.'[53] Although the Yale publication programme faltered somewhat in the 1960's and 1970's, Jonathan Edwards' star continued to rise in the academic world.[54] In 1988 Nathan O. Hatch

---

buhr: Theology, History, and Culture: Major Unpublished Writings, William Stacy Johnson, ed. (New Haven and London: Yale University Press, 1996), p. 133. This lecture was delivered by Niebuhr on March 9, 1958, in Northampton, Massachusetts. 'The description of Edwards as "anachronism",' explains Johnson in his 'Introduction', 'he had borrowed from Vernon Louis Parrington, who said that though Edwards was destined for intellectual eminence, he had remained, alas, a Calvinist. In contrast to Parrington, who saw in Edwards a great tragedy of brilliance turned to backwardness, Niebuhr suggests that Edwards' vision of divine sovereignty, human bondage, and the fragility of life had become, in an age of death camps and other looming holocausts, no longer as anachronistic as an earlier age had believed.' Ibid., p. xxix.

[47] *Works,* 9:85.

[48] Donald Weber, 'Introduction' to Perry Miller, *Jonathan Edwards* (Amherst: The University of Massachusetts Press, 1981), p. vi.

[49] Cited ibid., p. v. Weber is citing Stuart Pratt Sherman who, in 1915, was evaluating an essay on JE by the humanist critic, Paul Elmer More, for the Cambridge History of American Literature.

[50] C. Samuel Storms, *Tragedy in Eden: Original Sin in the Theology of Jonathan Edwards* (Lanham: University Press of America, 1985), p. 2.

[51] *Works,* 1:viii.

[52] Niebuhr, "Anachronism," p. 123.

[53] Edmund S. Morgan, *Visible Saints: The History of a Puritan Idea* (New York: New York University Press, 1963), p. 152.

[54] No volumes appeared in the Yale series during the 1960's and only three in the 1970's. John E. Smith, the general editor in 1979, explained that the two obstacles that lay in the way of more rapid progress were, firstly, the problem of insufficient funding for editors' leaves of absence, and, secondly, an underestimation of the time required in order to

and Harry S. Stout described him as 'one of America's great original minds',[55] while in the following year Ramsey wrote of him as being 'the founding father of philosophy and theology in America'.[56] In 1998 Michael J. McClymond described Edwards as 'the intellectual giant of colonial America'.[57] In 1999 Marsden reiterated the view articulated by Niebuhr that the New England divine should be regarded as 'the American Augustine'.[58] Interestingly, the very extent of the acclaim now accorded to the New England philosopher-theologian-preacher demonstrated, by contrast, the extent of the eclipse and the neglect from which he had undoubtedly suffered for a period of almost one hundred years.

It is important to note, however, that the revival of interest in and appreciation for the legacy of Jonathan Edwards in the United States in the second half of the twentieth century has not necessarily involved an endorsement of his theological position. Miller was careful to guard the Yale project from any potential misunderstanding in this respect: 'This is not to imply that today the precise doctrines that

---

transcribe, date, and edit the manuscripts. See John E. Smith, 'Summary Report of the Progress of the Yale Edition of the Works of Jonathan Edwards', *Early American Literature* 14 (Winter 1979): pp. 352-353. Smith also explained the somewhat slow appearance of the Sermons: 'The Sermons present special problems difficult to resolve. The enormous number of sermons extant seemed to indicate the need for selection, but that alternative presented a number of problems. A definitive edition must include all sermons published in Edwards' lifetime and it cannot reasonably exclude any sermons published in previous editions, especially when in many cases these sermons were not well edited. But no principle of selection can afford to overlook the fact that numerous sermons in the previous two categories are not up to the level of many unpublished sermons. Taking all these factors into account and upon discovering the inadequacy of several schemes for arranging the sermons – according to the biblical books of the texts, central topics, special occasions (e.g., funeral sermons), etc. – the Committee decided to attempt publication in chronological order of all sermons fully written out (after 1742, most are only in outline form); the estimate of twenty-five volumes for these is, if anything, conservative.' Ibid., p. 353. Ultimately, the Yale sermon corpus was limited to six volumes.

[55] Nathan O. Hatch and Harry S. Stout, 'Introduction', in *American Experience*, p. 3.

[56] *Works*, 8:120.

[57] McClymond, p. 3.

[58] Marsden, 'Jonathan Edwards, American Augustine', *Books and Culture* 5 (Nov/Dec 1999): 12. 'His importance for us is not only as a major figure in American history but also as a major figure in the history of Christian theology.' Ibid. See also Douglas A. Sweeney, '"Longing for More and More of It"? The Strange Career of Jonathan Edwards's Exegetical Exertions', in *Jonathan Edwards at 300*, pp. 31-32.

Edwards maintained, in the language in which he cast them, have been or should be extensively revived; indeed it is quite beyond the purpose of this edition to promulgate them.'[59] Miller clearly made a colossal contribution towards the reversing of the tide of what has been called 'the progressivist condemnation of Edwards as an "anachronism".'[60] But the very fact of Miller's avowed rejection of Christianity demonstrates that his interest in Edwards (and that of many of Miller's followers) was essentially intellectual, academic, and antiquarian.[61] Miller was enthralled by 'the intellect behind the doctrines'.[62]

The third source is surely the most significant of all, namely, the revival of interest in Edwards in *Reformed, Calvinistic circles* throughout the world in the last fifty years or so. Here the interest in his *Works* is not primarily intellectual, academic, or antiquarian, but *theological, spiritual,* and *homiletical.*[63] Pivotal in this revival of interest is the significance of Edwards' *Works* in the ministry of the great Welsh preacher, D. Martyn Lloyd-Jones (1899-1981), who, from 1938 to 1968, exercised such a powerful ministry at Westminster Chapel in the heart of London. Lloyd-Jones' discovery of the *Works* in Wales in 1929 is described by Iain H. Murray:

> Next to his Bible it was probably Jonathan Edwards' *Works* which provided the greatest stimulus to him at this date. While still in London he had asked a Welsh Presbyterian Minister for the name of books which would help him prepare for the ministry. One recommendation he received was *Protestant Thought Before Kant,* written by A. C. McGiffert. Although the book did not live up to his expectation, while reading it he came across the name

[59] *Works,* 1:viii.

[60] Weber, p. vi.

[61] In his introductory essay, 'Perry Miller and the Recovery of Jonathan Edwards', Weber makes this observation: 'Of course Perry Miller did not share either Niebuhr's or Edwards' faith in redemptive history or belief in the Gospels. Still, as an "atheist for Niebuhr" . . . Miller felt an intellectual kinship with the contemporary Jeremiah and clearly recognized in Niebuhr a type of America's first native artist.' Weber, p. xxi.

[62] Miller, *Edwards,* p. 328.

[63] Stephen J. Stein, the editor of *Notes on Scripture* in the Yale series, notes the different *loci* of interest in JE's biblical writings: 'Intellectual and historical curiosity about Edwards drives some of the expanding interest in his biblical writings; shared religious convictions motivate other researchers.' *Works,* 15:33.

of Jonathan Edwards for the first time. His interest aroused, Dr Lloyd-Jones relates: 'I then questioned my ministerial adviser on Edwards, but he knew nothing about him. After much searching I at length called at John Evans' bookshop in Cardiff in 1929, having time available as I waited for a train. There, down on my knees in my overcoat in a corner of the shop, I found the two-volume 1834 edition of Edwards which I bought for five shillings. I devoured these volumes and literally just read and read them. It is certainly true that they helped me more than anything else.'[64]

But if Edwards' *Works* played a very significant role in the ministry of the minister of Westminster Chapel, it is also true that Lloyd-Jones himself played a very significant role in the promotion and ultimate republication of the *Works* in a context quite different from that of Yale. *The Select Works of Jonathan Edwards*, vol. 1., was among the earliest titles published by The Banner of Truth Trust (founded in 1957) and was recommended by Lloyd-Jones to his congregation in the month that marked the bicentennial of Edwards' death, March 1958. Furthermore, in 1974 the two-volume Hickman edition of 1834 was republished by the Trust. Thus the ministries of Edwards and Lloyd-Jones have, in the providence of God, so acted and reacted upon one another as to produce increasingly, from the mid-twentieth century onwards, not only generations of Christians, but also generations of churches, by whom and in which the essential message of Edwards is both loved and proclaimed. Thus 'this towering edifice' of the legacy began to reach and touch the very ends of the earth; and the significance of the dissemination of Edwards' *Works* in a Reformed, Calvinistic context lies precisely in the fact that Edwards himself was neither neo-orthodox, nor an atheist, nor merely a scholar. He was above all else a Calvinistic preacher-theologian; and his truest heirs are, therefore, those that embrace his theology and preach his gospel.

There is, however, a surprising *lacuna* in the otherwise exponentially exploding field of Edwards scholarship; that *lacuna* relates to his

---

[64] Iain H. Murray, *David Martyn Lloyd-Jones: The First Forty Years 1899-1939* (Edinburgh: Banner of Truth, 1982), pp. 253-254.

preaching.[65] Ralph G. Turnbull, writing in 1958, made this observation: 'Edwards has been appraised by those who have been attracted by his philosophy. His worth as a preacher has been neglected.'[66] Sean Michael Lucas, writing in 2003, on the occasion of the tercentenary of Edwards' birth, notes that this neglect still persists: 'Surprisingly, there are not many studies of Edwards as a preacher.'[67] Indeed, one of the tacit tendencies in Edwards scholarship during the course of the last half-century has been that of belittling or minimizing the significance of his preaching. The tacit tendency of such scholarship has been that of ranking Edwards' philosophy first in importance, his theology second, and his preaching third. This tendency need not surprise. It was, surely, antecedently predictable that an 'atheists for Edwards' movement, for instance, would be predisposed to highlight his philosophy at the expense of his preaching of the word of God. Wilson H. Kimnach, writing in 2006, attributes this relative neglect of Edwards' preaching, at least on the part of the scholarly world, to the influential, but eccentric, views of Miller:

> Ever since Perry Miller insisted throughout his critical biography, *Jonathan Edwards* ... that JE was habitually secretive and verbally cryptic or gnomic in his pulpit utterances, composing statements that are 'almost a hoax, not to be read but to be seen through' ... scholars have tended to treat sermons as if they were less the 'essential Edwards' than notebook entries or learned treatises. However, sustained comparison of all three categories of writing reveals no disinclination on JE's part to reveal his deepest thoughts and values to any congregation, even one composed of frontiersmen and Indians ... His sermons were no hoaxes.[68]

[65] 'As an index to the quickening tempo of research, the total number of dissertations on Edwards increased in geometrical proportion during much of the last half century, doubling during each successive decade from 1940 to 1980.' McClymond, p. 3.

[66] Ralph G. Turnbull, *Jonathan Edwards the Preacher* (Grand Rapids, Michigan: Baker Book House, 1958), p. 20.

[67] Sean Michael Lucas, "Jonathan Edwards between Church and Academy: A Bibliographic Essay," in *The Legacy of Jonathan Edwards: American Religion and the Evangelical Tradition*, eds., D. G. Hart, Sean Michael Lucas, and Stephen J. Nichols (Grand Rapids, MI: Baker Academic, 2003), p. 234.

[68] *Works*, 25:46 n. 1.

Kimnach's assessment is both correct and shrewd; and it should be emphasized that his own analysis of Edwards' preaching is the most thorough and incisive yet to appear. Kimnach has, in his two volumes in the Yale edition, subjected Edwards' preaching to the most searching literary analysis.[69] But that is both the strength and the weakness of Kimnach's work. His approach savours more of the academic than the spiritual; it savours more of the literary than the homiletical; and its tendency is continually that of reducing Edwards' preaching to rhetorical theory. Yet even in Reformed, Calvinistic circles – circles in which Edwards' colossal homiletical legacy has been most valued – the *lacuna* persists. The Reformed world has itself been dilatory in analysing the preaching of this homiletical giant. This work attempts to supply that *lacuna*. Indeed, it seeks to provide a comprehensive analysis of Jonathan Edwards' preaching. It will cite extensively from his sermons and from other works in order to demonstrate something of the power of his preaching and of his thought. It will interact, both appreciatively and critically, with the now completed definitive edition of *The Works of Jonathan Edwards* produced by Yale and also with the rapidly burgeoning field of Edwards scholarship at large. It will seek to demonstrate from the vast corpus of sermonic material the remarkable strengths and qualities of the New England preacher; it will also seek to expose any weaknesses or flaws; and in the final chapter it will seek to evaluate the significance of those strengths and weaknesses for preachers and pastors today in the context of the twenty-first century.

[69] See *Works*, 10 & 25.

2

God-Centredness

One of the most fascinating differences between the era of Thomas Hooker (1586-1647) – the great-grandfather of Sarah Pierpont Edwards – and the era of Jonathan Edwards (1703-1758) is that they lie on opposite sides of the watershed of the Newtonian revolution. The latter half of the seventeenth century had been of monumental significance from the standpoint of science. 'In 1700', contends Bertrand Russell in his *History of Western Philosophy*, 'the mental outlook of educated men was completely modern; in 1600, except among a very few, it was still largely medieval.'[1] At the outset of the seventeenth century the Ptolemaic (geocentric) system, although shaken by the Copernican (heliocentric) system, still reigned supreme; by the commencement of the eighteenth century the Ptolemaic monolith had been toppled. Kepler's laws of planetary motion (1609-1619), Newton's three laws of motion together with his law of universal gravitation (1687), and Boyle's law in chemistry (1688) – these were the outstanding landmarks in a century that ushered in the modern, scientific world. It was in 1687 that Sir Isaac Newton (1642-1727) published his *Principia*, and the Copernican revolution was now complete.

But the history of science sometimes yields what has been termed 'the law of unintended consequence'.[2] Just as, in the early twentieth

---

[1] Bertrand Russell, *History of Western Philosophy and its Connection with Political and Social Circumstances from the Earliest Times to the Present Day* (London: George Allen and Unwin Ltd, 1961), p. 522.

[2] Paul Johnson, *A History of the Modern World from 1917 to the 1980's* (London: Weidenfeld and Nicolson, 1983), pp. 3-4, in the context of his discussion of Einstein's Special Theory of Relativity, refers to Karl Popper's concept of 'the law of unintended consequence'.

century, Einstein's theory of relativity was misconstrued by the popular mind as justifying relativism, so, in the late seventeenth and early eighteenth centuries, Newton's confirmation of the Copernican system was misconstrued by certain minds as a confirmation of deism. The astonishing absence of stellar parallax in a heliocentric system demonstrated the inconceivable vastness of the universe.[3] Douglas J. Elwood notes the impact of the Newtonian revolution upon theology and faith: 'While this marked an advance in experimental science, it had disastrous consequences outside the domain of pure science. God was pushed to the periphery of the knowable universe and relegated to the beginning of the temporal process ... Thus the deistic view of God arose.'[4] The central idea in deism was that God had, in the beginning, communicated self-subsistence and self-sustentation to the cosmos. God was the Supreme Being – the great Architect or Mechanic who had created the universe in the beginning, but who then left the universe to run its own course as a self-operating machine. Newtonian science had, albeit unintentionally, led to what has been described as 'the mathematization of nature'[5] and 'the depersonalization of Providence'.[6] 'The chief problem of the eighteenth century', observes Elwood, 'became one of relocating God in a post-Newtonian universe'.[7]

[3] In his essay 'Of the Prejudices of the Imagination', the first part of which was composed, it seems, in late 1721 or early 1722 and which thus antedates the 'New York period', Jonathan Edwards refers to the now superseded Ptolemaic system: 'Thus some men will yet say that they cannot conceive how the fixed stars can be so distant as that the earth's annual revolution should cause no parallax among them, and so are almost ready to fall back into antiquated Ptolemy, his system, merely to ease their imagination.' *Works*, 6:197.

[4] Douglas J. Elwood, *The Philosophical Theology of Jonathan Edwards* (New York: Columbia University Press, 1960), pp. 49–50.

[5] Richard S. Westfall, *Never at Rest: A Biography of Isaac Newton* (Cambridge: Cambridge University Press, 1980), p. 14.

[6] Norman Fiering, *Jonathan Edwards's Moral Thought and Its British Context* (Chapel Hill: The University of North Carolina Press, 1981), p. 93.

[7] Elwood, p. 51. Marsden, 'Jonathan Edwards in the Twenty-First Century', in *Jonathan Edwards at 300*, p. 154, makes this observation with regard to 'the context in which Edwards was working'. 'In my view it is especially important to view him as someone who was deeply loyal to the Puritan and wider Reformed or Calvinistic traditions of the seventeenth century and who was also informed by the Newtonian revolution and profoundly challenged by the British Enlightenment of his own era. One of the things that makes Edwards so interesting is that the Puritan side of him looks back to the Christendom of the Middle Ages and the Reformation, while the Newtonian and Enlightenment issues he was address-

The mechanization of the natural world gave rise to a new style of preaching in which the focus fell upon the wonders and the marvels of the stupendous machine which God had created. Stout describes this new style thus:

> To express the sense of mechanical order and cosmic vastness common to the age, preachers like Tillotson adapted a new 'aesthetics of the infinite' to their pulpits. The object of this new style was to stretch the imagination and overwhelm the soul with a sense of divine beauty and the 'natural sublime'. Terms like 'stupendous', 'great', 'sublime', 'vast', 'unlimited', 'spacious', or 'unbounded', recurred in descriptions of the visible universe to instill an intellectualized emotional response (or 'sentiment') of 'happiness', 'pleasure', 'joy', or, most frequently, 'delight'. God himself came to be referred to by such extrabiblical, mechanistic titles as 'the Almighty Being', the 'Father of Lights', 'the Great Governor of the Universe', the 'Almighty Hand', or the 'Supreme Architect' – epithets that rarely appeared in seventeenth-century preaching.[8]

The New England divine was clearly no deist. Indeed, Elwood emphasizes that 'his whole theology . . . rises in opposition to any view that tends to separate God from the world he has made.'[9] Edwards was responding to what McClymond describes as 'a growing tendency in eighteenth-century thought to marginalize God and remove God from significant involvement in nature, history, and human affairs.'[10] Indeed, such is Edwards' emphasis upon the concept of divine immediacy that this concept has justifiably been regarded as the controlling idea or principle of correlation that runs throughout his *Works*.[11]

---

ing look forward to the modern era. Facing the juxtaposition of these two vastly different outlooks so directly, he was acutely alert to some of the most significant implications of modernity.'

[8] Harry S. Stout, *The New England Soul: Preaching and Religious Culture in Colonial New England* (New York: Oxford University Press, 1986), p. 133.

[9] Elwood, p. 9.

[10] McClymond, p. 80.

[11] See Elwood, p. 3. 'The study in hand seeks to reunite Edwards the theologian and Edwards the philosopher by locating the principle of correlation in his doctrine of immediacy.'

It is interesting to note, however, that the New England preacher forges an 'aesthetics of the infinite' of his own. Edwards delights in ascribing greatness to God, and his constant use of the adjective *great* is very striking: 'the great Being who sees in secret';[12] 'that great Being, in whom you live and move, and have your being';[13] 'the great God of heaven and earth, and Governor of all things';[14] 'the great and almighty Creator and King of heaven and earth';[15] 'the great and original Spirit'.[16] Moreover, in his characteristically eclectic manner Edwards does not shrink from utilizing at times the language of the more deistical preachers to describe God. An analysis of his sermons reveals descriptions of God as 'the Supreme Being';[17] 'the supreme Governor of the world';[18] 'the First Being, the Being of beings, the great Creator and mighty possessor of heaven and earth';[19] 'Providence';[20] 'the great Author and Fountain of all good'.[21] Similarly, he demonstrates both a fascination with the concept of the *infinity* of God and a predilection for the adjective *infinite:* 'the Infinite Being, the Best of Beings, the Eternal Jehovah';[22] 'the infinite God, the great King of heaven and earth';[23] 'the Infinite Majesty of heaven';[24] 'an infinitely glorious being, a being of incomprehensible majesty and excellency';[25] 'the infinitely great and holy God';[26] 'an infinitely powerful, self-sufficient being';[27] 'the infinitely holy and wise Creator and Governor of the world'.[28] But it is Edwards'

---

[12] *Charity and Its Fruits: Christian Love as Manifested in the Heart and Life* (London: Banner of Truth, 1969), p. 139.

[13] *Works* (Hickman), 2:826.

[14] Ibid., 1:571.

[15] Ibid., 2:10.

[16] Ibid., p. 145.

[17] Ibid., p. 16.

[18] Ibid., p. 209.

[19] Ibid., p. 820.

[20] Ibid., pp. 138; 168.

[21] Ibid., p. 116.

[22] *Works*, 10:305.

[23] *Works*, (Hickman), 1:672.

[24] Ibid., 2:886.

[25] Ibid., p. 889.

[26] Ibid., p. 186.

[27] Ibid., p. 197.

[28] Ibid., p. 198.

insistence upon the sovereignty of God, and the Trinitarian framework in which it is expressed, that distinguishes his 'aesthetics of the infinite' from that of the more deistical and latitudinarian preachers of the late seventeenth and early eighteenth centuries. He refers to God as 'the supreme Lord and absolute Sovereign of the universe';[29] 'the great Jehovah, the infinite sovereign of the universe';[30] 'the common Father of spirits, the Lord and master and absolute sovereign of the creation';[31] 'this eternal Three in One'.[32] Thus whilst the Northampton preacher makes occasional use of the terminology of the deists and the latitudinarians, he moves far beyond both their terminology and their position. His constant emphasis upon the infinity and the absolute sovereignty of the Triune God demonstrates that his essential position is that of biblical, Calvinistic theism.

The powerful God-centredness of Jonathan Edwards' *Weltanschauung* (worldview) has not gone unnoticed by Edwards scholars. Holbrook notes 'this theocentric character of Edwards's thought';[33] Mark A. Noll refers to 'Edwards's painstakingly theocentric mind';[34] and Marsden observes that 'Edwards always begins with God'[35] – that he was 'a Puritan absolutely preoccupied with the centrality of God'.[36] Indeed, McClymond has recently suggested that a good case can be made that *theocentrism* constitutes the fundamental motif in Edwards' writings. Whilst noting that previous attempts on the part of Edwards scholars have not really been successful in establishing irrefutably any single concept that could be regarded as a correlating principle, McClymond tentatively proposes that 'the theocentric motif'[37] might well constitute the Ariadne's thread that runs throughout his *Works*. Although McClymond's immediate focus in this context is upon 'The Theocentric Metaphysics of *The Mind*', and although the general focus of his

---

[29] *Charity*, p. 147.

[30] *Works*, 25:558.

[31] Ibid., p. 557.

[32] *Charity*, p. 327.

[33] Holbrook, *Jonathan Edwards and His Detractors*, p. 388.

[34] Noll, *Freedom of the Will Abroad*, p. 108.

[35] Marsden, *Jonathan Edwards in the Twenty-First Century*, p. 154.

[36] Marsden, 'American Augustine', p. 11.

[37] McClymond, p. 28.

essay is one which deliberately bypasses *inter alia* Edwards' sermons, yet his articulation of this motif is one which applies to the entire corpus of Edwards' *Works*. 'Throughout his writings', McClymond insists, 'Edwards is unfailingly theocentric.'[38] McClymond emphasizes the essential unity of Edwards' thought and notes 'his pervasive concern with the reality, centrality, and supremacy of God'.[39] Indeed, there is an interesting connection between Edwards' theocentric *Weltanschauung* and his contemplative propensities. McClymond contends that 'Edwards fashioned a spirituality that was less anthropocentric and more theocentric than that of his Puritan forbears.'[40] 'The character of his spirituality was both theocentric and contemplative.'[41] In an observation that captures implicitly both God's transcendence and God's immediacy, McClymond observes that 'Edwards consistently strives to exalt God but not to distance God from the world.'[42] It should be noted, moreover, that in an age which emphasized reason and nature, and which therefore fostered rationalism and moralism, 'Edwards's theocentrism represents a turning of the tables on Enlightenment anthropocentrism and has therefore a polemical aspect.'[43] McClymond concludes his prize-winning essay by contending that 'Edwards's lifework might be seen as a massive attempt to . . . re-establish a theocentric perspective within a culture increasingly alienated from God . . . Edwards set for himself the prodigious task of rethinking the entire intellectual culture of his day and turning it to the advantage of God.'[44]

The consistent tendency of Edwards' preaching is, therefore, that of exalting, extolling, and magnifying the God of heaven. This tendency lies in solution throughout his sermons. Kimnach correctly identifies 'the grandeur of God' as 'a favorite theme'[45] of the North-

---

[38] Ibid., p. 5.

[39] Ibid., p. 35.

[40] Ibid., p. 38.

[41] Ibid., p. 46.

[42] Ibid., p. 30.

[43] Ibid., p. 29.

[44] Ibid., p. 112. McClymond's work was adjudged The Frank S. and Elizabeth D. Brewer Prize Essay of the American Society of Church History.

[45] *Works*, 10:414.

ampton preacher; but what contributes to this sense of the greatness, the grandeur, and the sheer magnificence of God is Edwards' striking use of *adjectives* – indeed, his unashamed use of *superlatives* – as he seeks to portray, *via* the limitations of language, the glory of that great Being who is ultimately incomprehensible and indescribable. Edwards' deliberate use of superlatives in his preaching has not gone unnoticed by Edwards scholars. Helen P. Westra pinpoints 'the rhetoric of . . . superlatives'[46] as an essential aspect of his homiletical style; she notes that 'many of Edwards's sermons derive their power from their striking . . . use of superlatives.'[47] Indeed, it would not be incorrect to speak of an Edwardsean hyperbole in his descriptions of God – an hyperbole that reflects the self-manifestation of God in the Scriptures, yet one that is cast in the language of his age. One of Edwards' great achievements as a preacher is his ability to convey to his hearers a sense of God.

'God's All-Sufficiency for the Supply of Our Wants', demonstrates this ability to display the greatness and the grandeur of God. The sermon was a Thanksgiving Day sermon that was preached in Northampton on November 13, 1729. Northampton, where Solomon Stoddard's grandson was to minister for twenty-three years, was 'the crown jewel of the Connecticut River Valley'.[48] The Northampton church was, therefore, extremely influential; it was the largest congregation west of Boston[49] – 'the one pulpit in New England', asserts Miller, 'that could challenge Boston's eight'.[50] Edwards' text on this occasion was Psalm 65:9 'Thou visitest the earth, and waterest it: thou greatly enrichest it with the river of God, which is full of water: thou preparest them corn, when thou hast so provided for it.' It appears that Edwards' choice of text on this occasion was significantly influenced by the fact of drought. Kenneth P. Minkema notes the following interesting fact: 'In New

[46] Helen P. Westra, 'Divinity's Design: Edwards and the History of the Work of Revival', in *Edwards in Our Time: Jonathan Edwards and the Shaping of American Religion*, Sang Hyun Lee and Allen C. Guelzo, eds. (Grand Rapids, Michigan: William B. Eerdmans Publishing Company, 1999), p. 144.

[47] Ibid., p. 140.

[48] *Works*, 14:10.

[49] I am indebted to Lesser for this piece of information. See *Works*, 19:6.

[50] Miller, *Edwards*, p. 13.

England, it seems, the year 1729 was without rain.'[51] Minkema describes this sermon as 'a meditation on the wonders of creation';[52] it demonstrates Edwards' 'personal vision of the magnificence of God':[53]

> God shows his great power in sending abroad at such a prodigious distance so powerful a light and heat from the sun, which is so great in its influences all over the face of the earth. How mighty and powerful is that globe of fire through so vast regions of the

[51] *Works*, 14:472. 'Several sermons besides this one use imagery that testifies to such a condition.' Ibid. 'See the fast sermon of 1729 on Amos 8:11 (95), in which JE contrasts a temporal drought to a "famine of the Word"; and the paired sermons on Jer. 17:5-6 (122) and 17:7-8 (123), which portray those who trust in the creature as living in a dry country and a barren heath, and those who trust in God as having an "ever-flowing" and "full fountain of good to live upon."' Ibid., n. 6.

[52] Ibid., p. 471. This sermon is of particular interest with regard to JE's views of the debate between the Ptolemaic system and the Copernican system. It is evident from his reference to 'antiquated Ptolemy, his system', *Works*, 6:197, that JE was, by the age of eighteen, convinced of the heliocentric Copernican system. It is, therefore, particularly interesting that in 'God's All-Sufficiency for the Supply of Our Wants', which was delivered about eight years later, he refers to 'the diurnal revolution of the sun round the earth in perpetual successions', *Works*, 14:477-478. Minkema, the Yale editor, makes this observation on this matter: 'Though Edwards was fully acquainted with the Copernican view of the solar system as well as the works of Newton and his expositors, he nonetheless retains references to the Ptolemaic cosmology. Why Edwards does this is uncertain; perhaps his congregation was still not ready to accept modern theory, or perhaps he deliberately subordinated scientific fact to the theological truth that humankind is the focal point of creation and that God arranges everything for humankind's benefit', Ibid., pp. 471-72. But it is very doubtful whether JE's words here actually commit him to the Ptolemaic system. Certainly this reference to 'the diurnal revolution of the sun round the earth in perpetual successions' is not one that overtly commits him to the Copernican system, but nor does it, in and of itself, overtly commit him to the Ptolemaic system. The viewpoint is *prima facie* anthropocentric or geocentric rather than heliocentric; but it should be noted that this is precisely the *prima facie* position of the Scriptures. Moreover, from man's perspective there is indeed a 'diurnal revolution of the sun round the earth'. There is, almost certainly, an element of homiletical tact here on JE's part; indeed, there is even, perhaps, a deliberate ambiguity on his part. But it should be noted that JE had clearly embraced the heliocentric Copernican system at least eight years earlier, and possibly ten. Wallace E. Anderson makes this observation: 'Whiston's *Astronomical Lectures* was used by tutors Samuel Johnson and Daniel Browne to introduce the Copernican astronomy to the Yale students at New Haven in 1717.' *Works*, 6:149. Anderson also notes that JE's contact with Whiston's *Lectures* probably did not occur before 1719. See ibid. Thus Avihu Zakai's conclusion, on the basis of this sermon, with regard to JE's 'rejection of the Copernican revolution', is clearly flawed. Avihu Zakai, *Jonathan Edwards's Philosophy of History: The Reenchantment of the World in the Age of Enlightenment* (Princeton and Oxford: Princeton University Press, 2003), p. 117.

[53] *Works*, 14:471.

universe, and shows the all-sufficient power of him that kindled it, and that maintains its light and heat!

God shows his great power in ordering of the atmosphere, or that body of air that encloses this globe and the things contained in it, for our good, as in raising and sustaining in the air such vast quantities of water in the clouds. He calls for the waters of the sea, and the waters of the sea obey him and mount up at his command, and he poureth it out on the dry land. Amos 5:8, 'Seek him that maketh the seven stars and Orion, and turneth the shadow of death into the morning, that maketh the day dark with night: that calleth for the waters of the sea, and poureth them out upon the face of the earth: the Lord is his name.'

God shows his great power in the winds, in moving such great portions of the atmosphere with such rapidity, whereby he fans and cleanses the air; and wafteth to and fro the clouds, those great quantities of waters above the firmament, whither he pleases they should go. Prov. 30:4, 'Who hath gathered the winds in his fists?'

He shows his mighty power in thunder and lightning, whereby he cleanses and sweetens the air. Job 26:14, 'The thunder of his power who can understand?'

God shows his great power in moving and managing the sea, that huge collection of waters, for the good of mankind, especially in the tides. He hereby shows he has his way in the sea, and his path in the great waters (Ps. 77:19).[54]

'Ruth's Resolution' was preached in Northampton in April 1735 at the time of the extraordinary awakening in the town and the surrounding area. The sermon was first published in *Five Discourses* in 1738. Edwards' text on this occasion was Ruth 1:16: 'And Ruth said, Entreat me not to leave thee, or to return from following after thee; for whither thou goest, I will go, and where thou lodgest, I will lodge; thy people shall be my people, and thy God, my God.' Edwards'

---

[54] Ibid., pp. 476-477.

'Main Proposition' demonstrates his readiness to utilize the concept of opportunity during times of revival: 'When those that we have formerly been conversant with, are turning to God, and joining themselves to his people, it ought to be our firm resolution, that we will not leave them; but that their people shall be our people, and their God, our God.'[55] Edwards then provides various reasons to reinforce the necessity of this 'firm resolution', the first of which focuses upon the excellencies and perfections of the most high God:

> Because their *God* is a glorious God. There is none like him, who is infinite in glory and excellency. He is the most high God, glorious in holiness, fearful in praises, doing wonders. His name is excellent in all the earth, and his glory is above the heavens. Among the gods there is none like unto him; there is none in heaven to be compared to him, nor are there any among the sons of the mighty that can be likened unto him. Their God is the fountain of all good, and an inexhaustible fountain; he is an all-sufficient God, able to protect and defend them, and do all things for them. He is the King of glory, the Lord strong and mighty, the Lord mighty in battle: a strong rock, and a high tower. There is none like the God of Jeshurun, who rideth on the heaven in their help, and in his excellency on the sky: the eternal God is their refuge, and underneath are everlasting arms. He is a God who hath all things in his hands, and does whatsoever he pleases: he killeth and maketh alive; he bringeth down to the grave and bringeth up; he maketh poor and maketh rich: the pillars of the earth are the Lord's. Their God is an infinitely holy God: there is none holy as the Lord. And he is infinitely good and merciful. Many that others worship and serve as gods, are cruel beings, spirits that seek the ruin of souls; but this is a God that delighteth in mercy; his grace is infinite, and endures for ever. He is love itself, an infinite fountain and ocean of it.[56]

'The Justice of God in the Damnation of Sinners' belongs, like 'Ruth's Resolution', to the latter part of the Northampton awakening in

---

[55] *Works*, 19:309.
[56] *Works* (Hickman), 1:665.

the spring of 1735; like 'Ruth's Resolution', it was published in 1738 at the request of the people of Northampton as one of the *Five Discourses*. Edwards himself emphasizes the fact of God's blessing upon this particular sermon: 'I never found so much immediate saving fruit, in any measure, of any discourses I have offered to my congregation, as some from these words, Rom. 3:19. "That every mouth may be stopped"; endeavouring to show from thence, that it would be just with God for ever to reject and cast off mere natural men.'[57] This sermon was clearly a favourite with Edwards; and but for its length (all the evidence suggests that the sermon was preached in five preaching units) it would almost certainly have been repreached elsewhere.[58] The sermon contains passages that greatly exalt, magnify, and glorify the Divine Being; early in his 'Doctrine' it is the *infinitude* of the attributes of God upon which the preacher expatiates:

> But God is a being infinitely lovely, because he hath infinite excellency and beauty. To have infinite excellency and beauty, is the same thing as to have infinite loveliness. He is a being of infinite greatness, majesty and glory; and therefore is infinitely honorable. He is infinitely exalted above the greatest potentates of the earth, and highest angels in heaven; and therefore is infinitely more honorable than they. His authority over us is infinite; and the ground of his right to our obedience, is infinitely strong; for he is infinitely worthy to be obeyed in himself, and we have an absolute universal and infinite dependence upon him.[59]

One of the most striking features of Edwards' preaching is that it constitutes a deliberate and powerful counterblast to the inveterate tendency in man to belittle and degrade the great God of heaven. 'The thing at bottom is', observes Edwards in 'The Justice of God', 'that men have low thoughts of God, and high thoughts of themselves; and therefore it is that they look upon God as having so little right, and they so much. Matt. 20:15, "Is it not lawful for me to do what I will with mine

---

[57] Ibid., p. 353.

[58] This sermon was also clearly a favourite both with editors and the public, having been reprinted half a dozen times from 1773 to 1814. See *Works*, 19:336 n. 1.

[59] Ibid., p. 342.

own?'"[60] Similarly, in 'Men Naturally God's Enemies', Edwards charges the non-Christian with this same trait: 'Particularly, you may be sensible that you have at least had a low and contemptible estimation of God; and that, in your esteem, you set the trifles and vanities of this world far above him.'[61] Edwards clearly regarded the tendency in man to belittle and degrade God as symptomatic of that 'disrelish and aversion towards God'[62] by which the natural man is characterized.

Similarly, in 'Divine Sovereignty' – a sermon based upon Psalm 46:10 ('Be still, and know that I am God'), and preached in June 1735 – Edwards charges those who oppose the doctrine of the sovereignty of God with entertaining 'mean', 'little', and 'diminutive thoughts of God'.[63] The sermon contains the following two passages:

> It is most evident by the works of God, that his understanding and power are infinite; for he that hath made all things out of nothing, and upholds, and governs, and manages all things every moment, in all ages, without growing weary, must be of infinite power. He must also be of infinite knowledge; for if he made all things, and upholds and governs all things continually, it will follow, that he knows and perfectly sees all things, great and small, in heaven and earth, continually at one view; which cannot be without infinite understanding.[64]

> In that he is God, he *will* be sovereign, and will act as such. He sits on the throne of his sovereignty, and his kingdom ruleth over all. He will be exalted in his sovereign power and dominion, as he himself declares: 'I will be exalted among the heathen, I will be exalted in the earth.' He will have all men to know, that he is most high over all the earth. He doth according to his will in the armies of heaven and amongst the inhabitants of the earth, and none can stay his hand. – There is no such thing as frustrating, or baffling, or undermining his designs; for he is great in counsel, and wonderful in working. His counsel shall stand, and he will do all his pleasure.

---

[60] Ibid., p. 373.
[61] *Works* (Hickman), 2:134.
[62] Ibid.
[63] Ibid., p. 109.
[64] Ibid., p. 107.

There is no wisdom, nor understanding, nor counsel against the Lord; whatsoever God doth, it shall be for ever; nothing shall be put to it, nor any thing taken from it. He will work, and who shall let it? He is able to dash in pieces the enemy. If men join hand in hand against him, to hinder or oppose his designs, he breaks the bow, he cuts the spear in sunder, he burneth the chariot in the fire. – He kills and he makes alive, he brings down and raises up just as he pleases. Isa. xlv. 6, 7. 'That they may know from the rising of the sun, and from the west, that there is none besides me. I am the Lord, and there is none else: I form the light and create darkness; I make peace and create evil; I the Lord do all these things.'[65]

One of the most interesting features of this striking theocentricity in Edwards' sermons is that it pertains even to those passages in which, it might be deemed, there is a *prima facie* anthropocentric focus. 'God Makes Men Sensible of Their Misery Before He Reveals His Mercy and Love' is a very interesting sermon on Hosea 5:15, 'I will go and return to my place, till they acknowledge their offence, and seek my face: in their affliction they will seek me early.' This sermon was delivered in the fall of 1730 and consists of four preaching units.[66] During the course of this sermon Edwards refers to numerous characters in the Bible in order to illustrate and demonstrate the ways and methods of God. He refers to Joseph, the children of Jacob, Jacob himself, the children of Israel in Egypt, the children of Israel at the Red Sea, the children of Israel in the wilderness, the times of the Judges, the woman of Canaan, Joseph's brethren, Peter's sermon, Paul, the jailer, David, and Elijah.[67] But what is so striking is Edwards' use of the following expressions throughout the sermon: 'It is God's manner to . . .' 'It is God's ordinary manner to . . .' 'God sometimes . . .' 'God oftentimes . . .' 'This is God's method.' 'This is God's ordinary way . . .':

And the experience of God's people in all ages corresponds with those examples. *It is God's usual method* before remarkable discoveries of his mercy and love to them, especially by spiritual mercies,

[65] Ibid., p. 109.
[66] See *Works*, 17:139.
[67] *Works* (Hickman), 2:830-832.

in a special manner to humble them, and make them sensible of their misery and helplessness in themselves, and of their vileness and unworthiness, either by some remarkably humbling dispensation of his providence or influence of his Spirit.[68]

The same ability to draw theocentric lessons from *prima facie* anthropocentric aspects of the sermon is also evident in 'The Unreasonableness of Indetermination in Religion'. This sermon is based upon 1 Kings 18:21, 'And Elijah came unto all the people, and said, How long halt ye between two opinions? if the Lord be God, follow him: but if Baal, then follow him. And the people answered him not a word.' The manuscript itself indicates that this sermon was one of Edwards' favourites. Dated June 1734, it was, interestingly, preached on three separate occasions to the people of Northampton, including 'a second time from Josh. 24:15', once 'at Windsor', and again to the Stockbridge Indians in July 1752.[69] The preacher introduces his sermon thus:

> 'Tis God's manner, before he bestows any signal or remarkable mercy on a people, first to prepare them for it; and before he removes any awful judgment that he has brought upon them for their sins, first to bring them to forsake those sins that procured those judgments.[70]

The significant phrase here is, once again, the phrase ''Tis God's manner . . .' The very use of the phrase demonstrates Edwards' concern to draw God-centred principles and lessons from the characters, examples, and narratives of the Scriptures. Thus Biblical material which might otherwise be deemed to be limited to the *exemplary* and the *experimental* is shrewdly invested by the preacher with a significant *theocentric* focus and thrust.

It is not surprising to find that this powerful theocentric focus continues in the Indian sermons at Stockbridge, although in a radically simplified manner.[71] This simplification was necessitated by the

---

[68] Ibid., p. 831. Emphasis added.

[69] See *Works*, 19:92.

[70] Ibid., p. 93.

[71] Marsden describes the village of Stockbridge thus: 'The village itself . . . was designed to be a model community, a prototype for future missions where English and Indians would

fact that Edwards was now ministering to Mahican Indians on the very borders of civilization. But it is part of the paradox of the Stockbridge years that this journey into virtual exile was also, in effect, as Kimnach puts it, the culmination of an intellectual and spiritual journey – 'a voyage from the world of the village pastor to that of the international community of thinkers and intellectual leaders in religious affairs.'[72] Thus his journey of some fifty or sixty miles from Northampton to Stockbridge in the summer of 1751 is itself vested with an almost symbolical significance. In addition to his preaching and pastoral duties, he produced in Stockbridge four major treatises, two of which are often regarded as classics in the history of Christianity and in the history of American intellectual life.[73] 'The seven years of exile were also years of intense labor', notes Ola Elizabeth Winslow, 'and labor toward an abundant harvest. In the small room known as the "study" – a tiny nook at the west end of the house, large enough only for a desk, a chair, and many books – Jonathan Edwards found the most effective rostrum he had ever known.'[74]

But the desk in his tiny study was not his only rostrum in Stockbridge. In addition to this rostrum the ousted Northampton minister

---

live side by side in peace ... The Stockbridge experiment centered around a couple of hundred Mahican Indians ..., the largest single part of the remnant of the once-great Mahican confederacy, now struggling for survival and willing to be under English protection ... Between 1736 and 1739 they [John Sergeant, the first missionary and thus JE's predecessor, and Timothy Woodbridge, a schoolmaster from Springfield] established Stockbridge, a town for the Mahicans that also included four English (New Englander) families. The idea was that the Indians might be more effectively evangelized if they learned to live with the English and according to English principles. Civilizing, it was believed, should go hand in hand with evangelizing. The government granted the Indians lots from some of the best land by the river, and the English families land in the hills above the meadows ... At the time of Sergeant's death, 218 Indians were living in Stockbridge, of whom 125 had been baptized and 42 were communicants in the church ... The town in 1749, much as Edwards would have found it when he visited the next year, had a single rambling main street with fifty-three Indian dwellings, twenty of which were English-style homes. The number of English families in the surrounding area had grown from the original four to around ten.' Marsden, *Edwards*, pp. 375-378.

[72] *Works*, 10:125.

[73] I am indebted to Marsden for this observation. See Marsden, *Edwards*, p. 389. Marsden is doubtless referring to *Freedom of the Will* and *The Nature of True Virtue*.

[74] Winslow, p. 292. Winslow indicates the diminutive size of this room in her reference to 'his four-by-eight foot study' at Stockbridge. Ibid., p. 241.

now had, in effect, two pulpits. He was now the pastor of a hamlet, in which he would have the charge both of an Indian mission and a white congregation. During the seven years spent at Stockbridge Edwards appears to have preached at two separate services – one for the English congregation and the other for the Indian mission – in the same meetinghouse each Sunday.[75] He had first preached at Stockbridge in October, 1750, and the sequence of events in the call to Stockbridge is described by Marsden thus: 'Now he had an invitation to consider the possibility of settling there as the pastor of the English congregation and missionary to the Indians. Despite his interest, Edwards moved cautiously, perhaps because of his doubts concerning his pastoral gifts. To test the situation, he left for Stockbridge in January and stayed until early spring, preaching to both whites and Indians and securing formal invitations to settle there.'[76] 'Edwards was finally installed in Stockbridge on August 8', notes Kimnach, 'although he did not actually move there until October 18, after preaching his last sermon as a supply preacher in Northampton on October 13, 1751.'[77]

In the providence of God Stockbridge afforded 'the advantages of isolation'[78] and thus unique opportunities for writing. There is a fascinating dualism about the activity of the Stockbridge years in that Edwards was now operating at two rather strangely juxtaposed levels – on the one hand, that of the philosopher-theologian who produced in the course of those years *Freedom of the Will, God's Chief End, The Nature of True Virtue,* and *Original Sin,* described by Sereno E. Dwight (1786-1850) as 'four of the ablest and most valuable works, which the Church of Christ has in its possession';[79] and, on the other hand, that of the missionary to the Indians who, week by week, preached the word of God with appropriate simplicity to a part of the remnant of the once great Mahican confederacy. In the Stockbridge ministry as a whole great profundity and great simplicity lie side by side.

The sermon 'God Is Infinitely Strong', the manuscript of which is

---

[75] I am indebted to Kimnach for this information. See *Works,* 25:73.
[76] Marsden, *Edwards,* p.364.
[77] *Works,* 25:28.
[78] Marsden, *Edwards,* p. 447.
[79] Cited *Works,* 1:8.

marked 'St [ockbridge] Ind [ians]. Jan 1753',[80] is particularly interesting in this respect. Edwards' text on this occasion was Job 9:4: 'He is wise of heart, and mighty in strength.' Kimnach describes this sermon as 'the meridian of Edwards' missionary effort'[81] at Stockbridge: 'This is one of three sermons Edwards preached to the Indians from the book of Job, suggesting his sense of the appeal of good biblical narrative to the Indians. Describing the difficulty of comprehending God's power, Edwards compares it to compressing the oceans into a nutshell . . . and stresses God's power of knowing above all other dimensions of his power.'[82] Early in the sermon the Stockbridge missionary describes, with a compelling simplicity and profundity, both the omniscience and the immensity of God:

> [God] sees all over this world: every man, woman, and child; every beast on earth, every bird in the air, [every] fish in the sea. There is not so much [as] a fly or worm or gnat [that is unknown to God]. [He] knows every tree, every leaf, every spire of grass; every drop of rain or dew; every single dust [mote] in the whole world. [God] sees in darkness [and] under ground. [A] thousand miles under ground [is] not hid [from his view]. [God] sees all that men [do] or say, sees their hearts [and] thoughts.

> [God] knows everything past, [even] things a thousand years ago. [He also knows] everything to come, [even] a thousand years to come. [He knows] all the men that will be, [and] all that they will do, say, or think. This is more than all the rest: he perfectly knows himself. God is so great that we can't know but little of him. They that know most [know almost nothing of God]. Man's knowledge is not large enough: it can't reach so far as the greatness of God. [A] nutshell can't contain all the waters of the sea: so the mind of man. The angels of heaven [cannot comprehend God]. But God knows him: knows himself altogether. We are so far from knowing all of God, that we know but little of ourselves: but little of our bodies, little of our souls. But God knows all things at

---

[80] *Works*, 25:642.
[81] Ibid., p. 30.
[82] Ibid.

all times; [he] don't sleep, is not weary of minding so many things; nothing is ever out of his mind. [He] knows all things at once: we can look but on one thing at once, but he [comprehends all things in a single glance] . . .

Because God made all things, he must see and know all things: all the stars, angels, all mankind; beast, birds, fishes, flies: every part of their bodies, their eyes, their legs, every bone, every vein. [He not only knows the] stars, [but] every tree leaf [and blade of] grass; [every] drop of water [and mote of] dust: [God] must see 'em all when he made [them]; otherwise, [he] could not make 'em. Did he not know what he did?[83]

Vitae interminabilis, tota, simul et perfecta possessio: twice in *Freedom of the Will* (1754) Edwards cites this great dictum of Boethius (*circa* A.D. 480-524).[84] It is a dictum that captures, in a profound, abstract manner, that truth that he taught the Indians in such a simple, concrete manner in this very sermon: *the total, simultaneous, and perfect comprehension of endless existence.* The genius of this particular dictum is that it conveys, with that remarkable economy characteristic of ecclesiastical Latin, a sense of the infinity, the immensity, the eternity, the immutability, the timelessness, the successionlessness, the immediacy, the omnipotence, the omnipresence, and the omniscience of the great God with whom men have to do. It is fascinating to reflect that, at the very time when Edwards was composing this sermon for the Indians, namely, January 1753, he was also pouring all his efforts and all his treasures of wisdom and knowledge amassed in a lifetime of study into the

[83] Ibid., pp. 643-644. Kimnach provides the following explanation concerning the preparation of the text: 'Omissions and *lacunae* in the manuscript text are filled by insertions in square brackets ([ ])'. Ibid., p. xiii.

[84] 'The very reason, why God's knowledge is without succession, is, because it is absolutely perfect, to the highest possible degree of clearness and certainty. All things, whether past, present, or to come, being viewed with equal evidence and fulness; future things being seen with as much clearness, as if they were present; the view is always in absolute perfection; and absolute constant perfection admits of no alteration, and so no succession; . . . Nothing is more impossible than that the immutable God should be changed, by the succession of time; who comprehends all things, from eternity to eternity, in one, most perfect, and unalterable view; so that his whole eternal duration is *vitae interminabilis, tota, simul et perfecta possessio.*' *Works* (Hickman), 1:39. See also ibid., p. 72.

writing of a treatise – *Freedom of the Will* – that would stun the world.[85] Thus, in instructing the transatlantic intellectual and clerical community of the mid-eighteenth-century Enlightenment the missionary-philosopher made use of the profound utterance of Boethius; and in instructing the Indians of Stockbridge concerning the omniscience of God he referred to 'flies', 'worms', 'gnats', 'leaves', 'spires and blades of grass', 'drops of rain or dew', and 'motes of dust'. It is a brilliant, extraordinary juxtaposition.

[85] Marsden notes that it was not until the winter of 1752-1753 that JE was able to return to his anti-Arminian project. See Marsden, *Edwards,* p. 437. In a letter written from Stockbridge on April 14, 1753, to the Reverend John Erskine, JE provides his Scottish correspondent with this news: 'After many hindrances, delays, and interruptions, divine providence has so far favored me, and smiled on my design of writing on the Arminian controversy, that I have almost finished the first draft of what I first intended.' *Works,* 16:594.

In 1889 Alexander V. G. Allen, 'The Freedom of the Will', in *Critical Essays on Jonathan Edwards,* William J. Scheick, ed. (Boston, Massachusetts: G. K. Hall & Co., 1980), p. 89, described *Freedom of the Will* as 'a work which produced so deep an impression that it still continues to be spoken of as "the one large contribution which America has made to the deeper philosophic thought of the world."' Allen goes on to describe this treatise as 'one of the literary sensations of the last century'. Ibid., p. 90.

3

THE PREACHING OF JUDGMENT

It is impossible to grasp the rationale for Jonathan Ewards' constant proclamation of the fact and the reality of judgment from
his Northampton pulpit apart from an understanding of the ecclesiastical situation that had developed in New England in the first century
of its history. It is important to note that, when Edwards became
assistant to his grandfather, Solomon Stoddard, in February 1727, the
churches of New England were no longer gathered churches of visible
saints; ironically, they often resembled that 'mixed multitude' from
which the Pilgrim Fathers had sought to escape. Interestingly, the
issue of the sacraments of baptism and the Lord's Supper lay at the
very centre of the spiritual malaise that had crept over the churches
of New England within just a couple of generations since the arrival
of the Pilgrim Fathers in 1620. The problem, contends Morgan, was
'the problem of biology'[1] or 'the problem of the next generation.'[2]
This rapidly developing situation is, perhaps, best understood in terms
of three successive generations within the churches. The first generation consisted of believers from overseas who had, let us say, arrived
in New England as part of the Great Migration of the 1630's; these
believers were, of course, already baptized and continued to have
access to the sacrament of the Lord's Supper. The second generation
consisted of the children of this first generation; as such, they were
baptized, but in many cases did not have access to the Lord's Supper
because, although now adult, they had not made a profession of faith
in Christ. The third generation consisted of the children of the latter
– they were the children of baptized unbelievers; and the question

[1] Morgan, *Visible Saints*, p. 125.
[2] Ibid., p. 136.

41

that inevitably arose with regard to them was whether or not they had a right to baptism.

'By the late 1640's', notes Morgan, 'an increasing number of children who had been baptized in New England churches were coming of age without a religious experience and starting families of their own. The synod which met at Cambridge in 1646-1648 had been asked to decide the status of these persons. Since it failed to do so, every church during the 1650's had to face the question for itself, and most of them seem to have adopted a do-nothing policy by neither expelling the second-generation adults nor baptizing their third-generation children.'[3] With the passage of every year, however, the situation became increasingly urgent, and when a full-scale synod convened in 1662, it delivered *inter alia* the following proposition:

> Proposition 5th. Church-members who were admitted in minority, understanding the Doctrine of Faith, and publicly professing their assent thereto; not scandalous in life, and solemnly owning the Covenant before the Church, wherein they give up themselves and their Children to the Lord, and subject themselves to the Government of Christ in the Church, their Children are to be Baptized.[4]

This 'owning the covenant' on the part of the second generation should not be confused with the concept of a genuine profession of faith in Christ. This fifth Proposition clearly required *notitia* and *assensus*, but was tailored in such a way that it deliberately fell short of an insistence upon the necessity of *fiducia*.[5] Such, then, was the essence of the ecclesiastical expedient known as the 'Halfway Covenant'. The term itself was, originally, a term of derision. Morgan describes the extent and the limitations of the blessings of 'halfway membership':

> The membership they retained, however, was not the full membership that had been granted in the Separatist churches. Rather it was the continuation of the membership they had had as children: they could not vote in church affairs, and they could not participate

[3] Ibid., p. 129.
[4] Cited ibid., p. 130.
[5] *Notitia* means *knowledge; assensus* means *assent;* and *fiducia* means *trust.*

in the Lord's Supper (they were not members in 'full communion'). What they gained was two privileges which had probably been hitherto denied them in most New England churches: the application of church discipline (they could be admonished or excommunicated for bad conduct) and baptism for their children. They were 'half-way' members, and the synod's whole solution to the question of their status was dubbed the 'half-way covenant.'[6]

This already complex and unsatisfactory situation was then further complicated and exacerbated by the fact that, in 1677, Edwards' own grandfather, Solomon Stoddard, introduced into the church in Northampton the practice of 'open communion'. Stoddard justified this innovation on the grounds that the Lord's Supper was, allegedly, a 'converting ordinance'. Thus, if the Halfway Covenant allowed the administration of the sacrament of baptism to infants who were not children of the covenant, Stoddardism allowed the administration of the sacrament of the Lord's Supper to adults who made no pretension to faith in Christ. The almost universal availability of both sacraments simply had the effect of cheapening the sacraments.

It should be noted that there is a real tension between Stoddard's soteriology and his ecclesiology and that there is a paradox about his ministry. On the one hand Jonathan Edwards' grandfather preached powerful evangelistic sermons from his Northampton pulpit; and on the other hand he played a colossal role in introducing into the churches of New England a conception of the church that was much more inclusive and comprehensive than that embraced by the New England churches at the beginning. Indeed, in 1700 Increase Mather predicted that, if Stoddard's views should gain ground as rapidly in the ensuing thirty years as they had in the preceding thirty, the people of God in New England would have to '"gather Churches out of churches"'.[7] C. C. Goen makes the interesting observation that 'on the eve of the Great Awakening most of the parish churches in New England, like the old English churches from which they had fled, harbored a mixed company. That explains why many of the Awakening's con-

---

[6] Morgan, *Visible Saints*, pp. 131-132.
[7] Cited ibid., p. 151.

verts were church members of one sort or another.'[8]

It also explains, in large part, the awakening character of many of the sermons of New England's leading preacher. In his treatise, *An Humble Inquiry into the Rules of the Word of God Concerning . . . Full Communion in the Visible Christian Church* (1749), Edwards made this incisive observation with regard to the practical consequences of this situation:

> The effect of this method of proceeding in the churches in New England, which have fallen into it, is actually this. – There are some that are received into these churches under the notion of their being in the judgment of rational charity visible saints or professing saints, who yet at the same time are actually open professors of heinous wickedness; I mean, the wickedness of living in known impenitence and unbelief, the wickedness of living in enmity against God, and in the rejection of Christ under the gospel.[9]

It is this fact, then, that, to a very large degree, constitutes the rationale for the powerfully awakening, evangelistic, and conversionist tone of Jonathan Edwards' preaching, with its tremendous emphasis upon the judgment of God, both in his own church in Northampton and more widely in the churches of New England itself. Edwards was convinced that many of the church members within New England Congregationalism were simply unconverted. His ministry was, in effect, a fulfillment of Increase Mather's prediction concerning the necessity of 'gathering churches out of churches'.

But it was not simply the realities of the domestic situation, but also those of the international situation, that convinced the New England preacher of the necessity of highlighting the judgment of God in his preaching. Edwards was a Puritan who lived in the Age of the Enlightenment; and it should be noted that, as such, he was a significant member of the transatlantic intellectual community of the first half of the eighteenth century. Through his wide, eclectic reading he was well aware of the rising tide of deism and the remarkable growth

---

[8] *Works*, 4:2.
[9] *Works* (Hickman), 1:478.

of scepticism in this period.[10] In *Freedom of the Will* (1754), for instance, he refers to 'gentlemen possessed of that noble and generous freedom of thought, which happily prevails in this age of light and inquiry'[11] and to 'the supposed rational and generous principles of the modern fashionable divinity'.[12] In *God's Chief End in Creation*, which was provisionally completed by February 1756, he refers, in his concluding observations, to 'our modern free-thinkers who do not like the talk about satisfying justice with an infinite punishment'.[13] In *Original Sin* (1758) he again comments in ironic and sardonic vein that 'it must be understood, that there is risen up now at length, in this happy age of light and liberty, a set of men, of a more free and generous turn of mind, of a more inquisitive genius, and of better discernment.'[14] This 'set of men' – these 'modern free-thinkers' – were men of latitudinarian or deistic tendency who were now flourishing in the Age of the Enlightenment; and the 'generosity' by which their principles were characterized applied *inter alia* to the biblical, Calvinistic doctrine of eternal judgment. 'For several generations prior to Edwards', observes McClymond, 'European intellectuals had been emancipating themselves from traditional notions of hell.'[15]

A significant member of the 'set of men' against which Edwards had set his face was John Tillotson (1630-1694). In 1691 Tillotson was appointed Archbishop of Canterbury in spite of the fact (or perhaps because of the fact) that in 1690 he had preached before the Queen a most significant sermon entitled 'The Eternity of Hell Torments'. This was a subtle, suggestive, insinuating sermon in which the future Archbishop, whilst purporting to defend the doctrine of the everlasting misery of the damned, in fact deliberately subverted it. The sermon, observes Norman Fiering, is marked by 'a kind of suave cleverness'.[16] Everlasting punishment, Tillotson suggested, was not so much a

---

[10] See my 'Jonathan Edwards and the Deists', *The Banner of Truth* magazine, 299-300 (August-Sept 1988): pp. 22-34.
[11] *Works* (Hickman), 1:89.
[12] Ibid., p. 86.
[13] Ibid., p. 121.
[14] Ibid., p. 233.
[15] McClymond, p. 140.
[16] Fiering, p. 228.

certainty as a possibility; indeed, he suggested that the Bible's teaching on eternal punishment was given to 'deter men' – it was a deterrent rather than retributive. In the same sermon Tillotson also flirts and toys with the heterodox notions of the Greek father, Origen, who held that punishment in the world to come is reformatory and rehabilitative, and who suggested that such punishment may only last for a thousand years. It is important to note that Tillotson's writings arrived in New England *circa* 1714 and began to exert an inevitably pernicious influence. 'He had been a scholar, a popular preacher and a most benign gentleman', notes Arnold Dallimore, 'and had been particularly effective in presenting Christianity as a sedate ethic and the Christian life as merely cultured, inoffensive behaviour.'[17] Indeed, Tillotson's fundamental position was that of moderatism and latitudinarianism. As far as Jonathan Edwards was concerned, however, the Archbishop was the fountain-head of much that was heterodox and dangerous in eighteenth-century Christianity; and in April 1739, almost half a century after the preaching of Tillotson's sermon, Edwards himself preached a sermon entitled 'The Eternity of Hell Torments' that was based on Tillotson's own text, Matthew 25:46: 'And these shall go away into everlasting punishment.'[18] 'Tillotson was dead', remarks Gerald R. Cragg, 'but his sermons were the ethical handbook of the new age.'[19] The Archbishop's sermons had proved to be very popular and highly influential. Thus in his counterblast the Northampton divine specifically referred to the Canterbury divine: 'Archbishop Tillotson, who has made so great a figure among the new-fashioned divines'.[20] In this sermon (as indeed in his *Miscellanies*) Edwards launched a powerful counter-attack upon 'the infidel humor'[21] of the age. Reasoning both

---

[17] Arnold A. Dallimore, *George Whitefield: The Life and Times of the Great Evangelist of the Eighteenth-Century Revival*, vol. 1 (Edinburgh: Banner of Truth Trust, 1970), p. 483.

[18] It is evident that 'The Eternity of Hell Torments' must have interrupted the series of thirty sermons, posthumously published as *A History of the Work of Redemption*, which was preached from March to August 1739.

[19] Gerald R. Cragg, *The Church and the Age of Reason 1648-1789* (Bristol: Hodder and Stoughton, 1960), p. 159.

[20] *Works* (Hickman), 2:86-87.

[21] Cited Fiering, p. 200. I am indebted to Fiering's fascinating chapter, 'Hell and the Humanitarians', in this work. See ibid., pp. 200-260.

from the Scriptures and also from the philosophical premises of opponents such as Tillotson and the Third Earl of Shaftesbury, he attacked the psychological optimism and the sentimental humanitarianism of the benevolist school. Edwards regarded the 'generosity' of Tillotson's views as a spurious and dangerous generosity; and in combating the views of the Archbishop, he sought to provide a reasoned and scriptural counterblast to the benevolist and humanitarian pull of the age.

It is important to note, however, that whilst the main thrust of the section entitled 'Doctrine' in this sermon is that of 'confutation', the main thrust of the section entitled 'Application' is evangelistic. 'The Eternity of Hell Torments' is not only a polemical sermon; it is also an awakening sermon. Like many of Edwards' sermons it deliberately aims to awaken sinners out of the slumbers of spiritual death. Indeed, the 'use of awakening' is one of the many different 'uses' that are found in Edwards' Applications. Similarly, 'The Future Punishment of the Wicked Unavoidable and Intolerable', dated April 1741 and based upon Ezekiel 22:14, ('Can thine heart endure, or can thine hands be strong, in the days that I shall deal with thee? I the Lord have spoken it, and will do it'), contains the following remarkable awakening passage:

This subject may be applied in a use of awakening to impenitent sinners . . . What art thou in the hands of the great God, who made heaven and earth by speaking a word? What art thou, when dealt with by that strength, which manages all this vast universe, holds the globe of the earth, directs all the motions of the heavenly bodies from age to age, and, when the fixed time shall come, will shake all to pieces? There are other wicked beings a thousand times stronger than thou: there are strong and proud spirits of a gigantic stoutness and hardiness. But how little are they in the hands of the great God! they are less than weak infants; they are nothing, and less than nothing, in the hands of an angry God, as will appear at the day of judgment. Their hearts will be broken; they will sink; they will have no strength or courage left; they will be as weak as water; their souls will sink down into an infinite gloom, an abyss of death and despair. Then what will become of thee, a poor worm, when thou shalt fall into the hands of that

God, when he shall come to show his wrath, and make his power known on thee?

If the strength of all the wicked men on earth, and of all the devils in hell, were united in one, and thou wert possessed of it all; and if the courage, greatness, and stoutness of all their hearts were united in thy single heart, thou wouldst be nothing in the hands of Jehovah. If it were all collected, and thou shouldst set thyself to bear as well as thou couldst, all would sink under his great wrath in an instant, and would be utterly abolished: thine hands would drop down at once, and thine heart would melt as wax. The great mountains, the firm rocks, cannot stand before the power of God. He can tear the earth in pieces in a moment; yea, he can shatter the whole universe, and dash it in pieces at one blow. How then will thine hands be strong, or thine heart endure?

Thou canst not stand before a lion of the forest; an angry wild beast, if stirred up, will easily tear such an one as thou art in pieces. Yea, not only so, but thou art crushed before the moth. A little thing, a little worm or spider, or some such insect, is able to kill thee. What canst thou do in the hands of God? It is vain to set the briers and thorns in battle-array against glowing flames; the points of thorns, though sharp, do nothing to withstand the fire.[22]

But the question that must be posed with regard to Edwards' doctrine of judgment is this: is he not vulnerable to the charge that, if his doctrine of hell is biblical, his emphasis upon hell is unbiblical? It is not that he focuses upon hell at the expense of heaven; his emphasis upon heaven is very considerable and his descriptions of heaven are very beautiful. It is rather that there is, surely, something excessive about the sometimes lurid, graphic detail in his descriptions of the eternal sufferings of the damned in hell. This tendency in Edwards emerges in the following passage found in the Application in 'The Eternity of Hell Torments':

---

[22] *Works* (Hickman), 2:81-82.

Do but consider what it is to suffer extreme torment for ever and ever; to suffer it day and night, from one year to another, from one age to another, and from one thousand ages to another, and so adding age to age, and thousands to thousands, in pain, in wailing and lamenting, groaning and shrieking, and gnashing your teeth; with your souls full of dreadful grief and amazement, with your bodies and every member full of racking torture, without any possibility of getting ease; without any possibility of moving God to pity you by your cries; without any possibility of hiding yourselves from him; without any possibility of diverting your thoughts from your pain; without any possibility of obtaining any manner of mitigation, or help, or change for the better.

Do but consider how dreadful despair will be in such torment. How dismal will it be, when you are under these racking torments, to know assuredly that you never, never shall be delivered from them; to have no hope; when you shall wish that you might be turned into nothing, but shall have no hope of it; when you shall wish that you might be turned into a toad or a serpent, but shall have no hope of it; when you would rejoice, if you might but have any relief, after you shall have endured these torments millions of ages, but shall have no hope of it. After you shall have worn out the age of the sun, moon, and stars, in your dolorous groans and lamentations, without rest day and night, or one minute's ease, yet you shall have no hope of ever being delivered; after you shall have worn a thousand more such ages, you shall have no hope, but shall know that you are not one whit nearer to the end of your torments; but that still there are the same groans, the same shrieks, the same doleful cries, incessantly to be made by you, and that the smoke of your torment shall still ascend up for ever and ever. Your souls, which shall have been agitated with the wrath of God all this while, will still exist to bear more wrath; your bodies, which shall have been burning all this while in these glowing flames, shall not have been consumed, but will remain to roast through eternity, which will not have been at all shortened by what shall have been past.[23]

---

[23] Ibid., p. 88.

Thus we would contend that, although Edwards' doctrine in this sermon is perfectly biblical and constitutes a very necessary counter-blast to the heterodox opinions of Archbishop Tillotson, the tone of this passage is not characterized by the measure, the sobriety, and the restraint found in the Scriptures. Paul Helm's general observations on this most solemn matter of hell are judicious and his observations concerning the danger of embroidering and embellishing the sober testimony of the Scriptures are not without relevance to the New England preacher:

> Hell is a dreadful topic, . . . Who would wish to dwell on this theme, on the fact of hell, the details, the prospect? And yet a certain type of religious personality has loved to dwell on the subject, to embellish it in lurid detail, to linger on the pains, and the hopelessness, in a way that tells us more about such a person's own psychological and spiritual state than about the sober and restrained witness of Scripture.[24]

Wednesday, July 8, 1741 was a very significant date in the ministry of Jonathan Edwards, for it was on that day – ten years exactly after delivering his discourse, 'God Glorified in Man's Dependence', at Boston – that he preached at Enfield, Massachusetts (now part of Connecticut) the sermon upon which, regrettably, his fame (and often his infamy) appears almost exclusively to rest, namely, 'Sinners in the Hands of an Angry God'. Indeed, this date places the preaching of this sermon right at the centre of the Great Awakening. The village of Enfield, however, had remained untouched by the fires of the revival – 'impious Enfield'[25] stood thus far in striking contrast to 'pious Suffield'[26] in this respect. Marsden describes the situation in the latter town thus: 'The neighbouring town of Suffield (where Edwards had heard Whitefield preach) was undergoing a tremendous revival; an amazing ninety-five persons had been added to the communicant roles the previous Sunday.'[27] A series of weekday meetings had, there-

[24] Paul Helm, *The Last Things: Death, Judgment, Heaven, Hell* (Edinburgh: Banner of Truth Trust, 1989), p. 108.

[25] Marsden, *Edwards*, p. 220.

[26] Ibid., p. 219.

[27] Ibid.

fore, been arranged in order that Enfield might be placed in the way of the blessing experienced at Suffield. In the providence of God Edwards was the preacher on that Wednesday and the sermon he decided to preach was one that he had preached at least once before, and certainly in June, to the people of Northampton.[28] His text was Deuteronomy 32:35: 'Their foot shall slide in due time.' But the circumstances in which this sermon was preached in Enfield contained little to suggest that its impact would be different from that upon the people of Northampton in the previous month; indeed, they seemed initially to promise a reception inferior to that of Northampton. In his *History of Connecticut* Benjamin Trumbull describes those circumstances thus:

> While the people in the neighbouring towns were in great distress for their souls, the inhabitants of that town were very secure, loose and vain. A lecture had been appointed at Enfield, and the neighbouring people, the night before, were so affected at the thoughtlessness of the inhabitants, and in such fear that God would, in his righteous judgment, pass them by, while the divine showers were falling all around them, as to be prostrate before him a considerable part of it, supplicating mercy for their souls. When the time appointed for the lecture came, a number of the neighbouring ministers attended, and some from a distance. When they went into the meeting-house, the appearance of the assembly was thoughtless and vain. The people hardly conducted themselves with common decency.[29]

'That quickly changed', observes Marsden. 'When Edwards started to preach, they fell under the gaunt pastor's almost hypnotic spell.'[30] Trumbull goes on to describe the astonishing effect of this sermon upon the people of Enfield:

> Before the sermon was ended, the assembly appeared deeply impressed and bowed down, with an awful conviction of their

[28] See ibid., p. 224.

[29] Benjamin Trumbull, *A Complete History of Connecticut Civil and Ecclesiastical from the Emigration of its First Planters, from England, in the Year 1630, to the Year 1764; and to the Close of the Indian Wars*, vol. 2 (New London: H. D. Utley, 1898), p. 112.

[30] Marsden, *Edwards*, p. 220.

sin and danger. There was such a breathing of distress, and weeping, that the preacher was obliged to speak to the people and desire silence, that he might be heard. This was the beginning of the same great and prevailing concern in that place, with which the colony in general was visited.[31]

It is interesting to analyse this sermon precisely because of the extraordinary effect that it clearly had upon the people of Enfield on this particular occasion. The following passage, for instance, is quite remarkable for the gripping, nervous brevity in the style; the vivid, graphic, solemnizing way in which the preacher puts words into the mouths of the lost in hell and engages them in dialogue; and the powerfully individualized, experimental note thus attained. The passage exemplifies well Edward J. Gallagher's observations concerning 'the sermon's pace, its pulse, or what we might call more precisely its pulsation':[32]

> If we could speak with them, and inquire of them, one by one, whether they expected, when alive, and when they used to hear about hell, ever to be the subjects of that misery, we, doubtless, should hear one and another reply, 'No, I never intended to come here: I had laid out matters otherwise in my mind; I thought I should contrive well for myself: I thought my scheme good. I intended to take effectual care; but it came upon me unexpected: I did not look for it at that time, and in that manner; it came as a thief: Death outwitted me: God's wrath was too quick for me. O my cursed foolishness! I was flattering myself, and pleasing myself with vain dreams of what I would do hereafter; and when I was saying, Peace and safety, then sudden destruction came upon me.'[33]

This sermon has recently been described by Stout and Hatch as 'arguably America's greatest sermon'.[34] It is certainly America's most

[31] Trumbull, p. 112.

[32] Edward J. Gallagher, '"Sinners in the Hands of an Angry God": Some Unfinished Business', *New England Quarterly* 73 (June 2000): p. 204.

[33] *Works* (Hickman), 2:9.

[34] *Works*, 22:34.

famous sermon. But fame is not necessarily synonymous with greatness, and the reason for its fame lies largely in the fact of its astonishing effectiveness at Enfield on this particular occasion. It is, however, quite possible that *if* the impact of this sermon had been no greater at Enfield in July than it had been in Northampton in June – in short, that if the sovereign blessing of God had *not* fallen upon the people at Enfield – this sermon might have lain in relative obscurity for the last two-hundred and sixty years. It is certainly a remarkable awakening sermon; but, as the history of the sermon itself demonstrates, its effectiveness must clearly not be deemed to work *ex opere operato*. Its effectiveness or non-effectiveness on any given occasion is inextricably connected with the sovereignty of the Spirit of God. Indeed, such is the greatness and sheer versatility of Edwards as a preacher that a case could be made that this particular sermon is not even *his* greatest sermon.[35] This is not to deny the unquestionable greatness of this sermon. Kimnach has justly described it as 'this shattering blast of the Gospel trumpet before the walled citadel of the natural heart.'[36]

The character of 'Sinners in the Hands of an Angry God' on the one hand and its reputation on the other are such that a very important distinction must be made. In the popular mind this sermon is doubtless the quintessential *hell-fire* sermon. But a careful analysis of the sermon demonstrates that it would be more aptly described as the

[35] Philip F. Gura, 'Lost and Found: Recovering Edwards for American Literature', in *Jonathan Edwards at 300*, p. 92, makes this interesting observation with regard to 'Sinners': 'In Edwards's lifetime not much was made of it. Samuel Hopkins, Edwards's first biographer, never mentions it, nor does Sereno Edwards Dwight in his study of 1829. Benjamin Trumbull was the first to bring this piece to wide attention, in 1818, in his *Complete History of Connecticut*, a central artifact of the Second Great Awakening. Like a burr that will not be shaken, the notion that this sermon somehow represents the apogee of Edwards's art has persisted.'

[36] Wilson H. Kimnach, 'The Brazen Trumpet: Jonathan Edwards's Conception of the Sermon' in *Jonathan Edwards: His Life and Influence,* Charles Angoff, ed. (Cranberry, New Jersey: Associated University Presses, Inc., 1975), pp. 39-40. The observation by Stout and Hatch to the effect that JE is 'almost out of control, when speaking for God' is regrettable. Indeed, the Yale co-editors flirt and toy with an essentially psychological interpretation of the sermon, or rather of the preacher, with their next observation: 'God, in Edwards' angry hands, can hardly contain his loathing, anger, and hatred of sinners.' *Works,* 22:37. The co-editors insinuate here the idea, which is undeveloped and unsubstantiated, of a projection of JE's extreme, unbalanced views and his own emotions on to God himself.

quintessential *awakening* sermon. Certainly, the sermon sets before the unconverted person the danger and the prospect of hell; but the major emphasis of the sermon falls, in fact, upon the precariousness of the sinner's position in the hands of God in this life. Kimnach is correct in noting that 'several manuscript sermons contain passages considerably more lurid than anything in "*Sinners*".[37] "'Sinners" is usually identified as the best of Edwards' "hell-fire" sermons; however, comparison with other examples of that genre among Edwards' sermons reveals that "Sinners" is not even a proper 'hell-fire' sermon, let alone the best. Sermons such as "The Eternity of Hell Torments" and "The Future Punishment of the Wicked Unavoidable and Intolerable" serve to mark the distinction between a true hell-fire sermon and the proto-eschatological formulation of "Sinners", focused as it is upon the here and now.'[38] The very title of the sermon – 'Sinners in the Hands of an Angry God' – highlights a very significant biblical and Edwardsean theme, namely, the immediacy of God. It is not just in hell that the sinner is in God's hands; he is in the hands of God now – in this life and in this world.

It is highly probable that the nineteenth-century Presbyterian theologian W. G. T. Shedd (1820-1894) had *inter alia* Edwards' preaching in mind and also the sometimes hysterical reaction to it on the part of certain men when he wrote his essay 'Hellphobia' in 1893. Referring to 'the sceptic's hellphobia',[39] Shedd contends that there is a certain 'irritability'[40] with which the doctrine of hell is met by certain 'literary men' – 'a kind of fear which shows itself in a certain species of literature, and in a certain class of persons'.[41] In his essay, 'Endless Punishment an Essential Doctrine of Christianity', Shedd demonstrates the crucial connection between the doctrine of hell and the

---

[37] *Works*, 10:114.

[38] Ibid., p. 168.

[39] W. G. T. Shedd, 'Hellphobia', in *Orthodoxy and Heterodoxy: A Miscellany* (New York: Charles Scribner's Sons, 1893; repr., Minneapolis: Klock and Klock Christian Publishers, Inc., 1981), p. 192.

[40] Ibid., p. 190.

[41] Ibid., p. 189. See Oliver Wendell Holmes, 'Jonathan Edwards', in *Critical Essays on Jonathan Edwards*, William J. Scheick, ed. (Boston, Massachusetts: G. K. Hall & Co., 1980), pp. 219-221, for an interesting example of this 'irritability'.

doctrine of the atonement: 'We affirm therefore that the doctrine of Christ's atonement stands or falls with that of endless punishment. He who denies the latter must logically deny the former ... Disbelievers in endless punishment are not believers in the atonement.'[42] Shedd emphasizes in that essay the indispensability of this doctrine to the gospel itself: 'But the fact is, that there is no doctrine more necessary in order to the integrity of the evangelical system than that future punishment is eternal. Vicarious satisfaction for sin is the keystone of the arch of Christianity, and if endless retribution for sin be taken out, the whole scheme of redemption by the sufferings of Christ falls to the ground.'[43] Moreover, the kind of piety that lies behind such objections to the doctrine of hell is, Shedd contends, not 'the piety of the gospel'; it is 'the piety of sentimentalism'.[44] 'Preaching about hell', observed H. R. Niebuhr shrewdly on the occasion of Edwards' bicentennial in Northampton in 1958, 'is always resented by men of so-called liberal mind.'[45]

---

[42] Shedd, 'Endless Punishment an Essential Doctrine of Christianity', in *Orthodoxy and Heterodoxy*, p. 185.

[43] Ibid., p. 183.

[44] Ibid., p. 186.

[45] Niebuhr, 'Anachronism', p. 130.

4

SOVEREIGNTY AND RESPONSIBILITY

Jonathan Edwards' lifelong preoccupation with and battle against Arminianism in his theology, philosophy, and preaching cannot be understood apart from a consideration of the rapidly developing theological climate of New England during his own lifetime. One of the most significant landmarks in this respect was the 'Great Apostasy' at Yale in 1722. The infant college, founded in 1701, just two years before Edwards' birth, had already suffered a troubled, chequered history which was reflected in the existence of three rival branches at Saybrook, Wethersfield, and New Haven. But the embarrassment of rival branches paled into insignificance in comparison with the public débacle of 1722:

> At the Commencement of 1722, just when it seemed that the college had overcome its turbulent birth pains, the trustees were faced with their greatest crisis. The Rector of Yale at the time, Timothy Cutler, along with one of the two tutors and five local ministers, had revealed their conversion to Anglicanism, made plain by Cutler's conspicuous conclusion of the Commencement prayer from the Book of Common Prayer – 'and let all the people say, Amen.'[1]

Marsden describes thus the significance of this citation from the *Book of Common Prayer*:

> This information resounded as though lightning had struck the podium. Some of the crowd might not have been surprised if lightning had struck the rector. It was as though, in a later era, . . .

[1] George G. Levesque, 'Introduction' to 'Quaestio: Peccator Non Iustificatur Coram Deo Nisi Per Iustitiam Christi Fide Apprehensam', *Works*, 14:49-50.

the commencement preacher at Bob Jones University had closed with a prayer to the Blessed Virgin. Cutler's words were straight out of the Anglican Book of Common Prayer. They were a signal that the very man chosen to be the chief guardian of New England orthodoxy had declared himself in the camp of the enemy.[2]

Anglicanism was, of course, 'the great Puritan nemesis';[3] and for the New England mind it was inextricably associated with Arminianism. 'In Puritan vocabulary', explains Minkema, 'Arminianism, Latitudinarianism, and Prelacy were synonymous with heresy, and Anglicanism possessed all three.'[4] Consequently, Rector Timothy Cutler and tutors Johnson and Browne were dismissed by the Yale trustees for their heresy on October 16, 1722. These events coincided with Edwards' eight-and-a-half months pastorate in New York City and it is unlikely that he was personally present to witness them. But news of these events would have reverberated throughout New England and would have inevitably soon reached the ears of the Yale graduate. 'The "Great Apostasy", observes Minkema, 'personally sensitized him to the alleged dangers of the importation of Arminian thought. He was drawn into an ideological and theological civil war that would occupy nearly his entire life.'[5]

The Commencement at Yale the following year gave Edwards an opportunity to strike the first blow in this 'ideological and theological civil war'. It was on September 20, 1723, that he delivered, in Latin, his oration, or academic disputation, in partial fulfilment of the M.A. degree requirements for Yale College: *Quaestio: Peccator Non Iustificatur*

---

[2] Marsden, *Edwards*, p. 83.

[3] Ibid., p. 35.

[4] *Works*, 14:50.

[5] Ibid., p. 8. Kimnach also emphasizes the connection between the 'Great Apostasy' and JE's early preoccupation with the threat of Arminianism: 'There can be little doubt that JE's early focus upon Arminianism was in part a response to the very recent debacle at Yale College when Rector Timothy Cutler and tutors Johnson and Browne espoused the Church of England and were dismissed by the Yale trustees for their heresy on Oct. 16, 1722. Like Cutler, Johnson, and Browne, JE had been a great reader of the new books from England and was deeply impressed with both new ideas and new rhetoric, but JE was determined to stand for the New England Way, and anti-Arminianism seems to have become his banner.' *Works*, 10:287 n. 7.

Coram Deo Nisi Per Iustitiam Christi Fide Apprehensam.[6] Edwards' bold selection of the doctrine that lay at the very centre of the Reformation of the sixteenth century clearly signalled his intention to take up the cudgels on behalf of the orthodoxy of Yale. 'In a climate in which free will and self-determination were gaining favor', observes Levesque, 'Edwards defended the Calvinist proposition that a sinner is completely dependent upon God for salvation. Everyone in the audience doubtless recognized this as a frontal assault on the Arminian tendencies of the recent "Apostacie."'[7] There can be little doubt that Edwards' election to a tutorship at Yale on May 21, 1724, was in no small part due to both the courage and the ability displayed in his anti-Arminian oration of the previous September.

The twenty-eight months that Edwards spent as a tutor at Yale between May 1724 and September 1726 are marked, perhaps not surprisingly, by an almost complete absence of sermon composition. This period is marked, however, by 'prodigious intellectual growth'.[8] 'His connections with Yale College', explains Minkema, '. . . and his access to the new treasures of the Yale library, supplied a rich soil for his burgeoning ideas. During these years his working notebooks expanded geometrically to include studies on scriptural exposition, natural philosophy, typology, and the nature of faith and conversion. In the process, a larger form began taking shape: a theological system which, while grounded in orthodox Calvinism, was peculiarly his own.'[9] 'All God's Methods Are Most Reasonable' demonstrates this theological system. The evidence suggests that Edwards began the preaching of this sermon at Northampton on September 24, 1727.[10] The sermon itself consists of three preaching units on Isaiah

---

[6] 'The Question: The Sinner is not Justified before God except by the Righteousness of Christ Appropriated by Faith.'

[7] Levesque, p. 51.

[8] *Works*, 14:3.

[9] Ibid.

[10] 'The date Edwards began the series can be pinpointed with some accuracy because of the existence of auditor's notes, probably made by Joseph Hawley, Sr., that record the first preaching unit. The notes immediately prior in the volume, on sermons by both Stoddard and Edwards, are from early and mid-September 1727. This sermon was probably begun on September 24.' Ibid., p. 163. Kimnach also refers to this 'note-taker'. *Works*, 10:34-36. 'Joseph Hawley, Sr.', was, of course, JE's uncle and the man whose tragic suicide on June 1,

1:18-20: 'Come now, let us reason together, saith the Lord: though your sins be as scarlet, they shall be as white as snow; though they be red like crimson, they shall be as wool. If ye be willing and obedient, ye shall eat the good of the land: but if you refuse and rebel, ye shall be devoured with the sword: for the mouth of the Lord hath spoken it.' The sermon reflects the considerable intellectual maturation that had occurred during the years of the Yale tutorship. In the course of his Doctrine Edwards demonstrates the essential compatibility of 'necessity' and 'liberty':

> God may order that a thing shall certainly be done, so that it is impossible but that the thing should come to pass, and yet not force the doing. The certainty and necessity of events is very consistent with the liberty of action. Necessity and liberty ben't contradictory terms, though compulsion and liberty are. A thing may be certain and necessary from all eternity, as to the futurity of it, and the action be done with as much freedom and liberty as ever anything was done in the world. It was from all eternity certain, absolutely certain, that Judas should betray Christ; but yet when he did it, he did it freely because he himself chose it, and did it because he of his own free choice had determined it.
>
> Necessity is not opposed to liberty, but to contingency, to the accidentalness of a thing. And compulsion is opposed to liberty. Liberty don't consist in an exact indifference to an action, so that when it is done it shall be done merely accidentally; but it consists in acting according to one's own choice, to the counsel of our own will. And he that acts according to his own choice, acts freely, however God has determined that choice; and it was absolutely certain from all eternity that the man should make such a choice.[11]

In this passage the twenty-three-year-old preacher anticipates the central tenet that he was later to defend in *Freedom of the Will* (1754), namely, that 'necessity is not inconsistent with liberty'.[12] 'In Edwards'

1735, effectively marked the *terminus ad quem* of the Northampton awakening.

[11] *Works*, 14:168.

[12] *Works* (Hickman), 1:9.

view', observes Marsden, 'the only sensible way to talk of the free will was that one is free to do what one wants to do . . . If having free will, then, meant being free to do what one wanted to do, that was another way of saying that one was free to follow one's own strongest motive.'[13] This passage also demonstrates the astonishing intellectual and spiritual precocity and maturity of Stoddard's young assistant. The passage itself is perhaps atypical of Edwards' preaching considered as a whole; but it demonstrates, in passing, the unashamedly theological and, on rare occasions, even philosophical character of his preaching. Indeed, a good case could be made that the thought expressed in the above passage is really too philosophical and too profound for the pulpit, and belongs more to the treatise.

Eight years after delivering his *Quaestio* at Yale Edwards had an opportunity to turn his attention to Harvard. On Thursday July 8, 1731 – during the week of the Commencement at Harvard – he delivered in Boston a public lecture on 1 Corinthians 1:29-31: 'That no flesh should glory in his presence. But of him are ye in Christ Jesus, who of God is made unto us wisdom, and righteousness, and sanctification, and redemption: that, according as it is written, He that glorieth, let him glory in the Lord.' The lecture was entitled 'God Glorified in the Work of Redemption, by the Greatness of Man's Dependence upon Him in the Whole of it.' New England had been for some time very conscious of the gathering storm clouds of Arminianism. It was a highly strategic time, town, and text. The 'Great Apostasy' at Yale had clearly stunned the New England mind; but, as Marsden observes, 'everyone . . . knew that for decades some Harvard students toyed with Arminian notions and that a few of the more liberal clergy were rumoured to be tainted with Arminian and rationalist tendencies . . . Those who designed the occasion were well aware of the symbolic significance of inviting not only Stoddard's young successor but also a thoroughly orthodox Yale man to address an audience overwhelmingly of Harvard graduates.'[14] In his lecture Edwards stated the following as his Doctrine: 'God is glorified in the work of redemption in this,

---

[13] Marsden, *Edwards*, pp. 440-441.
[14] Ibid., p. 140.

that there appears in it so absolute and universal a dependence of the redeemed on him.'[15] One of the most remarkable features of this lecture was that it delivered, on behalf of Calvinism, a resounding counterblast to Arminianism without ever mentioning either theological system specifically by name. The lecture was published in Boston within a month.[16]

The following passage in the section of the lecture entitled 'Use' demonstrates that Edwards clearly had Arminianism and its correlates in view:

> Hence those doctrines and schemes of divinity that are in any respect opposite to such an absolute and universal dependence on God, derogate from his glory, and thwart the design of our redemption. And such are those schemes that put the creature in God's stead, in any of the mentioned respects, that exalt man into the place of either Father, Son, or Holy Ghost, in anything pertaining to our redemption. However they may allow of a dependence of the redeemed on God, yet they deny a dependence that is so *absolute* and universal. They own an entire dependence on God for *some* things, but not for others; they own that we depend on God for the gift and acceptance of a Redeemer, but deny so absolute a dependence on him for the obtaining of an *interest* in the Redeemer. They own an absolute dependence on the Father for giving his Son, and on the Son for working out redemption, but not so entire a dependence on the Holy Ghost for *conversion*, and a being in Christ, and so coming to a title to his benefits. They own a dependence on God for *means* of grace, but not absolutely for the benefit and success of those means; a partial dependence on the power of God, for obtaining and exercising holiness, but not a mere dependence on the arbitrary and sovereign grace of God. They own a dependence on the free grace of God for a reception into his favour, so far that it is without any proper merit, but not as it is without being attracted, or moved with any excellency. They own a partial dependence on Christ, as he through whom we have life, as having purchased new terms of

---

[15] *Works* (Hickman), 2:3.
[16] See Miller, *Edwards*, p. 15.

life, but still hold that the righteousness through which we have life is inherent in ourselves, as it was under the first covenant. Now whatever scheme is inconsistent with our *entire* dependence on God for all, and of having all of him, through him, and in him, it is repugnant to the design and tenor of the gospel, and robs it of that which God accounts its lustre and glory.[17]

The crucial phrases here are 'an absolute and universal dependence on God' on the one hand and 'a partial dependence' on the other. It is Calvinism that posits the former and Arminianism that posits the latter. Thus, although the twenty-seven-year-old Yale graduate did not specifically mention 'the absolute sovereignty of God' in this lecture, it is clearly implied, for the 'absolute sovereignty of God' is a corollary of 'the absolute dependence of man'. Similarly, the corollary of 'a partial dependence' is a partial sovereignty; and a partial sovereignty is ultimately no sovereignty at all.

It is an interesting fact that Edwards never flaunts the term 'Calvinist' or 'Calvinism' in his sermons; indeed, he demonstrates a certain reserve with regard to the terms Calvinism and Arminianism not only in his sermons, but also in that treatise, which, above all others, sets forth the Calvinistic scheme over against Arminianism, namely, *Freedom of the Will*. In his Preface to that treatise, however, he emphasizes that, if he were to avoid terms such as Calvinism and Arminianism, his discourse 'would be too much encumbered with circumlocution'.[18] It is very evident that even here Edwards' use of these terms is 'for distinction's sake'[19]; it is equally true, however, that he is not at all ashamed to be identified by the term Calvinism:

> However the term *Calvinistic* is, in these days, among most a term of greater reproach than the term *Arminian;* yet I should not take it at all amiss, to be called a *Calvinist,* for distinction's sake: though I utterly disclaim a dependence on *Calvin,* or believing the doctrines which I hold, because he believed and taught them;

---

[17] *Works* (Hickman), 2:7.
[18] Ibid., 1:3.
[19] Ibid.

and cannot justly be charged with believing in every thing just as he taught.[20]

'Edwards occasionally used "Calvinistic" as a description of his theology', observes Marsden, 'but he seldom cited or mentioned John Calvin by name. Edwards' theology was refracted mostly through Reformed, or Calvinistic, writers of the seventeenth or early eighteenth centuries, especially Puritan and Scottish Presbyterian writers from Great Britain and Reformed theologians from the continent.'[21]

But if Edwards demonstrates a certain reserve in his sermons concerning the term Calvinism, he shows no reserve at all concerning the doctrines of Calvinism.[22] 'God's Sovereignty in the Salvation of Men' – a sermon on Romans 9:18 ('Therefore hath he mercy on whom he will have mercy, and whom he will he hardeneth') – was preached *circa* 1732. In this sermon he asserts clearly and categorically the doctrine of 'the absolute sovereignty of God'. 'The glory of God is his absolute sovereignty',[23] he insists. 'The sovereignty of God is his absolute, independent right of disposing of all creatures according to his own pleasure.'[24] He goes on to express the truth of God's sovereignty very beautifully: 'Christ in his sovereignty passes by the gates of princes and nobles, and enters some cottage and dwells there, and has communion with its obscure inhabitants.'[25]

Moreover, in this sermon Edwards demonstrates very cogently from the Scriptures that 'God does actually exercise his sovereignty in men's salvation'[26] in the following remarkable passage which relates *inter alia* to the salvation of children:

> God sometimes will bless weak means for producing astonishing effects, when more excellent means are not succeeded. God some-

---

[20] Ibid.

[21] Marsden, *Edwards*, p. 514, n. 3.

[22] Mark Valeri makes this observation with regard to the period 1730-1733: 'Nowhere in his sermons from this period ... did Edwards state the classical Calvinist scheme explicitly.' *Works*, 17:12.

[23] *Works* (Hickman), 2:853.

[24] Ibid., p. 850.

[25] Ibid., p. 852.

[26] Ibid., p. 851.

times will withhold salvation from those who are the children of very pious parents, and bestow it on others, who have been brought up in wicked families. Thus we read of a good Abijah in the family of Jeroboam, and of a godly Hezekiah, the son of wicked Ahaz, and of a godly Josiah, the son of a wicked Amon. But on the contrary, of a wicked Amnon and Absalom, the sons of holy David, and that vile Manasseh, the son of good Hezekiah. Sometimes some, who have had eminent means of grace, are rejected, and left to perish, and others, under far less advantages, are saved. Thus the scribes and Pharisees, who had so much light and knowledge of the Scriptures, were mostly rejected, and the poor ignorant publicans saved. The greater part of those, among whom Christ was much conversant, and who heard him preach, and saw him work miracles from day to day, were left; and the woman of Samaria was taken, and many other Samaritans at the same time, who only heard Christ preach, as he occasionally passed through their city. So the woman of Canaan was taken, who was not of the country of the Jews, and but once saw Jesus Christ. So the Jews, who had seen and heard Christ, and saw his miracles, and with whom the apostles laboured so much, were not saved. But the Gentiles, many of them, who, as it were, but transiently heard the glad tidings of salvation, embraced them, and were converted.[27]

It is important to note, however, that, for all his vigorous assertion of 'the absolute sovereignty of God', Edwards never degenerates into Hyper-Calvinism. Indeed, both in his theological writings and in his sermons he steers a very careful *via media* between the Scylla of Hyper-Calvinism on the one hand and the Charybdis of Arminianism on the other. This balance between his emphasis upon the sovereignty of God and the responsibility of man is expressed beautifully in one of his *Miscellanies:*

In efficacious grace we are not merely passive, nor yet does God do some, and we do the rest. But God does all, and we do all. God produces all, and we act all. For that is what he produces, *viz.* our own acts. God is the only proper author and fountain; we only

[27] Ibid., p. 852.

are the proper actors. We are, in different respects, wholly passive and wholly active . . . These things are agreeable to that text, 'God worketh in you both to will and to do.'[28]

Man's total passivity in salvation reflects the sovereignty of God; man's total activity in salvation reflects the responsibility of man. It should be noted that Edwards' preaching consistently lays great emphasis upon this responsibility of man, whether that of the sinner or of the saint.

The most sophisticated analysis of the due relationship between and the proper adjustment of the sovereignty of God and the responsibility of man is, of course, found in his *magnum opus, Freedom of the Will* (1754). Written, astonishingly, in just four and a half months in Stockbridge, this treatise represents the matured distillation of the study and the reflection of a lifetime; it is a devastating assault upon 'Arminian liberty of will, consisting in indifference, and sovereign self-determination'.[29] Edwards regarded 'the Arminian notion of self-determination'[30] as utterly destructive of this doctrine of the absolute sovereignty of God and as powerfully corrosive of the gospel scheme of salvation. The Arminian concept of man's will insisted that the will enjoyed a state of equilibrium, indifference, and sovereignty over itself – in short, that it was wholly unfettered and was characterized by a power of self-determination. 'By the 1750's', observes Marsden, 'what we call "the Enlightenment" and what Edwards called sardonically "this age of light and inquiry", was waxing towards its meridian.'[31] In a letter to John Erskine on August 3, 1757, the Stockbridge philosopher-theologian articulated his assessment of the danger of the Arminian position thus: 'I think the notion of liberty, consisting in a contingent self-determination of the will, as necessary to the morality of men's dispositions and actions, almost inconceivably pernicious.'[32]

Over against 'sovereign self-determination' Edwards asserts 'the absolute and most perfect sovereignty of God'.[33] 'There is no other

[28] Ibid., p. 557.
[29] Ibid., 1:68.
[30] Ibid.
[31] Marsden, *Edwards*, p. 433.
[32] *Works*, 16:719.
[33] *Works* (Hickman), 1:70.

divine sovereignty but this',[34] he insists. 'The sovereignty of God is his ability and authority to do whatever pleases him.'[35] The corollary of this absolute, divine sovereignty is 'the doctrine of *absolute, eternal, personal election*'.[36] Edwards' position with regard to liberty is simply 'the opinion of the *Calvinists,* who place man's liberty *only in a power of doing what he will*'[37] 'In other words', explains Ramsey, 'a man is free to do what he wills, but not to do what he does not will.'[38] Thus the Calvinistic doctrine of man's inability is essentially *an inability of the will;* man is, by nature, unable to be willing in the great things of Christ and the gospel.

But the fact that man is unable to be willing in the great things of Christ and the gospel does not mean that he is not responsible for this inability of the will; nor does it mean that man cannot be validly addressed with and confronted by God's counsels, promises, threatenings, commands, exhortations, invitations, and persuasions. It is crucial to note that the doctrine of the absolute sovereignty of God does not, in Edwards' mind, preclude the concept, and indeed the necessity, of choice. Man is 'an intelligent and voluntary agent',[39] and, as such, he can and should be addressed with and confronted by the commands and the invitations of the gospel:

> The things which have been already observed, may be sufficient to answer most of the objections, and silence the great exclamations of *Arminians* against the *Calvinists,* from the supposed inconsistence of *Calvinistic* principles with the moral perfections of God, as exercised in his government of mankind. The consistence of such a doctrine of necessity as has been maintained, with the fitness and reasonableness of God's commands, promises and threatenings, rewards and punishments, has been particularly considered. The cavils of our opponents, as though our doctrine of necessity made God the author of sin, have been answered; and

[34] Ibid., p. 71.
[35] Ibid.
[36] Ibid., p. 88.
[37] Ibid., p. 18.
[38] *Works*, 1:13.
[39] *Works* (Hickman), 1:6.

also their objections against these principles, as inconsistent with God's sincerity, in his counsels, invitations and persuasions, has already been obviated, in what has been observed respecting the consistence of what *Calvinists* suppose, concerning the secret and revealed Will of God. By that it appears, there is no repugnance in supposing it may be the secret Will of God, that his ordination and permission of events should be such, that it shall be a certain consequence, that a thing never will come to pass; which yet it is man's duty to do, and so God's preceptive Will, that he should do; and this is the same thing as to say, God may sincerely command him and require him to do it. And if he may be sincere in commanding him, he may, for the same reason, be sincere in counselling, inviting, and using persuasions with him to do it. Counsels and invitations are manifestations of God's preceptive Will, or what God loves, and what is in itself, and as man's act, agreeable to his heart; and not of his disposing Will, and what he chooses as a part of his own infinite scheme of things. It has been particularly shewn, . . . that such a necessity as has been maintained, is not inconsistent with the propriety and fitness of divine commands; and for the same reason, not inconsistent with the sincerity of invitations and counsels, . . . Yea, it has been shown, . . . that this objection of *Arminians,* concerning the sincerity and use of divine exhortations, invitations, and counsels, is demonstrably against themselves.[40]

'Edwards', insists Marsden, '. . . wanted to make clear his most fundamental point: that he was not denying free will but defending it in the highest intelligible meaning of the term.'[41] Marsden develops this crucial issue thus:

The crucial point for Edwards was how God governs the universe. Far from creating a purely mechanistic universe and then letting it run by some inexorable natural laws, as some Deists might posit, in Edwards' conception God governs by multiple means. For inanimate things God normally governs by natural laws, so in the Newtonian universe every motion is related by natural laws to

---

[40] Ibid., pp. 82-83.
[41] Marsden, *Edwards,* p. 445.

every other motion, except when God occasionally intervenes miraculously. With persons, who are higher on the scale of being, however, God governs increasingly through moral necessity. God allows them choices that are their own choices. Ultimately, of course, their wills, like everything else in the universe, are subject to God's will and design – Edwards saw no escape from that if God is eternal, omniscient, and all powerful. Yet the crucial point was that God exercised that sovereignty in a variety of ways. So he created intelligent beings who were free to choose what they wanted in the most significant ways possible in a God-governed universe. Their choices were fully their own, and they were morally responsible for their choices.[42]

This emphasis upon the choice of man is set forth as a formal principle in the proclamation of the gospel in 'Heaven is a World of Love':

> God gives men their choice. They may have their inheritance where they choose it, and may obtain heaven if they will seek it by patient continuance in well-doing, Rom. 2:7. We are all of us, as it were, set here in this world as in a large wilderness with divers countries about it, with several ways or paths leading to these different countries, and we are left to our choice what course we will take. If we heartily choose heaven, and set our hearts chiefly on that blessed Canaan, that land of love, and love the path which leads to it, we may walk in it; and if we continue so to do, it will certainly lead us to heaven at last.[43]

Edwards' emphasis upon the concept of 'choice' and his reiteration both of the verb 'to choose' and the word 'if' demonstrate that he proclaims the gospel in terms of a certain *prima facie* conditionalism or contingency. If it be asked – 'How is this apparent emphasis upon choice, conditionalism, and contingency compatible with his belief in the "absolute sovereignty" of God? How is it compatible with the position of his great treatise *Freedom of the Will* in which he demolishes "the

---

[42] Ibid., pp 443-444.
[43] *Works*, 8:392-393. The differences between the Yale edition (cited here) and Tryon Edwards' 1852 edition at this point are minimal.

Arminian doctrine of contingence and self-determination"?'[44] – the answer lies in the fact that it is one thing to assert (as Edwards does consistently) the *necessity of choice;* it is quite another to assert (as he never does) the *liberty of self-determination.*

It is very evident both from his formal statements and from his actual practice that Edwards was a passionate believer in the free offer of the gospel. In 'Great Guilt No Obstacle to the Pardon of the Returning Sinner' – a sermon on Psalm 25:11 ('For thy name's sake, O Lord, pardon my iniquity; for it is great') – he emphasizes the universality of the terms of the gospel[45]:

> Pardon is as much *offered* and *promised* to the greatest sinners as any, if they will come aright to God for mercy. The invitations of the gospel are always in universal terms: as, 'Ho, every one that thirsteth'; 'Come unto me, all ye that labour and are heavy laden'; and, 'Whosoever will, let him come.' And the voice of Wisdom is to men in general; Prov. viii. 4. 'Unto you, O men, I call, and my voice is to the sons of men.' Not to moral men, or religious men, but to you, O men. So Christ promises, John vi. 37. 'Him that cometh to me, I will in no wise cast out.' This is the direction of Christ to his apostles, after his resurrection, Mark xvi. 15, 16. 'Go ye into all the world, and preach the gospel to every creature: he that believeth, and is baptized, shall be saved.' Which is agreeable to what the apostle saith, that the gospel was preached to every creature which is under heaven, Col. i. 23.[46]

It is very important to note that the New England Calvinistic preacher had no compunction whatsoever about utilizing the language of invitation and responsibility in his preaching. Indeed, his sermons are replete with phrases such as 'making a choice',[47] 'choosing him for your Saviour',[48] 'believing in him',[49] 'receiving Christ as one's

---

[44] *Works* (Hickman), 1:67.

[45] This sermon is not dated and is, therefore, presumed to have been preached before the year 1733, as it was in that year that JE began to date his sermons. See *Works,* 17:455.

[46] *Works* (Hickman), 2:112.

[47] Ibid., p. 60.

[48] Ibid., p. 686.

[49] Ibid., p. 89.

Saviour',[50] 'accepting of him',[51] 'embracing Christ as a Saviour',[52] 'going to Christ',[53] 'coming to Christ',[54] 'coming to such a Saviour as this',[55] 'coming to him in your heart',[56] 'coming and putting one's trust in him',[57] 'running to him',[58] 'closing with him as your Saviour',[59] 'casting yourself upon him',[60] 'venturing your soul upon Christ',[61] 'committing your souls to him',[62] and 'letting him in'.[63] It should be noted that, in his sermons, Edwards does not *merely* utilize the language of divine command and human inability; indeed, in his sermons he does not *mainly* utilize the language of divine command and human inability. Rather he utilizes the language of divine invitation and human responsibility. In his preaching he constantly presents the wooings of God in the gospel.

This 'wooing note',[64] as Turnbull terms it, is a very significant feature of Edwards' preaching, as is evident from the following extracts from five different sermons:

> Christ is represented in Scripture, as wooing the souls of sinners. He uses means to persuade them to choose and accept of their own salvation. He often invites them to come to him that they may have life, that they may find rest to their souls; to come and take of the water of life freely. He stands at the door and knocks; and ceases not, though sinners for a long time refuse him. He bears repeated repulses from them, and yet mercifully continues knock-

---

[50] Ibid., p. 45.
[51] Ibid., 1:686.
[52] Ibid., 2:45.
[53] Ibid., 1:686.
[54] Ibid., 2:113.
[55] Ibid., 1:686.
[56] Ibid.
[57] Ibid.
[58] Ibid.
[59] Ibid.
[60] Ibid.
[61] Ibid.
[62] Ibid., 2:89.
[63] Cited Marsden, *Edwards*, pp. 393-394. Marsden cites the following from one of the Indian sermons at Stockbridge: "'Let him in", Edwards pled. 'Will you shut him out of doors when he comes to you and knocks at your door with his wounded, bleeding hands?'"
[64] Turnbull, p. 122.

ing, saying, 'Open to me, that I may come in and sup with you, and you with me.' At the doors of many sinners he stands thus knocking for many years together. Christ is become a most importunate suitor to sinners, that he may become their sovereign.[65]

Salvation is ready brought to your door; and the Saviour stands, knocks, and calls that you would open to him, that he might bring it in to you. There remains nothing but your consent ... And the wisdom of God has provided us a Saviour that woos in a manner that has the greatest tendency to win our hearts. His word is most attractive. He stands at our door and knocks. He does not merely command us to receive him: but he condescends to apply himself to us in a more endearing manner. He entreats and beseeches us in his word and by his messengers.[66]

Christ condescends not only to call you to him, but he comes to you; he comes to your door, and there knocks. He might send an officer and seize you as a rebel and vile malefactor; but instead of that, he comes and knocks at your door, and seeks that you would receive him into your house, as your Friend and Saviour. And he not only knocks at your door, but stands there waiting, while you are backward and unwilling.[67]

This glorious person has been offered to you times without number, and he has stood and knocked at your door, till his hairs were wet with the dews of the night; but all that he has done has not won upon you; you see no form nor comeliness in him, no beauty that you should desire him. When he has thus offered himself to you as your Saviour, you never freely and heartily accept of him.[68]

Now, now, then, is the time, now is the blessed opportunity to escape those everlasting burnings. Now God hath again set open the same fountain among us, and gives one more happy opportunity for souls to escape. Now he hath set open a wide door, and

[65] *Works* (Hickman), 2:212.
[66] Ibid., p. 156.
[67] Ibid., 1:687.
[68] Ibid., 2:887.

he stands in the door-way, calling and begging with a loud voice to the sinners of Zion: Come, saith he, come, fly from the wrath to come; here is a refuge for you; fly hither for refuge; lay hold on the hope set before you.[69]

It is surely undeniable that this language is remarkable, and even daring.[70] What is so striking in the above extracts is not simply the emphasis upon the commands and the invitations of Christ in the gospel, but also the preacher's unashamed use of the metaphor of Christ standing at the door of men's hearts – indeed, his representation of Christ as standing, knocking, waiting, wooing, calling, and even begging for an entry; and what might seem, at first sight, to make it more remarkable still is the fact that this is the language of the author of that great Calvinistic *tour de force, Freedom of the Will*. It should be noted, however, that it is, *inter alia*, precisely the validity of this note that Edwards is concerned to establish in that treatise. One of the major objections levelled by Arminians against the Calvinistic position was that of the issue of the *sincerity of God:*

It is objected against the absolute decrees respecting the future actions of men, and especially the unbelief of sinners, and their rejection of the gospel, that this does not consist with the sincerity of God's calls and invitations to such sinners; as he has willed, in his eternal secret decree, that they should never accept of those invitations.[71]

---

[69] Ibid., p. 205.

[70] Mark Valeri makes this observation: 'Individual sermons were not systematic theologies, and at one time Edwards stressed one side of the equation (human responsibility) or the other (divine sovereignty). He could sound like an Arminian.' *Works*, 17:9. Marsden goes somewhat further: 'Calvinist revivalists, such as Edwards himself, were part of the eighteenth-century revolution that accentuated individual choice ... Yet rigorous Calvinists, such as Edwards and his Puritan forbears, kept such modern individualizing tendencies in severe check, balanced against their even greater insistence that one's status was defined only in relation to the absolutely sovereign God ... Remove divine sovereignty from the emphasis on individual choice and the whole system would collapse.' Marsden, *Edwards,* p. 439.

[71] *Works* (Hickman), 2:528. JE deals with the issue of the sincerity of God in *Freedom of the Will*, Ibid., 1:78-79. I have chosen, however, to cite from the *Miscellany* as it expresses this particular issue so succinctly.

Edwards responds to this objection along a number of different, although related, lines of argument. Firstly, he insists, *contra* Arminianism, that there are 'two wills of God': 'And thus it must needs be, and no hypothesis whatsoever will relieve a man, but that he must own these two wills of God.'[72] These 'two wills of God' are, on the one hand, 'God's revealed will' or 'God's preceptive will', and, on the other, 'his secret will' or 'his disposing will'. In *Freedom of the Will* Edwards demonstrates incontrovertibly the validity of this distinction by pointing to 'Joseph's brethren selling him into Egypt'[73] and to 'the crucifixion of Christ'.[74] In each case God's revealed or preceptive will insisted that these actions were wicked; but in each case God's secret or disposing will permitted and even utilized these evil acts for the sake of the greater good that flowed from them. Thus God's revealed or preceptive will coheres with the responsibility of man; it coheres with the free offer of the gospel. Conversely, God's secret or disposing will coheres with the sovereignty of God; it coheres with the doctrine of election.

The New England preacher-theologian would almost certainly have concurred with John Murray's incisive treatment of this issue in the latter's 'The Free Offer of the Gospel' in which he emphasizes the multiformity and the manifoldness of the divine will:

> There is a multiformity to the divine will that is consonant with the fullness and richness of his divine character, and it is no wonder that we are constrained to bow in humble yet exultant amazement before his ineffable greatness and unsearchable judgments. To deny the reality of the divine pleasure directed to the repentance and salvation of all is to fail to accept the witness borne by such a text as this [*Isa.* 45:22] to the manifoldness of God's will and the riches of his grace.[75]

---

[72] Ibid. Similarly, in *Freedom of the Will* JE makes this assertion: 'The Arminians themselves must be obliged, whether they will or no, to allow a distinction of God's will, amounting to just the same thing that Calvinists intend by their distinction of a secret and revealed will.' Ibid., 1:79.

[73] Ibid., 1:78.

[74] Ibid.

[75] John Murray, *Collected Writings of John Murray*, vol. 4 (Edinburgh: Banner of Truth, 1982), p. 127.

We have found that God himself expresses an ardent desire for the fulfilment of certain things which he has not decreed in his inscrutable counsel to come to pass. This means that there is a will to the realization of what he has not decretively willed, a pleasure towards that which he has not been pleased to decree. This is indeed mysterious, and why he has not brought to pass, in the exercise of his omnipotent power and grace, what is his ardent pleasure lies hid in the sovereign counsel of his will. We should not entertain, however, any prejudice against the notion that God desires or has pleasure in the accomplishment of what he does not decretively will.[76]

Secondly, Edwards emphasizes the crucial importance of 'means and endeavours'.[77] In *Freedom of the Will* he demonstrates that there is a general and almost universal connection between 'means and end',[78] 'causes and effects',[79] 'antecedents and consequents',[80] 'endeavours and success'.[81] Means and endeavours, in a general sense, 'belong to the general chain of events'.[82] The conversion of sinners is the end; the preaching of the gospel is the means to that end. With the exception of the rare, immediate interposition or intervention of God, the preaching of the gospel, with its commands and invitations, is essential to the conversion of sinners. 'God influences persons by means',[83] Edwards insists. 'The effect is *with* the Means, and not *without* them.'[84] Indeed, D. Bruce Hindmarsh has argued that, over against the tendency towards passivity found in Hyper-Calvinistic circles, Edwards' writings and his example led to the affirmation, within English evangelicalism, of 'a larger role for human agency in evangelism and salvation.'[85]

---

[76] Ibid., pp. 131-132.
[77] *Works* (Hickman), 1:67.
[78] Ibid., p. 68.
[79] Ibid., p. 67.
[80] Ibid.
[81] Ibid., p. 68.
[82] Ibid., p. 67.
[83] Ibid., p. 657.
[84] Ibid., p. 67.
[85] Hindmarsh, p. 216.

The great New England preacher was, as John H. Gerstner expresses it, a 'predestinarian evangelist'.[86] In this context it is important to note that, *contra* Hyper-Calvinism, his belief in predestination did not have a negative repercussive effect upon his belief in evangelism; and that, *contra* Arminianism, his belief in evangelism did not have a negative repercussive effect upon his belief in predestination. 'He opposed Hyper-Calvinism and was equally opposed to Arminianism',[87] notes Lloyd-Jones. This very fact reflects Edwards' essentially compatibilist position. The language of the sermons, with their remarkable emphasis upon the knocking, the waiting, and the wooing of Christ, clearly presupposes the perfect compatibility in Edwards' mind between the highest possible emphasis upon the sovereignty of God and the highest possible emphasis upon the responsibility of man. Thus, in *Freedom of the Will* he establishes as a fundamental principle the axioms implicit in his homiletical practice, namely, that 'command and obligation to obedience [are] consistent with moral inability to obey.'[88] 'If things for which men have a moral inability may properly be the matter of precept or command, then they may also of invitation and counsel. Commands and invitations come very much to the same thing; the difference is only circumstantial . . . The main difference between command and invitation consists in the enforcement of the will of him who commands or invites. In the latter it is his *kindness*, the goodness from which his will arises: in the former it is his *authority* . . .; therefore, a person being directed *by invitation*, is no more an evidence of insincerity in him that directs – in manifesting either a will or expectation which he has not – than a person being known to be morally unable to do what he is directed by command is an evidence of insincerity.'[89] 'It has been particularly shewn', Edwards concludes, 'that such a necessity as has been maintained, is not inconsistent with the propriety and fitness of divine commands; and for the same reason, not

[86] John H. Gerstner, *Jonathan Edwards, Evangelist* (Morgan, PA: Soli Deo Gloria Publications, 1995), p. 13.

[87] D. M. Lloyd-Jones, 'Jonathan Edwards and the Crucial Importance of Revival', in *The Puritans: Their Origins and Successors: Addresses Delivered at the Puritan and Westminster Conferences 1959-1978* (Edinburgh: Banner of Truth, 1987), p. 356.

[88] *Works* (Hickman), 1:47.

[89] Ibid., p. 51.

inconsistent with the sincerity of invitations and counsels, . . .'[90] It is this cogent reconciliation of the sovereignty of God and the responsibility of man – this incisive harmonization of necessity and liberty – that constitutes one of the greatest achievements of the Stockbridge philosopher-theologian-preacher in *Freedom of the Will*; it also constitutes a crucial aspect of the power and the appeal of his sermons.

[90] Ibid., p. 83.

5

THE CONCEPT OF SEEKING

It is evident from Jonathan Edwards' own statements that he had no brief for the preparationism which, historically, had developed in the preaching of New England by the mid-seventeenth century. Pivotal in the emergence of preparationism in New England were Thomas Hooker (1586-1647) and Thomas Shepard (1604-1649). Educated at Cambridge University at a time when the town was still filled 'with the discourse of the power of Mr. Perkins' ministry',[1] Hooker arrived in New England in 1633. He was to become one of the patriarchs of New England and the founder of Connecticut. Shepard, who was also educated at Cambridge, was later to marry Hooker's daughter. Norman Pettit emphasizes with regard to these two divines that 'each was to become a leading exponent in America of the concept of preparation.'[2] It is a fact of great significance that the conversion of both of these divines was, as Pettit expresses it, 'long and painful'.[3] There can be little doubt but that their own experience in this respect exerted a vital formative influence upon their theology. Thomas Hooker, whose great-granddaughter Jonathan Edwards was to marry eighty years after the latter's death, emphasized the necessity of preparation for Christ; he insisted upon the preparatory stages of *contrition* (consisting of 'the sight of sin', 'meditation', 'brokenness of heart', and 'separation from sin') followed by *humiliation* (consisting

[1] Cited Robert M. Horn, 'Thomas Hooker – The Soul's Preparation for Christ', in *The Puritan Experiment in the New World* (Rushden, England: The Westminster Conference, 1976), p. 19.
[2] Norman Pettit, *The Heart Prepared: Grace and Conversion in Puritan Spiritual Life* (New Haven and London: Yale University Press, 1966), p. 87.
[3] Ibid., p. 107.

of 'help sought', 'failure confessed', 'submission given', and 'content-ment reached').[4] Hooker was the theologian *par excellence* responsible for establishing a 'morphology of conversion' in seventeenth-century New England.

But Edwards was no respecter of grandfathers. Indeed, the eight-eenth-century New England preacher-theologian demonstrates a very striking independence of mind, not only with regard to the issue of the Lord's Supper, but also with regard to the issue of preparation-ism. He constantly sought to bring the ecclesiastical and homiletical traditions of New England to the bar of Holy Scripture. It is an inter-esting fact that Edwards was clearly exercised about the preparationist scheme of salvation as early as the 'New York period':

Dec. 18 [1722] . . . The reason why I, in the least, question my interest in God's love and favor, is, –

1. Because I cannot speak so fully to my experience of that pre-paratory work, of which divines speak: –

2. I do not remember that I experienced regeneration, exactly in those steps, in which divines say it is generally wrought . . .[5]

Monday morning, Aug. 12. [1723] The chief thing, that now makes me in any measure to question my good estate, is my not having experienced conversion *in those particular steps,* wherein the people of New England, and anciently the Dissenters of Old England, used to experience it. Wherefore, now resolved, never to leave searching, till I have satisfyingly found out the very bottom and foundation, the real reason, why they used to be converted in those steps.[6]

It is evident from these two entries that, from the very outset of his ministry, Edwards entertained distinct reservations with regard to the steps and stages in which, allegedly, conversion ought to be experienced. Indeed, it is evident that the weighty tradition of the New England preparationist scheme of conversion was such that it initially impinged

---

[4] See Horn, pp. 25-32.
[5] Cited *Works*, 10:269.
[6] Cited ibid., pp. 269-270.

upon his own assurance of salvation – hence his determination to pursue this issue until he had resolved it to his own satisfaction. McClymond summarizes the situation thus:

> He became aware quite early on that his experiences did not conform to the received theory. The *Diary* for 1722 expressed the worry 'I do not remember that I experienced regeneration, exactly in those steps, in which divines say it is generally wrought.' He specifically mentioned the lack of a full 'preparatory work.' Yet he soon stopped trying to fit experience to doctrine and instead altered his doctrine. *Personal Narrative* implicitly, and *Religious Affections* explicitly, repudiated the old morphology by making the *nature* of one's spiritual experiences rather than their *order* the discriminating factor in determining whether or not they were gracious.[7]

Thus it is in *Religious Affections* (1746) that Edwards expresses most clearly and persistently his opposition to preparationism. This treatise was published in Boston in 1746 in the aftermath of the Great Awakening. 'According to Dwight', observes John E. Smith, '"it was a series of sermons, which he preached from his own desk."'[8] The text upon which the series was based was 1 Peter 1:8 ('Whom having not seen, ye love; in whom, though now ye see him not, yet believing, ye rejoice with joy unspeakable and full of glory'). 'The *Affections*', contends Smith, 'contains his most acute and detailed treatment of the central task of defining the soul's relation to God.'[9] 'It has unquestionably been Edwards' most widely read book.'[10] Early in the treatise Edwards delivers an initial salvo against the preparationist concept of a 'morphology of conversion':

> It is to be feared that some have gone too far towards directing the Spirit of the Lord, and marking out his footsteps for him, and limiting him to certain steps and methods. Experience plainly

---

[7] McClymond, p. 42.

[8] *Works*, 2:73.

[9] Ibid., p. 1. 'The *Affections* represents a probing of the nature of piety with a finer instrument than Edwards had used in other revival writings.' Ibid., p. 6.

[10] Ibid., p. 78.

shows that God's Spirit is unsearchable and untraceable, in some of the best of Christians, as to the method of his operations in their conversion. Nor does the Spirit of God proceed discernibly in the steps of a particular established scheme, one half so often as is imagined. A scheme of what is necessary, and according to a rule already received and established by common opinion, has a vast, though to many a very insensible, influence in forming men's notions of the steps and method of their own experiences ... Very often, at first, their experiences appear like a confused chaos, as Mr. Shepard expresses it: but then, those passages of their experience are picked out, that have most of the appearance of such particular steps that are insisted on; and these are dwelt upon in the thoughts, and from time to time, in the relation they give. These parts grow and brighten in their view; and others, being neglected, grow more and more obscure. What they have experienced is insensibly strained to bring all to an exact conformity to the scheme established. And it becomes natural for ministers, who have to deal with and direct them while insisting upon distinctness and clearness of method, to do so too. But yet there has been so much to be seen of the operations of the Spirit of God, of late, that they who have had much to do with souls, and are not blinded with a sevenfold vail of prejudice, must know that the Spirit is so exceeding various in his manner of operating, that in many cases it is impossible to trace him, or find out his way.[11]

In this section of the treatise he makes a crucial distinction between the *nature* of divine things and the *order* of divine things. It was Edwards' conviction that the preparationist tradition of New England laid far too much emphasis upon the supposed steps and stages of its scheme – in short, upon a certain preconceived method of conversion.[12] Thus it was, in his judgment, an artificial scheme that tended to force the experience of the converted into its own mould. The scheme not only ignored the variety of the operations of the Spirit of God; it also ignored, in effect, the sovereignty of the Spirit and the profoundly mysterious and

---

[11] *Works* (Hickman), 1:254-255.
[12] See ibid., p. 254.

unsearchable character of his ways. Indeed, so far is Edwards from any stereotypical 'morphology of conversion' that twice in *Religious Affect-ions* he cites, interestingly, Thomas Shepard himself to the effect that the change in or the experience of the saints is, at first work, 'like a confused chaos'.[13]

Lloyd-Jones observes that 'Jonathan Edwards would have nothing to do with the teaching of preparationism. He belongs here to John Cotton rather than to Thomas Hooker.'[14] This assessment is just. It is, therefore, all the more surprising to note that some scholars have regarded Edwards' preaching as a continuation of the preparationist tradition. 'Jonathan Edwards', asserts Goen, 'inherited a tradition which had long occupied itself with analyses of the conversion experience.'[15] Goen follows Morgan in alleging that Edwards essentially adopted a 'morphology of conversion'[16] from the preparationists. This morphol-ogy had classically laid down certain steps by which the Spirit's work in the soul of any given individual could supposedly be identified. Goen continues his analysis thus:

> The Great Awakening revived this pattern of conversion. Still more, it established a morphology which would become normative in the evangelical churches; and as the revivalism then aborning brought those churches to dominance in American Christianity, this pattern of conversion came to be widely accepted as the normal mode of entry into the Christian life. Credit for such a development goes chiefly to Jonathan Edwards, for three reasons: (1) far more than any of his predecessors, he had vast opportunities for clinical observation of sinners in the throes of the conversion experience; (2) he refracted his data through the insights of a new psychology derived from John Locke (1632-1704), thus achieving an interpretation of religious experience that commended the evan-gelical scheme to many thoughtful persons; and (3) he published a testimonial history of the first wave of revivalism, with the result that the pattern of the Northampton conversions became fixed

---

[13] Ibid.
[14] Lloyd-Jones, 'Crucial Importance of Revival', p. 350.
[15] *Works*, 4:25.
[16] Ibid.

in the popular mind . . . When he gave his narrative to the world, the simple fact is that no revival could ever be a surprise again.[17]

But the problem here is that the reasons adduced by Goen do not establish the point for which they are adduced; they do not establish that Edwards was chiefly responsible for re-establishing a 'morphology of conversion' in the New England churches. More precisely, they ignore his own insistence upon the *variety* by which the operations of the Spirit of God are characterized. Indeed, in *A Faithful Narrative* (1737) – the very work to which Goen appeals in order to substantiate his point concerning the 'morphology of conversion' – Edwards himself insists very strongly upon this fact of variety. 'There is an endless *variety* in the particular manner and circumstances in which persons are wrought on; and an opportunity of seeing so much will show, that God is further from confining himself to a particular method in his work on souls, than some imagine.'[18] Moreover, it must be insisted upon that in *A Faithful Narrative* Edwards was simply describing what he had observed. It is essential to note that it is one thing to *describe* a set of experiences in the act of conversion; it is quite another thing to *prescribe* such a set of experiences. The *de facto* is being confused here with the *de jure*.

Again, in 'The Spirit of Charity the Opposite of a Censorious Spirit' – a sermon on 1 Corinthians 13:5 ('Charity . . . thinketh no evil') – Edwards criticizes the censoriousness of some who fail to allow for such variety:

---

[17] Ibid., pp. 26-27. Goen does acknowledge that JE's position was essentially one of *description* rather than *prescription*. Goen's position appears to be that JE's *description* in *A Faithful Narrative* was later fossilized by his evangelical successors into a *prescription*: 'Careful interpreters of Edwards observe that he was hardly attempting to "fix the work of the Spirit to an inflexible series of stages" or restrict conversion to a uniform pattern. He was always unwilling to reject an experience just because it failed to follow a certain presupposed order, for, as he put it in *Religious Affections*, "no order or method of operations and experiences is any certain sign of their divinity." But in *A Faithful Narrative* he was only reporting what he had actually observed; and notwithstanding the many varieties of religious experience at Northampton, the three-stage pattern which can be extrapolated from his report is a fair summary of what he described.' Ibid., p. 29.

[18] *Works* (Hickman), 1:357.

84

And so persons are censorious when . . . they are ready to reject all as irreligious and unconverted men, because their experiences do not in everything quadrate with their own; setting up themselves, and their own experience, as a standard and rule to all others; not being sensible of that vast variety and liberty which the Spirit of God permits and uses in his saving work on the hearts of men, and how mysterious and inscrutable his ways often are, and especially in this great work of making men new creatures in Christ Jesus. In all these ways, men often act, not only censoriously, but as unreasonably (in not allowing any to be Christians who have not their own experiences) as if they would not allow any to be men who had not just their own stature, and the same strength, or temperament of body, and the very same features of countenance with themselves.[19]

Similarly, in the Preface to his 'Farewell Sermon' (1750) he deliberately corrects the 'slanderous representations'[20] of his position which had circulated in the midst of the Communion controversy. Amongst these 'gross misrepresentations'[21] was the allegation that, as the dismissed Northampton pastor puts it, 'I required a particular relation of the method and order of a person's inward experience, and of the time and manner of his conversion, as the test of his fitness for Christian communion.'[22] 'I ever declared against insisting on a relation of experiences, in this sense (*viz.* a relation of the particular time and steps of the operation of the Spirit, in first conversion) as the terms of communion.'[23] It is evident from the entire corpus of Edwards' writings that his position was that, *contra* the tradition of the churches of New England, it was not a relation or narration of the steps or method of the work of the Spirit that was necessary, but a sincere profession of faith in Christ himself.

Sermon notebook 45 contains an entry that is of great significance with regard to Edwards' concept of *seeking salvation:* 'To choose some

[19] *Charity,* pp. 206-207.
[20] *Works,* 25:489.
[21] Ibid., p. 488.
[22] Ibid., p. 489.
[23] Ibid., p. 493.

subject on purpose to show how unreasonable it is that persons should strive less in religion after conversion than before.'[24] Clearly implicit in this homiletical note is the conviction on his part that the pulpits and the churches of New England reflected a certain imbalance with regard to this doctrine. By clear implication it was his conviction that far more emphasis was being placed upon the seeking of salvation on the part of the *unconverted* than upon such seeking on the part of the *converted*. Such an emphasis was in Edwards' mind as unreasonable as it was unscriptural; indeed, such an emphasis was, in his mind, the reverse of the scriptural emphasis. It is quite possible that the sermon 'The Character of Paul an Example to Christians' is the sermon projected in the notebook. This lengthy sermon, which consisted of four preaching units and which is dated February 1740, was based on Philippians 3:17 ('Brethren, be followers together of me, and mark them which walk so as ye have us for an example'). The sermon is remarkable not only for its very thorough treatment of the concept of *example*, but also for its incisive treatment of the concept of *seeking*. Indeed, the very first aspect of the example of the Apostle Paul that is set before the people of Northampton is that of his *seeking salvation*. 'We should follow him in his earnestness in seeking his own salvation.'[25] Edwards goes on to develop his thesis concerning the seeking of salvation by emphasizing the 'violence and resolution' of the Apostle:

> And in this way he sought the kingdom of heaven. He acted in this matter very much as one that is running a race for some great prize, who makes running his great and only business, till he has reached the end of the race, and strains every nerve and sinew, and suffers nothing to divert him, and will not stand to listen to what any one says to him, but presses forward. Or as a man that is engaged in battle, sword in hand, with strong and violent enemies, that seek his life. 1 Cor ix. 26. 'I therefore so run, not as uncertainly; so fight I, not as one that beateth the air' . . . Now those, who seek their salvation, ought to follow this example . . .

---

[24] *Works*, 10:62. According to Kimnach this notebook 'was probably begun in late 1738 or early 1739.' Ibid.

[25] *Works* (Hickman), 2:856. Emphasis added.

Let them do as did the apostle Paul; seek salvation in the way he did, with the like violence and resolution.[26]

The New England preacher lays a foundation here for his ensuing emphasis – that which he specified in the entry in his sermon notebook – namely, that of the necessity of 'earnestness and violence for the kingdom of heaven' *after* conversion. Indeed, the very Scriptures that he has already cited, which depict the Christian life as a race and as a battle in which the believer is *even now* vigorously engaged and which is not yet won, anticipate this particular emphasis:

> The apostle did not only thus earnestly seek salvation *before* his conversion and hope, *but afterwards also* . . . To see one of the most eminent saints that ever lived, if not the most eminent of all, so exceedingly engaged in seeking his own salvation, ought for ever to put to shame those who are a thousand degrees below him, and are but mere infants to him, if they have any grace at all; who yet excuse themselves from using any violence after the kingdom of heaven now, because they have attained already, who free them-selves from the burden of going on earnestly to seek salvation with this, that they have finished the work, they have obtained a hope. The apostle, as eminent as he was, did not say within himself, 'I am converted, and so am sure of salvation. Christ has promised it me; why need I labour any more to secure it? Yea, I am not only converted, but I have obtained great degrees of grace.' But still he is violent *after* salvation . . . The apostle knew that though he was converted, yet there remained a great work that he must do, in order to his salvation. There was a narrow way to eternal glory, through which he must pass, and never could come to heaven in any other way. He knew it was absolutely necessary for him earn-estly to seek salvation still; he knew there was no going to heaven in a slothful way. And therefore he did not seek salvation the less earnestly, for his having hope and assurance, but a great deal more. We nowhere read so much of his earnestness and violence for the kingdom of heaven *before* he was converted, as *afterwards*.[27]

---

[26] Ibid.
[27] Ibid., pp. 856-857.

In the light of Edwards' consistent emphasis upon the importance of seeking *after* conversion there is reason to question the following assertion by Gerstner: 'The evangelical cutting edge of Edwards' preaching was the Puritan doctrine of seeking.'[28] The context of Gerstner's observation demonstrates that by 'evangelical' he means 'evangelistic'. According to Gerstner this doctrine of seeking permeated Edwards' preaching throughout his ministerial career; and its prevalence is demonstrated by the interesting and revealing fact that, between the spring of 1728 and December 1751, he preached four times on the first part of Ecclesiastes 9:10 ('Whatsoever thy hand findeth to do, do it with thy might'). These sermons, the first of which was preached not long after the commencement of his ministry at Northampton and the last of which not long after the commencement of his ministry at Stockbridge, are of great significance with regard to Edwards' concept of the seeking to be undertaken by the unconverted. 'It may well be that the most important general writings of Edwards on the whole theme of preparation', Gerstner writes, 'are the four unpublished sermons on Ecclesiastes 9:10 . . . In a comprehensive fashion, he enumerates what the seeking sinner can and cannot do. In so explicating he spells out the Calvinistic rationale for preparation.'[29] Gerstner goes on to summarize the essence of these sermons in which Edwards defines the parameters of the sinner's seeking, both from the negative and the positive standpoint:

> It is true, Edwards maintains, that fallen man suffers moral inability and there are certain things that he simply cannot do. First, (Edwards explains to the Indians in the latest preaching on this text), [December 1751] men cannot make satisfaction for their sins; only God can do that. Second, men cannot earn a righteousness that makes them acceptable before God; only he can provide that. Third, men cannot change their hearts which, yet, must be changed by God. This alone is enough to demonstrate that Edwards was no incipient Arminian. John Calvin never enunciated

---

[28] John H. Gerstner, *The Rational Biblical Theology of Jonathan Edwards*, vol. 3 (Powhatan, Virginia: Berea Publications, 1993), p. 50.

[29] Ibid., p. 66.

the sinner's moral inability more explicitly and lucidly. The sinner suffers total moral inability to save himself or to cooperate in his regeneration.

Yet there are many things the sinner can do without new faculties or principles. If Edwards lists three things that he cannot do, we find no less than ten things he can do enumerated in the earlier sermon on our text [Spring 1728–Winter 1729[30]] . . .

1. A man can abstain from the outward gratifications of his lusts.

2. A man can in many respects keep out of the way of temptation.

3. Persons can perform outward duties of morality towards their neighbours.

4. Persons can search the Scripture.

5. Persons can attend all ordinances.

6. Persons can use their tongues to the purpose of religion.

7. Persons have in a great measure the command of their thoughts.

8. Persons can set apart a suitable proportion of their time for these things.

9. Persons can improve divine assistance that is given.

10. They can lay out their strength in these things as well as other things.[31]

Edwards' basic position here is that the sinner is able to put himself in the way of the blessing of conversion by making use of means. Moreover, the very fact that Edwards utilized here the verb 'can' rather than the verb 'must' demonstrates that he is setting forth *possibilities*, not *laws*. It might be retorted, of course, that the verb 'can' still raises significant problems for a Calvinistic doctrine of seeking; for if the

---

[30] Thomas A. Schafer has narrowed the possible time range for the preaching of this sermon to 'Summer 1728-Winter 1729.' See *Works*, 14:546.

[31] Gerstner, *Rational Biblical Theology*, 3:66-67. It should be noted that there is nothing in the above list that belongs exclusively to the domain of the Christian. There is, however, a potential ambiguity about the fifth recommendation: 'Persons can attend all ordinances.' In view of the position that JE espoused in the late 1740's with regard to participation in the Lord's Supper one might well conclude that JE is simply referring here to the desirability of being present at the celebration of this ordinance; but in view of the fact that this sermon was preached in the late 1720's, when Stoddard's position that the Lord's Supper was a 'converting ordinance' held sway, one might conclude that JE is not excluding participation in the sacrament.

verb 'must' savours of *law*, the verb 'can' savours of *ability;* and *moral ability* is the very thing that Calvinism utterly denies.

Edwards deals with this very issue in 'All That Natural Men Do Is Wrong'. Dated April 1736, this sermon is a very significant exposition of Romans 3:11-12 ('There is none that understandeth, there is none that seeketh after God. They are all gone out of the way, they are together become unprofitable; there is none that doeth good, no, not one'). In the course of his 'Introduction' Edwards makes the following statement with regard to *seeking:*

> In the text there are five things predicated of natural men . . . That they don't seek after God. Many of them seem to seek after God: they attend on the ordinances of religion; yea, and some of them have their minds very much engaged in it. But yet they don't seek after God. They may pray to God earnestly, and beg mercy of him; but yet they don't seek after God. They seek themselves, and not God.[32]

Edwards concludes the doctrinal section of this sermon with the following passage in which he emphasizes that the doctrine and the practice of seeking must have an essentially Christocentric focus:

> Persons ought to seek salvation only in and through Christ, looking to God for it through him, depending on his merits and righteousness alone for the attainment of it: but so natural men don't seek it. They seek it through their own righteousness and worthiness. So that all natural men seek salvation in a way that is altogether wrong. 'They are all gone out of the way. There is none that seeketh after God'; as it is said in the text. Those of them that are most concerned and engaged, they may be seeking in such a way as, through the infinite grace [of God], if they continue, may be likely legally to prepare 'em for converting grace, and so to issue in it. But indeed all natural men seek salvation in a wrong way; not only wrong in some low degree, but exceeding wrong in a way that is in many respects diametrically contrary to the rule.[33]

---

[32] *Works,* 19:519.
[33] Ibid., p. 530.

It is important to note that in this sermon Edwards somewhat tentatively limits that seeking, of which the natural man is capable, to the positing of the possibility of 'a legal preparation for converting grace'. He makes it clear that the natural man does not seek after God and that 'all that natural men do is wrong.'[34] What, then, is the seeking to which Edwards so often refers and which he so often advocates? Natural men, he asserts, can do those things that are 'comparatively right'; they can do those things that are 'externally and naturally right'; and they can do those things that are 'likely to issue in the good of their souls'. The goodness of which they are capable is 'rather a natural than a moral goodness'.[35] At the close of the sermon he returns to this theme of *natural, relative, unregenerate goodness* with his technique of objection and answer:

> Here some may be ready to make an objection, and say, 'If it be so that all that I do is wrong, then what signifies for me to do any longer? Why had not I better leave off doing?' . . .
>
> [Ans.] 2. This objection has been already obviated in the beginning of this discourse, where it was observed that natural men could do what was negatively and comparatively right. {They do} that by which they avoid doing what is more wrong, as they do by attending, as far as in them lies, all moral and religious duties. [They] do [what is] materially right; [for it is] better [to] do that which is materially right than do what is both materially [and] finally wrong.
>
> [Natural men] can do what is right according to a rule of providence; {for it is} in a way likely to issue in saving good, though in itself wrong. [It] may be a legal preparation and, by sovereign grace, be the way to obtain mercy.[36]

The problem in this sermon is that it is difficult to escape the impression of a certain incoherence in Edwards' thought with regard

---

[34] Ibid., p. 520.

[35] Ibid., p. 521.

[36] Ibid., p. 536. This passage is, in effect, the 'Conclusion' of the sermon. We have, however, omitted the final sentence as it is not germane to the concept of seeking. Moreover, the final sentence does not enhance the conclusion because it is distinctly anti-climactic: 'But having already spoken particularly to these things, I shall not further insist on them.' Ibid.

to the seeking undertaken by the unconverted – in short, the impression that Edwards himself is struggling with the internal tensions of this particular doctrine – even an impression of logical inconsistency. Indeed, the very title of the sermon suggests that the natural man can do nothing of any value. It is almost as if Edwards argues himself out of the possibility and viability of such a doctrine, only to concede it in the closing lines of the sermon. This sermon is clearly very important; but it is not one of his best, and at times it is even somewhat convoluted.

Edwards returns to this emphasis upon the importance of seeking *after* conversion in *Religious Affections:*

> Hence there is an end to many persons' earnestness in seeking, after they have once obtained that which they call their conversion; . . . Before, while they looked upon themselves as in a state of nature, they were engaged in seeking after God and Christ, and cried earnestly for grace, and strove in the use of means: but now they act as though they thought their work was done; they live upon their first work, or some high past experiences; and there is an end to their crying, and striving after God and grace. Whereas the holy principles that actuate a true saint, have a far more powerful influence to stir him up to earnestness in seeking God and holiness, than servile fear. Hence seeking God is spoken of as one of the distinguishing characters of the saints; and *those that seek God,* is one of the names by which the godly are called in Scripture: Ps. xxiv. 6. 'This is the generation of them that seek him, that seek thy face, O Jacob.' Ps. lxix. 6. 'Let not those that seek thee, be confounded for my sake.' Ver. 32. 'The humble shall see this, and be glad; and your heart shall live that seek God.' And lxx. 4. 'Let all those that seek thee, rejoice, and be glad in thee: and let such as love thy salvation say continually, The Lord be magnified.' And the Scriptures every where represent the seeking, striving, and labour of a Christian, as being chiefly *after* his conversion, and his conversion as being but the beginning of his work. And almost all that is said in the New Testament, of men's watching, giving earnest heed to themselves, running the race that is set before them, striving and agonizing, wrestling not with flesh and blood, but principalities and powers, fighting, putting on the whole armour

of God, and standing, having done all to stand, pressing forward, reaching forth, continuing instant in prayer, crying to God day and night; I say, almost all that is said in the New Testament of these things, is spoken of and directed to the saints. Where these things are applied to sinners' seeking conversion once, they are spoken of the saints' prosecution of the great business of their high calling ten times. But many in these days have got into a strange anti-scriptural way, of having all their striving and wrestling over before they are converted; and so having an easy time of it afterwards, to sit down and enjoy their sloth and indolence.[37]

Edwards thus demonstrates irrefutably from the Scriptures not only that the concept of seeking is not restricted to man's duty *in his natural state,* but also that the preponderance of the biblical usage of the terminology of seeking (and its cognates) points to man's duty to continue to seek *in his regenerate state.* Indeed, a very strong case can be made that the major emphasis in Edwards' doctrine of seeking is not that of *seeking regeneration,* but rather that of *seeking glorification.* It is at this point that we differ from John H. Gerstner in his findings with regard to Edwards' doctrine of seeking. Certainly, Gerstner acknowledges that the history of the concept of seeking or preparation in Reformed theology does indeed distinguish between two different usages of the term 'seeking', namely, that of 'preparation for regeneration'[38] on the one hand and 'preparation for glorification'[39] on the other. Moreover, Gerstner acknowledges that strand in Edwards' preaching that focuses upon this 'preparation for glorification': 'We are aware', writes Gerstner, 'that Edwards often represents Christians as seekers.'[40] 'There is no ground for Christians thinking that because they have found God they are thereafter to cease seeking for him.'[41] The problem with Gerstner's analysis of the concept of seeking in Edwards' preaching and treatises is that, while he acknowledges the emphasis upon *seeking glorification,* he does not sufficiently develop his analysis of this par-

---

[37] *Works* (Hickman), 1:313-314.
[38] Gerstner, *Rational Biblical Theology,* 3:51.
[39] Ibid.
[40] Gerstner, *Evangelist,* p. 79.
[41] Ibid., p. 82.

ticular emphasis. For instance, Gerstner appears to have missed the very significant statements made by Edwards in this respect in *Religious Affections:* 'Where these things are applied to sinners' seeking conversion once, they are spoken of the saints' prosecution of the great business of their high calling ten times.' Gerstner virtually ignores this major strand in Edwards' thinking and thus loses sight of one of the keys that unlocks the doctrine of seeking in the thought of the preacher-theologian.[42]

Charles E. Hambrick-Stowe has recently sought to qualify the traditional scholarly understanding of New England preparationism: 'Scholars have limited discussion of preparation for salvation to argument over whether Hooker and his colleagues intended that unregenerate sinners could prepare themselves for conversion . . . Conversion was but the point of departure for a life of devotional practice and spiritual progress . . . As with Bunyan's pilgrim who set out after first conversion, salvation was the goal of a life journey rather than an achieved state.'[43] Thus Hambrick-Stowe's reassessment of preparationism places the emphasis not so much upon preparation for conversion as upon the concept of 'pilgrimage as preparation'.[44] 'By means of conversion God readied the pilgrim for the journey; as sanctification enabled the soul to follow God's will increasingly "on its own", through the life of devotion the saint anticipated arrival at the heavenly destination.'[45] 'New England preparationism began with preparation for conversion but stretched out, Sabbath to Sabbath, toward death and

---

[42] In the subtitle to his chapter on 'Seeking', Gerstner defines seeking as 'preparation for salvation'. But Gerstner demonstrates a certain incoherence in his treatment of this theme. On the one hand, he makes 'seeking' and 'preparation for salvation' synonymous, interchangeable terms in his title and subtitle; on the other hand, he cites with approval Joseph Tracy who asserts that, according to JE, "'God has not appointed any thing for men to do before coming to Christ by faith.'" Gerstner, *Rational Biblical Theology*, 3:63. Thus Gerstner himself implies in this citation that seeking should not be confused with preparationism! We concur with this latter position. JE's position is, indeed, essentially that of a doctrine of seeking; it is not that of seventeenth century New England preparationism. But the problem of incoherence in Gerstner's position remains unresolved. See ibid., pp. 50-107.

[43] Charles E. Hambrick-Stowe, *The Practice of Piety: Puritan Devotional Disciplines in Seventeenth-Century New England* (Chapel Hill: The University of North Carolina Press, 1982), pp. 198-199.

[44] Ibid., p. 197.

[45] Ibid., p. 202.

beyond . . . It is crucial to recognize this breadth and unity in New England preparationism.'[46]

These observations capture well Edwards' own concept of seeking. It is evident from Edwards' own usage that his concept of seeking is a general, collective, all-embracing, comprehensive concept which includes potentially the whole spectrum of the *ordo salutis*. Thus in his doctrine of seeking salvation the Christian life is viewed not so much as a series of steps and stages, but as a continuum. It embraces both the idea of repentance and faith and the idea of continuing in the grace of God; it tends to view salvation as a journey or a pilgrimage. Thus the concept embraces both the idea of setting out and of persevering on that journey; it even embraces implicitly the thought of arriving at the ultimate goal of glory itself. Thus it includes both the *terminus a quo* and the *terminus ad quem*. The concept of seeking is, for this reason, a concept that is applicable and relevant to both unbeliever and believer alike. There is a sense in which the homiletical genius of the concept of seeking salvation lies in its very non-specificity. The non-Christian must seek salvation; the Christian must also seek salvation. The non-Christian must set out on the narrow way that leads to life; the Christian must continue on that narrow way.

It is important to note, therefore, that more recent Edwardsean scholarship has exonerated Edwards from the charge of imposing a 'morphology of conversion' and from the related charge of preparationism. David D. Hall makes this significant observation:

Historians of religion in early New England have frequently assumed that Edwards wanted to restore the requirement of a relation of spiritual experience. His contemporary critic Solomon Williams said as much in accusing his cousin of requiring an 'account of experiences' of candidates for membership. But as Edwards strenuously insisted in his letter of May 1750 to Peter Clark, he

[46] Ibid., pp. 202-203. McClymond, summarizing Hambrick-Stowe, makes the following observation: 'Salvation for the Puritans . . . was never a given or a fully achieved state but always a journey and a goal. While theologically it may be true that union with God was realized at the beginning of the Christian life, experientially this union became a conscious fact only through a lengthy process of spiritual development. Conversion was only one event in the Puritan life-pilgrimage.' McClymond, p. 40.

did not specify the procedure of a relation. *The Humble Inquiry* is infused with a distrust of narratives of spiritual experience, a distrust rooted in his long-standing discontent with the traditional vocabulary of stages . . . He turned, therefore, to the traditional alternative, the act of profession.[47]

Kimnach notes 'his opposition to the notion of predictable steps in conversion'[48]; Hambrick-Stowe calls attention to 'Edwards' abrogation of seventeenth-century Puritan teaching on God's work in the stages of "preparation for salvation"';[49] and McClymond describes 'his rejection of the Puritan morphology of conversion that made humiliation for sin a necessary prelude to consolation and assurance' as 'Edwards's most noteworthy departure from convention.'[50] Indeed, it is difficult to imagine how Jonathan Edwards could have set his face any more steadfastly or emphatically against a 'morphology of conversion' or against preparationism than he in fact did. It must be insisted upon, therefore, that, *if* a 'morphology of conversion' has been developed out of his writings, then this is *in spite of* the New England divine, and not *because of* him.

---

[47] *Works*, 12:61.

[48] *Works*, 25:606.

[49] Charles Hambrick-Stowe, 'The "Inward, Sweet Sense" of Christ in Jonathan Edwards', in *The Legacy of Jonathan Edwards*, p. 84 n. 7.

[50] McClymond, p. 41.

6

CHRIST-CENTREDNESS

'This verse is a proof of the indestructibility of the Church.'[1] This entry in Jonathan Edwards' 'Blank Bible' was a single entry relating to Isaiah 51:8: 'For the moth shall eat them up like a garment, and the worm shall eat them like wool: but my righteousness shall be for ever, and my salvation from generation to generation.' But this one verse constituted, remarkably, Edwards' text for a series of thirty lecture/sermons that were delivered between March and August 1739.[2] Although these sermons were never prepared for publication by the preacher's own hand, it is evident from his fascinating letter to the Trustees of the College of New Jersey, dated October 19, 1757, that he had every intention of turning his attention again to the material of this particular series. After setting forth certain preliminary objections in his own mind to his accepting the invitation

---

[1] Cited *Works*, 9:37.

[2] It is important to note what Kimnach has termed 'the intimate relation between sermon and treatise'. *Works*, 10:163. Indeed, there is a very intimate connection between JE's sermons and at least three of his major treatises. The series *A History of the Work of Redemption* was preached between March and August 1739 and published posthumously in 1774; the sermon *The Distinguishing Marks of a Work of the Spirit of God* was delivered at the Yale Commencement on September 10, 1741 and was published shortly afterwards in expanded form; and his *Treatise on the Religious Affections*, which finally appeared in 1746, similarly had its genesis in a series of sermons which were delivered *circa* 1742-1743.

Similarly, Stout and Hatch make the following observation with regard to a sermon preached in April 1742: '*Keeping the Presence of God* illustrates two trends in Edwards' sermonic writing. First, he tended to deliver the substance, if not the exact content, of treatises in sermon form first. This was a habit of his going back to *Justification by Faith Alone*. The second trend, however, was something new. Beginning with the waning of the Great Awakening, he devoted more and more time to the production of treatises. He increasingly perceived his audience as larger than his local setting. This sermon charts that shift.' *Works*, 22:522.

of the Trustees to become President of the College of New Jersey, the Stockbridge theologian specifies his main objection:

> But besides these, I have had on my mind and heart (which I long ago began, not with any view to publication) a great work, which I call *A History of the Work of Redemption*, a body of divinity in an entire new method, being thrown into the form of an history, considering the affair of Christian theology, as the whole of it, in each part, stands in reference to the great work of redemption by Jesus Christ; which I suppose is to be the grand design of all God's designs, and the *summum* and *ultimum* of all the divine operations and degrees.[3]

In the sovereign and profoundly mysterious providence of God, Edwards was ultimately to accept the invitation to go to Princeton. Within five weeks of his commencing his labours as president, his frail, emaciated, and now lifeless body was laid to rest in Princeton cemetery.

The treatise, *A History of the Work of Redemption*, was published posthumously in Edinburgh in 1774. The original sermons that comprise this treatise appear to have been transcribed by his son, Jonathan Edwards, Jr., and to have been edited into this form by Edwards' Scottish correspondent, John Erskine.[4] The uniqueness of this series of sermons lay, firstly, in its sheer length – it was twice the length of the longest series prior to 1739, namely, the fifteen sermons on 1 Corinthians 13 preached in the previous year and published as *Charity and Its Fruits* (1852); secondly, in the fact that this series (unlike *Charity and Its Fruits*, which is essentially consecutive exposition) was preached on a single verse of Scripture; and thirdly, in the relative lack of application that characterizes the series as a whole. 'Not only was there little explicit theology in the sermons', observes Marsden, they 'also contained relatively little that was directly practical'.[5] It is on account of differences such as these that Wilson, the Yale editor, has written of 'the metamorphosis of the sermon form'.[6] Indeed, all the

---

[3] *Works*, 16:727-728.
[4] See *Works*, 9:20-25.
[5] Marsden, *Edwards*, p. 194.
[6] *Works*, 9:34.

evidence indicates that these sermon/discourses constituted, in fact, what Wilson terms 'a proto-treatise'.[7]

It must be conceded that, temporarily, for the duration of this series, the sermon form was indeed significantly modified. It is an interesting homiletical fact that, whereas each sermon in *Charity and Its Fruits* was a structurally complete unit, each sermon in *A History of the Work of Redemption* was, as Stout and Hatch put it, 'structurally incomplete – a Doctrine without an Application, or an Application without a Use'.[8] It is also true that throughout this extended series Edwards' emphasis falls upon the objective aspects of redemption; it falls much more upon *redemption accomplished* than upon *redemption applied*, or much more upon *historia salutis* than upon *ordo salutis*. It is, therefore, not in the least surprising that such a treatise from such a pen should contain a number of Christ-centred passages of great beauty. Edwards concludes 'Period I. From the Fall to the Incarnation' with the following striking passage concerning the 'great and extraordinary person' for whose entry into the world such remarkable preparations were made:

> What has been said, may show us how great a person Jesus Christ is, and how great his errand into the world, seeing there was so much done to prepare the way for his coming. God had been preparing the way for him through all ages of the world from the very beginning. If we had notice of a certain stranger being about to come into a country, and should observe that a great preparation was made for him, great things were done, many alterations made in the state of the whole country, many hands employed, persons of great note engaged in making the preparation; and all the affairs and concerns of the country ordered so as to be subservient to the design of entertaining that person, it would be natural for us to think, surely this is some extraordinary person, and it is some very great business that he is coming upon. How great a person then must he be, for whose coming the great God of heaven and earth, and Governor of all things, spent four thousand years in prepar-

[7] Ibid., p. 61. Kimnach, for his part, notes the development of the following trend in the later 1730's: 'Indeed, it seems obvious that, at least from 1735, there is an increased tendency to preach treatises from the pulpit.' *Works*, 10:105.

[8] *Works*, 22:11.

ing the way! Soon after the world was created, and from age to age, he has been doing great things, bringing mighty events to pass, accomplishing wonders without number, often overturning the world in order to it. He has been causing every thing in the state of mankind, and all revolutions and changes in the habitable world, from generation to generation, to be subservient to this great design. – Surely this must be some great and extraordinary person, and a great work indeed it must needs be, about which he is coming.[9]

In 'Period II. From Christ's Incarnation to His Resurrection', Edwards gives this very beautiful general assessment of the significance of the incarnation of Christ:

The next thing that I would observe concerning the incarnation of Christ, is the greatness of this event. Christ's incarnation was a greater and more wonderful thing than ever had yet come to pass. The creation of the world was a very great thing, but not so great as the incarnation of Christ. It was a great thing for God to make the creature, but not so great as for the Creator himself to become a creature. We have spoken of many great things that were accomplished between the fall of man and the incarnation of Christ: but God becoming man was greater than all. Then the greatest person was born that ever was or ever will be.[10]

The following passage from the same 'Period' is, again, a very beautiful analysis of the so-called 'years of obscurity' in Nazareth:

Christ was subject to great humiliation in his private life at Nazareth. He there led a servile, obscure life, in a mean, laborious occupation; for he is called not only the *carpenter's son*, but the *carpenter:* Mark vi. 3. 'Is not this the carpenter, the brother of James and Joses, and Juda, and Simon?' By hard labour he earned his bread before he ate it, and so suffered that curse which God pronounced on Adam, Gen. iii. 13. 'In the sweat of thy face shalt thou eat bread.' Let us consider how great a degree of humiliation the glorious Son of God, the Creator of heaven and earth,

[9] *Works* (Hickman), 1:571.
[10] Ibid., p. 573.

was subject to in this, that for about thirty years he should live a private obscure life among labouring men, and all this while be overlooked, not taken notice of in the world, more than other common labourers. Christ's humiliation in some respects was greater in private life than in the time of his public ministry. There were many manifestations of his glory in the word he preached, and the miracles he wrought: but the first thirty years of his life he spent among ordinary men, as it were in silence. There was not any thing to make him to be taken notice of more than any ordinary mechanic, only the spotless purity and eminent holiness of his life; and that was in a great measure hid in obscurity; so that he was little taken notice of till after his baptism.[11]

This further passage from the same 'Period' further develops the theme of the humility and the voluntary self-humiliation of the Lord Jesus Christ:

In this work he most wonderfully manifested those *virtues which more immediately respected himself;* as humility, . . . Christ, though he was the most excellent and honourable, yet was the most *humble;* yea, he was the most humble of all creatures. No angel or man ever equalled him in humility, though he was the highest in dignity and honourableness. Christ would have been under the greatest temptations to pride, if it had been possible for any thing to be a temptation to him. The temptation of the angels that fell was the dignity of their nature, and the honourableness of their circumstances; but Christ was infinitely more honourable than they. The human nature of Christ was so honoured as to be in the same person with the eternal Son of God, who was equal with God; and yet that human nature was not at all lifted up with pride. Nor was the man Christ Jesus at all lifted up with pride with all those wonderful works which he wrought, of healing the sick, curing the blind, lame, and maimed, and raising the dead. And though he knew that God had appointed him to be the king over heaven and earth, angels and men, as he says, Matt. xi. 27. 'All things are delivered unto me of my Father'; though he knew

11 Ibid., p. 578.

he was such an infinitely honourable person, and thought it not robbery to be equal with God; and though he knew he was the heir of the Father's kingdom: yet such was his humility, that he did not disdain to be abased and depressed down into lower and viler circumstances and sufferings than ever any other elect creature was; so that he became least of all, and lowest of all. The proper trial and evidence of humility, is stooping or complying with those acts or circumstances, when called to it, which are very low, and contain great abasement. But none ever stooped so low as Christ, if we consider either the infinite height that he stooped from, or the great depth to which he stooped. Such was his humility, that though he knew his infinite worthiness of honour, and of being honoured ten thousand times as much as the highest prince on earth, or angel in heaven; yet he did not think it too much when called to it, to be bound as a malefactor, to become the laughing-stock of the vilest of men, to be crowned with thorns, to have a mock robe put upon him, and to be crucified like a slave and malefactor, as one of the meanest and worst of vagabonds and miscreants, and an accursed enemy of God and men, who was not fit to live. And this was not for himself, but for some of the meanest and vilest of creatures, even some of those accursed wretches that crucified him. Was not this a wonderful manifestation of humility, when he cheerfully and most freely submitted to this abasement?[12]

There can be no question but that Edwards' reputation in the popular mind is inextricably associated with his so-called 'terror preaching' in which he sets forth at considerable length and in considerable detail the fact and the reality of eternal judgment; he is not so well known for his preaching of Christ. Yet it is essential to note that his great purpose in his preaching of judgment was precisely to drive the sinner to Christ. In his *Thoughts on the Revival*, published in 1743 in the immediate aftermath of the Great Awakening in New England, he insists upon the intimate connection between these two emphases in preaching:

[12] Ibid., pp. 577-578.

Indeed something besides terror is to be preached to them whose consciences are awakened. They are to be told that there is a Saviour provided, who is excellent and glorious; who has shed his precious blood for sinners, and is every way sufficient to save them; who stands ready to receive them, if they will heartily embrace him; for this is also the truth, as well as that they now are in an infinitely dreadful condition. This is the word of God. Sinners, at the same time that they are told how miserable their case is, should be earnestly invited to come and accept of a Saviour, and yield their hearts unto him, with all the winning, encouraging arguments, that the gospel affords. But this is to induce them to escape from the misery of their condition, not to make them think their present condition to be less miserable than it is, or to abate their uneasiness and distress, while they are in it. That would be the way to quiet them, and fasten them there, and not to excite them to flee from it. Comfort in one sense, is to be held forth to sinners under awakenings of conscience, i.e. comfort is to be offered to them in Christ, on their fleeing *from their present miserable state* to him. But comfort is not to be administered to them, *in their present state,* or while out of Christ.[13]

It is important to note, therefore, not only that Edwards constantly points to Christ in his preaching, but also that he provides what must rank as some of the loveliest detailed descriptions of Christ in the whole range of homiletical literature. 'The Wisdom of God Displayed in the Way of Salvation' was preached in March 1733. It is one of Edwards' greatest sermons. His text on this occasion was Ephesians 3:10: 'To the intent that now unto the principalities and powers in heavenly places might be known by the church the manifold wisdom of God.' In the following passage the twenty-nine year old preacher displays a remarkable ability to depict the glory of Christ's incarnation:

And if God had revealed to them, that it was possible, and even that it should be, but left to them to find out how it should be; we may well suppose that they would all have been puzzled and con-

---

[13] Ibid., p. 392.

founded, to conceive of a way for so uniting a man to the eternal Son of God, that they should be but one person: that one who is truly a man in all respects, should indeed be the very same Son of God, that was with God from all eternity. This is a great mystery to us. Hereby, a person that is infinite, omnipotent, and unchangeable, is become, in a sense, a finite, a feeble man; a man subject to our sinless infirmities, passions, and calamities! The great God, the sovereign of heaven and earth, is thus become a worm of the dust. (Psal. xxii. 6.) 'I am a worm, and no man.' He that is eternal and self-existent, is by this union born of a woman! He who is the great original Spirit, is clothed with flesh and blood like one of us! He who is independent, self-sufficient, and all-sufficient, now is come to stand in need of food and clothing: he becomes poor, 'has not where to lay his head'; – stands in need of the charity of men; and is maintained by it! It is far above us, to conceive *how* it is done. It is a great wonder and mystery to us; but it was no mystery to divine wisdom.[14]

In the same sermon Edwards proceeds to describe the wonderful wisdom of God in Christ's atonement:

The next thing to be considered is the death of Christ. This is a means of salvation for poor sinners, that no other but divine wisdom would have pitched upon; and when revealed, it was doubtless greatly to the surprise of all the hosts of heaven, and they never will cease to wonder at it. How astonishing is it, that a person who is blessed for ever, and is infinitely and essentially happy, should endure the greatest sufferings that ever were endured on earth! That a person who is the supreme Lord and judge of the world, should be arraigned, and should stand at the judgement-seat of mortal worms, and then be condemned. That a person who is the living God, and the fountain of life, should be put to death. That a person who created the world, and gives life to all his creatures, should be put to death by his own creatures. That a person of infinite majesty and glory, and so the object of the love, praises, and adoration of angels, should be mocked and spit upon by the vilest of men. That a person, infinitely good, and who is love itself, should suffer the greatest cruelty. That a person who is infinitely beloved of the Father, should be put to inexpressible anguish under his own Father's wrath. That he who is king of heaven, who hath heaven for his throne, and the earth for his footstool, should be buried in the prison of the grave. How wonderful is this! And yet this is the way that God's wisdom hath fixed upon, as the way of sinners' salvation; as neither unsuitable nor dishonourable to Christ.[15]

It will be noted that in each of these two passages Edwards sets forth very beautifully the contrast between the circumstances of the Son's exaltation as the second Person of the Godhead and those of his humiliation as the God-Man in the days of his flesh. Indeed, such is the skill with which he develops this juxtaposition that the effect is powerfully doxological.

'The Excellency of Christ', which was preached as a sacramental sermon in August 1736 and published in 1738 as part of *Five Discourses on Important Subjects,* demonstrates Edwards' remarkable versatility as a preacher. Although this sermon (unlike the other four discourses) was not preached in the immediate context of the revival of 1734-1735, Edwards deliberately included the sermon with this notice: 'What is published at the end, concerning the excellency of Christ, is added on my own motion; thinking that a discourse on such an evangelical subject, would properly follow others that were chiefly awakening, and that something of the excellency of the Saviour was proper to succeed those things that were to show the necessity of *salvation*.'[16] His text on this occasion was Revelation 5:5-6: 'And one of the elders saith unto me, Weep not: behold, the Lion of the tribe of Judah, the Root of David, hath prevailed to open the book, and to loose the seven seals thereof. And I beheld, and, lo, in the midst of the throne, and of the four beasts, and in the midst of the elders, stood a Lamb as it had been slain.' In this sermon Edwards analyses 'two distinct appellations' of Christ in which he is described by the Apostle John both as a Lion and as a Lamb. The

---

[15] Ibid., p. 144.
[16] Ibid., 1:621.

following passage is a beautiful analysis of the humility and meekness of Christ:

> But however he is above all, yet he is lowest of all in humility. There never was so great an instance of this virtue among either men or angels, as Jesus. None ever was so sensible of the distance between God and him, or had a heart so lowly before God, as the man Christ Jesus. Matt. xi. 29. What a wonderful spirit of humility appeared in him, when he was here upon earth, in all his behaviour! In his contentment in his mean outward condition, contentedly living in the family of Joseph the carpenter, and Mary his mother, for thirty years together, and afterwards choosing outward meanness, poverty, and contempt, rather than earthly greatness; in his washing his disciples' feet, and in all his speeches and deportment towards them; in his cheerfully sustaining the form of a servant through his whole life, and submitting to such immense humiliation at death!
>
> In the person of Christ do meet together infinite *majesty* and transcendent *meekness*. These again are two qualifications that meet together in no other person but Christ. Meekness, properly so called, is a virtue proper only to the creature: we scarcely ever find meekness mentioned as a divine attribute in Scripture; at least not in the New Testament; for thereby seems to be signified a calmness and quietness of spirit, arising from humility in mutable beings that are naturally liable to be put into a ruffle by the assaults of a tempestuous and injurious world. But Christ being both God and man, hath both infinite majesty and superlative meekness.
>
> Christ was a person of infinite majesty. It is he that is spoken of, Psalm xlv. 3. 'Gird thy sword upon thy thigh, O most mighty, with thy glory and thy majesty.' It is he that is mighty, that rideth on the heavens, and his excellency on the sky. It is he that is terrible out of his holy places; who is mightier than the noise of many waters, yea, than the mighty waves of the sea: before whom a fire goeth, and burneth up his enemies round about; at whose presence the earth quakes, and the hills melt; who sitteth on the circle of the earth, and all the inhabitants thereof are as grasshoppers; who rebukes the sea, and maketh it dry, and drieth up the rivers;

whose eyes are as a flame of fire; from whose presence, and from the glory of whose power, the wicked shall be punished with everlasting destruction; who is the blessed and only Potentate, the King of kings, and Lord of lords, who hath heaven for his throne, and the earth for his footstool, and is the high and lofty One who inhabits eternity, whose kingdom is an everlasting kingdom, and of whose dominion there is no end.

And yet he was the most marvellous instance of meekness, and humble quietness of spirit, that ever was; agreeable to the *prophecies* of him, Matt. xxi. 4, 5. 'All this was done, that it might be fulfilled which was spoken by the prophet, saying, Tell ye the daughter of Sion, Behold, thy King cometh unto thee, meek, and sitting upon an ass, and a colt the foal of an ass.' And, agreeable to what Christ declares of himself, Matt. xi. 29 'I am meek and lowly in heart.' And agreeable to what was manifest in his behaviour: for there never was such an instance seen on earth, of a meek behaviour, under injuries and reproaches, and towards enemies; who, when he was reviled, reviled not again. He had a wonderful spirit of forgiveness, was ready to forgive his worst enemies, and prayed for them with fervent and effectual prayers. With what meekness did he appear in the ring of soldiers that were contemning and mocking him; he was silent, and opened not his mouth, but went as a lamb to the slaughter. Thus is Christ a Lion in majesty, and a Lamb in meekness.[17]

This juxtaposition of the excellencies of Christ as Lion and those of Christ as Lamb lies at the very foundation of 'The Excellency of Christ'. Later in this sermon Edwards develops further the contrast between the veiling and the unveiling of the outward glory of Christ in the days of his flesh:

This admirable conjunction of excellencies appears in the acts and various passages of Christ's life. Though Christ dwelt in mean outward circumstances, whereby his condescension and humility especially appeared, and his majesty was veiled; yet his divine dignity and glory did in many of his acts shine through the veil, and it

---

[17] Ibid., pp. 681-682.

illustriously appeared, that he was not only the Son of Man, but the great God.

Thus, in the circumstances of his infancy, his outward meanness appeared; yet there was something then to show forth his divine dignity, in the wise men's being stirred up to come from the east to give honour to him, their being led by a miraculous star, and coming and falling down and worshipping him, and presenting him with gold, frankincense, and myrrh. His humility and meekness wonderfully appeared in his subjection to his mother and reputed father when he was a child. Herein he appeared as a lamb. But his divine glory broke forth and shone when, at twelve years old, he disputed with the doctors in the temple. In that he appeared, in some measure, as *the Lion of the Tribe of Judah*.

And so, after he entered on his public ministry, his marvellous humility and meekness was manifested in his choosing to appear in such mean outward circumstances; and in being contented in them, when he was so poor that he had not where to lay his head, and depended on the charity of some of his followers for his subsistence; as appears by Luke viii. at the beginning. How meek, condescending, and familiar his treatment of his disciples; his discourses with them, treating them as a father his children; yea, as friends and companions. How patient, bearing such affliction and reproach, and so many injuries from the scribes and Pharisees, and others. In these things he appeared *as a Lamb*. And yet he at the same time did in many ways show forth his divine majesty and glory, particularly in the miracles he wrought, which were evidently divine works, and manifested omnipotent power, and so declared him to be *the Lion of the Tribe of Judah*. His wonderful and miraculous works plainly showed him to be the God of nature; in that it appeared by them that he had all nature in his hands, and could lay an arrest upon it, and stop and change its course as he pleased. In healing the sick, and opening the eyes of the blind, and unstopping the ears of the deaf, and healing the lame; he showed that he was the God that framed the eye, and created the ear, and was the author of the frame of man's body. By the dead's rising at his command, it appeared that he was the author and fountain of life, and that 'God the Lord, to whom belong the issues from death.' By his walking on the sea in a storm, when the waves were raised, he showed himself to be that God spoken of in Job ix. 8. 'That treadeth on the waves of the sea.' By his stilling the storm, and calming the rage of the sea, by his powerful command, saying, 'Peace, be still', he showed that he has the command of the universe, and that he is that God who brings things to pass by the word of his power, who speaks and it is done, who commands and it stands fast.[18]

'Jesus Christ the Same Yesterday, Today, and Forever' is, as the title suggests, a sermon on Hebrews 13:8. It was delivered in April 1738. The sermon is a very beautiful analysis of the immutability of Christ. Edwards develops his doctrine thus:

Christ is thus unchangeable in two respects.
I. In his divine nature . . .
II. Christ is unchangeable in his office. He is unchangeable as the Mediator and Saviour of his church and people. That unchangeableness of Christ in his office of Mediator, appears in several things.

This office never ceases to give place to any other to come in his room: Christ is the only Mediator between God and man, that ever has been or ever shall be. He is an everlasting Saviour. There have been typical mediators many, that have continued but a little while, and then have passed away, and others have come in their room; but the great antitype continues for ever. There have been prophets, that have been raised up, and these have died, and others have succeeded them. Moses was not suffered to continue by reason of death; and the dispensation which he introduced was abolished, to give place to another which Christ should introduce. Moses gives place to Christ, but Christ never gives place to any other. John the Baptist was a great prophet. He was Christ's forerunner; like the morning star, the forerunner of the sun, he shone bright a little while, but his ministry by degrees ceased, and gave way to the ministry of Christ, as the morning star by little and little goes out as the sun rises. John iii. 30. John the Baptist says, 'He must increase, but I must decrease.' But Christ's ministry never

---

[18] Ibid., p. 683.

ceases. So the ancient legal priests, they had but a changeable and shortlived priesthood. Aaron died, and his son Eleazar succeeded in his room; and so there were many priests, one after another; but Christ continues a priest for ever . . . In that respect, Melchizedek is a type of Christ, of whom the Scriptures give us an account, that he was a priest, but seems not to have been a priest by inheritance, as the sons of Aaron were: . . . Those things that appertain to Christ's priesthood are everlasting. The tabernacle at which the priests of old officiated, was a tabernacle that men pitched, and therefore a tabernacle that was taken down. It was the holy of holies of old; but Christ is a minister of the true tabernacle and the true sanctuary, which the Lord hath built, and not man. Heb. v. 2 The holy of holies he entered into was *heaven;* he is a priest in a tabernacle that shall never be taken down, and in a temple that shall never be demolished. So the altar on which he offers incense, the priestly garments or robes in which he officiates, are not of a corruptible nature. And so Christ is everlasting with reference to his kingly office. David and Solomon were great kings, and eminent types of Christ: but death put an end to their kingdom and greatness. Earthly monarchies that ever have been, those that have ruled over the bigger part of the known world, as particularly the Grecian and Roman monarchies, they have come to an end, but Christ's is an everlasting kingdom, his throne is for ever and ever; . . .[19]

In this passage Edwards establishes a very striking, reiterated contrast between type and antitype; and he achieves this by means of his sustained use of the adversative 'but'. 'But the great antitype continues for ever . . .; but Christ never gives place to any other . . .; but Christ's ministry never ceases . . .; but Christ continues a priest for ever . . .; but Christ's is an everlasting kingdom, his throne is for ever and ever.' It is important to note, however, that in this Edwards has simply taken his cue from the Scriptures. The prophets, Moses and John the Baptist, were great men; but Christ is greater than they. The priests, Aaron and Eleazar, were the very first priests under the law. They died and were succeeded by others; but Christ has no successor. The kings, David and Solomon, were great kings, yet they too succumbed to death; but

<hr>

[19] Ibid., 2:949-950.

Christ's kingdom is an everlasting kingdom. 'The great antitype' is 'one greater' than all those that preceded him. All these men were mortal; but Christ is possessed of immortality. He is 'from everlasting to everlasting'.

It is evident from Edwards' sermons that his preaching was powerfully Christ-centred and Christ-exalting. 'What deserves attention', observes Wilson, 'is his high and conventional Christology. In this he stood securely in the Calvinist tradition, and his Christocentric position is evident.'[20] It is important to note, moreover, that this Christocentricity on Edwards' part never degenerates into Christomonism precisely because of the power of his Applications; it is also important to note that his Applications never degenerate into moralism precisely because of the power of his Christocentricity. In his Preface to *Fifteen Sermons on Various Subjects,* published in 1779, Jonathan Edwards, Jr., (1745-1801) contrasts the sermons of his father with 'those modern fashionable discourses which are delivered under the name of sermons, but really are mere harangues on such moral subjects as have been much better handled by Cicero, Seneca, or the Spectator, and contain very little more of the gospel than is to be found in the heathen philosophers.'[21] This assessment of the father by the son is just. The great eighteenth-century New England preacher was no preacher of moralism – he was no peddler of ethics without the gospel. He was a preacher of the gospel of Christ; and it is his powerful and undeniably beautiful Christocentricity that both establishes his evangelical orthodoxy and distinguishes him from the moralists of Rome and (more significantly still) from the moralists of the eighteenth century.

It is, therefore, very important to note that the New England preacher, whose reputation rests so powerfully on the *minatory,* also excelled in the *consolatory.* It is, moreover, precisely because of the recalcitrant issue of the general perception of Edwards as a preacher of judgment, and even of terror, that it is so important to note the sweetness and the beauty of his descriptions of Christ. It was clearly a fundamental part of his homiletical philosophy that he should not only provide

[20] *Works,* 9:54.
[21] *Works* (Hickman), 2:51.

what might be described as 'the element of attack', but that he should also administer the healing 'balm of Gilead' to the soul. Indeed, his sermons, considered *in toto*, reveal what might be described as a kind of homiletical pincer movement. 'For by the law is the knowledge of sin', insists the Apostle; and Edwards' great concern in preaching the law of God was that men should 'flee from the wrath to come' into the open arms of Christ. Thus, if in his sermons there is often great emphasis upon the terrors of Mount Sinai, there is also great emphasis upon the wonder and the glory of Calvary's hill. This balance may not always be evident in the same sermon; it is, however, evident in his preaching ministry as a whole. The sweetness of his preaching at this point is, of course, no saccharine sentimentalism about the universal fatherhood of God and the universal brotherhood of man. The New England preacher never says, 'Peace, peace, when there is no peace'; he never 'heals the hurt of the daughter of my people slightly'. The encouragement, the consolation, and the peace that Edwards offers in his preaching are always on the basis of the gospel of Christ. It is important to note that he has no encouragement or consolation to offer *apart* from Christ; he has, therefore, no hope to offer to those who persist in remaining *outside* of Christ. The encouragement and the consolation that he repeatedly holds forth in his sermons are rooted and grounded in 'Jesus Christ and him crucified'.

Moreover, it is this rare ability to depict the beauty and the glory of Christ that many have found to be so attractive and so winsome in Edwards' preaching. In 1825, on the morning of his sudden death, John Williams, the first pastor of the Oliver Street Baptist Church in New York City, made this observation to a friend: 'I love President Edwards; he always speaks so sweetly of Christ.'[22]

---

[22] Cited Iain H. Murray, *Revival and Revivalism: The Making and Marring of American Evangelicalism 1750-1858* (Edinburgh: Banner of Truth, 1994), p. 322.

7

THE PREACHING OF HEAVEN

'There are three worlds. One is this, which is an intermediate world – a world in which good and evil are so mixed together as to be a sure sign that this world is not to continue for ever. Another is heaven, a world of love, without any hatred. And the other is hell, a world of hatred, where there is no love, which is the world to which all of you who are in a Christless state properly belong.'[1] This statement in 'Heaven is a World of Love' captures what Stout has described as 'Jonathan Edwards' tri-world vision.'[2] At first glance Stout's description of Edwards' *Weltanschauung* might well be deemed to be a statement of the obvious; but it should be noted that in the aforementioned letter to the Trustees of the College of New Jersey in October 1757 the future President of that College wrote of the *magnum opus* that lay much upon his heart: it was 'a great work'[3] which would set forth the history of redemption by Jesus Christ as it relates to 'all three worlds, heaven, earth and hell':

This history will be carried on with regard to all three worlds, heaven, earth and hell: considering the connected, successive events and alterations, in each so far as the Scriptures give any light; introducing all parts of divinity in that order which is most scriptural and most natural: which is a method which appears to me the most beautiful and entertaining, wherein every divine doctrine will appear to greatest advantage in the brightest light, in

[1] *Charity*, pp. 358-359.
[2] Harry S. Stout, 'Jonathan Edwards' Tri-World Vision', in *The Legacy of Jonathan Edwards*, p. 27.
[3] *Works*, 16:727.

the most striking manner, showing the admirable contexture and harmony of the whole.[4]

Edwards' emphasis upon the world of hell is, of course, well known; his emphasis upon the world of heaven is not so well known. Recent scholarship has, however, recognized the prevalence of this emphasis. Amy Plantinga Pauw notes 'Jonathan Edwards' deep fascination with heaven'.[5] It is interesting to note that a number of Edwards' greatest sermons deal with this theme. 'Heaven is a World of Love'; 'True Saints, When Absent from the Body, Are Present with the Lord'; 'The Portion of the Righteous'; 'The Pure in Heart Blessed'; 'Praise, One of the Chief Employments in Heaven' – each of these sermons demonstrates, in varying degrees, this deep interest in the heavenly world. McClymond has, however, if anything, veered to the opposite extreme in his observation concerning what, in his view, is 'one of the puzzling themes in Edwards's writings, namely, his near obsession with "the saints in heaven".'[6] But why, we ask, should it be deemed puzzling that a Reformed preacher-theologian of the stature of the New England divine should be profoundly interested in the life and the world to come? His interest was not merely in 'the church militant' here on earth; it was also in 'the church triumphant' in heaven. These are 'not indeed two churches', he insisted in his Thanksgiving Sermon on November 7, 1734. They are 'the same society'.[7] Edwards' profound fascination and preoccupation with heaven is, we contend, simply a vital aspect of his profound other-worldliness; and it is the positive counterpart of his preoccupation with hell.

'Heaven is a World of Love' – the concluding sermon in Edwards' great expository series entitled *Charity and Its Fruits* - is described by Hughes Oliphant Old as 'one of the classics of the American pulpit'.[8]

[4] Ibid., p. 728.

[5] Amy Plantinga Pauw, '"Heaven is a World of Love": Edwards on Heaven and the Trinity,' *CTJ* 30 (1995): p. 392.

[6] McClymond, p. 77.

[7] *Works* (Hickman), 2:916.

[8] Hughes Oliphant Old, *The Reading and Preaching of the Scriptures in the Worship of the Christian Church*, vol. 5 (Grand Rapids, Michigan: William B. Eerdmans Publishing Company, 2004), p. 269.

It is a very beautiful sermon. The text upon which the sermon is based is 1 Corinthians 13:8-10: 'Charity never faileth; but whether there be prophecies, they shall fail; whether there be tongues, they shall cease; whether there be knowledge, it shall vanish away. For we know in part, and we prophesy in part. But when that which is perfect is come, then that which is in part shall be done away.' Although the sermon has not received the attention given to 'Sinners in the Hands of an Angry God', it is often compared with the Enfield sermon. Ramsey observes that 'the rhetorical power' of the former sermon is such that it is 'rivaled only by his other "virtuoso performance", "Sinners in the Hands of an Angry God."'[9] "'Heaven is a World of Love'", asserts Kimnach, '. . . is a sermon of Dantean simplicity, scope, and grandeur.'[10] The 'Doctrinal' section of the sermon contains the following passage in which Edwards defines heaven as the dwelling-place of the Triune God:

> Here I remark that the God of love himself dwells in heaven. Heaven is the palace or presence-chamber of the high and holy One, whose name is love, and who is both the cause and source of all holy love. God, considered with respect to his essence, is everywhere – he fills both heaven and earth. But yet he is said, in some respects, to be more especially in some places than in others. He was said of old to dwell in the land of Israel, above all other lands; and in Jerusalem, above all other cities of that land; and in the temple, above all other buildings in the city; and in the holy of holies, above all other apartments of the temple; and on the mercy-seat, over the ark of the covenant, above all other places in the holy of holies. But heaven is his dwelling-place above all other places in the universe; and all those places in which he was said to dwell of old, were but types of this. Heaven is a part of creation that God has built for this end, to be the place of his glorious presence, and it is his abode for ever; and here will he dwell, and gloriously manifest himself to all eternity . . .
>
> There, even in heaven, dwells the God from whom every stream of holy love, yea, every drop that is, or ever was, proceeds. There

---

[9] *Works*, 8:61.
[10] *Works*, 10:220.

dwells God the Father, God the Son, and God the Spirit, united as one, in infinitely dear, and incomprehensible, and mutual, and eternal love. There dwells God the Father, who is the father of mercies, and so the father of love, who so loved the world as to give his only-begotten Son to die for it. There dwells Christ, the Lamb of God, the prince of peace and of love, who so loved the world that he shed his blood, and poured out his soul unto death for men. There dwells the great Mediator, through whom all the divine love is expressed toward men, and by whom the fruits of that love have been purchased, and through whom they are communicated, and through whom love is imparted to the hearts of all God's people. There dwells Christ in both his natures, the human and the divine, sitting on the same throne with the Father. And there dwells the Holy Spirit – the Spirit of divine love, in whom the very essence of God, as it were, flows out, and is breathed forth in love, and by whose immediate influence all holy love is shed abroad in the hearts of all the saints on earth and in heaven. There, in heaven, this infinite fountain of love – this eternal Three in One – is set open without any obstacle to hinder access to it, as it flows for ever. There this glorious God is manifested, and shines forth, in full glory, in beams of love. And there this glorious fountain for ever flows forth in streams, yea, in rivers of love and delight, and these rivers swell, as it were, to an ocean of love, in which the souls of the ransomed may bathe with the sweetest enjoyment, and their hearts, as it were, be deluged with love![11]

One of the most striking features about Edwards' descriptions of heaven is their lovely Christ-centredness, for it is in heaven that the risen, ascended, and glorified Christ is seated at the right hand of God. 'There dwells Christ in both his natures, the human and the divine, sitting on the same throne with the Father.'[12] This theme of the Christ-centredness of heaven is developed very beautifully in 'True Saints, When Absent from the Body, Are Present with the Lord' – the sermon preached on October 12, 1747, on the occasion of the funeral of the

---

[11] *Charity*, pp. 326-328.
[12] Ibid., p. 327.

saintly David Brainerd, who had spent his last days in the Edwards home in Northampton as he lay dying of tuberculosis, and whose remarkable spirituality and extraordinarily self-denying labours in the gospel amongst the American Indians have since become part of the great evangelical and Reformed heritage.[13] Edwards' text on this occasion was 2 Corinthians 5:8: 'We are confident, I say, and willing rather to be absent from the body, and to be present with the Lord.' The souls of true saints', emphasized the preacher, 'when they leave their bodies at death, go to be with Christ, to dwell in the immediate, full, and constant view of him'[14]:

> Their beatific vision of God is in Christ, who is that brightness or effulgence of God's glory, by which his glory shines forth in heaven, to the view of saints and angels there, as well as here on earth. This is the Sun of righteousness, that is not only the light of this world, but is also the sun that enlightens the heavenly Jerusalem; by whose bright beams it is that the glory of God shines forth there, to the enlightening and making happy all the glorious inhabitants. 'The Lamb is the light thereof; and so the glory of God doth lighten it', Rev. xxi. 23. None sees God the Father immediately, who is the King eternal, immortal, invisible: Christ is the image of that invisible God, by which he is seen by all elect creatures. The only-begotten Son that is in the bosom of the Father, he hath declared him, and manifested him. None has ever immediately seen the Father but the Son; and none else sees the Father any other way, than by the Son's revealing him. And in heaven, the spirits of just men made perfect behold his glory. They see the glory of his divine nature, consisting in all the glory of the Godhead, the beauty of all his perfections; his great majesty, almighty power, his infinite wisdom, holiness, and grace, and they see the beauty of his glori-fied human nature, and the glory which the Father hath given him, as God-man and Mediator. For this end, Christ desired that his saints might 'be with him, that they might behold his glory,' John

---

[13] The manuscript is labelled, 'Prepared for Mr. Brainerd's funeral, appointed October 12, 1747.' See *Works*, 25:330. Kimnach also notes that the sermon is written 'on rice paper, though the first and last two leaves are of heavier paper.' Ibid.

[14] *Works* (Hickman), 2:28.

xvii. 24. And when the souls of the saints leave their bodies, to go to be with Christ, they behold the marvellous glory of that great work of redemption, and of the glorious way of salvation by him; which the angels desire to look into.[15]

In her article '"Heaven is a World of Love": Edwards on Heaven and the Trinity' Pauw observes, correctly, that 'heaven . . . has sharply receded from the forefront of Western consciousness, even from the consciousness of most contemporary Christians.'[16] The essentially other-worldly character of the Christian faith has, especially from the latter part of the nineteenth century onwards, been eroded; and it has been replaced by an essentially this-worldly interpretation. Thus the focus in much modern theology falls, increasingly, upon man at the expense of God and upon this life and this world at the expense of the life and the world to come. There is, therefore, in an age of horizontalism in theology, something very refreshing and very salutary about the powerful verticalism of Edwards' theology. He does not, as some of his critics have contended, neglect the horizontal aspects of Christianity; *Charity and Its Fruits* alone, quite apart from the rest of the sermon corpus, demonstrates this incontestably. But his major emphasis falls, as in the Scriptures, upon the vertical, Godward dimension. There is, in his sermons, a tremendous emphasis upon heaven and hell, upon the life and the world to come, in short, upon eternity. He constantly views life in this world *sub specie aeternitatis*. Indeed, there is an obvious correlation between his powerful verticalism and his powerful theocentricity:

God is the highest good of the reasonable creature; and the enjoyment of him is the only happiness with which our souls can be satisfied. – To go to heaven, fully to enjoy God, is infinitely better than the most pleasant accommodations here. Fathers and mothers, husbands, wives, or children, or the company of earthly friends, are but shadows; but the enjoyment of God is the substance. These are but scattered beams; but God is the sun. These

---

[15] Ibid.
[16] Pauw, p. 392.

are but streams; but God is the fountain. These are but drops; but God is the ocean.[17]

---

[17] *Works* (Hickman), 2:244.

8

INTRODUCTIONS

Jonathan Edwards' sermons generally consist of three major divisions: firstly, the 'Text'; secondly, the 'Doctrine'; thirdly, the 'Application'. This basic structure closely follows what Lesser terms 'the triadic Puritan form of Text, Doctrine, and Application'.[1] The Text, for its part, generally consists of the text of Scripture under consideration and a contextual introduction. Kimnach gives the following helpful analysis of Edwards' contextual introductions:

> In the vast majority of sermons . . . there is a brief passage (a page, more or less) of comment and explication following the scriptural passage which Edwards designates the Opening of the Text. The Opening consists of several, brief numbered heads, frequently designated 'Observation' or 'Inference', in which Edwards defines difficult terms, cites other Scripture passages that parallel or complement the textual passage, and generally explains its meaning. In explication, he is never pedantic, even on those rare occasions when he introduces Hebrew or Greek words to clarify definitions; he explains carefully, but does not belabor small points. Indeed, some students of Edwards have felt the Opening of the Text to be the finest part of the sermon because of Edwards' remarkable ability to narrate the statements and events of the text as immediate experience, and in his narrations he not infrequently displays the talent of a first-rate journalist or novelist. But his narrations present concise sketches rather than murals, and the Text is never long.[2]

[1] *Works*, 19:6.
[2] *Works*, 10:37.

Thus Edwards' general method in the contextual introduction stands firmly in the English Puritan tradition. J. I. Packer describes that tradition thus: 'The Puritan method of "opening" a text . . . was first to explain it in its context.'[3] Gerstner confirms that Edwards' general method was that of the contextual introduction: 'For him first came a contextual introduction but with this difference: like an eagle Edwards circled over the context until he found his point and then descended deeply to snatch his homiletic prey and hold it up to the full view of all. For the next hour or more, Jonathan Edwards' only interest was to dissect the text, to analyze it, to feed his hungry people with it.'[4]

'The Nakedness of Job' – a sermon on Job 1:21 ('Naked came I out of my mother's womb, and naked shall I return thither') – belongs to the so-called 'New York period' in Edwards' ministerial career when, for some eight and a half months, between August 1722 and April 1723, the Yale graduate ministered to a small Presbyterian congregation that gathered in a meeting-place on Williams Street, near the docks, on the southern tip of Manhattan Island. 'The English Presbyterians who had come to New York from New England', writes Kimnach, 'constituted a minority among the Scottish Presbyterians, and the disaffected separating group who employed the eighteen-year old Edwards as an unordained supply preacher were probably more like an extended family than an institutional church, worshipping in houses or a rented room.'[5] Kimnach describes this period as 'a brief golden age in the springtime of his career: an eight month sojourn during which he left Yale College, the Connecticut Valley, and even New England to become minister to a Presbyterian congregation in a community where he was no one's son, grandson, or nephew.'[6] 'When he went to New York', Kimnach adds, 'Edwards probably carried fewer than a dozen sermons with him,

---

[3] J. I. Packer, 'Puritan Preaching', in *A Quest for Godliness: The Puritan Vision of the Christian Life* (Wheaton, Illinois: Crossway Books, 1990), p. 284.

[4] John H. Gerstner, *The Rational Biblical Theology of Jonathan Edwards*, vol. 1 (Powhatan, Virginia: Berea Publications, 1991), p. 486.

[5] Ibid., p. 262. It is an interesting fact that JE both began and ended his ministerial career in a Presbyterian context, namely, at New York in 1722-1723 and at Princeton in 1758 respectively.

[6] Ibid., p. 261.

although he would have had to supply nearly forty preaching occasions during his stay there.'[7]

The fact that he was just nineteen when he preached 'The Nakedness of Job' simply highlights the remarkable spiritual and homiletical maturity by which the sermon is characterized – a maturity which is reflected in the Introduction:

We have an instance in this chapter of one of the greatest men in the world, in the most prosperous worldly estate and condition, brought to be externally one of the meanest of men; brought from seven thousand sheep, and three thousand camels, and five hundred yoke of oxen, and five hundred she-asses, and a very great household, all at once to nothing at all, as poor as the meanest beggar: a most remarkable instance of the vanity of worldly honor, riches, and prosperity. How soon is it gone and lost; how many hundred, yea thousands of accidents, may deprive the most prosperous of all in a little time, and make him most miserable and forlorn!

Here is a man that sat like a king and dwelt as a prince, but, as yesterday and today, is become a miserable and forlorn beggar. Before the messenger had finished his bad news, another came with more of the like upon the back of it. First, he has the news of his servants' being killed and his oxen and asses being taken, as you may see in the fourteenth and fifteenth verses; but before he had done telling this sad news to Job, there comes in another and brings him tidings that fire from heaven had burnt up all his sheep, and servants that kept them; and before he had done speaking there comes in another, and tells him that the Chaldeans had carried away all his camels and killed his servants; and before he had done, there came another with the yet more dreadful news that his children were all suddenly killed, as they were feasting together in their eldest brother's house.

And to what circumstances is this man, that just now was one of the richest men in the world, brought to? Now most that read or hear this remarkable history will doubtless acknowledge that,

---

[7] Ibid., p. 282.

if such a catastrophe was to happen to every man's estate, it would be enough quite to wean him from the world. Almost every man will doubtless say that, if they knew they should lose all their great estate and be deprived entirely of all their outward prosperity, as Job was, they would entertain no thought of striving and laying themselves out for a great estate in the world, seeing they must certainly in this manner be deprived of it, and they know not how soon. If it were so, men would not be so eager and earnest after riches, but would strive only for that that they could not be deprived of; all will grant [that] it would not be worth the while to do more.

But we may speak of it not only as a thing supposed, but as a thing that shall certainly be, for thus every man, however rich, shall certainly be deprived of all his goods, whether sheep, or oxen, or camels, or asses, or servants, or children; they shall be deprived of them as much as Job was, and he knows not how soon. Perhaps, when you read the history of Job, you read it as a strange thing that happened but once in the world; but, for the time to come, read it as a thing that happens daily, and frequently, for every man at death is as much deprived of all his worldly goods as Job was. The great men in the world, as kings, princes, and lords, when they die are as much deprived of all their outward prosperity as Job was: 'tis lost at once, and gone forever, never to be possessed more. Job's losses came indeed sudden, and in a little time one messenger came after another in a very strange manner, but the dying man is deprived of all his external prosperity and worldly good at once, at one breath, even his last breath. This history of Job is only a shadow of death; it is no more than happens to every man in the world.[8]

This is a very impressive, although in some respects atypical, Edwardsean Introduction. What is particularly striking is that it does not consist of the usual sober, generalized, contextual summary; it is in fact a dramatic renarration of the events of the first chapter of the Book of Job. The young preacher does not shrink from utilizing

---

[8] Ibid., pp. 403-404.

the details of the chapter and thus reproduces, almost in journalistic fashion, something of the dramatic and tragic momentum of the Book of Job itself. Moreover, this Introduction is unusual in that it does not reflect the normal compartmentalization by which Edwards' sermons are generally characterized. Whereas the basic pattern in his sermons is that the Introduction utilizes the first person plural pronoun 'we', the Doctrine the third person pronoun 'he' or 'they', and the Application often the second person pronoun 'you', this particular Introduction actually mingles the various pronouns. Thus in the fourth paragraph Edwards shifts to the second person pronoun: 'Perhaps, when *you* read the history of Job, *you* read it as a strange thing that happened but once in the world; but, for the time to come, read it as a thing that happens daily, and frequently, for every man at death is as much deprived of all his worldly goods as Job was.'[9] Indeed, what is unusual here is that not only does the preacher shift from the first person plural pronoun 'we' to the second person pronoun 'you', he also shifts from the indicative mood to the imperative mood. This very fact reflects the rather unusual mingling, in this Introduction, of the characteristics of the various categories of Text, Doctrine, and Application. In these four paragraphs the young preacher not only narrates the events of Job's calamities with great skill; he also reflects upon the events, draws generalized principles from them, and even begins to apply them. This particular Introduction even has an awakening tendency.

The Introduction to *Christian Cautions; or, The Necessity of Self-Examination* demonstrates beautifully Gerstner's observation concerning the circling of the eagle over its prey. Edwards' text on this occasion was Psalm 139:23-24: 'Search me, O God, and know my heart; try me, and know my thoughts; and see if there be any wicked way in me, and lead me in the way everlasting.' A footnote in the Hickman edition of 1834 provides the following details: 'This Tract contains the substance of four posthumous discourses, on the text prefixed, first printed at Edinb. 1788.'[10] The evidence suggests that these four

---

[9] Ibid., p. 404.
[10] *Works* (Hickman), 2:173 n.

preaching units were delivered in September 1733.[11] The sermon contains one of the finest examples of Edwards' general method in his contextual Introductions:

> This psalm is a meditation on the omniscience of God, or upon his perfect view and knowledge of every thing, which the psalmist represents by that perfect knowledge which God had of all his *actions*, his downsitting and his uprising; and of his *thoughts*, so that he knew his thoughts afar off; and of his *words*, 'There is not a word in my tongue', says the psalmist, 'but thou knowest it altogether.' Then he represents it by the impossibility of fleeing from the divine presence, or of hiding from him; so that if he should go into heaven, or hide himself in hell, or fly to the uttermost parts of the sea, yet he would not be hid from God; or if he should endeavour to hide himself in darkness, yet that would not cover him; but the darkness and light are both alike to him. Then he represents it by the knowledge which God had of him while in his mother's womb, ver. 15, 16. 'My substance was not hid from thee, when I was made in secret; thine eyes did see my substance, yet being imperfect; and in thy book all my members were written.'
>
> After this the psalmist observes what must be inferred as a necessary consequence of this omniscience of God, viz. that he will slay the wicked, since he seeth all their wickedness, and nothing of it is hid from him. And last of all, the psalmist improves this meditation upon God's all-seeing eye, in begging of God that he would search and try him, to see if there were any wicked way in him, and lead him in the way everlasting.[12]

This is a classic Edwardsean contextual introduction. Characteristically, the preacher provides the context, summarizes the essence of the psalm, and states the salient truths contained in it as a whole. Thus in this particular sermon, where the last two verses constitute the text, Edwards states the truths contained in the previous verses and then returns to the emphasis and thrust of his selected text. It is a general statement of the truth both of the text and of the context.

---

[11] See *Works*, 17:457.
[12] *Works* (Hickman), 2:173.

The original composition of 'The Final Judgment: or, The World Judged Righteously by Jesus Christ' can be assigned to 1729. In this sermon Edwards takes as his text Acts 17:31: 'Because he hath appointed a day, in the which he will judge the world in righteousness by that man whom he hath ordained.' It contains another fine example of an Edwardsean contextual introduction:

> These words are a part of the speech which Paul made in Mars' hill, a place of concourse of the judges and learned men of Athens. Athens was the principal city of that part of Greece which was formerly a commonwealth by itself, and was the most noted place in the whole world for learning, philosophy, and human wisdom; and it continued so for many ages; till at length the Romans having conquered Greece, its renown from that time began to diminish; and Rome having borrowed learning of it, began to rival it in science, and in the polite and civil arts. However, it was still very famous in the days of Christ and the apostles, and was a place of concourse for wise and learned men.
>
> Therefore, when Paul came thither, and began to preach concerning Jesus Christ, a man who had lately been crucified at Jerusalem, (as in the 18th verse,) the philosophers thronged about him, to hear what he had to say. The strangeness of his doctrine excited their curiosity; for they spent their time in endeavouring to find out new things, and valued themselves greatly upon their being the authors of new discoveries, as we are informed in ver. 21. They despised his doctrine in their hearts, and esteemed it very ridiculous, calling the apostle a babbler; for the preaching of Christ crucified was to the Greeks foolishness, 1 Cor. i. 23. Yet the Epicurean and Stoic philosophers, two different sects, had a mind to hear what the babbler had to say.[13]

Edwards' contextual introduction in this sermon is particularly thorough and therefore quite lengthy. Having considered Athens and then the Athenians, he now proceeds to analyse the Apostle's general approach to the preaching of the gospel in such a city and to such men.

---

[13] Ibid., p. 190.

He then concludes his Introduction with a summary of the specific content of the Mars Hill sermon:

> Upon this Paul rises up in the midst of them, and makes a speech; and as he speaks to philosophers and men of learning, he speaks quite differently from his common mode of address. There is evidently, in his discourse, a greater depth of thought, more philosophical reasoning, and a more elevated style, than are to be found in his ordinary discourses to common men. His speech is such as was likely to draw the attention and gain the assent of philosophers. He shows himself to be no babbler, but a man who could offer such reason, as they, however they valued themselves upon their wisdom, were not able to gainsay. His practice here is agreeable to what he saith of himself, 1 Cor. ix. 22 'that he became all things to all men, that he might by all means save some.' He not only to the weak became as weak, that he might gain the weak; but to the wise he became as wise, that he might gain the wise.
>
> In the first place, he reasons with them concerning their worship of idols. He declares to them the true God, and points out how unreasonable it is to suppose, that he delights in such superstitious worship. He begins with this, because they were most likely to hearken to it, as being so evidently agreeable to the natural light of reason, and also agreeable to what some of their own poets and philosophers had said, (ver. 28.). He begins not immediately to tell them about Jesus Christ, his dying for sinners, and his resurrection from the dead; but first draws their attention with that to which they were more likely to hearken; and then, having thus introduced himself, he proceeds to speak concerning Jesus Christ.
>
> He tells them, the times of this ignorance concerning the true God, in which they had hitherto been, God winked at; he suffered the world to lie in heathenish darkness; but now the appointed time was come, when he expected men should everywhere repent; 'because he had appointed a day, in the which he will judge the world in righteousness by that man whom he hath ordained.' As an enforcement to the duty of turning to God from their ignorance, superstition, and idolatry, the apostle brings in this, that

God had appointed such a day of judgment. And as a proof of this, he brings the resurrection of Christ from the dead.[14]

It will be noted that in this contextual introduction the verse selected is placed in the context of the entire Mars Hill sermon. Edwards provides basic background information of an historical and geographical nature. Characteristically, he summarizes the details of both the situation and the sermon preached by the Apostle. There is an element of narration here; and interwoven into this is an element of analysis, with observation and comment.

An interesting exception to his general method is the Introduction to the sermon 'The Duty of Self-Examination' which, according to the dating of Thomas A. Schafer, also belongs to the 'New York period' of 1722-1723 and which was, therefore, preached in close proximity to 'The Nakedeness of Job'. The evidence indicates that this sermon was repreached on at least three further occasions, two of which were at Bolton and at Northampton.[15] Edwards' text for this sermon was Haggai 1:5: 'Now therefore thus saith the LORD of hosts: Consider your ways.' He begins the sermon thus:

> It is the property of a beast to do things without any reflection or consideration, but to go just as their animal appetites lead them. They neither premeditate what to do in time to come, nor reflect on what they have done in time past. God has made their sense and their natural instinct their guide, and therefore hath made these far more perfect in them than in man. But the Almighty has given us something to be guided by, besides outward impulses upon our senses. He has given us a higher faculty, even reason and understanding, that we might be guided by consideration in things that we set about. The bees and ants, they have natural instinct to prompt them to provide in summer against winter, and diligently to improve their best opportunities for gathering and laying up their food. Natural instinct teaches the swallow to know the time of her coming and going.

---

[14] Ibid., pp. 190-191.
[15] I am indebted to Kimnach for this information. See *Works*, 10:481.

But God has left us without these instincts because he expects we should use those powers he has given for our own safety and advantage; he expects that we should improve our power of thinking and considering, that he has given us, by looking forward to see what is like to befall a little while hence, and make preparation for it against it comes. He expects, seeing he has made us capable of understanding and knowing future things that he has revealed, that we should consider them and provide for them: that we should make provision not only for this life, like the beasts that perish and have no other state to provide for, but also for the life that is to come, and consider what will become of us after death as well as before it.

'Tis this duty of consideration that God presses on the people of Israel by his prophet, Haggai . . .[16]

Kimnach makes the following observation on the Introduction to this sermon: 'The Exordium or opening of the sermon is interesting for its meditation upon animals and the natural world, eschewing for a space the usual textual exegesis.'[17] It is, however, an exception that proves the rule; and the rule is that of textual exegesis. Thus Edwards' almost universal concern in his Introductions is to expound the text in its context and there are virtually no topical or anecdotal introductions in his sermons. There is, moreover, a simplicity, a sobriety, and a thoroughness about his contextual introductions which reflect the 'plain style' by which his sermons are characterized. Sereno E. Dwight makes this general observation concerning his great-grandfather's Introductions:

> The plan of his sermons is most excellent. In his introduction, which is always an explanation of the passage, he exhibits uncommon skill, and the sagacity with which he discovers, and the power with which he seizes at once, the whole drift and meaning of the passage in all its bearings, has rarely if ever been equalled.[18]

---

[16] Ibid., p. 482.
[17] Ibid., p. 480.
[18] *Works* (Hickman), I:cxc.

9

DOCTRINAL EXPOSITION

'Christianity', notes J. Gresham Machen (1881–1937), 'begins with a triumphant indicative.'[1] This grammatical-theological observation by the Princeton theologian captures the genius and the glory of the gospel of Christ. The indicative mood is, as the *Oxford English Dictionary* emphasizes, 'assertive of objective fact'.[2] It stands in contrast to the imperative mood, which signifies a command or a request, and to the subjunctive mood, which signifies that which is contingent or hypothetical. Thus the indicative mood is the fundamental mood of history. Machen is, therefore, emphasizing here the essential historicity and factuality of the gospel message. That gospel does not begin by telling the sinner what *he* must do; it begins by telling him what *God* has done in Christ. It does not begin with an urgent imperative; it begins with a triumphant indicative. Certainly, Christianity does not neglect man's responsibility, man's duty, man's response. It is very important to note that, both in the preaching and in the theology of the New Testament, the indicative mood moves on to the imperative mood. Indeed, the theology of the New Testament, considered *in toto*, is that of an indicative-imperative pattern or structure.[3] But there is, within this pattern or structure, a fundamental primacy or priority about the indicative mood. Indeed, this pattern or structure constitutes the tacit theological rationale for the Puritan concept of preaching as

---

[1] J. Gresham Machen, *Christianity and Liberalism* (Grand Rapids: Eerdmans, 1977), p. 47.

[2] Ibid.

[3] For an analysis of this indicative-imperative pattern or structure of New Testament Christianity see my *The Imperative of Preaching: A Theology of Sacred Rhetoric* (Edinburgh: Banner of Truth, 2002).

explicatio et applicatio verbi Dei; it constitutes the tacit theological rationale for the classic Doctrine-Application pattern or structure of the Puritan sermon. It has been noted that there is, within this relationship between the indicative and the imperative moods, both an *irreversibility* and an *inseparability;* and it is the fact of *irreversibility* that insists upon the primacy and the priority of Doctrine in the sermon.

The New England Puritan preacher of the eighteenth century was heir to this tradition of the sermon as *explicatio et applicatio verbi Dei.* His sermons are, accordingly, invariably divided into Doctrine and Application. The Doctrine, observes Kimnach, is 'a major portion of most sermons and, structurally, often the most complex.'[4] It should be noted, however, that there is a touch of ambiguity in Edwards' use of the category Doctrine in his sermons. On the one hand, the term denotes that substantial section in his sermons in which the text is explained and expounded and which thus sets the stage for the Application. On the other hand, the term is virtually synonymous with what is known, homiletically, as the Main Proposition. Thus it is generally at the outset of the Doctrine that Edwards makes a doctrinal observation which captures the essence of the text and which thus announces the theme of the sermon:

> The Doctrine usually begins with a single statement of doctrine, carefully labeled 'Doc[trine]'. In his inclination to formulate the entire doctrinal message of the sermon in a single statement of doctrine, Edwards was, it seems, a little unusual for his day. Most contemporary preachers tended to formulate two or more equally important statements and list them in parallel at the head of the Doctrine. Although it is Edwards' custom to draw two, three, or four Propositions or Observations from the doctrine immediately after its statement, thus dividing it for 'clearing' or full discussion in the body of the Doctrine, the single statement of doctrine brings the entire sermon into a sharp thematic focus, like light rays passing through a lens, if only for a vivid moment.[5]

[4] *Works,* 10:37.
[5] Ibid., pp. 37-38.

There are, however, occasional exceptions to this general rule concerning the single statement of doctrine. In 'The Church's Marriage to her Sons, and to her God', for instance, where he takes as his text Isaiah 62:4-5: 'Thy land shall be married. For as a young man marrieth a virgin, so shall thy sons marry thee: and as the bridegroom rejoiceth over the bride, so shall thy God rejoice over thee', Edwards unusually resolves the truth of the text into two Propositions:

> The text thus opened affords these two propositions proper for our consideration on the solemn occasion of this day.
> I. The uniting of faithful ministers with Christ's people in the ministerial office, when done in a due manner, is like a young man's marrying a virgin.
> II. This union of ministers with the people of Christ is in order to their being brought to the blessedness of a more glorious union, in which Christ shall rejoice over them, as the bridegroom rejoiceth over the bride.[6]

Edwards' normal practice is, however, that of the single statement of Doctrine, as the following examples demonstrate:

> 'Living Peaceably One With Another':
> Rom 12:18: 'If it be possible, as much as lieth in you, live peaceably with all men.'
> Doctrine: 'It is an indispensable duty incumbent upon us to endeavor, to the utmost of our power, to live peaceably with all men.'[7]

> 'God's Sovereignty in the Salvation of Men':
> Rom. 9:18: 'Therefore hath he mercy on whom he will have mercy, and whom he will he hardeneth.'
> Doctrine: 'God exercises his sovereignty in the eternal salvation of men.'[8]

---

[6] *Works* (Hickman), 2:19.
[7] *Works*, 14:120.
[8] *Works* (Hickman), 2:850.

'A Divine and Supernatural Light':

Matt. 16:17: 'And Jesus answered and said unto him, Blessed art thou, Simon Bar-jona; for flesh and blood hath not revealed it unto thee, but my Father which is in heaven.'

Doctrine: 'That there is such a thing as a spiritual and divine light, immediately imparted to the soul by God, of a different nature from any that is obtained by natural means.'[9]

'Charity More Excellent than the Extraordinary Gifts of the Spirit':

1 Corinthians 13:1-2: 'Though I speak with the tongues of men and of angels, and have not charity, I am become as sounding brass, or a tinkling cymbal. And though I have the gift of prophecy, and understand all mysteries, and all knowledge; and though I have all faith, so that I could remove mountains, and have not charity, I am nothing.'

Doctrine: 'The ordinary influence of God's Spirit, working saving grace in the heart, is a more excellent blessing than any of the extraordinary gifts of the Spirit.'[10]

'The Spirit of Charity the Opposite of a Selfish Spirit':

1 Cor. 13:5: 'Charity . . . seeketh not her own.'

Doctrine: 'A Christian spirit is opposite to a selfish spirit.'[11]

'The Nature and End of Excommunication':

1 Cor. 5:11: 'But now I have written unto you not to keep company, if any man that is called a brother be a fornicator, or covetous, or an idolater, or a railer, or a drunkard, or an extortioner; with such an one no not to eat.'

Doctrine: 'Those members of the visible christian church who are become visibly wicked, ought not to be tolerated in the church, but should be excommunicated.'[12]

---

[9] Ibid., p. 13.

[10] Works, 8:152.

[11] Ibid., p. 252. Although this sermon is the eighth in Tryon Edwards' edition of 1852, it is, in fact, the seventh in the original manuscript. Tryon divided the fourth sermon – 'Long-suffering and Kindness' - into two Lectures. See footnote in the chapter 'Use of Exhortation.'

[12] Works (Hickman), 2:118.

The above examples are representative of Edwards' ability to capture succinctly and concisely the essence of his text in his Doctrine. Indeed, his sermons are characterized by a striking textual fidelity. It is an interesting fact, however, that some of his Main Propositions do not fully capture the truth of the entire text. Some of them capture a part or an aspect of the text. 'Man's Natural Blindness in the Things of Religion' is based on Psalm 94:8-11: 'Understand, ye brutish among the people: and ye fools, when will ye be wise? He that planted the ear, shall he not hear? He that formed the eye, shall he not see? He that chastiseth the heathen, shall he not correct? He that teacheth man knowledge, shall he not know? The LORD knoweth the thoughts of man, that they are vanity.' In this sermon Edwards makes the following doctrinal observation: 'That there is an extreme and brutish blindness in things of religion, which naturally possesses the hearts of mankind.'[13] It is significant that Edwards does not deal here with the omnipotence and the omniscience of God, but simply with the brutish blindness of man. His focus in the sermon falls upon an isolated aspect of the text. Indeed, the sermon is essentially a textual-topical consideration of the blindness and the foolishness of man in the things of religion.

'The Justice of God in the Damnation of Sinners' is unquestionably one of Edwards' greatest sermons. It is, however, interesting to note that the text for this sermon – 'That every mouth may be stopped' - is, in fact, just part of Romans 3:19; indeed, it is simply a subordinate clause within that verse. Edwards states as his Doctrine the following Main Proposition: ''Tis just with God eternally to cast off, and destroy sinners.' The preacher then proceeds to divide his doctrinal treatment of the text into two themes: 'The truth of this doctrine may appear, by the joint consideration of two things, *viz.* man's sinfulness, and God's sovereignty.'[14] It should be noted that, on the one hand, Edwards has narrowed his text here, but also that, on the other hand, he has expanded and amplified his doctrinal consideration beyond the scope of the text. The validity of considering 'man's sinfulness' is clearly not in question; but the validity of considering 'God's sovereignty' on the

---

[13] Ibid., p. 247.
[14] Works, 19:341.

basis of such a text is somewhat questionable. There is a certain lack of coherence between the text, the Main Proposition, and the doctrinal content.

Other sermons capture an inference from the text. This is particularly evident in 'Degrees of Glory', which is dated 'Feb. 1736, 7' [sic].[15] This sermon is based upon 2 Corinthians 9:6: 'But this I say, He which soweth sparingly shall reap also sparingly; but he which soweth bountifully shall reap also bountifully. His Doctrine here is the following: 'We ought to seek high degrees of glory in heaven.'[16] Since the context of this text is clearly that of giving for the relief of the poor, it will be immediately evident that this Main Proposition does not capture the essence of the text, but constitutes rather an inference from the text. In other words, Edwards has, in effect, bypassed the *telos* and the fundamental meaning of the text, and has focused instead upon what could legitimately be described as a good and necessary consequence of the text. Lesser makes this interesting observation concerning this sermon:

> Sometimes Edwards begins a sermon with a chronicle of events, often stretching over several texts before coming to the one at hand, *but seldom does he cast his proof text aside entirely, as he seems to here.* In 'Degrees of Glory' he recounts the plight of the impoverished churches in Judea, Galatia, Macedonia, and Achaia and the efforts at relief, citing texts from Acts, Romans, Galatians, and I Corinthians as ancient examples of 'charity to the poor'; yet the phrase turns up again only at the end of the sermon, and mention of the impoverished churches not at all. Although his text from II Corinthians broadly hints at charity, his doctrinal statement avoids it altogether – 'We ought to seek high degrees of glory in heaven' – and he settles instead on . . . the just correlation between work and reward.[17]

In the light of these facts, it is not in the least surprising that the matter in the Doctrinal section appears to belong more appropriately to the

[15] See ibid., p. 611.
[16] Ibid., p. 614.
[17] Ibid., p. 609. Emphasis added.

Application. This is the perhaps inevitable result of turning an inference from the text into a Main Proposition.

In 'The Excellency of Christ' Edwards states the following as the subject of his discourse: 'There is an admirable conjunction of diverse excellencies in Jesus Christ.'[18] It will be noted that he again isolates from the text one particular point, namely, the fact that the Lord Jesus Christ is described in this text both as a *Lion* and as a *Lamb*. Indeed, the preacher himself virtually acknowledges this:

> Many things might be observed in the words of the text; but it is to my present purpose only to take notice of the two distinct appellations here given to Christ.
> 1. He is called a *Lion* . . .
> 2. He is called a *Lamb* . . .[19]

It is this juxtaposition of the dual images of the *Lion* and the *Lamb* that constitutes the basis for the inference stated in the Main Proposition which is then powerfully developed. Very often, as in this particular sermon, Edwards' doctrinal exposition is developed and amplified in such an expansive manner that his sermons are perhaps best described as textual-topical. The great strength of the textual-topical approach is that it is powerfully conducive to that unity which is such a vital ingredient in the sermon.

A significant procedure utilized by Edwards in his doctrinal exposition is that of 'Questions' (or 'Inquiries') and 'Answers'. This procedure is, in effect, simply a more formal use of the analytical question and the analytical-question response.[20] The analytical question is, as the term suggests, a question that analyses a proposition. It engages in a kind of dialogue with the proposition and thus, by means of both question and response, assists in the exposition and development of the proposition. Edwards utilizes this approach in one of his earliest sermons, 'Wicked Men's Slavery to Sin'. This sermon was preached at some point between the summers of 1721 and 1722 when Edwards

[18] *Works* (Hickman), 1:680.
[19] Ibid.
[20] For a consideration of the analytical question and the analytical-question response see my *The Imperative of Preaching*, pp. 57-61.

was merely 17 or 18 years of age; indeed, the sermon possibly antedates the 'New York period'. His text on this occasion was John 8:34: 'Jesus answered them, Verily, verily, I say unto you, Whosoever committeth sin is the servant of sin.' Edwards' Main Proposition is as follows: 'Wicked men are servants and slaves to sin.' He commences his Doctrine thus: 'We shall explain and clear up this doctrine by answering these two queries: first, how does it appear that wicked men are slaves to sin, and second, in what respects are they so?'[21] He then gives three answers to each of these two questions. Thus the questions prompt and set up the answers. Indeed, these two questions and the six answers provided constitute the entirety of the doctrinal exposition in this sermon. His second answer to the first question is as follows:

> The wicked man is devoted to the commands of sin, and there-fore may be said to be under slavery to it. Wicked men are very obedient servants to sin. All things in the world must give way to the commands thereof: the commands of God must not stand in competition with them, but must all bow down and be tramp-led upon by sin. His own interest and happiness must also give place when sin requires it, and so devoted are wicked men to their lord and master, sin, that they will rather burn in hell forever than disobey him and rebel against him. They stand ready to be sent on any errand that sin requires them to go; they wait at sin's gates, and watch at the posts of his doors, like an obedient lackey, to hear what commands he has for them to do. Thus, if sin requires them to steal, swear, defraud, or commit fornication, it is done; if sin commands them to do that which tends to their own ruin and destruction, it is done; if sin commands them to run and jump into the bottomless pit, the sinner immediately obeys, and runs with all his might towards this pit of fire and brimstone. And whatever fears and dreadful apprehensions he may have on his mind, yet he is such a devoted servant to sin that it shall be performed. Thus he is entirely given up to obey this tyrant, sin.[22]

---

[21] *Works*, 10:340.
[22] Ibid., p. 342.

This method of Questions and Answers is virtually the doctrinal counterpart to the applicatory method of Objections and Answers; just as the latter is found invariably in the Application, so the former is invariably found in the Doctrine. Both procedures enhance the dialogical aspect of Edwards' preaching.[23]

Edwards' ability in analysing a concept is well exemplified in 'Christ Exalted: or, Jesus Christ Gloriously Exalted Above All Evil in the Work of Redemption'. In this sermon (described in a footnote in the Hickman edition as a 'Lecture, August 1738')[24] Edwards takes as his text 1 Corinthians 15:25-26: 'For he must reign, till he hath put all enemies under his feet. The last enemy that shall be destroyed is death.' In the course of expounding the Doctrine, Edwards analyses the phrase 'all enemies' under the following headings, the last of which we cite in full:

1. Satan . . .
2. Guilt . . .
3. Corruption and wickedness of heart . . .
4. Many of the devil's instruments . . .
5. Affliction and misery . . .
6. Death . . .[25]

Death is an evil which has greatly prevailed, and made dreadful havoc in this world. How does it waste and devour mankind, one age after another; sparing none, high or low, rich or poor, good or bad! Wild beasts have destroyed many; many cruel princes have taken away the lives of thousands, and laid waste whole countries: but death devours all; none are suffered to escape. And the bodies of the saints as well as others, fall a prey to this great devourer. Yea, so high did this enemy rise, that he took hold on Christ himself, and swallowed him among the rest. He became the prey of

---

[23] For further examples of the procedure of Questions (or Inquiries) and Answers see 'The Manner in which the Salvation of the Soul is to be Sought', *Works* (Hickman), 2:52-53; 'The Future Punishment of the Wicked Unavoidable and Intolerable', ibid., p. 81; 'The Most High a Prayer-Hearing God, ibid., pp. 115-116; 'The Nature and End of Excommunication', ibid., pp. 119-120.

[24] Ibid., p. 213.

[25] Ibid., pp. 213-215.

this great, insatiable monster. By his means, was his bodily frame destroyed, and laid dead in the dark and silent grave. And death still goes on destroying thousands every day. And therefore the grave is one of those things which Agur says, never has enough. – So have evils of every kind prevailed; and to such a degree have they exalted themselves in the world.[26]

This ability to analyse a concept thoroughly, indeed exhaustively, is again demonstrated in 'Self-Flatteries'. The text for this undated sermon was Psalm 36:2: 'For he flattereth himself in his own eyes, until his iniquity be found to be hateful.' In the course of the main body of the doctrinal section the preacher analyses the central idea of *self-flattery* into the following propositions, the third of which we cite:

1. Some flatter themselves with a secret hope, that there is no such thing as *another world* . . .
2. Some flatter themselves that *death* is a great way off, and that they shall hereafter have much opportunity to seek salvation; . . .
3. Some flatter themselves that they lead *moral* and orderly lives, and therefore think that they shall not be damned . . .
4. Some make the *advantages* under which they live an occasion of self-flattery . . .
5. Some flatter themselves with their own *intentions* . . .
6. There are some who flatter themselves, that they *do*, and have *done*, a great deal for their salvation, and therefore hope they shall obtain; . . .
7. Some hope by their strivings to obtain salvation *of themselves* . . .
8. Some sinners flatter themselves, that they are *already* converted . . .[27]

3. Some flatter themselves that they lead moral and orderly lives, and therefore think that they shall not be damned. They think with themselves that they live not in any vice, that they take care to wrong no man, are just and honest dealers; that they are not addicted to hard drinking, or to uncleanness, or to bad language; that they keep the sabbath strictly, are constant attendants on the

---

[26] Ibid., pp. 214-215.
[27] Ibid., pp. 218-19.

public worship, and maintain the worship of God in their families. Therefore they hope that God will not cast them into hell. They see not why God should be so angry with them as that would imply, seeing they are so orderly and regular in their walk! they see not that they have done enough to anger him to that degree. And if they have angered him, they imagine they have also done a great deal to pacify him.

If they be not as yet converted, and it be necessary that they should experience any other conversion in order to their salvation, they hope that their orderly and strict lives will move God to give them converting grace. They hope that surely God will not see those that live as they do go to hell. Thus they flatter themselves, as those (Luke xviii. 9.) 'that trusted in themselves that they were righteous.'[28]

Edwards' capacity for the relentless, logical analysis of an idea is perhaps supremely manifested in 'Wicked Men Inconsistent with Themselves', unquestionably one of his most brilliant sermons. Preached in December 1738, this sermon belongs to a period which some have regarded as the apogee of his preaching career.[29] 'At no time in a preaching career that spanned more than thirty-five years', contends Lesser, 'did Jonathan Edwards achieve such sustained mastery of the sermon form as during the five years from 1734 to 1738.'[30] A significant number of Edwards' greatest sermons were composed and first preached during these years.[31] This period, which significantly

---

[28] Ibid., p. 218.

[29] 'The literary legacy of sermons from this period is of great importance, for in the long trajectory of Edwards' preaching career the period of 1734-1738 represents the apogee.' Wilson H. Kimnach, 'Note to the Reader', *Works*, 19:XI.

[30] Ibid., p. 3.

[31] Note especially the following: 'The Unreasonableness of Indetermination in Religion'; 'Wicked Men Useful in their Destruction Only'; 'Natural Men in a Dreadful Condition'; 'Justification by Faith Alone'; 'Praise One of the Chief Employments of Heaven'; 'The Preciousness of Time'; 'Pressing into the Kingdom of God'; 'Ruth's Resolution'; 'The Folly of Looking Back in Fleeing out of Sodom'; 'The Justice of God in the Damnation of Sinners'; 'When the Wicked Shall have Filled Up Themselves of their Sin', 'Wrath Will Come upon them to the Uttermost'; 'The Sole Consideration that God is God, Sufficient to Fill All Objections to his Sovereignty'; 'The Portion of the Wicked'; 'The Portion of the Righteous'; 'The Most High a Prayer-Hearing God'; 'God the Best Portion of the Christian'; 'Unbe-

straddles the Northampton awakening of 1734-1735, was clearly one of tremendous homiletical creativity and productivity on his part. 'Wicked Men Inconsistent with Themselves' was preached right at the close of this period. The latter sermon is a remarkable analysis of Matthew 11:16-19: 'But whereunto shall I liken this generation? It is like unto children sitting in the markets, and calling unto their fellows, and saying, We have piped unto you, and ye have not danced; we have mourned unto you, and ye have not lamented. For John came neither eating nor drinking, and they say, He hath a devil. The Son of Man came eating and drinking, and they say, Behold a man gluttonous, and a winebibber, a friend of publicans and sinners. But wisdom is justified of her children.' Edwards states as his Doctrine the following:

> Wicked men are very inconsistent with themselves. They are so in the following respects:
> 1. The dictates of their darkened understandings are inconsistent with themselves.
> 2. Their wills are inconsistent with their reason.
> 3. Their wills are inconsistent with themselves.
> 4. Their outward show is inconsistent with their hearts.
> 5. Their profession is inconsistent with their practice.
> 6. Their practice is inconsistent with their hopes.
> 7. Their practice is inconsistent with itself.[32]

It should be noted that, in characteristic fashion, Edwards takes his cue in this sermon from the text. He explains in his introductory remarks that, in this passage, 'Christ reproves the unreasonableness of the Jews in rejecting God's messengers.'[33] But it is his ability to move from the particular to the general that is so strikingly demonstrated in this sermon. On the basis of the negative, unreasonable response of

---

lievers Contemn the Glory and Excellency of Christ'; 'Men Naturally God's Enemies'; 'The Excellency of Christ'; 'Hope and Comfort Usually Follow Genuine Humiliation and Repentance'; 'Joseph's Great Temptation and Glorious Deliverance'; 'Jesus Christ the Same Yesterday, Today, and Forever'; *Charity and Its Fruits;* 'Jesus Christ Gloriously Exalted Above All Evil in the Work of Redemption'; and 'Wicked Men Inconsistent with Themselves'.

[32] *Works* (Hickman), 2:919.
[33] Ibid., 918.

the Jews to both John the Baptist and Christ, Edwards makes incisive observations and generalizations concerning man. Thus the sermon consists essentially of an analysis of 'the woeful confusion of the nature of all men now in their fallen state'[34] as manifested continually by the 'impossibilities, and self-contradictions, and self-inconsistencies'[35] by which they are characterized. In the third section the Northampton preacher provides a brilliant analysis of the inconsistencies of men with regard to the will:

> They do not like God as he is, and yet they would not like him if he were otherwise. They would not like him if he were otherwise than he is in those very things for which they most dislike him.
>
> 1. They dislike God because he is a holy God. This is the main foundation of the enmity that wicked men have against God. His perfect purity and holiness make them enemies to him, because from this perfection of his nature he necessarily hates sin, and so hates their sins, which they love, and he will not and cannot allow of any sin in them. They are utter enemies to such a holy God. And yet they would not like him if they supposed him to be an unholy being, or if they supposed him to be at all wanting in perfect holiness, for then he could not be depended upon . . .
>
> 2. They do not like God, because he is a God of justice. This indeed is a branch of his holiness, for being strictly and perfectly just, he is disposed to execute just punishment on all iniquity . . .; and yet they would not like God if he were an unjust God. If he were an unjust being, that would be an insuperable objection with them against accepting him as their God, for then they would think with themselves, 'how do I know how unjustly he may deal with me'; and wicked men, however unjust they are, never like injustice against themselves . . .
>
> 3. They do not like God because, he is an Almighty God, and is able to destroy them when he pleases; nor yet would they like him if he were a weak being and of but little power . . .
>
> 4. They do not like God because he is an omniscient God, for

---

[34] Ibid., p. 926.
[35] Ibid.

hereby he sees all their wickedness. But yet neither would they like him if he did not know all things, for then in many cases he would not know what their case is, and what it requires, and what is best for them. He might ruin them in the disposal of them through mistake, he might not know how to extricate them out of difficulties in which they are or may be involved.

5. Natural men oftentimes dislike God in the exercises of his infinite sovereign mercy, when it is exercised towards others. They are greatly displeased at God's being so gracious to others; they dislike it much that God bestows converting grace upon them and pardoning mercy, and a title to eternal life upon them. When they hear of their conversion it is unpleasant news, and they find fault with it the more when the persons who seem to have received such mercy are very unworthy, and have been very great sinners; . . . And yet they would not like God if he were not infinitely merciful, for then they would have less hopes of obtaining mercy themselves. They are angry because God appears so merciful in the exercises of his grace to others; but yet they would have God merciful, and are at the same time afraid that he is not merciful enough to be willing to pardon their sins, and bestow his blessing on them. Thus natural men do not like God as he is, nor yet would they like him if he were otherwise.[36]

'Related to his logical analysis', observes Kimnach, 'is Edwards's ability to define his intended subject. Here, perhaps the most distinctive procedure is his clearing the field through negation of alternatives prior to declaring that which is affirmed.'[37] This procedure is known as the *via negationis*.[38] Classically, this method makes deliberate use of negatives in the matter of definition or explanation. Thus in the *via negationis* the process of definition moves from the negative to the positive; it thus involves a process of elimination in which the focus narrows rapidly. This is precisely Edwards' method in 'A Divine and Supernatural Light': 'I would show what this spiritual and divine

---

[36] Ibid., pp. 920-921.

[37] Wilson H. Kimnach, 'Jonathan Edwards's Pursuit of Reality', in *American Experience*, p. 112.

[38] *The way of negation*. This method is also known as the *via negativa*.

light is. And in order to it, would show, First, In a few things what it is not . . .'[39] Edwards' approach here is virtually diagnostic:

> This spiritual and divine light does not consist in any impression made upon the imagination. It is no impression upon the mind, as though one saw any thing with the bodily eyes. It is no imagination or idea of an outward light or glory, or any beauty of form or countenance, or a visible lustre or brightness of any object. The imagination may be strongly impressed with such things; but this is not spiritual light. Indeed when the mind has a lively discovery of spiritual things, and is greatly affected by the power of divine light, it may, and probably very commonly doth, much affect the imagination; so that impressions of an outward beauty or brightness may *accompany* those spiritual discoveries. But spiritual light is not that impression upon the imagination, but an exceedingly different thing. Natural men may have lively impressions on their imaginations; and we cannot determine but that the devil, who transforms himself into an angel of light, may cause imaginations of an outward beauty, or visible glory, and of sounds and speeches, and other such things; but these are things of a vastly inferior nature to spiritual light.[40]

Kimnach remarks that this technique of the *via negationis* is suggestive of 'a metaphysical plow that moves slowly and methodically, yet inexorably and effortlessly to the goal, clearing away all obstacles in its passage.'[41] Then, after the negation, comes the affirmation: 'Secondly, Positively what this spiritual and divine light is . . .'[42]

---

[39] *Works* (Hickman), 2:13. Kimnach observes that 'perhaps Edwards' logic is rhetorically most impressive when it is presented as logic, specifically, in the 'rational proof' of the Doctrine where he argues not only a positive proof, but first eliminates alternatives in a negative proof. In many such negative-to-positive proofs, Edwards moves grandly through the whole range of evident possibilities until the espoused principle is left standing alone and dominant.' *Works*, 10:253. Kimnach goes on to refer, in a footnote, to this very sermon: 'A representative example would be the first proposition of the Doctrine in "A Divine and Supernatural Light", . . .' Ibid., n. 8.

[40] Ibid. See also 'The End of the Wicked Contemplated by the Righteous', ibid., pp. 208-209.

[41] *Works*, 10:253.

[42] *Works* (Hickman), 2:14.

Closely related to the *via negationis* is Edwards' use of antithesis or contrast. In 'Heaven is a World of Love' he sets in antithesis the inveterate turbulence of this world with the eternal peacefulness and rest of the heavenly world:

There are many principles contrary to love, that make this world like a tempestuous sea. Selfishness, and envy, and revenge, and jealousy, and kindred passions keep life on earth in a constant tumult, and make it a scene of confusion and uproar, where no quiet rest is to be enjoyed except in renouncing this world and looking to another. But oh! what rest is there in that world which the God of peace and love fills with his own gracious presence, and in which the Lamb of God lives and reigns, filling it with the brightest and sweetest beams of his love; where there is nothing to disturb or offend, and no being or object to be seen that is not surrounded with perfect amiableness and sweetness; where the saints shall find and enjoy all that they love, and so be perfectly satisfied; where there is no enemy and no enmity, but perfect love in every heart and to every being; where there is perfect harmony among all the inhabitants, no one envying another, but every one rejoicing in the happiness of every other; where all their love is humble and holy, and perfectly Christian, without the least carnality or impurity; where love is always mutual and reciprocated to the full; where there is no hypocrisy or dissembling, but perfect simplicity and sincerity; where there is no treachery, or unfaithfulness, or inconstancy, or jealousy in any form; where there is no clog or hindrance to the exercises or expressions of love, no imprudence or indecency in expressing it, and no influence of folly or indiscretion in any word or deed; where there is no separation wall, and no misunderstanding or strangeness, but full acquaintance and perfect intimacy in all; where there is no division through different opinions or interests, but where all in that glorious and loving society shall be most nearly and divinely related, and each shall belong to every other, and all shall enjoy each other in perfect prosperity and riches, and honour, without any sickness, or grief, or persecution, or sorrow, or any enemy to molest them, or any busybody to create jealousy or misunderstanding, or mar the perfect, and holy, and blessed peace that reigns in heaven![43]

It will be noted that, before he proceeds to describe the holy perfections of heaven, Edwards emphasizes the unholy passions of this world. Thus by means of contrast he sets in relief the beauties of the heavenly state; he thus highlights them. The use of contrast here is very much akin to that of the *via negationis* in that it proceeds to the positive description *via* the negative. Once again affirmation follows a species of negation.

Edwards' predilection for the use of contrast in his sermons has been noted by Kimnach: 'He seems always to have liked juxtaposition of opposites and other varieties of parallelism.'[44] Indeed, Kimnach specifies 'parallelism' as a crucial element in 'Edwards' essential rhetorical arsenal.'[45] The Doctrinal section of *The Portion of the Righteous* contains the following striking passage in which the preacher sets in juxtaposition the present frail state of the believer's body and its future glorious state. The impressiveness of the juxtaposition or contrast is enhanced by the repetition of the formula 'Now ... But then ...':

> Now the body is in need of food and sleep continually, to recreate it, but it shall not be so then; now the body is subject to weariness, and to diseases, but it shall not be so then; now if God lets in any great matter of divine light into the soul, the body is ready to sink under it, but it shall not be so then. The glorified body of the saints shall not then fail or flag at all by the most powerful exercises of mind. Now no man can see God and live, but the body would immediately sink and be dissolved; but then the body shall not fail at all by the immediate beholding of God. Now the saints can see but little. When God a little reveals himself, as he doth at times, the saints are forced to beseech God either to strengthen them to see it, or to stay his hand; but then the body shall be so vigorous and spiritual, that the constant and everlasting view of the glory of God shall not in any wise overcome it, or cause it in the least to fail.[46]

[43] *Charity*, pp. 350-351.
[44] *Works*, 10:97.
[45] Ibid., p. 294.
[46] *Works* (Hickman), 2:894.

Indeed, Edwards' use of contrast is so pervasive in his sermons and is used in such a variety of contexts that it merits special attention at this point. This simple, yet highly effective rhetorical technique appears to have been almost instinctive with the New England preacher. In his sermons God's omniscience is contrasted with man's ignorance; God's omnipotence in judgment is contrasted with man's utter impotence; the rationality of man is contrasted, positively, with the instincts of the beasts; man's natural inability to glorify God is contrasted, negatively, with the natural ability of the beasts in this respect; man's ingratitude to his Owner is contrasted, negatively, with the gratitude of the beasts to theirs; the foolishness of men is contrasted, negatively, with the wisdom of the beasts in providing for the future; 'the concerns of this world' are contrasted with 'the concerns of [men's] souls'; the young people of Northampton who are still alive are contrasted with a young man who is now dead; past awakening is contrasted with present carelessness; 'then' (in the past) is contrasted with 'now'; 'now' is contrasted with 'then' (in the future); the present needs and burdens of the body are contrasted with its future emancipation; the turbulence of this world is contrasted with the eternal rest of the heavenly world; type is contrasted with 'the great antitype'; 'fallen man' is contrasted with 'Christ . . . the Lion of the tribe of Judah'; the Lion is contrasted with the Lamb; the glory of Christ before the world was is contrasted with his shameful treatment in this world. The great value of such contrasts is that they set in relief both elements in the contrast – the superior element (if any) is set in relief against the inferior element and *vice versa*. There can be no doubt that such a use of contrast is eminently biblical; indeed, there is an essential timelessness about this simple homiletical technique.

Another device utilized by Edwards in his Doctrinal exposition is that of the *reductio ad absurdum*. This classic technique, the use of which again reflects Edwards' formidable logical powers, essentially reasons from the premises of an opponent in such a way that the position itself is reduced to absurdity. A notable example of this is to be found in 'The Eternity of Hell Torments'. In this sermon the Northampton preacher deals specifically with one of the subtle insinuations made by Archbishop Tillotson with regard to the doctrine of everlasting punishment, namely, that although God is obliged to fulfil his promises, he is not obliged to fulfil his threatenings. The absurdity to which Edwards reduces this position lies in the fact that, if the position were true, the conclusion would be inevitable that God has made use of a fallacy to govern the world – a fallacy, moreover, in which God has apparently been detected!

> The doctrine of those who teach, that it is not certain that God will fulfil those absolute threatenings, is *blasphemous* another way; and that is, as God, according to their supposition, was obliged to make use of a *fallacy* to govern the world. They own, that it is needful that men should *apprehend* themselves liable to an eternal punishment, that they might thereby be restrained from sin, and that God has threatened such a punishment, for the very end that they might *believe* themselves exposed to it. But what an unworthy opinion does this convey of God and his government, of his infinite majesty, and wisdom, and all-sufficiency! – Beside, they suppose, that though God has made use of such a fallacy, yet it is not such an one but that they have *detected* him in it. Though God *intended* men should believe it to be certain, that sinners are liable to an eternal punishment; yet they suppose, that they have been so cunning as to find out that it is not certain: and so that God had not laid his design so deep, but that such cunning men as they can discern the cheat, and defeat the design: because they have found out, that there is no necessary connexion between the threatening of eternal punishment, and the execution of that threatening.[47]

There can be no doubt that Edwards was *inter alia* what Robert L. Dabney (1820-1898) describes as a "'reasoning preacher'".[48] Edwards' reasoning is often very close and his argumentation very tight. This very

---

[47] Ibid., p. 86.

[48] Robert L. Dabney, *Sacred Rhetoric or A Course of Lectures on Preaching* (repr., Edinburgh: Banner of Truth, 1979), p. 196. Dabney, in arguing against 'the popular prejudice against "reasoning preachers"', makes this observation: 'But, in truth, he who does not reason is no preacher: he establishes no conviction . . . The attractive preacher is the true reasoner, for he argues skilfully and tersely. He is interesting, not because he gives the understanding no logical grounds, but because he gives them aright.' Ibid., pp. 196-197.

fact highlights an interesting paradox with regard to his attitude to reason. On the one hand, he demonstrates an inveterate opposition to the rationalism of the Enlightenment; on the other hand, he demonstrates a constant appeal to reason. 'As much by his actual practice of reasoning as by his overt statements', contends McClymond, 'he exhibited a tremendous rational confidence.'[49] The solution to this paradox lies, McClymond insists, in 'Edwards's sharp distinction between regenerate and unregenerate reason.'[50] 'Regeneration', McClymond observes, 'is the epistemological foundation of Edwards's entire religious outlook.'[51] 'A thinker who reasoned from biblical principles was wholly different from one who argued from natural reason alone. There was vast scope for the exercise of reason, but only after reason had embraced the truths of revelation by faith.'[52] Thus Edwards' attitude to reason is essentially the Augustinian or Anselmian approach as expressed in the principle *credo ut intelligam*[53] or *fides rationem praecedit*.[54] There can be no question but that regeneration or faith is the fundamental presupposition of Edwards' reasoning. Obviously, in contradistinction to the rationalists, he does not reason *against* the Scriptures; he reasons *from* the Scriptures; and he reasons *against* the enemies of the truth. In so doing he does not shrink from turning the formidable powers of his logic upon the purveyors of rationalism and upon the thinking of the unregenerate. Kimnach observes that 'most of his sermons, including the imprecatory ones, contain at least a few passages of fine logical argumentation, and many sermons contain displays of logical brilliance.'[55] 'The power of most of Edwards's sermons', insists Marsden, 'was in their logic'[56] – logic (we might add) sovereignly set ablaze by the Spirit of power.

---

[49] McClymond, p. 95.

[50] Ibid.

[51] Ibid., p. 111.

[52] Ibid., p. 95.

[53] *I believe in order that I may understand.*

[54] *Faith precedes reason.*

[55] *Works*, 10:253.

[56] George M. Marsden, 'Foreword', in *The Salvation of Souls: Nine Previously Unpublished Sermons on the Call of Ministry and the Gospel by Jonathan Edwards*, Richard A. Bailey and Gregory A. Wills, eds.(Crossway Books: Wheaton Illinois, 2002), p. 12.

10

Illustrations

The *Miscellanies* were essentially Edwards' theological notebooks. 'For thirty-five years', notes Schafer, 'these notebooks trace the intellectual development and maturation of one of America's foremost theologians, providing valuable insights into his mind and spirit.'[1] 'Taken together', observes Wallace E. Anderson, 'the series probably comprises one of the most complete and continuous records in existence of the intellectual history of a single person.'[2] Entry 652 in Edwards' *Miscellanies* is entitled 'Christian Religion. Mysteries in Religion', and is particularly interesting from the standpoint of the issue of illustration:

> I once told a boy of about thirteen years of age that a piece of any matter of two inches square was eight times so big as one of but one inch square, or that it might be cut into eight pieces, all of them as big as that of but an inch square. He seemed at first to think me not in earnest, and to suspect that I only went to make a game of him. But when I had taken considerable pains to convince him that I was in earnest, and that I knew what I said to be true, he seemed to be astonished at my positiveness, and cried out of the impossibility and absurdity of it, and would argue how was it possible for two inches to be eight inches; and all that I could say did [not] at all prevail upon him to make him believe it. I suppose it seemed to him as great and evident a contradiction as that twice one makes eight, or any other absurdity whatsoever, that that [which] was but twice so long, and twice so broad, and twice

[1] *Works*, 13:1.
[2] *Works*, 6:28.

so thick, but just so big every way, should yet be eight times so big. And when I afterwards showed him the truth of it by cutting out two cubes, one an inch and another two inches square, and let him examine the measures and see that the measures were exact, and that there was no deceit, and took and cut the two-inch cube into eight equal parts, and he counted the parts over and over, and took the parts one by one and compared them with the one inch cube, and spent some time in counting and comparing; he seemed to [be] astonished as though there were some witchcraft in the case and hardly to believe it after all, for he did not yet at all see the reason of it. I believe it was a much more difficult mystery to him than the Trinity ordinarily is to men. And there seemed to him more evidently to be a contradiction in it than ever there did in any mystery of religion to a Socinian or deist.

And why should we not suppose that there may be some things that are true, that may be as much above our understandings and as difficult to them, as this truth was to this boy. Doubtless, there is a vastly greater distance between our understanding and God's, than between this boy's and that of the greatest philosopher or mathematician.[3]

It is interesting to note, however, that there is no evidence that Edwards ever made use of this incident in any sermon. Indeed, there is in his preaching not only a distinctly self-effacing quality, but also a distinct reserve in his use of anecdotal illustration from the world of personal experience. Whereas the modern preacher, and indeed the modern hearer, would tend to snatch eagerly at an incident so familiar as a most suitable homiletical illustration, the Northampton preacher apparently disregarded it for any homiletical purpose. 'Edwards', notes Kimnach, 'has hardly any references to domestic life'.[4] 'Nor did he indulge in any personal reflections', observes Gerstner. 'One would never know he was married not to mention the father of eleven children. No domestic anecdotes were ever heard in Northampton.'[5] Doubtless

---

[3] *Works*, 18:192-193.
[4] *Works*, 10:284.
[5] Gerstner, *Rational Biblical Theology*, 3:82.

the homiletical atmosphere of eighteenth-century New England was different, in this respect, from twenty-first century America; and doubtless the latter has gone too far in the opposite extreme in its predilection for personal anecdote. But might not the Northampton pastor have mitigated somewhat his rather austere image if he had felt able to make use of such an incident as a sermon illustration?

This Miscellany does, however, demonstrate a general interest in and fascination with mathematics on Edwards' part; and it is important to note the presence in his sermons of what might be termed the *mathematical illustration*.[6] Such illustrations are, of course, inseparably connected with logic. In 'The Justice of God in the Damnation of Sinners' Edwards illustrates – indeed, he demonstrates – the infinite evil of the least sin:

> If there be any evil or faultiness in sin against God, there is certainly infinite evil: for if it be any fault at all, it has an infinite aggravation, *viz.* that it is against an infinite object. If it be ever so small upon other accounts; yet if it be anything, it has one infinite dimension; and so is an infinite evil. Which may be illustrated by this: if we suppose a thing to have infinite length, but no breadth and thickness, but to be only a mere mathematical line, it is nothing: but if it have any breadth and thickness at all, though never so small, yet

---

[6] Interestingly, both at the outset of his career and at the end of his life JE was remarkably frank about his self-perceived deficiency in mathematics. The cover of JE's notebook, *Notes on Natural Philosophy*, contains the following entry which appears to have been written at some point between 1724 and 1726: 16. 'Always, when I have occasion to make use of mathematical proof, to acknowledge my ignorance in mathematics, *and only propose it to 'em that are skilled in that science whether or no that is not a mathematical proof.' Works*, 6:194.

Similarly, in his letter to the Trustees of the College of New Jersey, written at Stockbridge on October 19, 1757, he again acknowledges a deficiency in this area: 'I am also deficient in some parts of learning, particularly in algebra, and the higher parts of mathematics, and in the Greek classics; my Greek learning having been chiefly in the New Testament.' *Works*, 16:726.

Wallace E. Anderson endorses JE's own verdict in this: 'In fact, it appears that Edwards never acquired much skill in mathematics, and his reading of Newton was largely confined to the more general and philosophical discussions.' *Works*, 6:22. No doubt there is a significant element of truth in this position; but it is important to note that the self-confessed ignorance of a modest genius must be deemed to be somewhat relative. JE's knowledge of the basic principles of mathematics was clearly sufficient to enable him to make use of *mathematical illustration* with ease.

if it have but one infinite dimension, *viz.* that of length, the quantity of it is infinite; it exceeds the quantity of anything, however broad, thick and long, wherein these dimensions are all finite.[7]

Similarly, in 'All That Natural Men Do Is Wrong' he again illustrates his central thesis by means of the logic of mathematics. Essentially his position is that, if *infinitude times something* yields an infinite quantity, then *infinitude times nothing* yields nothing; but this truth is expressed with beautiful simplicity:

> If all that natural man does is wrong, then nothing that he does deserves anything; and if it deserves nothing, then a great deal of it deserves no more than a little. Nothing that they do has any goodness in it, and a great deal of that which has no goodness in it has no more goodness than a little of it. A thousand dead bodies have no more life in them than one dead body. If there be no life in the particulars, there is no life in the aggregate of 'em all. Five, or ten, or twenty, or forty years spent in doing wrong is no better than one day so spent, and deserves no more. And those that have spent a long time in such doing have no reason to complain, because that God don't show 'em mercy, or do so much for them, as for some that have spent but a little time in so doing. If all that natural men do is wrong, then God is not to blame for acting arbitrarily and sovereignly in the bestowment of his grace on sinners without any regard to their doings, whether they have done much or little.[8]

In 'Wicked Men Useful in their Destruction Only', dated July 1744, Edwards took as his text Ezekiel 15:2-4: 'Son of man, What is the vine-tree more than any tree? or than a branch which is among the trees of the forest? Shall wood be taken thereof to do any work? or will men take a pin of it to hang any vessel thereon? Behold, it is cast into the fire for fuel; the fire devoureth both the ends of it, and the midst of it is burned. Is it meet for any work?' Edwards states as his Doctrine or Main Proposition the following: 'If men bring forth no fruit to God,

---

[7] *Works*, 19:343.
[8] Ibid., p. 535.

they are wholly useless, unless in their destruction.'[9] This sermon is unusual in that it contains, not just a single, but a threefold illustration, from the realm of familiar, material things. He insists that it is precisely because man is 'so noble a creature'[10] that his being of use or benefit in temporal things merely answers his subordinate or inferior end; it does not answer his ultimate or highest end, which is that of bringing glory to God. Edwards then carefully illustrates this principle by referring successively to 'the underpinning of a house', 'the husbandman in ploughing and sowing', and 'the parts of a clock':

> I will illustrate this by two or three examples. The subordinate end of the underpinning of a house, is to support it, and the subordinate end of the windows, is to let in the light. But the ultimate end of the whole, is the benefit of the inhabitants. Therefore, if the house be never inhabited, the whole is in vain. The underpinning is in vain, though it be ever so strong, and support the building ever so well. The windows also are wholly in vain, though they be ever so large and clear, and though they obtain the subordinate end of letting in the light: they are as much in vain, as if they let in no light.
>
> So the subordinate end of the husbandman in ploughing and sowing, and well manuring his field, is, that it may bring forth a crop. But his more ultimate end is, that food may be provided for him and his family. Therefore though his inferior end be obtained, and his field bring forth ever so good a crop, yet if after all it be consumed by fire, or otherwise destroyed, he ploughed and sowed his field as much in vain, as if the seed had never sprung up ...
>
> Thus if the parts of a clock subserve ever so well one another, mutually to assist each other in their motions; one wheel moving another ever so regularly; yet if the motion never reach the hand or the hammer, it is altogether in vain, as much as if it stood still. So one man was made to be useful to another, and one part of mankind to another; but the use of the whole is to bring glory to God the maker, or all else is in vain.[11]

[9] *Works* (Hickman), 2:125.
[10] Ibid., p. 126.
[11] Ibid.

These three illustrations of the same principle are particularly important in this sermon precisely because the principle itself is somewhat complex, namely, the concept of 'the subordinate end' and its relationship to 'the ultimate end'. These illustrations doubtless greatly facilitated the comprehension of a people that clearly did not move with such ease in the rarefied intellectual atmosphere of the graduate and tutor from Yale.

'Approaching the End of God's Grand Design' is a sermon based on Revelation 21:6: 'And he said unto me, It is done.' It was preached in December 1744. Kimnach describes the sermon as 'a systematic tour of the many dimensions of God's "one scheme".'[12] Edwards defines 'this one great design'[13] thus:

> 'Tis to present to his Son a spouse in perfect glory from amongst sinful, miserable mankind, blessing all that comply with his will in this matter and destroying all his enemies that oppose it, and so to communicate and glorify himself through Jesus Christ, God-man. This I take to be the great design of the work of creation [and the] work of providence.[14]

In the following passage he illustrates the essential unity of 'God's grand design' by means of the imagery both of the clock and of the river:

> God's design in all his works is one, and all his manifold and various dispensations are parts of one scheme. God not only is acting for some end in all things he does, so as not to act for nothing, but his end in all that he does is one. His works are various and manifold, but the end ultimately aimed at in all is the same. He han't different and separate designs that have no relation one to another in his various works, but has one great design in all . . . As we see in the work of creation, the whole creation is but one world.

---

[12] *Works*, 25:111. Kimnach makes this further observation: 'A complex and ambitious undertaking, this sermon might have been one of Edwards' more impressive homiletical achievements had it been fully developed in the manner of the sermons of the 1730's.' Ibid.

[13] Ibid., p. 116.

[14] Ibid.

from one another, yet all bear a relation one to another and all is united together so as to make one frame and to be all together, one building. So it is in the works of providence: all are the various parts of one scheme, different motions all conspiring together to help one another to bring forth some one great event. As 'tis with the different motions of the various parts of a clock, all conspire together to turn one hand and to move one hammer . . . 'Tis with the train and series of the various and manifold works and dispensations of God through all ages of the world as it is with a great river: there are innumerable streams, [but] all have relation [and] come together [to] make one river. [They] empty themselves [as] by one will into the ocean. Thus the grand design and scheme and work of God in all his manifold works and dispensations is one.[15]

One of his favourite illustrations – and one that is, of course, very much drawn from the world of personal experience – is that of *the taste of honey;* indeed, Marsden refers to this as 'his most repeated illustration'.[16] It lies at the centre of Edwards' argument in 'A Divine and Supernatural Light'. This sermon was preached at Northampton in August 1733 and was 'published at the desire of some of the hearers, in the year 1734'.[17] It was one of his earliest publications. 'This is', observes Mark Valeri, 'perhaps his most sophisticated, and certainly his most celebrated, sermon from the period.'[18] Its significance lies in the fact that Edwards sets forth here his concept of the immediacy, the spirituality, and the supernaturalism of the operations of the Spirit of God in the soul of the regenerate. His text on this occasion was Matthew 16:17: 'And Jesus answered and said unto him, Blessed art thou, Simon Bar-jona; for flesh and blood hath not revealed it unto thee, but my Father which is in heaven.' His Doctrine or Main Proposition is the following: 'That there is such a thing as a spiritual and divine light, immediately imparted to the soul by God, of a different

---

[15] Ibid., pp. 114-116.
[16] Marsden, *Edwards*, p. 96.
[17] *Works* (Hickman), 2:12 n.
[18] *Works*, 17:40. The period to which Valeri is referring is that of 'the early 1730's'. Ibid. Valeri's volume covers 1730-1733.

nature from any that is obtained by natural means.'[19] The significance of this particular illustration is that *the taste of honey* is analogous to *the sense of the heart*. Edwards emphasizes that it is one thing to have *a merely notional* opinion concerning honey; it is quite another thing to taste honey. Similarly, it is one thing to have a merely notional opinion that 'Jesus is the Christ, the Son of the living God'; it is quite another thing to have a 'sense of the excellency of Christ'.[20] Thus the illustration of *the taste of honey* lies at the centre of Edwards' doctrine of regeneration:

> There is a twofold knowledge of good of which God has made the mind of man capable. The first, that which is merely notional; as when a person only speculatively judges that anything is, which, by the agreement of mankind, is called good or excellent, *viz.* that which is most to general advantage, and between which and a reward there is a suitableness, – and the like. And the other is, that which consists in the sense of the heart; as when the heart is sensible of pleasure and delight in the presence of the idea of it. In the former is exercised merely the speculative faculty, or the understanding, in distinction from the will or disposition of the soul. In the latter, the will, or inclination, or heart are mainly concerned.
>
> Thus there is a difference between having an *opinion*, that God is holy and gracious, and having a *sense* of the loveliness and beauty of that holiness and grace. There is a difference between having a rational judgment that honey is sweet, and having a sense of its sweetness. A man may have the former that knows not how honey tastes; but a man cannot have the latter unless he has an idea of the taste of honey in his mind. So there is a difference between believing that a person is beautiful, and having a sense of his beauty. The former may be obtained by hearsay, but the latter only by seeing the countenance. When the heart is sensible of the beauty and amiableness of a thing, it necessarily feels pleasure in the apprehension. It is implied in a person's being heartily sensible of the loveliness of a thing, that the idea of it is pleasant to his

---

[19] *Works* (Hickman), 2:13.
[20] Ibid., p. 15.

soul; which is a far different thing from having a rational opinion that it is excellent.[21]

The twenty-nine year old preacher returns to the illustration of the taste of honey at the close of the doctrinal section:

> It is out of reason's province to perceive the beauty or loveliness of any thing: such a perception does not belong to that faculty. Reason's work is to perceive truth and not excellency. It is not ratiocination that gives men the perception of the beauty and amiableness of a countenance, though it may be many ways indirectly an advantage to it; yet it is no more reason that immediately perceives it, than it is reason that perceives the sweetness of honey: it depends on the sense of the heart. – Reason may determine that a countenance is beautiful to others, it may determine that honey is sweet to others; but it will never give me a perception of its sweetness.[22]

Indeed, 'A Divine and Supernatural Light' (1734), with its emphasis upon 'the sense of the heart', anticipates a theme that was to be developed more fully in his great work, *The Religious Affections* (1746).[23] Thus, if the sermon of 1733 represents Edwards' earliest treatment of this theme, the treatise of 1746 represents his most mature treatment. *The Religious Affections* is unquestionably a masterpiece of experimental divinity, and in its pages Edwards once again makes use of the illustration of the taste of honey:

---

[21] Ibid., p. 14.

[22] Ibid., p. 17.

[23] 'His treatise on *Religious Affections* picks up many of the ideas from "A Divine and Supernatural Light". In sum, his expression of the nature of spiritual knowledge in this 1733 lecture became an integral part of his theology.' Mark Valeri, *Works,* 17:406. It should be noted, however, that Valeri's rather laboured analysis of JE's theology of regeneration and revival in the Yale volume simply demonstrates that he has not grasped that this theology was, as far as JE was concerned, rooted and grounded in God's revelation, and not in some pragmatic adjustment on JE's part to *the personal, the local, and the sociological.* 'Conversion, in effect, was his answer to, rather than a retreat from, social problems', Valeri insists. 'That Edwards led his congregation into a revival in 1734 suggests that he achieved a rapport with at least some of the citizens of Northampton.' Ibid., p. 44. Valeri's editorial Preface leaves much to be desired in this area.

There is given to the regenerated a new supernatural sense, a certain divine spiritual taste. This is in its whole nature diverse from any former kinds of sensation of the mind, as tasting is diverse from any of the other five senses, and something is perceived by a true saint in the exercise of this new sense of mind, in spiritual and divine things, as entirely different from any thing that is perceived in them by natural men, as the sweet taste of honey is diverse from the ideas men get of honey by looking on it or feeling of it. Now the beauty of holiness, is that which is perceived by this spiritual sense, so diverse from all that natural men perceive in them; or, this kind of beauty is the quality that is the immediate object of this spiritual sense; this is the sweetness that is the proper object of this spiritual taste.[24]

The value of this particular illustration lies in the fact that it enables the philosopher-theologian-preacher to demonstrate very simply the truth of a somewhat complex distinction. The distinction itself is essentially that between two different kinds of knowledge: the one is that of 'mere *speculative* knowledge'[25] such as that of 'knowing what a triangle or a square is'[26]; the other is that of '*sensible* knowledge'[27] such as that of 'perceiving the sweet taste of honey'.[28] In regeneration, which by definition involves 'the sense of the heart', Edwards insists that 'the mind not only *speculates* and *beholds*, but *relishes* and *feels*'.[29] Moreover, the theological appropriateness of this illustration lies in the fact that the Scriptures themselves utilize the vocabulary and the concept of *savouring* and *relishing* in the context of the doctrine of regeneration: 'For they that are after the flesh do *mind* the things of the flesh; but they that are after the Spirit the things of the Spirit.'[30]

It is an interesting fact that, with the exception of those illustrations drawn from the Scriptures (and these are innumerable in his sermons),

---

[24] Ibid., 1:280.
[25] Ibid., p. 283.
[26] Ibid.
[27] Ibid.
[28] Ibid.
[29] Ibid.
[30] Romans 8:5.

Edwards' illustrations are very seldom drawn from history. There are, however, a few exceptions to this general rule. The theme of 'Wicked Men's Slavery to Sin' – a sermon which possibly antedates the 'New York period' – is that of the 'self-destructive enslavement to evil',[31] and in the Application, as the young preacher develops the idea of 'the cruel service of sin',[32] he provides a striking (and even rather shocking) illustration from the cruelty of the cannibals of Guinea:

> They do by you as I have heard they do in Guinea, where at their great feasts they eat men's flesh. They set the poor ignorant child who knows nothing of the matter, to make a fire, and while it stoops down to blow the fire, one comes behind and strikes off his head, and then he is roasted by that same fire that he kindled, and made a feast of, and the skull is made use of as a cup, out of which they make merry with their liquor. Just so Satan, who has a mind to make merry with you.[33]

Kimnach describes this illustration as 'the rhetorical climax of the sermon'.[34] 'This climactic scene, suggestive of a black mass, encapsulates the plight of the paradoxically child-like sinner who seeks a feast only to become one.'[35] Kimnach goes on to speculate on the possible sources of the illustration: 'This extraordinary illustration may have come to hand in some collection of emblems or even in a travel narrative, though no source has been discovered in books to which JE is known to have had access. Of course it is possible that he means just what he says in "I have heard", and that the tale came from conversation with sailors or travelers in the port city of New York.'[36]

'God's Excellencies' similarly makes use of a striking illustration from history. The text upon which this remarkable sermon was based is Psalm 89:6: 'For who in the heaven can be compared unto the LORD,

[31] *Works,* 10:337.
[32] Ibid., p. 348.
[33] Ibid., p. 349.
[34] Ibid., p. 338.
[35] Ibid., p. 337.
[36] Ibid., p. 349 n.5. Of course, if the sermon does antedate the 'New York period', then the possibility that the tale was originally heard in 'the port city of New York' is effectively precluded.

and who among the sons of the mighty can be likened unto the LORD?' The sermon was composed at some point between the summers of 1722 and 1723 and thus was almost certainly preached at New York. Edwards states his intention right at the outset of his Doctrine: 'My design at this time [is] to endeavor, by God's help, to exhibit and set forth the greatness, gloriousness, and transcendent excellency of that God who made us, and whom we worship and adore.'[37] The Doctrinal section of the sermon consists of a 'survey of seven divine attributes',[38] namely, 'duration', 'greatness', 'excellency and loveliness', 'power', 'wisdom', 'holiness', and 'goodness'.[39] 'A poignant practical discourse and an untrammeled meditative excursion', observes Kimnach, 'this long sermon is finally evidence of Edwards' great ambition, personally and professionally, during this early phase of his career as he unabashedly tackled in its totality what was to become a favorite theme, the grandeur of God.'[40] In his consideration of the 'excellency and loveliness' of God, Edwards demonstrates the glory of the Creator from the glory of the sun; his illustration refers to a Christian martyr incarcerated in darkness for three years during the Spanish Inquisition:

> We admire at the beauty of creation, at the beautiful order of it, at the glory of the sun, moon and stars. The sun appears very bright and glorious; so beautiful doth it appear that many nations take it to be the supreme God, and worship it accordingly, but we have much more reason from the beauty of the sun to admire at the invisible glory of that God whose fingers have formed it, and to say, as one that was imprisoned by virtue of the Spanish Inquisition and was kept in a dark dungeon three years from the sight of the sun, when he was brought forth into the light to his martyrdom, he, greatly admiring at the beauty of the sun which he had not seen so long, being astonished at it, cries out that he wondered any man could worship anything but the maker of that glorious creature, having respect to the idolatry of the papists.[41]

[37] Ibid., p. 416.
[38] Ibid., p. 413.
[39] Ibid., pp. 418-424.
[40] Ibid., p. 414.
[41] Ibid., pp. 420-421. We disagree with Kimnach's assertion that this reference to 'the

'Peaceable and Faithful amid Division and Strife' – a two-unit ser-mon based upon 2 Samuel 20:19 ('I am one of them that are peace-able and faithful in Israel') was preached (as the upper right-hand corner of the first leaf of the manuscript indicates) in 'May 1737'.[42] In this sermon Edwards addresses with characteristic boldness and frankness one of the perennial sins of the people of Northamp-ton, namely, contentiousness. 'Contention and party strife', observes Miller, 'were "the old iniquity" of Northampton, and increased with the years.'[43] Lesser notes that this particular sermon was preached in the context of 'the fractious debate over the new meetinghouse the past spring'.[44] For the last four years the people of Northampton had quar-relled firstly over the need, then over the site, then over the seating of the meetinghouse, and finally over the question of the separation of the sexes. At the time of the preaching of this sermon Northampton's third meetinghouse had not yet been completed, but the contention, the wrangling, and the feuding still continued. Marsden describes this sermon as 'a scathing sermon on the party spirit, envy, and backbiting that set neighbor against neighbor in the small town'.[45] Towards the close of this sermon Edwards illustrates the great dangers of contention by means of an historical reference to Nero:

> There are many men in the world that, when they are opposed and crossed, will contend, let what will become of the honor and inter-ests of religion, yea, though heaven itself should go to rack. Nero, the Roman emperor, wished that all the people of Rome had one neck, that he might cut it off at one blow. So there is a sort of men, that if the honor of religion has as it were but one neck, and their contending would cut it off at one blow, yet they would con-tend, rather than not get their wills. And 'tis well if there be none

---

Spanish Inquisition' and to 'the idolatry of the papists' constitutes a 'gratuitous swipe at the Roman Catholic Church'. 10:421 n.1. It should not be forgotten that the Edict of Nantes had been revoked by Louis XIV in 1685 and that during his eight and a half months at New York JE actually met some of the French Huguenots upon whom the severest persecution had thus been unleashed. See Marsden, *Edwards*, p. 47.

[42] *Works*, 19:657.
[43] Miller, *Edwards*, p. 101.
[44] *Works*, 19:656.
[45] Marsden, *Edwards*, pp. 185-186.

amongst us too much akin to 'em, if not some of 'em. The honor of religion in this land never had more one neck than now, and that betrusted with us, our practice shows how careful we are of it.[46]

Lesser points out, interestingly, that 'Suetonius attributes this sentiment to Caligula, not Nero'[47] – a fact which demonstrates the somewhat free, unverified, *memoriter* character of some of Edwards' citation and references.[48]

'Charity Disposes us Meekly to Bear the Injuries Received from Others' is the fourth of the fifteen sermons in *Charity and Its Fruits*. It is an exposition of 1 Corinthians 13:4: 'Charity suffereth long, and is kind.' In the course of his 'brief improvement of the subject'[49] Edwards presents various motives by which he might, by the power of God's Spirit, induce and persuade his hearers to the cultivation of this Christian longsuffering and meekness in the face of injuries. We cite here the third of these motives. Once again the reference – on this occasion, to the Persians and the city of Babylon – is historical in nature:

> In this way *we shall be most above injuries*. He that has established such a spirit and disposition of mind that the injuries received from others do not exasperate and provoke him, or disturb the calmness of his mind, lives, as it were, above injuries, and out of their reach. He conquers them, and rides over and above them, as in triumph, exalted above their power. He that has so much of the exercise of a Christian spirit, as to be able meekly to bear all injuries done him, dwells on high, where no enemy can reach him. History tells us, that when the Persians besieged Babylon, the walls of the city were so exceeding high, that the inhabitants used to stand on the top of them, and laugh at their enemies; and so one whose soul is fortified with a spirit of Christian meekness, and a disposition calmly to bear all injuries, may laugh at the enemy that would injure him.[50]

---

[46] *Works*, 19:678.

[47] Ibid., p. 678 n.5.

[48] Kimnach notes, for instance, 'JE's frequent disregard of verbal exactitude when quoting scripture.' *Works*, 10:341 n.1.

[49] *Charity*, p. 82.

[50] Ibid., p. 86.

Edwards' use of historical or anecdotal illustration is, however, relatively rare, except perhaps in his earliest sermons. As he matured as a preacher (and, indeed, as a thinker) he appears to have moved away somewhat from the historical or anecdotal *genre* of illustration, and towards the more conceptual and intellectual.

Thus in *A History of the Work of Redemption* he employs the metaphor of the building of a temple to illustrate the divine construction involved in the great scheme of redemption:

> The work of redemption with respect to the grand design in general, as it respects the universal subject and end, is carried on – not merely by repeating or renewing the same effect in the different subjects of it, but – by many successive works and dispensations of God, all tending to one great effect, united as the several parts of a scheme, and all together making up one great work. Like a temple that is building; first, the workmen are sent forth, then the materials are gathered, the ground is fitted, and the foundation laid; then the superstructure is erected, one part after another, till at length the top-stone is laid, and all is finished. Now the work of redemption in this large sense, may be compared to such a building. God began it immediately after the fall, and will proceed to the end of the world. Then shall the top-stone be brought forth, and all will appear complete and glorious.[51]

Indeed, towards the close of the treatise, as he describes 'the marriage of the Lamb' and the consummation of redemption, Edwards returns to the metaphor of 'the top-stone': 'And now the whole work of redemption is finished. Now the top-stone of the building is laid.'[52]

If, however, he makes virtually no reference to himself and his family in his sermons and only very occasional reference to the events of extra-biblical history, he frequently, in characteristic Puritan fashion, utilizes the characters of the Bible as illustrations. In such illustrations the exemplaristic note – and thus the latent, implied imperative – is suppressed. In other words, Edwards often makes use of the characters of the Bible not imperativally, but illustratively. The following

[51] *Works* (Hickman), 1:535.
[52] Ibid., p. 615.

passage from 'Charity More Excellent than the Extraordinary Gifts of the Spirit' demonstrates well this particular distinction:

> *That grace which is the effect of the ordinary influences of the Spirit of God, is a privilege which God bestows only on his own favourites and children, but the extraordinary gifts of the Spirit are not so.* – It has been observed before, that though God most commonly has chosen saints, and eminent saints, to bestow extraordinary gifts of the Spirit upon, yet he has not always done so; but these gifts are sometimes bestowed on others. They have been common to both the godly and the ungodly. Balaam is stigmatized in Scripture as a wicked man (2 Pet. ii. 15; Jude 11; Rev. ii. 14), and yet he had the extraordinary gifts of the Spirit of God for a while. Saul was a wicked man, but we read, once and again, of his being among the prophets. Judas was one of those whom Christ sent forth to preach and work miracles; he was one of those twelve disciples of whom it is said, in Matt. x. 1, 'And when he had called unto him his twelve disciples, he gave them power against unclean spirits, to cast them out, and to heal all manner of sickness, and all manner of disease.' And in the next verses we are told who they were; their names are all rehearsed over, and 'Judas Iscariot, who also betrayed him,' among the rest. And in ver. 8, Christ says to them, 'Heal the sick, cleanse the lepers, raise the dead, cast out devils.' The grace of God in the heart is a gift of the Holy Ghost peculiar to the saints: it is a blessing that God reserves only for those who are the objects of his special and peculiar love. But the extraordinary gifts of the Spirit are what God sometimes bestows on those whom he does not love, but hates; which is a sure sign that the one is infinitely more precious and excellent than the other. That is the most precious gift, which is most of an evidence of God's love. But the extraordinary gifts of the Spirit were, in the days of inspiration and miracles, no sure sign of the love of God.[53]

It will be noted that Edwards refers *inter alia* in this passage to Balaam, Saul, and Judas. None of them, however, is set forth as an example, whether to be imitated or to be shunned. Edwards is clearly

---

[53] *Charity*, pp. 37-38. See also *Works*, 8:159-160.

not saying, in effect, with regard to them, 'Go and do likewise'; nor is he saying, in effect, 'Be warned to avoid the example of these men.' Rather he sets them forth as illustrations, for distinction's sake. In other words, Balaam, Saul, and Judas illustrate cogently the very point upon which he is insisting, namely, that the mere possession of extra-ordinary gifts is, in and of itself, no certain evidence whatsoever of the possession of saving grace, since each of these three was a wicked man. Indeed, not only do these three characters *illustrate* the point; they actually *prove* the point. Edwards' use of these characters is clearly more doctrinal than applicatory.

It is an interesting fact that many of Edwards' illustrations that are not drawn directly from the Scriptures are analogical.[54] Such illust-rations are not actual, personal, or historical, but imaginary, theoreti-cal, and hypothetical. Indeed, at times they are almost parabolic. 'God's All-Sufficiency for the Supply of Our Wants' contains a classic example of the analogical illustration. In the course of his Application Edwards utilizes his favourite analogy of a king:

> If a king should take a poor man from the street that had nothing to eat or wear, and should build a stately house for him with every-thing convenient for his necessity and comfort within doors and without, and should every day, as duly as the day came, send him provision and everything he needed, and so as long as he lived: would it not be a stupid thing in the man if he never or seldom reflected upon it, that it was this king's gracious kindness that he lived upon?
>
> The very cattle and dogs and other brute creatures seem to be more sensible of man's kindness to 'em, than some men do of the kindness of God. Is. 1:3, 'The ox knows his owner, and the ass his master's crib: but Israel doth not know, my people doth not consider.'[55]

'A Warning to Professors: or, The Great Guilt of Those who Attend on the Ordinances of Divine Worship, and yet Allow Themselves in

---

[54] 'Imagery and analogy were his most powerful weapons.' Marsden, *Edwards*, p. 98.
[55] *Works*, 14:482.

any Known Wickedness' was, according to Valeri, 'probably a sacrament sermon'.[56] It was preached at some point between August 1731 and December 1732.[57] The text upon which this sermon was based was Ezekiel 23:37-39: 'That they have committed adultery, and blood is in their hands, and with their idols have they committed adultery, and have also caused their sons, whom they bare unto me, to pass for them through the fire to devour them. Moreover this they have done unto me: they have defiled my sanctuary in the same day, and have profaned my Sabbaths. For when they had slain their children to their idols, then they came the same day into my sanctuary to profane it; and, lo, thus have they done in the midst of mine house.' In this sermon Edwards utilizes essentially the same analogy of the wicked servant in his relationship to his king:

> It would show a great irreverence in any person towards a king, if he should not care how he came into his presence, and if he should come in a sordid habit, and in a very indecent manner. How much more horrid irreverence doth it show, for persons willingly and allowedly to defile themselves with that filth which God infinitely hates, and so frequently to come into the presence of God! . . .
>
> If a rebel or traitor should send addresses to his king, making a show of great loyalty and fidelity, and should all the while openly, and in the king's sight, carry on designs of dethroning him, how could his addresses be considered as any other than mockery? If a man should bow and kneel before his superior, and use many respectful terms to him, but at the same time should strike him, or spit in his face, would his bowing and his respectful terms be looked upon in any light than as done in mockery? When the Jews kneeled before Christ, and said, *Hail, King of the Jews,* but at the same time spit in his face, and smote him upon the head with a reed; could their kneeling and salutations be considered as any other than mockery? . . .
>
> A servant would affront his master by wilfully disobeying his

[56] *Works,* 17:453.

[57] Mark Valeri provides the following footnote with regard to the paper on which this sermon was written: 'Sermons in this batch are written on paper with an English/GR watermark.' Ibid., p. 452 n.2.

commands in any wise. But he would affront him much more, if he should on every occasion come to him to inquire his will, as though he were ready to do whatever his master would have him do, and then should immediately go away and do the contrary.[58]

It will be noted that, although the nuance in the analogy varies somewhat during the course of this passage, involving, either implicitly or explicitly, the concept of 'subject', 'rebel', and 'traitor', the analogy remains, to all intents and purposes, the same.

'Men Naturally God's Enemies' is one of the great sermons composed and preached by the Northampton minister in the mid-to-late 1730's. Delivered in August 1736 and based upon Romans 5:10 ('For if, when we were enemies, we were reconciled to God by the death of his Son'), this sermon again employs the analogy of a wicked servant. The very frequency with which Edwards utilizes the verb 'to suppose' demonstrates that this illustration is a hypothetical supposition:

If you yourself had a servant that carried it towards you, as you do towards God, you would not think there was need of any greater evidence of his being your enemy. Suppose your servant should manifest much contempt of you; and disregard your commands as much as you do the commands of God; should go directly contrary, and in many ways act the very reverse of your commands; should seem to set himself in ways that were contrary to your will obstinately and incorrigibly, without any amendment from your repeated calls, warnings, and threatenings; and should act so cross to you day and night, as you do to God; would he not be justly deemed your enemy? Suppose, further, when you sought one thing, he would seek the contrary; when you did any work, he would, as much as in him lay, undo and destroy; and suppose he should continually drive at such ends, as tended to overthrow the ends you aimed at: when you sought to bring to pass any design, he would endeavour to overthrow your design; and set himself as much against your interest, as you do yourself against God's honour. And suppose you should moreover see him, from time to time, with those who were your declared mortal enemies; making

---

[58] *Works* (Hickman), 2:187.

them his counsellors, and hearkening to their counsels, as much as you do to Satan's temptations: should you not think you had sufficient evidence that he was your enemy?[59]

Edwards' obvious predilection for the analogical illustration is powerfully demonstrated by 'The Justice of God in the Damnation of Sinners'. This remarkable sermon contains no less than six analogical illustrations, of which we cite three:

> If a king should condemn a man to some exceeding tormenting death, which the condemned person thought himself not deserving of, but looked upon the sentence unjust and cruel, and the king, when the time of execution drew nigh, should offer him his pardon, under the notion of a very great act of grace and clemency, the condemned person never could willingly and heartily allow it under that notion, because he judged himself unjustly condemned.[60]

> If a man should hate you, and devour you, and exalt himself, and smite you in the face, and tell you that he did it voluntarily, and because he had a mind to, but only should tell you at the same time, that he hated you so much that he could not help choosing and willing so to do, would you take it the more patiently for that? Would not your indignation be rather stirred up the more?[61]

> If any of you see cause to show kindness to a neighbor, do all the rest of your neighbors come to you, and tell you that you owe them so much as you have given to such a man? But this is the way you deal with God![62]

It will be evident that in the first of these illustrations the main figure in the illustration ('a king') sustains an analogical relationship to *God*; in the second illustration the main figure ('a man') sustains an analogical relationship to the *sinner*; and in the last illustration the neighbour implied by the words 'you' and 'your' clearly sustains an

[59] Ibid., p. 135.
[60] *Works*, 19:362-363.
[61] Ibid., p. 365.
[62] Ibid., p. 373. For the other three analogical illustrations see ibid., p. 364 (twice) and pp. 366-367.

initial analogical relationship to *God*, since this is the neighbour that has shown the kindness. Interestingly, however, this last brief analogy contains another example of 'the manipulated point of view' or 'the shift in perspective' that we analyse elsewhere.[63] Suddenly, the neighbour that has hitherto sustained an analogical relationship to *God* is the one that now sustains an analogical relationship to the *sinner*: 'But this is the way you deal with God!'

'In Charity Contrary to a Selfish Spirit', based upon 1 Corinthians 13:5 ('Charity . . . seeketh not her own'), Edwards illustrates the way in which the God-given principle of self-love in man has, as a consequence of the Fall, become inordinate and has degenerated into self-ishness. The illustration here is again analogical; it is that of a servant who becomes the master:

> To illustrate this: if a servant in a family, who was formerly kept in the place of a servant, and his influence in family affairs was not inordinate while his master's strength was greater than his; yet if afterwards his master grows weaker and loses his strength, and the rest of the family loses their former power, though the servant is not at all increased, yet the proportion of his strength having increased, his influence may become inordinate; and from being a servant he may become master in that house. And so self-love becomes inordinate. Man before the Fall loved himself or his own happiness, I suppose, as much as after his fall. But then a superior principle of divine love had the throne, it being in such strength that it wholly regulated and directed self-love. But since the Fall this principle of divine love has lost its strength, or rather is dead. So that self-love continuing in its former strength, and having no superior principle to regulate it, becomes inordinate in its influence, and governs where it should be only a servant.[64]

In 'The Great Concern of a Watchman for Souls', preached at the ordination of Jonathan Judd to the new church in Northampton on June 8, 1743, (in 1753 the church would be made part of the separate district of Southampton), Edwards takes as his text a part of Hebrews

---

[63] See the chapter 'The Use of the Indicative'.
[64] *Works*, 8:256.

13:17: 'They watch for your souls, as they that must give account.' In the course of the sermon he employs the familiar images of a prince and his subject to emphasize the tremendous responsibility involved in the care of souls:

> If a prince should commit some great treasure, consisting of most precious jewels, to the care of a subject, to keep for him, and carry through an enemy's country, and bring home safe to his palace, and knew that the enemies by the way would be sensible that the treasure was committed to him, and would be aware of the great value of it, and therefore would be exceeding greedy of it, and incessant in their endeavours to get it from him; would not the prince expect that he, with whom he had entrusted this treasure, should use great care in keeping it? Would he be esteemed faithful to his trust, in the care of so great a treasure, and in such circumstances, without keeping up a continual watch?[65]

It is evident that in this passage the prince sustains an analogical relationship to Christ, whilst the subject sustains an analogical relationship to the minister of the gospel. It is a classic example of that 'analogy *a fortiori*' that is so frequently employed by the Northampton preacher. It should be noted, moreover, that the sheer persuasiveness of this 'analogy *a fortiori*' is further enhanced by Edwards' use of two rhetorical questions, the answers to which are characteristically self-evident.

Between February 15 and March 22, 1750, Edwards delivered a series of five Thursday lectures which have recently been published for the first time in the Yale edition as *Lectures on the Qualifications for Full Communion in the Church of Christ*. The very fact that this was a series of lectures rather than a series of sermons is significant; indeed, it is symptomatic of the profound ecclesiastical turmoil in which the issue of the Lord's Supper was by now embroiled in the town of Northampton. It was in early 1749 that Edwards formally announced to the committee of the church that he now regarded the 'Stoddardean way' as unscriptural and requested permission to preach in explanation and defence of his position. 'Although a few members supported his

---

[65] *Works*, 25:68.

proposal', comments Kimnach, 'the majority were opposed, and after some deliberation the committee instructed Edwards to publish his argument through the press. Curiously, they were willing to have a sensitive internal dispute aired before the world rather than risk Edwards' preaching to the church. There have been many tributes to the power of Edwards' preaching, but few stronger attestations than this, and none from more expert authorities.'[66] After the denial of some half-a-dozen further requests, Edwards finally announced a series of five Thursday lectures on the issue. It is interesting to note that, in this context, unusually, but not surprisingly, the treatise preceded the lectures.[67] These lectures, upon the success of which Edwards' future ministry and even livelihood depended, are characterized by a more familiar, illustrative style than the treatise and they contain a quite stunning analogy – that between, as Kimnach puts it, 'allowing a natural man to take communion and seating a dead body at the dinner table':[68]

> And this makes the Apostle's reason natural, plain and exceeding strong against such men's coming to the Lord's Supper: for why should we bring those to a feast that can't taste the food, any more than a dead man? For 'tis indeed just with a natural man, with regard to discerning spiritual food, as 'tis with a dead corpse with regard to discerning or tasting outward food. And 'tis just so unreasonable to bring those who are spiritually dead to God's table, to a spiritual feast of his children, as those that are temporally dead to a king's table, to a temporal feast with his children.[69]

[66] Ibid., p. 349.

[67] 'Preached several months after the publication of *An Humble Inquiry*, the lectures were clearly designed to complement the treatise. While the conceptual burden of the two works is the same insistence upon a sincere profession of godliness as a prerequisite to complete standing in the church, the treatise is primarily an exegetical argument from Scripture, including learned secondary sources, designed to persuade a public who might be persuaded by biblical learning and forensic argument; the lectures, on the other hand, are pastoral, employing simple analogies and practical examples from common experience to illustrate each point so that ordinary people might readily identify with the argument ... In any event, the lecture series has the stamp of the pulpit while the treatise does not.' Ibid., pp. 349-350.

[68] Ibid., p. 21.

[69] Ibid., p. 393.

It is evident, then, that Edwards' illustrations are frequently analogical. 'It must . . . be conceded', insists Dabney, 'that there are illustrations which are at the same time true analogies: they present a real parallelism of relations to those of the argument illustrated, in that respect wherein the force of the deduction resides. In such a case there is more than the force of mere illustration: there is analogical argument – a species of experimental evidence which is conclusive in proportion to the perfectness of the parallelism.'[70] Moreover, Kimnach has pinpointed 'analogy *a fortiori*[71] as part of 'Edwards' essential rhetorical arsenal'.[72] 'The *a fortiori* or "all the more reason" construction . . . is employed by Edwards as his primary supplement to simile and metaphor in developing analogical bridges between the seen and the unseen.'[73] Thus Edwards frequently establishes an analogy between the physical, temporal world and the spiritual, eternal world. It is important to note that such analogical illustrations are suggested, generated, and governed by the doctrine, and thus very appropriately reflect light back on to the doctrine. Thus his use of analogical illustration is perhaps, in certain respects, the reverse of the more common use of illustration; that is to say, instead of *discovering* an event, an incident, a situation that is illustrative of a doctrine, Edwards appears to *invent* a hypothetical event, incident, or situation which represents the doctrine analogically. It is important to note that these analogical illustrations beautifully represent the truth precisely because they are carefully chiselled by the doctrine itself. The very frequency with which he utilizes the analogical illustration, however, demonstrates perhaps its only weakness, namely, the impression of a certain predictability in its use.

---

[70] Dabney, *Sacred Rhetoric*, p. 197.
[71] *Works*, 10:294.
[72] Ibid.
[73] Ibid., p. 250.

11

Conclusions

Homiletical theory has generally insisted that, just as the Introduction is of vital significance to the sermon, so too is the Conclusion. Indeed, many homileticians contend that the Conclusion is even more significant than the Introduction precisely because it is, by definition, the final note of the sermon. For this reason the Conclusion, in the very nature of things, constitutes the climax of the sermon; it is essential, therefore, that it be climactic, not anti-climactic. Indeed, the whole concept of movement, progress, and development in the sermon generally presupposes a transition in the course of the sermon from the doctrinal to the practical, from the more objective to the more subjective, from the more indirect to the more direct. The general movement from the indicative mood to the imperative mood in a well constructed sermon demonstrates that a well constructed Conclusion will often be hortatory and parenetic in emphasis; the climactic note will often be expressed *via* exhortation.

The Conclusion to the sermon 'The Preciousness of Time', which was preached in December 1734 at the outset of the revival in Northampton, is impressive on a number of counts. In the first place, Edwards issues here a series of three exhortations through his repeated use of the imperative mood; in the second place, he concludes the sermon on a note of great solemnity; and in the third place, he enhances the unity of the sermon by means of a striking juxtaposition of the text of the sermon – 'Redeeming the time' – and the final clause of the sermon – 'that there should be time no longer':

> 1. Improve the *present* time without any delay. If you delay and put off its improvement, still more time will be lost; and it will be an

evidence that you are not sensible of its preciousness. Talk not of more convenient seasons hereafter; but improve your time while you have it, after the example of the psalmist, Psal. cxix. 60. 'I made haste, and delayed not to keep thy commandments.'

2. Be especially careful to improve *those parts* of time which are most precious. Though all time is very precious, yet some parts are more precious than others; as, particularly, holy time is more precious than common time. Such time is of great advantage for our everlasting welfare; therefore, above all, improve your sabbaths, and especially the time of public worship, which is the most precious part. Lose it not either in sleep, or in carelessness, inattention, and wandering imaginations. How sottish are they who waste away, not only their common, but holy time, yea the very season of attendance on the holy ordinances of God! – The time of youth is precious, on many accounts. Therefore, if you be in the enjoyment of this time, take heed that you improve it. Let not the precious days and years of youth slip away without improvement. A time of the strivings of God's Spirit is more precious than other time. Then God is near; and we are directed, in Isa. lv. 6. 'To seek the Lord while he may be found, and to call upon him while he is near.' Such especially is an accepted time, and a day of salvation: 2 Cor. vi. 2. 'I have heard thee in a time accepted, and in a day of salvation have I succoured thee: behold, now is the accepted time; behold, now is the day of salvation.'

3. Improve well your time of *leisure* from worldly business. Many persons have a great deal of such time, and all have some. If men be but disposed to it, such time may be improved to great advantage. When we are most free from cares for the body, and business of an outward nature, a happy opportunity for the soul is afforded. Therefore spend not such opportunities unprofitably, nor in such a manner that you will not be able to give a good account thereof to God. Waste them not away wholly in unprofitable visits, or useless diversions or amusements. Diversion should be used only in subserviency to business. So much, and no more, should be used, as doth most fit the mind and body for the work of our general and particular callings.

You have need to improve every talent, advantage, and opportunity, to your utmost, while time lasts; for it will soon be said concerning you, according to the oath of the angel, in Rev. x. 5, 6. 'And the angel which I saw stand upon the sea and upon the earth lifted up his hand to heaven, and sware by him that liveth for ever and ever, who created heaven, and the things that therein are, and the earth, and the things that therein are, and the sea, and the things which are therein, *that there should be time no longer.*[1]

Edwards' ability to create a striking juxtaposition between the text of the sermon and one of the final clauses of the sermon emerges again in 'The Justice of God in the Damnation of Sinners'. His text on this occasion was Romans 3:19 ('That every mouth may be stopped'). The counterpart of 'stopping the mouth' is, of course, that of 'opening the mouth'; and the theme of 'opening the mouth' is a *leitmotiv* that runs throughout this sermon. It is precisely because the sinner 'opens his mouth' in boasting, objections, and excuses before God that his mouth must be stopped. In the final paragraph of the sermon, however, Edwards gives an interesting and striking twist to the concept of 'opening the mouth'; he turns the negative connotation into one that is positive. The *sinner's* mouth needs to be *stopped;* but the mouth of the *saint* needs to be *opened:*

> O! what cause is here for praise! What obligations you are under to bless the Lord who hath dealt bountifully with you, and magnify his holy name! What cause for you to praise God in humility, to walk humbly before him. Ezek. xvi. 63. 'That thou mayest remember and be confounded, and never open thy mouth any more, because of thy shame, when I am pacified toward thee for all that thou hast done, saith the Lord God!' You shall never open your mouth in boasting, or self-justification; but lie the lower before God for his mercy to you. You have reason, the more abundantly, to open your mouth in God's praises, that they may be continually in your mouth, both here and to all eternity, for his rich, unspeak

---

[1] *Works* (Hickman), 2:236.

able, and sovereign mercy to you, whereby he, and he alone, has made you to differ from others.[2]

This deliberate, skilful playing upon the theme of 'stopping' and 'opening the mouth' is such that it greatly enhances that 'unity' which Kimnach describes as one of 'his distinguishing traits as a master of the sermon'.[3]

It is an interesting fact, however, that some of Edwards' Conclusions appear to be somewhat mediocre. Particularly striking in this respect is the Conclusion of 'God Makes Men Sensible of Their Misery'. In the sermon as published in the Hickman edition Edwards concludes by 'briefly mentioning' 'those things which are common occasions of persons losing their convictions':

1. Persons falling into sin is very often the occasion of their losing their convictions ...

2. Sometimes there happens some diverting occasion; ...

3. Some change in their circumstances takes off their minds from the concerns of their souls. Their minds are diverted by the new circumstances with which they are attended; or are taken up with new pleasures and enjoyments, or with new cares and business, in which they are involved. It may be they grow richer. They prosper in the world, and their worldly good things crowd in, and take possession of their minds. Or worldly cares are increased upon them, and they have so many things to look after, that their minds are taken up, and they have not time to look after their souls.[4]

The matter here is typically Edwardsean. But a good case could be made to the effect that, as it stands, this section belongs more appropriately to the main body of the sermon, whether in the Doctrine or in the Application, than to the Conclusion. There is clearly nothing climactic about it; in fact, it is somewhat abrupt and disappointing as a Conclusion. Indeed, it is really rather mysterious.

[2] Ibid., 1:679. It is difficult to understand why this passage in the Yale edition (19:376) commences with two *question marks* rather than two *exclamation marks*. It is surely evident both from the specific exclamative 'O!' and from the general context itself that JE is not, at this point, searching his hearers, but is exclaiming; it is an apostrophe.

[3] Kimnach, 'Pursuit of Reality', p. 111.

[4] *Works* (Hickman), 2:838.

The mystery is solved, however, when the sermon in the Hickman edition (1834) is compared with the sermon in the recently published Yale edition (1999). A comparison of the traditional version of the sermon with the actual manuscript version reveals immediately that this supposed Conclusion is not in fact the original Conclusion. The passage just cited belongs, in fact, to 'Use II' in the Application. Mark Valeri provides this observation in the Yale edition: "'God Makes Men Sensible of Their Misery' was first printed by Sereno Dwight (8, 44-69). Dwight's version omits several passages toward the end of the sermon, namely, the second through fifth subpoints under the first use, the final two subpoints of the third use, and the entirety of the fourth and fifth uses.'[5] The Yale edition demonstrates that the sermon concludes, in fact, with a much more appropriate use of self-examination; and it is evident that the sermon *as originally published* had been subjected to a degree of posthumous editorial tampering.[6]

'The Folly of Looking Back in Fleeing out of Sodom', which was preached in May 1735 at the very close of the revival in Northampton, is based upon the text 'Remember Lot's wife.' In his Conclusion the preacher mingles the note of exhortation and the note of warning:

> You belong to that city which is appointed to an awful, inevitable, universal, swift, and sudden destruction; a city that hath a storm of fire and wrath hanging over it. Many of you are convinced of the awful state you are in while in Sodom, and are making some attempts to escape from the wrath which hangs over it. Let such be warned by what has been said, to escape for their lives, and not to look back. Look not back, unless you choose to have a share in the burning tempest that is coming down on that city. – Look not back in remembrance of the enjoyments which you have had in Sodom, as hankering after the pleasant things which you have

---

[5] *Works,* 17:141. The only residual problem here is that, although Valeri writes of 'the fourth and fifth uses', there is in fact no fifth use in his edition.

[6] John H. Gerstner makes this observation with regard to the issue of editorial alteration: 'There is considerable difference between the original manuscripts and the various editions of them that have appeared since Edwards' death. In a great many instances the phraseology of Edwards is altered, and in some cases the very thought itself.' *Evangelist,* p. 11.

had there, after the ease, the security, and the pleasure which you have there enjoyed.

Remember Lot's wife, for she looked back, as being loth utterly and for ever to leave the ease, the pleasure, and plenty which she enjoyed in Sodom, and as having a mind to return to them again; remember what became of her. – Remember the children of Israel in the wilderness, who were desirous of going back again into Egypt. Numb. xi. [5]. 'We remember the flesh which we did eat in Egypt freely, the cucumbers, and the melons, and the leeks and onions, and the garlick.' Remember what was the issue. You must be willing for ever to leave all the ease, and pleasure, and profit of sin, to forsake all for salvation, as Lot forsook all, and left all he had, to escape out of Sodom.[7]

It should be noted that Edwards' deliberate use of the second person in both the indicative and the imperative moods contributes very significantly to the striking directness of this Conclusion.

'The Portion of the Wicked' – a sermon on Romans 2:8-9 ('But unto them that are contentious, and do not obey the truth, but obey unrighteousness, indignation and wrath, tribulation and anguish, upon every soul of man that doeth evil, of the Jew first, and also of the Gentile') – was preached in November 1735. Edwards' Conclusion, in which he deals with the concept of the justice of the punishment of the wicked, is very fine:

You have no cause to complain of the punishment being greater than is just; for you have many and many a time provoked God to do his worst. If you should forbid a servant to do a given thing, and threaten that if he did it you would inflict some very dreadful punishment upon him, and he should do it notwithstanding, and you should renew your command, and warn him in the most strict manner possible not to do it, and tell him you would surely punish him if he persisted, and should declare that his punishment should be exceedingly dreadful, and he should wholly disregard you, and should disobey you again, and you should continue to repeat your commands and warnings, still setting out the dreadfulness of the punishment, and he should still, without any regard to you, go on again and again to disobey you to your face, and this immediately on your thus forbidding and threatening him: could you take it any otherwise than as daring you to do your worst? But thus have you done towards God; you have had his commands repeated, and his threatenings set before you hundreds of times, and have been most solemnly warned; yet have you notwithstanding gone on in ways which you knew were sinful, and have done the very things which he has forbidden, directly before his face. Job xv. 25, 26. 'For he stretcheth out his hand against God, and strengtheneth himself against the Almighty. He runneth upon him, even on his neck, upon the thick bosses of his buckler.' You have thus bid defiance to the Almighty, even when you saw the sword of his vindictive wrath uplifted, that it might fall upon your head. Will it, therefore, be any wonder if he shall make you know how terrible that wrath is, in your utter destruction?[8]

It should be noted that this Conclusion contains the following elements: firstly, a directness and a pointedness which derive from Edwards' use of the indicative mood in the second person. Secondly, a cogent illustration which is typically Edwardsean precisely because it is analogical. In this analogy the hearer, who has been quarreling *with* God, is made to sustain an analogical relationship *to* God. Thus the analogy puts the hearer temporarily in the same position, as it were, as God himself over against his rebellious servant. The analogy emphasizes in a remarkable way, by means of its shift in perspective, both the utter reasonableness of God and the utter unreasonableness of the sinner. Edwards then reverts back to the normal perspective with the words: 'But thus have you done towards God.' It is a striking example of what Kimnach calls 'the manipulated point of view'. Thirdly, the use of a rhetorical question in the final sentence: 'Will it, therefore, be any wonder if he shall make you know how terrible that wrath is, in your utter destruction?' In this rhetorical question the answer is, characteristically, self-evident; it is a foregone conclusion. Thus the hearer is virtually driven to indict himself before the Almighty.

[8] Ibid., pp. 887-888.

In the following month, December 1735, Edwards preached a sermon that was the counterpart of 'The Portion of the Wicked', namely, 'The Portion of the Righteous'.[9] This sermon on Romans 2:10 ('But glory, honour, and peace, to every man that worketh good') is a most spiritual, heavenly sermon on the theme of the coming glory. Edwards' sustained use of the imperative mood results in one of his finest hortatory Conclusions:

> This subject furnishes ground of solemn exhortation to the godly, to strive earnestly after holiness of life. What manner of persons ought you to be in all holy conversation and godliness, who have received such infinite mercy of God, and entertain such glorious hopes; seeing God has admitted you to such happiness, earnestly labour that you may walk in some measure answerably; seeing God has admitted you to the happiness of children, walk as children. Eph. v. [1]. Be ye therefore followers of God as dear children; imitate your heavenly Father; be ye holy, for he is holy. Seeing that you are admitted to the blessedness of disciples and friends of Jesus, walk as the friends of Christ, imitate your glorious Lord and Head. Here consider several things: particularly,
>
> What great love God hath bestowed upon you in choosing you to such unspeakable blessedness before the foundation of the world. How wonderful was the love of God in giving his Son to purchase this blessedness for you, and how wonderful was the love of the Son of God in shedding his own blood to purchase such glory for you! how ought you therefore to live to God's glory! Let me therefore beseech, by those great mercies of God, that you give yourself up a living sacrifice, holy and acceptable to God, which is your reasonable service. And be not slothful in business, but fervent in spirit, serving the Lord. Give the utmost diligence that you may keep all the commandments of God: study that you may prove what is that good, and acceptable, and perfect will of God; study that in all things you may be found approved: seeing God hath so loved you, strive earnestly that you may bring forth the fruits

---

[9] Although the Hickman edition (1834) contains a footnote to the effect that the sermon was preached in 'December, 1740', the Yale edition gives the date as 'Dec. 1735'. Compare ibid., p. 888 with *Works*, 19:803.

of the love of God; and seeing Christ hath so loved you, see that you love one another; let love be without dissimulation; be kindly affectioned one with another with brotherly love; be of the same mind one towards another, in honour preferring one another; have fervent charity among yourselves. Seeing God hath mercy on you, be ye merciful as your Father which is in heaven is merciful. Look not every one on his own things; be pitiful, be courteous; be ready to distribute, willing to communicate; be kind one to another, tender-hearted, forgiving one another. Christ hath thus loved you while an enemy; therefore recompense to no man evil for evil, but contrariwise blessing; do good to them that do evil to you. Such things as these become those that are the heirs of the glory that we have heard of.

Consider how much above the world that blessedness is which God has given; how therefore ought you to live above the world. God has redeemed you out of the world, and therefore do not live as though you had your portion in this life. Live as pilgrims and strangers; as those that are not at home; as fellow-citizens with the saints and of the household of God. Be ye not conformed to this world, but be ye transformed by the renewing of your mind. How dishonourable will it be to you that God had so advanced and entitled you to such glory, to set your heart upon the dust of the earth; how you dishonour the grace of God in giving you such blessedness; and how will you dishonour the blessedness that God has given, no more to set your heart on it, and to set it so much on the world!

Consider what a vast difference has God made between you and other men, how vastly different is your relative state from theirs, how much more has God done for you than for them. Seek therefore those things which are above, where God is. Will it be a shame if one that is entitled to such glory conducts no better than a child of the devil? Consider it seriously; and let it not be asked with reference to you, Matt. v. 47. What do ye more than others? Other men love those that love them; other men do good to those that do good to them: walk worthy of the vocation wherewith ye are called; and let it appear that you are of a spirit more excellent than your neighbour; manifest more love, and more meekness, and more

humility, with all lowliness and meekness, with longsuffering, forbearing one another in love; walk worthy of the Lord to all pleasing,
strengthened with all might according to his glorious power unto
all patience and longsuffering. Put ye on as the elect of God, holy
and beloved, bowels of mercies, kindness, gentleness of mind,
meekness, long-suffering, forbearing one another, forgiving one
another; and let your light so shine before men, that they, seeing
your good works, may glorify your Father who is in heaven. Seeing God has given you so much, God and men may well expect
of you, that you should be greatly distinguished in your life from
other men.[10]

'Hope and Comfort Usually Follow Genuine Humiliation and Repentance', dated September 1737, is one of the most profoundly experimental
of Edwards' sermons. His text on this occasion was Hosea 2:15 ('And
I will give her her vineyards from thence, and the valley of Achor for a
door of hope: and she shall sing there, as in the days of her youth, and as
in the day when she came up out of the land of Egypt'). The Doctrine
that Edwards draws from this text is this: 'God is wont to cause hope
and comfort to arise in the soul after trouble and humbling for sin, and
according as the troubler is slain and forsaken.'[11] This fine sermon contains a fine Conclusion:

> When you have found out the troubler, be sure thoroughly to destroy
> it. Renounce it with detestation, as a vile serpent that has secretly
> lain under your head for a long time, and infected you with his
> poisons time after time, and bit you, when you were asleep, made
> you sick and filled you with pain, and you knew it not. Would not
> a man, when he has found out the serpent in such a case, destroy
> it with indignation, and be for ever afterwards thoroughly watch-
> ful that he is not caught with such a calamity again? You cannot
> be too thorough in destroying such an enemy, and labouring to
> root it out, and extirpate all its race. Whoever of you are under
> darkness and trouble, I am bold to say, if God help you to follow
> these directions, your darkness will soon be scattered, and hope and

[10] Ibid., pp. 904-905.
[11] Ibid., p. 839.

comfort will arise. And this is the surest, and readiest, and most direct course which any of you can take in order to the renewing of comfort in your soul. And without this, do not promise yourself any considerable degree of light or comfort while you live, however many examinations of past experiences and prayers to God for light you may make.[12]

This paragraph is the final paragraph under the third and final 'use' – 'Use of direction' – in the Application. It is notable for its combination of a number of different elements often advocated by homileticians in Conclusions: the element of recapitulation; the directive, imperatival note; a rhetorical question that demonstrates the folly of not heeding the exhortation given; and the note both of warning and encouragement.

'Christ's Agony' – a sermon on Luke 22:44 ('And being in an agony he prayed more earnestly, and his sweat was as it were great drops of blood falling down to the ground') – was preached in October 1739 at Northampton and also 'repreached "winter and spring" 1757',[13] presumably to the white congregation at Stockbridge. The sermon provides a striking instance of the exemplaristic preaching of Christ that was clearly dear to the heart of the New England preacher. The Conclusion makes powerful imperatival use of the example of Christ by means of the verbs of obligation *ought* and *should*; it also addresses different categories of hearers. After addressing Christians in general, Edwards proceeds to insist that the example of Christ in the matter of prayer is 'an example for ministers', 'an example for parents', 'an example for neighbours', and 'an example for us':

Hence we may learn how earnest Christians ought to be in their prayers and endeavours for the salvation of others. Christians are the followers of Christ, and they should follow him in this. We see from what we have heard, how great the labour and travail of Christ's soul was for others' salvation, and what earnest and strong cries to God accompanied his labours. Here he hath set us an example. Herein he hath set an example for ministers, who should as co-workers with Christ travail in birth with them till Christ be

---

[12] Ibid., p. 849.
[13] See *Works*, 22:539.

found in them. Gal. iv. 19. 'My little children, of whom I travail in birth again, until Christ be formed in you.' They should be willing to spend and be spent for them. They should not only labour for them, and pray earnestly for them, but should, if occasion required, be ready to suffer for them, and to spend not only their strength, but their blood for them. 2 Cor. xii. 15. 'And I will very gladly spend and be spent for you, though the more abundantly I love you, the less I be loved.' Here is an example for parents, showing how they ought to labour and cry to God for the spiritual good of their children. You see how Christ laboured and strove and cried to God for the salvation of his spiritual children; and will not you earnestly seek and cry to God for your natural children?

Here is an example for neighbours one towards another how they should seek and cry for the good of one another's souls, for this is the command of Christ, that they should love one another as Christ loved them. John xv. 12. Here is an example for us, showing how we should earnestly seek and pray for the spiritual and eternal good of our enemies, for Christ did all this for his enemies, and when some of those enemies were at that very instant plotting his death, and busily contriving to satiate their malice and cruelty, in his most extreme torments, and most ignominious destruction.[14]

It is interesting to note the close proximity in some of Edwards' sermons between the adduction of motives and the Conclusion. The rationale for this close proximity in his mind was almost certainly his conviction that *'volition [is] necessarily connected with the influence of Motives'*[15] and that *'the Will always follows the last dictate of the understanding'*.[16] Thus, when Edwards presents motives, he often places them at the end of the sermon so that the motives thus presented to the understanding might, under the influence of the Spirit of God, move the will. Thus in the Conclusion to the sermon 'Procrastination, or, The Sin and Folly of Depending on Future Time' Edwards announces: 'Here I shall offer you two motives.' One of these motives is positive; the other is negative.

---

[14] *Works* (Hickman), 2:877.
[15] Ibid., 1:26.
[16] Ibid., p. 7.

Edwards goes on to end the sermon with a characteristically solemnizing Conclusion:

> And what is worse yet than all the disquietude and terror of conscience in this world; the consequence of a contrary behaviour, with respect to the bulk of mankind, is their eternal perdition. They flatter themselves that they shall see another day, and then another, and trust to that, until finally most of them are swallowed up in hell, to lament their folly to all eternity, in the lake that burneth with fire and brimstone. – Consider how it was with all the foolish virgins who trusted to the delay of the bridegroom's coming: when he came they were surprised, and found unprepared, having no oil in their lamps; and while they went to buy, those who were ready went in with him to the marriage; and the door was shut against them, and they came afterwards crying in vain, *Lord, Lord, open to us.*[17]

'The Manner in which the Salvation of the Soul is to be Sought' is dated 'September, 1740' – a date which places the sermon in the period of the Great Awakening. Edwards' text on this occasion was Genesis 6:22: 'Thus did Noah; according to all that God commanded him, so did he.' The sermon is a characteristically awakening Edwardsean sermon and it contains a very impressive Conclusion:

> If you will not hearken to the many warnings which are given you of approaching destruction, you will be guilty of more than *brutish madness*. 'The ox knoweth his owner, and the ass his master's crib.' They know upon whom they are dependent, and whom they must obey, and act accordingly. But you, so long as you neglect your own salvation, act as if you knew not God, your Creator and Proprietor, nor your dependence upon him. – The very beasts, when they see signs of an approaching storm, will betake themselves to their dens for shelter. Yet you, when abundantly warned of the approaching storm of divine vengeance, will not fly to the *hiding-place from the storm, and the covert from the tempest.* The sparrow, the swallow, and other birds, when they are forewarned of approaching winter, will betake themselves to a safer climate.

[17] Ibid., 2:242.

Yet you who have been often forewarned of the piercing blasts of divine wrath, will not, in order to escape them, enter into the New Jerusalem, of most mild and salubrious air, though the gate stands wide open to receive you. The very ants will be diligent in summer to lay up for winter: yet you will do nothing to lay up in store a good foundation against the time to come. Balaam's ass would not run upon a drawn sword, though his master, for the sake of gain, would expose himself to the sword of God's wrath; and so God made the dumb ass, both in words and actions, to rebuke the madness of the prophet, 2 Pet. ii. 16. In like manner, you, although you have been often warned that the sword of God's wrath is drawn against you, and will certainly be thrust through you, if you proceed in your present course, still proceed, regardless of the consequence.

So God made the very beasts and birds of the old world to rebuke the madness of the men of that day: for they, even all sorts of them, fled to the ark, while the door was yet open: which the men of that day refused to do; God hereby thus signifying, that their folly was greater than that of the very brute creatures. – Such folly and madness are you guilty of, who refuse to hearken to the warnings that are given you of the approaching flood of the wrath of God.

You have been once more warned today, while the door of the ark yet stands open. You have, as it were, once again heard the knocks of the hammer and axe in the building of the ark, to put you in mind that a flood is approaching. Take heed therefore that you do not still stop your ears, treat these warnings with a regard-less heart, and still neglect the great work which you have to do, lest the flood of wrath suddenly come upon you, sweep you away, and there be no remedy.[18]

The sheer spiritual power of this Conclusion lies, in large measure, in Edwards' very skilful and sustained use of contrast. It will be noted that in the course of this Conclusion Edwards sets in antithesis the *beasts and birds* on the one hand and *men* on the other. In particular, he emphasizes the innate wisdom of 'the ox', 'the ass', 'the very beasts', 'the

[18] Ibid., pp. 56-57.

sparrow, the swallow, and other birds', 'the very ants', 'Balaam's ass', 'the very beasts and birds of the old world', and 'the very brute creatures'; and by way of contrast he emphasizes the innate foolishness of men: 'But you ...''Yet you ...''Yet you ...''Yet you ...'Moreover, this contrast contains an implicit *a fortiori* argument; it is an argument from the lesser to the greater. The Northampton preacher is saying, in effect, 'If the birds of the air and the beasts of the field demonstrate such wisdom, prudence, and foresight in the physical and temporal realm, how much more should men demonstrate the same qualities in the spiritual and eternal realm.'The appropriateness of this contrast lies in the fact that it coheres beautifully with the text and the theme:

> So God made the very beasts and birds of the old world to rebuke the madness of the men of that day: for they, even all sorts of them, fled to the ark, while the door was yet open: which the men of that day refused to do.

Similarly, contends the New England preacher, the very beasts and birds of the New World rebuke the madness of men today in their refusal to flee to the ark of Christ while the door is still open.

There is, however, a certain elusiveness about Edwards' Conclusions, considered *in toto*. Whereas his Introductions generally constitute a formal, and therefore easily identifiable, entity in his sermons, his Conclusions tend to be much more amorphous; they do not, generally, constitute a formal unit within the sermon. Obviously, the *terminus ad quem* of the Conclusion is easily recognizable; but the *terminus a quo* is much more difficult to pinpoint. There is often no obvious beginning to his Conclusions. Thus in analysing Edwards' Conclusions one is reduced to considering the final paragraph or the final few paragraphs. An analysis of the final paragraph or paragraphs reveals, however, certain patterns. On the one hand, the note of recapitulation, often advocated by homi-leticians, is essentially absent from his Conclusions. On the other hand, the applicatory note, also advocated by homileticians, is often power-fully present. Indeed, in view of his fundamental Doctrine-Application division of the sermon, Edwards' Conclusions are, by definition, part of his Application. Thus many of his Conclusions are hortatory and parenetic in emphasis. Some make sustained use – others occasional use

– of the imperative mood. Within this category some are framed in the classic second person in the imperative mood; others are framed in the first person plural ('let us'); and others are framed in the third person subjunctive ('let him'; 'let them'; 'let it'; 'let all'; 'let every one'). In some Conclusions the note of judgment preponderates; in others the note of grace. Thus some are powerfully awakening and solemnizing; others are strongly consoling and uplifting. Some Conclusions are powerfully doxological. Others make cogent use of the rhetorical question. On occasion Edwards deliberately enhances the unity of the sermon by creating a striking juxtaposition (involving a thematic twist) between the text and one of the final clauses of the sermon. But some of his Conclusions are distinctly anti-climactic. It is an interesting fact that there appears to be no stereotypical approach in his Conclusions; thus, if they display a certain variety in terms of approach, they also display a certain variableness in terms of quality.

12

IMAGERY

'Of all the materials Edwards borrowed from the Bible or from life', observes Kimnach, 'he seems to have done more with imagery in composing his discourses than with any other device. Possessed of an intensely concrete and particularistic imagination, Edwards' abstract logic and his metaphors are alike vivified by simple but poignant (usually visual) images.'[1] 'Vivid imagery',[2] Kimnach contends, constitutes an integral part of 'Edwards' essential rhetorical arsenal'.[3] Particularly striking in this respect is 'Christ, the Light of the World'. This sermon belongs to the 'New York period' and was preached *circa* 1723. The text upon which the young preacher based his sermon was John 8:12: 'I am the light of the world.' 'The sermon', writes Marsden, '. . . is a gem of his early writing, sustaining his favorite metaphor of light throughout.'[4] Indeed, it is quite remarkable for the way in which the image of light – central both to the Bible and to the Age of the Enlightenment – is elaborated; the sermon exemplifies what Marsden terms 'Edwards' almost poetic sensibilities'.[5] 'For Edwards', observes Kimnach, 'the "most excellent and glorious similitude" of light is not only scriptural, but it links Scripture and nature in such a way that simple phenomena relating to the sun metaphorically interpret Scripture to the informed heart. In the third subhead under the second Proposition of the Doctrine, Edwards illustrates the process in five parallels or analogies which constitute

---

[1] *Works*, 10:213.
[2] Ibid., p. 294.
[3] Ibid.
[4] Marsden, *Edwards*, p. 54.
[5] Ibid.

a remarkable extended simile.'⁶ We cite here the second, third, and fourth analogies:

> As the sun by his returning influences causes clouds and storms and cold to fly before it, so doth Jesus Christ, the cold, tempests, and clouds of the soul. In the winter season, the heavens are frequently overcast with clouds that hide the pleasing light of the sun; the air is disturbed with winds, storms and tempests, and all things are chilled with frost and cold. The rivers and streams are shut up with ice, the earth is covered with snow, and all things look dreadful; but when the sun returns with its warming influences, the heavens are cleared of dark clouds and the air stilled from tempests, the ice and cold and snow are fled. So the souls of men in their natural state are like winter, perpetually disturbed with the storms of lust and vice, and a raging conscience; their souls are all beclouded with sin and spiritual darkness. But when Christ comes with his warming influences, things are far otherwise: their minds are calm and serene, warmed with holiness and religion, and the clear sunshine of spiritual comfort.

> As when the sun returns in the spring, the frozen earth is opened, mollified and softened, so by the beams of the Sun of Righteousness the stony, rocky, adamantine hearts of men are thawed, mellowed and softened, and made fit to receive the seeds of grace. In the winter, the face of the earth is closed and shut up as a stone, unfit for anything to be sown in it, but is loosened in the spring by the warm beams of the sun; so [is] the heart in its natural state frozen and like the stony ground, so that the seeds of God's Word take no rooting in it, but is as if we should cast seed upon the bare rock. But when Christ melts the heart by shining upon it, the seed then sinks into it and takes root and begins to germinate and spring forth.

> As the sun revives the plants and trees and fruits of the earth, so Christ Jesus by his spiritual light revives the soul and causes it to bring forth fruit. In the winter, the trees are stripped of their leaves and fruit, and stand naked, cease growing, and seem to be dead; the grass and herbs are killed, and all things have the appearance

---

⁶ *Works*, 10:533.

of death upon them. But when the sun returns, then all things have the appearance of a resurrection: things revive again, the trees and fields put on their green livery and begin to bud forth, anew, and flourish and grow. The grass and herbs begin to peep forth out of the ground, and all things look green and flourishing: the fields, meadows, and woods seem to rejoice, and the birds sing a welcome to the returning spring. The fields and trees are adorned with beautiful and fragrant flowers.

Just such an alteration is made in the soul at conversion by Jesus Christ, only far more glorious: . . .[7]

In May 1739 the Northampton pastor interrupted his series on *The History of Redemption* in order to return to this image of the sun. The text upon which he based the sermon 'Christ the Spiritual Sun' was Malachi 4:1-2: 'For, behold, the day cometh, that shall burn as an oven; and all the proud, yea, and all that do wickedly, shall be stubble: and the day that cometh shall burn them up, saith the LORD of hosts, that it shall leave them neither root nor branch. But unto you that fear my name shall the Sun of righteousness arise with healing in his wings; and ye shall go forth, and grow up as calves of the stall.' Edwards begins the Doctrine thus: 'Christ is as it were the Sun [of] the spiritual world. The natural world is full of images of things in the spiritual world, but the most bright and glorious image of Christ that we have in the whole natural world is the sun.'[8] This image of the sun is, as the text in Malachi demonstrates, clearly biblical; yet, as in 'Christ, the Light of the World', so here, it is Edwards' development and elaboration of the implications of the image of the sun that are so striking.

It was *circa* 1756, towards the close of his ministry at Stockbridge, that Edwards wrote entry 209 in 'Images of Divine Things': 'The sun, a type of Christ. Cudworth's *Intellectual System*, p. 25.'[9] This simile of the sun – a simile that is so remarkably extended in 'Christ, the Light of the World' and in 'Christ the Spiritual Sun' – is representative of Edwards'

[7] Ibid., pp. 540-541.
[8] *Works*, 22:52.
[9] *Works*, 11:129.

basic philosophy of natural imagery. 'For indeed the whole outward creation', contends Edwards in his *Miscellanies,* 'which is but the shadows of beings, is so made as to represent spiritual things.'[10] Mason I. Lowance, Jr., notes 'the representative, symbolic, *typological* language of nature'[11] in Edwards' thought. 'Edwards would propose that a new system of "types" was to be found in the world of nature, Platonic in character, not pre-figurative entirely, but timeless, . . . so that the true believer provided with the "new sense of things" . . . could "read" the book of nature as previous exegetes had read the Book of Scripture for revelation of God's will.'[12] It is not simply that Edwards notes and utilizes the types and shadows of the Scriptures; in a manner that is virtually Platonic he makes a remarkable correlation between the natural and the spiritual world. 'His universe', Marsden observes, 'was filled with signs and types.'[13]

'Images of Divine Things' (variously called by its author 'Shadows of Divine Things', 'The Book of Nature and Common Providences', and 'The Language and Lessons of Nature')[14] contains 212 numbered entries in all. The evidence indicates that this work was begun shortly after Edwards' settling in Northampton in 1727 and it was continued throughout his life.[15] Entry no. 8, which was 'probably written . . . near the beginning of 1729',[16] reads as follows:

> Again, it is apparent and allowed that there is a great and remark-able analogy in God's works. There is a wonderfull resemblance in the effects which God produces, and consentaneity in His man-ner of working in one thing and another, throughout all nature. It is very observable in the visible world. Therefore 'tis allowed that God does purposely make and order one thing to be in agreeable-ness and harmony with another. And if so, why should not we suppose that he makes the inferior in imitation of the superior, the material of the spiritual, on purpose to have a resemblance and shadow of them? We see that even in the material world God

[10] Ibid., p. 7.
[11] Ibid., p. 181.
[12] Ibid., p. 161.
[13] Marsden, *Edwards,* p. 353.
[14] See *Works,* 11:34-35.
[15] See ibid., pp. 37-47.
[16] Ibid., p. 53 n.2.

makes one part of it strangely to agree with another; and why is it not reasonable to suppose he makes the whole as a shadow of the spiritual world?[17]

Thus, in effect, Edwards infers from 'the consent of all the parts' in the natural world a 'consentaneity' between the natural, visible world and the spiritual, invisible world. But his reasoning here is, strictly speaking, mere assertion and constitutes a *non sequitur*. It simply does not follow from 'the consent of all the parts' in the natural world that there is necessarily a 'consentaneity' between the natural, visible world and the spiritual, invisible world; and even if such a 'consentaneity' could be established in principle, it would still be virtually impossible (apart from an external authority such as the Scriptures) to establish in practice its precise extent and limits or to establish the precise correspondences that pertain between these two worlds. This is not to deny that there is a certain analogy between these two worlds; but there can be little doubt that 'Edwards' natural typology',[18] as Wallace E. Anderson has called it, involves a much more extensive or expansive approach to typology than that normally entertained in Reformed circles and that it is vulnerable to the charge of subjectivism on his part.[19] Anderson assesses Edwards' approach thus:

> Traditionally, typology involved the exercise of matching biblical 'types' – prophetic figures, events, or circumstances – in the Old Testament with their 'antitypes' or fulfilling figures, events, or circumstances in the New. In Edwards' hands, however, typology took on a broadened significance that comprehended not only Scripture but also nature and history . . . For Edwards, types were found not only in the Old Testament; the phenomenal world also declared divine truths.[20]

---

[17] Ibid., p. 53.

[18] Ibid., p. 14.

[19] 'Another group that Edwards implicitly addressed was the Reformed evangelicals, those who shared with him his heritage of Puritan dissent. With their typological approach based on the literal, historical sense, those in this camp would have objected to Edwards' expansion of types beyond Scripture into the natural world.' Ibid., p. 32.

[20] Ibid., p. 3.

Edwards' approach, as preserved most fully in 'Images of Divine Things' and the notebook on 'Types', represented an important innovation in Christian typology and philosophy. Edwards attempted to free typology from the narrow correspondences of the two testaments without reverting to exaggerated medieval allegory. In the process, he transcended philosophical dualism, linking the natural and the supernatural in a compelling and dynamic unity in God.[21]

The interesting feature in Edwards' approach to imagery drawn from the natural world is that it borders on the Platonic. It was *circa* 1756 that he copied into 'The Mind' a passage from Cudworth's *Intellectual System* (1678) in which Cudworth refers to Plato's subterranean cave:

> Plato [and] his subterranean Cave, so famously known, and so elegantly described by him, [where he] supposes men tied with their backs towards the Light, placed at a great distance from them, so that they could not turn about their Heads to it neither, and therefore could see nothing but the shadows (of certain Substances behind them) projected from it, which shadows they concluded to be the only Substances and Realities, and when they heard the sounds made by those Bodies that were betwixt the Light and them, or their reverberated Echoes, they imputed them to those shadows which they saw. [I say,] all this is a Description of the State of those Men, who take Body to be the only Real and Substantial thing in the World, and to do all that is done in it; and therefore often impute Sense, Reason and Understanding, to nothing but Blood and Brains in us.[22]

This Neoplatonic strand in Edwards' thought thus anticipates the *Weltanschauung* of the Romantic movement that was to emerge so powerfully in England forty years after Edwards' death.[23] Edwards' 'vertical typology',[24] as Kimnach terms it, appears to have been, in

---

[21] Ibid., p. 33.

[22] Cited *Works*, 6:359. See also ibid., pp. 36, 329.

[23] The year 1798 marks the *terminus a quo* of the Romantic movement in England with the publication of the *Lyrical Ballads* by William Wordsworth. See Encyclopedia of Philosophy, 1972 ed., s.v. 'Romanticism'.

[24] *Works*, 10:229.

large part, a reaction to – indeed, a deliberate counterblast to – the spirit of the Age of the Enlightenment. The latter posited what Avihu Zakai has described as a desacralized, disenchanted world; the New England divine promoted in its place a resacralized, re-enchanted world.[25] There is a significant element of truth in Miller's assertion that 'out of Edwards' work might be compiled an indictment of the eighteenth century that would rival Blake's and delight the heart of every Romantic.'[26] It is, of course, evident that Edwards did not share the theological position of the English Romantic poet, Samuel Taylor Coleridge (1772-1834); but to what extent, if any, one wonders, would he have differed from the view expressed in these lines of Coleridge, with their clear reference to Plato's allegory of the Cave?

> For all that meets the bodily sense I deem
> Symbolical, one mighty alphabet
> For infant minds: and we in this low world
> Placed with our back to bright Reality,
> That we may learn with young unwounded ken
> The substance from its shadow.[27]

[25] 'In his scientific and philosophical writings, Edwards reacted against these metaphysical and theological consequences [the deistic concept of a universe that ran like clockwork] of the new scientific thought. He was alarmed by the basic postulate of mechanical philosophers that nature operates according to mere mechanical principles, or natural laws, formulated in mathematical terms, envisioning the world of nature as a huge machine that runs by itself according to abstract, universal laws of nature, freed from subordination to God's dominion and not affected by his unceasing watchful eyes. With great dismay Edwards observed that mechanical philosophy's notion of a homogeneous, uniform, and symmetrical, one-dimensional world of nature not only deprived the created order of any teleological end and purpose, but stipulated that nature could no longer manifest the presence of God. Sadly he observed the mechanical philosophers' claim that the Almighty had created the world and then retired, releasing the realm of nature from its subordination to God and establishing it as a 'self-moving engine.' In sum, Edwards reacted against the growing tendency to differentiate sharply between nature and God. In response, he constructed his own theology of nature, or typology, interpreting the physical world as a representation or a "shadow" of the spiritual, which celebrates God's glory and sovereignty as they are evidenced in the coherence and beauty, order and harmony, of world phenomena. Against the scientific disenchantment of the world of nature, Edwards's quest was for its reenchantment.' Zakai, p. 89. See also Marsden, *Edwards*, p. 79.

[26] Miller, *Edwards*, p. 119.

[27] Cited David Newsome, *Two Classes of Men: Platonism and English Romantic Thought* (London: John Murray, 1974), p. 36.

Wallace E. Anderson notes that 'Cudworth's *Intellectual System* . . . was probably one of the last major works he read before going to Princeton in February 1758.'[28] It is almost as if the Stockbridge divine found in the writings of the Cambridge Platonist a late confirmation of that approach to imagery and symbolism which he had, almost instinctively, it appears, adopted from the beginning.[29] There can be little doubt but that one of Edwards' major concerns underlying his approach both to biblical and natural typology was that of providing a counterblast to the deistic distancing of God from the world that was so prominent in the eighteenth century; he was also concerned to provide a counterblast to the metaphysical materialism of Thomas Hobbes.[30] In 'Things to Be Considered and Written Fully About' – notes on Natural Philosophy drawn up *circa* 1722 – Edwards made the following entry: 'To bring in an observation somewhere in a proper place, that instead of Hobbes' notion that God is matter and that all substance is matter; that nothing that is matter can possibly be God, and that no matter is, in the most proper sense, matter.'[31] Hobbes' materialism denied outright the existence and reality of spiritual entities and therefore, by definition, denied any suggestion that the material world might contain correspondences with that spiritual world. Conversely, Edwards' immaterialism highlighted the existence and reality of spiritual entities and thus paved the way for a strong emphasis upon correspondences between the insubstantial physical world (which ultimately is mind-dependent or perceiver-dependent) and the greater reality of the spiritual world. 'Speaking most strictly', Edwards wrote in his 'Natural Philosophy' papers, 'there is no proper substance but God himself . . . How truly, then, is he said to be *ens entium*.'[32] Mc-

---

[28] *Works*, 11:46.

[29] The main philosophical enemy of the Cambridge Platonists was Thomas Hobbes (1588-1679). In their opposition to Hobbes' materialism they initially welcomed the dualism of René Descartes (1596-1650), but came eventually to fear the influence of the latter because they felt that he threatened the spiritual interpretation of the universe. See *Encyclopedia of Philosophy*, 1972 ed., s.v. 'Cambridge Platonists'.

[30] See *Works*, 11:13-14.

[31] *Works*, 6:235.

[32] Ibid., p. 215. McClymond, p. 33, explains the meaning of JE's term 'substance' thus: 'To him "substance" denotes something complete in itself, self-contained, and self-sufficient, and thus any understanding of creatures as themselves substances presents a direct chal-

Clymond argues that 'the connection between his idealism and his theological interests has not been fully appreciated. Edwards's idealism was in part a reaction to the threat of a mechanistic and materialistic universe, as most alarmingly illustrated in the writings of Hobbes, the *bête noire* of the eighteenth-century Christian philosophers.'[33] 'The speediest way for Edwards to cut the Gordian knot of atheistic materialism was to deny the very existence of independent matter, and with it the independent efficacy of material causation ... Idealism reflected a theocentric strategy of turning the tables on materialism, making God as immaterial into the central and defining reality and rendering matter a merely derivative phenomenon of consciousness.'[34] There is a very significant logical connection between Edwards' powerful theocentrism, his immaterialism, the influence of the Cambridge Platonists, and his 'vertical typology.'

The question that arises, however, is this: does Edwards, in his opposition to deism and metaphysical materialism, over-react and thus espouse an approach to typology and imagery that is exaggerated and that exceeds the bounds of Reformed orthodoxy? He clearly recognized that his approach to imagery and symbolism was one that made him vulnerable to the charge of being speculative and fanciful, and his somewhat weary defence of this approach in a late entry in the 'Types' notebook is not entirely convincing:

> I expect by very ridicule and contempt to be called a man of a very fruitful brain and copious fancy, but they are welcome to it. I am not ashamed to own that I believe that the whole universe, heaven and earth, air and seas, and the divine constitution and history of the holy Scriptures, be full of images of divine things, as full as a language is of words; and that the multitude of those things that I have mentioned are but a very small part of what is really intended to be signified and typified by these things: but that there is room for persons to be learning more and more of this language and

---

lenge to his theocentric vision of a world in every respect derived from and dependent upon God.'
[33] McClymond, p. 32.
[34] Ibid.

seeing more of that which is declared in it to the end of the world without discovering all.[35]

It is, however, important to note that his homiletical practice with regard to imagery is superior to his philosophical theory. Thus, if his philosophical theory is vulnerable to the charge of subjectivism and innovation, his homiletical practice must be regarded as significantly more conservative. Indeed, his use of imagery in his sermons constitutes one of his great strengths as a preacher. The Yale co-editors, Stout and Hatch, regard 'verbal imagery' as lying at the very centre of the mystery of Edwards' power as a preacher: 'What Whitefield accomplished in sheer drama, Edwards achieved in verbal imagery. In some of his greatest awakening sermons, most notably "Sinners in the Hands of an Angry God", ... Edwards employed a great panoply of images and metaphors designed to reach all the human emotions.'[36] Indeed, the Yale co-editors regard 'Edwards' rhetorical genius in using verbal imagery'[37] as lying at the centre of the mystery of the power of that sermon: 'What is it about this sermon that inspired rigid Calvinists to scream from their pews? Certainly not the delivery. Edwards preached all his sermons in a "natural way of delivery, and without any agitation of body, or anything else in the manner to excite attention" (as reported by Thomas Prince, in 1744). Rather, Edwards' rhetorical genius in using verbal imagery was nowhere better illustrated than here.'[38] Stout and Hatch go on to emphasize that 'in "Sinners in the Hands of an Angry God" he employs no less than twenty metaphors or descriptive adjectives to express God's wrath and hell's torments. The metaphors include a pit, an oven, a mouth, a furnace, a sword, flames, a serpent, a troubled sea, black clouds approaching, waters damned by a floodgate, a bow bent with an arrow ready to be "made drunk with your blood", an ax, and a heavy load that cannot be

[35] *Works*, 11:152. 'This curious passage', observes Kimnach, 'with its combination of self-conscious defensiveness and passionate affirmation, seems to reflect Edwards' final doubt about the probability of his mastering the divine idiom while never once doubting the reality of its existence.' *Works*, 10:236.

[36] *Works*, 22:262-263.

[37] Ibid., p. 401.

[38] Ibid.

held.'[39] It is this 'massing of several different images about a thematic point'[40] or 'the centripetal focusing of massed images'[41] that Kimnach regards as integral to the remarkable success of this sermon:

> As he elaborates each of several images, often in an interlocking pattern, the dynamic of the argument assumes a centripetal character wherein the complementary conjunctions of the several images coincide precisely with the connotations of the theme that the images are intended to vivify. Thus, the more images added, the sharper the sense of theme or doctrine, and the greater the diversity of images the more intense the light at the central point of fusion. 'Sinners' is the renowned exemplar of this technique and certainly the purest example.[42]

There is, however, one image in particular that has tended to dominate discussion of this sermon; it is the image of the spider held over the fire:

> The God that holds you over the pit of hell, much as one holds a spider, or some loathsome insect, over the fire, abhors you, and is dreadfully provoked: his wrath towards you burns like fire; he looks upon you as worthy of nothing else, but to be cast into the fire; he is of purer eyes than to bear to have you in his sight; you are ten thousand times more abominable in his eyes, than the most hateful venomous serpent is in ours. You have offended him infinitely more than ever a stubborn rebel did his prince: and yet, it is nothing but his hand that holds you from falling into the fire every moment. It is to be ascribed to nothing else, that you did not go to hell the last night; that you was suffered to awake again in this world, after you closed your eyes to sleep. And there is no other reason to be given, why you have not dropped into hell since you arose in the morning, but that God's hand has held you up. There is no other reason to be given why you have not gone to hell, since you have sat here in the house of God, provoking his pure eyes by your sinful wicked manner of attending his solemn wor-

[39] Ibid.
[40] *Works*, 10:217.
[41] Ibid., p. 224.
[42] Ibid., p. 217.

ship. Yea, there is nothing else that is to be given as a reason why you do not this very moment drop down into hell.

O sinner! consider the fearful danger you are in . . .[43]

This passage is, as Marsden observes, 'the infamous passage'.[44] Moreover, it is almost certainly this passage more than any other in this sermon that has generated the almost hysterical denunciation of Jonathan Edwards which regrettably constitutes the keynote of many of his detractors. It is true that this is not a biblical, but Edwards' own image. But the question that arises is this: Does this image of the spider held over the fire capture the biblical truth of the sinner's position in the hands of God? An analysis of the implications of the image reveals an emphasis upon God's blazing holiness, his righteous judgment, his infinite power, and his absolute sovereignty. It also reveals an emphasis upon the abominableness of man's sin, man's utter impotence, and the appalling precariousness of man's plight as he is only preserved from being cast into 'the fire that never shall be quenched'[45] by what the visiting preacher calls 'the mere arbitrary will, and uncovenanted, unobliged forbearance, of an incensed God'.[46] Men may not like this image of the spider held over the fire nor its implications; but they cannot easily deny that the image's implications are, in fact, revealed in the Bible as the darker aspects of the gospel of Christ – indeed, as the fundamental presupposition of that gospel. Kimnach is, we believe, correct when he contends that 'the importance of the spider image has been greatly exaggerated.'[47]

But if there has been an over-emphasis upon this particular image on the part of Edwards' detractors, there has also, we believe, been an over-emphasis upon the significance of imagery in general on the part of some of his admirers. It is interesting to note that, just as 'Sinners in the Hands of an Angry God' has been incorporated into anthologies of American literature and has been read, as a piece of literature, by countless American students, so too this sermon has, in the last sixty

[43] *Works* (Hickman), 2:10.
[44] Marsden, *Edwards*, p. 223.
[45] Mark 9:45.
[46] *Works* (Hickman), 2:9.
[47] *Works*, 10:175.

years or so, been analysed by a number of significant literary critics. In an influential article published in 1949 and entitled 'The Artistry of Jonathan Edwards', Edwin H. Cady argued that the springs of the success of 'Sinners in the Hands of an Angry God' lie in the fact that 'it is in the widest sense a work of literary art.'[48] 'By all the ordinary tests, "Sinners in the Hands of an Angry God" is a genuine work of literary art and testifies to Jonathan Edwards' right to the name of artist.'[49] More precisely, Cady pinpoints the preacher's imagery as lying at the heart of this artistry: 'Although thought, form, and imagery in the sermon are one, the great emotional power of the discourse comes primarily from the rich and versatile imagery.'[50] Cady insists that 'the secret of the effectiveness, then and since, of "Sinners in the Hands of an Angry God" resides first in the organic oneness of theme, image, and "application." More directly, the emotional force of the sermon springs from the imagery itself, especially from the freshly imaginative, native figures which burned into the minds of his audience Edwards' vision of the horrible predicament of the sinner without grace.'[51] Cady is somewhat dismissive of what he regards as the more outworn, conventional, biblical images employed by the visiting preacher at Enfield; conversely, he emphasizes the 'surprisingly homely and immediate'[52] character of what he regards as the most striking images utilized in the sermon, namely, the image of slipping – 'a condition then as now realizable every New England winter'[53] – and also 'the climactic figure of the entire sermon',[54] that of the spider held over the fire – an image which would have been familiar 'to a people who lived long months by the hearth'.[55]

In similar vein J. A. Leo Lemay has more recently observed that 'the images add to the suspense because they are, almost invariably, suspenseful: walking on air, the waters dammed up, the drawn bow

[48] Edwin H. Cady, 'The Artistry of Jonathan Edwards', *New England Quarterly* 22 (March 1949): p. 61.

[49] Ibid., p. 72.

[50] Ibid., p. 63.

[51] Ibid., p. 71.

[52] Ibid., p. 66.

[53] Ibid.

[54] Ibid., p. 67.

[55] Ibid.

and pointed arrow, the spider images, and the falling, slipping, slid-ing images. The most tension-filled images are found in the Applica-tion.'[56] Lemay insists that it is *inter alia* 'because of its suspenseful and archetypal imagery' that 'Sinners in the Hands of an Angry God' is 'a masterpiece of rhetorical strategies'.[57]

In response to such evaluations of 'Sinners' we would emphasize that we have no wish to deny Edwards' considerable literary or rhetorical skills. Indeed, in our own analysis of his preaching we have sought to demonstrate these skills from a wide range of his sermons. There is indeed an artistry about his sermons and there is indeed an artistry about this particular sermon. But the consistent tendency here – indeed, the frequent tendency of modern Edwardsean scholar-ship – is that of interpreting the astonishing effectiveness of 'Sinners' in terms of (as Stout and Hatch express it) his 'rhetorical genius in using verbal imagery'.[58] In short, the problem with these evaluations by Cady, Lemay, Kimnach, Stout, and Hatch is that, in their emphasis upon Edwards' imagery, there is virtually no recognition of the Spirit of God. Their approach tends to be *reductionistic* rather than *nuanced;* its tendency is *naturalistic* rather than *supernaturalistic.* This inter-pretation does not, in principle, exclude the implication that any skilful literary artist or homiletician could, almost at will, reproduce such effects as those displayed at Enfield, provided that he accumulate a sufficient number of powerful rhetorical metaphors.

Edwards' use of imagery in the course of his ministry to the Indians of Stockbridge is of particular interest. Indeed, his strategic employ-ment of nature imagery is a crucial element in the simplicity by which the Indian sermons are characterized. 'Christ is to the Heart like a River to a Tree Planted by It' is a sermon based on Psalm 1:3: 'He shall

---

[56] J. A. Leo Lemay, 'Rhetorical Strategies in Sinners in the Hands of an Angry God and Narrative of the Late Massacres in Lancaster County', in *Benjamin Franklin, Jonathan Edwards, and the Representation of American Culture,* Barbara B. Oberg and Harry S. Stout , eds. (New York: Oxford University Press, 1993), p. 190.

[57] Ibid., p. 191. 'Because of its extraordinarily increasing immediacy, because of its inexo-rably increasing tension and suspense, because of its exhaustively and inescapably convinc-ing logic, and because of its suspenseful and archetypal imagery, "Sinners in the Hands of an Angry God" is a masterpiece of rhetorical strategies.' Ibid.

[58] *Works,* 22:401.

be like a tree planted by the rivers of water.' The sermon was preached in Stockbridge in August 1751. 'He employed the most familiar nature imagery', notes Kimnach, '– a tree standing by a river.'[59] The sermon manuscript is, in contrast with the great sermons of the 1730's, characteristically rather sketchy and under-developed; but the following section is somewhat more fully developed and demonstrates well the simplicity and the spirituality with which the Stockbridge missionary explores such imagery:

> Waters of a river don't fail; [it] flows constantly, day and night. Waters that run upon the ground from showers of rain or melting of the snows soon dry up, but [waters from rivers do not]. Little brooks dry up in a very dry time, but the waters of a great river continue running continually, and from one age to another, and are never dry.
> So Christ never [leaves] his saints that love him and trust in him: the love of Christ never [ceases].[60]

Kimnach makes these interesting observations on the sermon: 'In this sermon, then, Edwards may have found an imagistic idiom common to himself and the Indians.'[61] 'Such an imagistic *tour de force* may be seen as another instance of Edwards' ability to find biblical metaphors that seem to speak directly to the Indian mentality, but if he develops the imagery brilliantly, it is more likely because Edwards himself found this image particularly moving. His notebooks attest to his fascination with images of rivers and trees in defining a Christian cosmology.'[62]

In 'Heaven's Dragnet', one of the earliest of the Indian sermons, he again makes use of an image that is not only biblical but also familiar to Indian culture – it is 'the master image of the net'.[63] His text is a verse drawn from the Parable of the Dragnet, namely, Matthew 13:47: 'Again, the kingdom of heaven is like unto a net.' Edwards develops the

[59] *Works*, 25:600.
[60] Ibid., p. 603.
[61] Ibid., p. 601.
[62] Ibid., p. 600. See also 'Images of Divine Things', nos. 77 and 78, and also the 'Miscellanies' notebook, no. 991.
[63] Ibid., p. 575.

implications of the image with a beautiful simplicity:

> 'Tis said that this kingdom of heaven is like a net that was cast into the sea. The sea is the whole world of mankind. As a net that is cast into the sea don't take all the fish in the sea, but only goes 'round and fences in a few, so the kingdom of Christ don't take all the world, but only a part.
>
> The people of Christ are separated from the rest of the world to be a peculiar people to him, to be Christ's part, as the net cast into the sea separates the fish that are in it from all the rest in the sea that they may belong to the fisherman and be his part of the fish of the sea, while the rest are let alone and are not meddled with.[64]

Kimnach notes that Edwards had preached an eight-sermon series on the Parable of the Dragnet at Northampton in May, June, and July of 1746. The sermon at Stockbridge, however, clearly involved an attempt at 'radical simplification'[65] on his part as he deliberately appeals to what Kimnach terms 'the hunter-gatherer culture of the Indians'.[66] 'This sermon ... demonstrates Edwards' aptitude for composing abstracts of much more expansive discourses and theological schemes, reducing the large and complicated for the consumption of Indian congregations – preparing 'milk for babes', as the seventeenth-century Puritans put it.'[67] 'Although the master image of the net was biblical and had been used in the Northampton sermon series on conversion, Edwards' selection of it for use in one of his first Indian sermons may have been an attempt to engage the hunter-gatherer culture of the Indians.'[68]

'Warring with the Devil', dated 'St [ockbridge] Ind [ians]. April 1754',[69] is based on Luke 11:21: 'When a strong man armed keepeth his palace.' In this sermon Edwards selects a text in which the central biblical image appeals to 'the Indian warrior culture'.[70] In the early

[64] Ibid., p. 577.
[65] Ibid., p. 575.
[66] Ibid.
[67] Ibid.
[68] Ibid.
[69] Ibid., p. 677.
[70] Ibid., p. 676.

explanatory or doctrinal part of the sermon the preacher again develops this central image with a beautiful simplicity:

> The devil is an enemy that is like a strong man armed. [He is an] enemy to God [and an] enemy to men ...
> The devil lives in [a] wicked man as in his house. A man's house is his own; he has it in possession [with all] his goods: [he] lives there [and] rules over [it] ...
> Christ is stronger than the devil.
> When a sinner is converted, Christ fights with the devil [and] overcomes [him].
> When a sinner is converted, he turns the devil out of his house where he lived, and takes possession himself.[71]

It is in the context of this sermon that Kimnach notes the way in which Edwards adjusted and adapted his use of imagery:

> Edwards' ability to adjust his analyses of the spiritual life and moral conduct to the congregation before him was tested by his Indian ministry. While he might seem to have expended most of his missionary energy defending the interests of his Indian congregants from the depredations of the Williams cabal in Stockbridge – writing good enough political letters to qualify as a professional lobbyist – he also worked hard at attuning his homiletics to the Indian culture. While his method did not involve oversimplification of essential concepts, or patronizing the Indians with a belittling gentleness, he often did adjust his diction and, most effectively, his imagery. In this case, the Indian warrior culture provided his rhetorical opportunity.[72]

In a recent analysis of Edwards' preaching to the Indians at Stockbridge, Rachel M. Wheeler has highlighted Edwards' deliberate, strategic use of imagery:

> In preaching to the Stockbridge Indians, the basic preaching of Calvinism had not changed, but the rhetoric, the style, and the subjects of the sermons had. Edwards tailored his sermons to fit

---

[71] Ibid., p. 678.
[72] Ibid., p. 676.

with what he saw as the particular needs of his congregation. At Stockbridge, he came to rely more heavily on metaphor and imagery. Drawing on the parables of the New Testament, Edwards preached of sowers of seed, of fishermen, of ground too dry for a seed to take, of trees fed by rivers that never ran dry, and of briars and thorns that impeded a traveler's way.[73]

Edwards' sermons to the Indians are overwhelmingly drawn from New Testament texts, with a heavy reliance on the Gospels of Matthew and Luke . . . Many of these sermons rely on the use of parables and biblical stories to explain the particular doctrine Edwards had chosen for explication. It is clear in his earlier sermons that Edwards understood the power of story and imagery. But in the Stockbridge sermons, parables and metaphors dominate, suggesting that he believed this method particularly adapted to his Indian audience.[74]

Wheeler emphasizes that 'Edwards was not trying to reach the heads of his listeners, but their hearts.'[75] 'Images, stories, metaphors – all were capable of striking straight to the heart of the listener, bypassing the intellect.'[76] She insists that 'his preaching at Stockbridge displays a decisive move away from metaphysical reasoning and towards a reliance on metaphor, images and narrative. The shift reflects the demands of a new audience, but perhaps the maturing of a preacher.'[77] There is some truth in Wheeler's evaluation. The sermons of the Stockbridge philosopher-theologian-preacher are indeed characterized by a radical simp-

---

[73] Rachel M. Wheeler, 'Living upon Hope: Mahicans and Missionaries, 1730-1760' (Ph.D. diss., Yale, 1999), p. 163. Marsden gives this general assessment of the Stockbridge Indian ministry: 'Edwards' sermons to the Indians reflect a good sense of his audience. For one thing, he did not just preach simpler versions of his sermons to the English, which were almost all old Northampton sermons. Rather, consistent with his advice regarding Indian education, he picked themes that involved narratives and plain vivid metaphors.' Marsden, *Edwards*, p. 393. Marsden notes that in his ministry to the Indians 'Edwards preached predominantly on New Testament texts, especially from Matthew and Luke. Some of his most effective sermon series were from the parables.' Ibid.

[74] Ibid., p. 167.

[75] Ibid., p. 163.

[76] Ibid., p. 168.

[77] Ibid., p. 166.

lification on his part and there is, accordingly, a much greater use made of images, metaphors, and narrative. But this very shift surely reflects the shrewdness and the adaptability of the preacher in a situation that was itself radically different from that at Northampton. Thus it is one thing to contend that this shift 'reflects the demands of a new audience'; it is quite another thing to suggest that the shift reflects 'perhaps the maturing of a preacher', as if metaphysical reasoning or a more abstract presentation of the truth were somehow intrinsically less desirable and merely belong to an earlier, less mature phase in his ministry. Indeed, Wheeler's analysis reflects elements of a certain anti-intellectualism on her part. Was it not antecedently probable, indeed, was it not antecedently predictable, that, in his ministry to the Mohawk and Mahican Indians, Edwards would realize immediately that metaphysical reasoning would be above their heads, indeed, that the Indian language itself would not be able to sustain the inevitably more abstract modes of thought involved in such reasoning? Wheeler's suggestion at this point is naïve and her conclusion superficial. She repeatedly sets up a false antithesis between the head and the heart and thus creates a false dichotomy between the more intellectual aspects and the more affective aspects of the proclamation of the truth of God. Thus whilst it is undeniable that Edwards' homiletical strategy changed in the new situation at Stockbridge, it is also evident from the entire corpus of his writings that his constant concern, whether in Northampton or in Stockbridge, and whether in the pulpit or with the pen, was that of producing what McClymond has described as 'a total cognitive-affective-practical response to God'.[78]

In *Jonathan Edwards the Preacher* (1958) Turnbull made this assertion: 'He was not suited to the pioneer work of a missionary on the frontier and did not master the language of the Indians.'[79] It is true, of course, that Edwards did not master the Indian language; indeed, he preached to the Indians *via* an interpreter, John Wauwaumpequun-aunt, who had been baptized by Edwards' predecessor, John Sergeant, at the age of 17 in 1740.[80] But the issue of Edwards' suitability as a

[78] McClymond, p. 108.
[79] Turnbull, p. 26.
[80] I am indebted at this point to Wheeler, p. 165.

pioneer missionary on the frontier is quite a different matter. We concede that there is a certain *prima facie* incongruity about New England's greatest intellect, premier theologian, and leading preacher living in virtual exile on the very borders of civilization as a missionary to the Indians. But God's thoughts are not our thoughts, neither are our ways his ways; and a very good case can be made that Jonathan Edwards' ministry as a whole during his seven years at Stockbridge was far more successful than might have been expected and, indeed, that it was far more successful than has often been acknowledged.[81] Indeed, the Stockbridge philosopher-theologian-missionary's strategy amongst the Indians reveals a sensitivity and a shrewdness at the pastoral and homiletical level for which, historically, he has seldom been given credit. His ministry to the Indians at Stockbridge demonstrates him to have been, as a preacher, 'wise as a serpent, and harmless as a dove'.[82]

It is evident, then, that imagery constitutes a major rhetorical device in Edwards' sermons, whether preached at New York, Northampton, or Stockbridge. Such a use of imagery is, of course, indicative of a strong imagination. Particularly striking in this respect are what Marsden refers to as 'images of the tenuousness of life'.[83] Conrad Cherry also notes this strand in his imagery: 'Edwards made dramatic use of everyday images to convey this sense of life's uncertainty: an insect suspended over a fire by a slender thread, men walking on a rotten covering stretched over a deep pit, a rock hurled toward a delicate

---

[81] Winslow, for instance, asserts that 'Jonathan Edwards was in almost all ways unfitted for the appointment.' It should be noted, however, that, for all her profound admiration for JE, she clearly had little sympathy with the cause of the gospel of Christ for which the missionary-theologian stood. Winslow, p. 271.

Conversely, Stephen J. Nichols, 'Last of the Mohican Missionaries: Jonathan Edwards at Stockbridge', in *The Legacy of Jonathan Edwards*, pp. 57, 58, gives this assessment: 'Edwards' work at Stockbridge is typically overlooked or even dismissed by most historians or other observers. The chief criticism is that because Edwards never learned the language, his work was of limited impact and importance. Examining the case a little further reveals, however, that such estimates are misguided . . . Additionally, Edwards' sermons reflect his sensitivity to his audience by using numerous metaphors and analogies from nature . . . He uses such imagery as waters and rivers and the motifs of light and darkness profusely.'

[82] Matthew 10:16.

[83] Marsden, *Edwards*, p. 222.

spider's web.'[84] It is important to note, however, that a significant number of his sermons are not characterized by this striking imagery. Indeed, Marsden notes that some of the previously unpublished sermons seem, in comparison with 'Sinners in the Hands of an Angry God', 'calmly intellectual',[85] 'seemingly staid',[86] 'with few emotive images'.[87] Thus it is important that Edwards' use of imagery be put in perspective.

Nevertheless, it is evident that he had at his disposal a powerful imaginative faculty; and that is all the more remarkable when it is considered that it is found in conjunction with an 'analytical subtlety' and 'reasoning powers'[88] which, in the opinion of B. B. Warfield, were probably unsurpassed. That such a master-logician should be able to balance relentless logic with poetic sensibility is intrinsically remarkable; but this remarkable balance or juxtaposition is itself a part of the secret of the effectiveness of his greatest sermons. Many of the images utilized are biblical; many of them are non-biblical in the sense that they are images of his own devising; and some of the images are purportedly divinely-given shadows, but questionably so. Some of the images are relatively sophisticated; and others, as in the case of the Stockbridge Indian sermons, are radically simplified. Sometimes, as in 'Christ, the Light of the World', the images are significantly extended and brilliantly elaborated; and at other times, as in 'Sinners in the Hands of an Angry God', they are strikingly and brilliantly massed. There can be no doubt, however, that, considered *in toto*, Jonathan Edwards' use of imagery reveals on his part a remarkable versatility, flexibility, and adaptability.

---

[84] Conrad Cherry, 'Imagery and Analysis: Jonathan Edwards on Revivals of Religion', in *Jonathan Edwards: His Life and Influence*, p. 23.

[85] Marsden, 'Foreword', in *The Salvation of Souls*, p. 12.

[86] Ibid.

[87] Ibid.

[88] Warfield, p. 528.

13

REPETITION

Jonathan Edwards' *Notes on Scripture* contain an interesting entry that relates to Genesis 2:17: 'Dying, thou shalt die . . .' In this entry he observes that 'such a repetition or doubling of a word, according to the idiom of the Hebrew tongue, is as much as our speaking a word once with a very extraordinary emphasis. But such a great emphasis . . . sometimes signifies certainty, at other times extremity, and sometimes both.'[1] There can be no doubt but that the skilful use of repetition is a very significant feature of Edwards' preaching. Kimnach, who, of all the Yale editors, has engaged in the most detailed literary analysis of Edwards' Sermons and Discourses, acknowledges this fact when he refers to 'repetition' as part of 'Edwards' essential rhetorical arsenal'.[2] Indeed, Kimnach describes 'repetition' as 'the most pervasive of all Edwards's literary devices'[3]:

> Simple and incremental repetition, sanctioned in Edwards's eyes by Hebrew poetry, are employed widely and effectively for the same end: to induce a maximum of contemplation with a minimum of verbal deflection from the subject of meditation. Thus Edwards is inclined to employ repetition not only when exhorting and inculcating, but likewise in the most contemplative passages. By restating, the preacher achieves both increased emphasis and the sense of continuity in time, dramatizing both the importance and the endurance of the subject handled.[4]

---

[1] Cited *Works*, 15:310.
[2] *Works*, 10:294.
[3] Kimnach, 'Pursuit of Reality', p. 114.
[4] Ibid., pp. 114-115.

'The Free and Voluntary Suffering and Death of Christ' is a sermon on John 10:18: 'No man taketh it from me, but I lay it down of myself.' There are, in fact, two manuscripts of this sermon extant, the first of which is undated and was, therefore, probably preached prior to 1733, and the second of which was first preached in April 1736. Edwards' Doctrine commences thus: 'Christ did not kill himself: the death of Christ was a murder.'[5] But it is in the course of his Application that his rhetorical intensity, which is *inter alia* often reflected in his use of repetition, first emerges:

> Christ as God perfectly knew the sins of men all eternity. But it has been meet that he also as man should have an extraordinary view of the wickedness of men given him at the time when he died for the wickedness of men, and this he had given him in the cruelty of those that put him to death. That so Christ might, at the time when he suffered to make atonement for the sins of men, have the sins of men set before him in its own colors, it pleased God so to order it that these sufferings should be caused by the sins of men. *It was the wickedness or corruption that is in men* that Christ died to make atonement for, and Christ had enough to impress upon him a sense of the vileness, and hatefulness, and unreasonableness of men's corruption and wickedness in the time of his suffering; *for it was the wickedness of men* that contrived and effected his sufferings. *It was the wickedness of men* that agreed with Judas: *it was the wickedness of men* that betrayed him, and apprehended him, and bound him, and led him away like a malefactor; and *[it] was by men's wickedness* that he was arraigned, and falsely accused, and unjustly judged; *it was by men's wickedness* that he was reproached, mocked, buffeted, and spit upon; *it was by the sins of men* that Barabbas was preferred before him. And *it was the sins of men* that scourged him, and led him away to crucify him; *it was {the sins of men}* that laid the cross on him to bear: *it was {the sins of men}* that nailed him to the cross, and put him to so cruel and ignominious a death. This tended to give Christ as man a lively sense of the greatness and . hatefulness of the sins and depravity of men, and what wickedness

there was in the heart of men, at the same time that he died to make atonement for men's wickedness it tended to make him then to see clearly what that sin was that he suffered for; . . . [6]

'Intensity permeates the prose',[7] observes Lesser with regard to this sermon – an intensity that is unquestionably enhanced by the use of repetition. Indeed, 'intensity' is described by Kimnach as one of 'his distinguishing traits as a master of the sermon'.[8] It is interesting to note that Edwards himself appears often to have assigned, in retrospect, what the Yale editors have interpreted as a 'decibel rating'.[9] This appears to be an 'intensity rating'. 'The Free and Voluntary Suffering and Death of Christ' received the very high rating of nine symbols. Lesser makes this observation with regard to the sermons of 1734-1738 in general and this sermon in particular:

> Just above the text on the first leaf of each of three sermon manuscripts in this volume, Edwards entered a series of successive symbols in later ink, a 'decibel rating' of sorts, a gauge (and recollection) of its rhetoric: in 'Light in a Dark World,' a 'Dark Heart'... he logged four such symbols to signify a fairly powerful rhetoric, in 'The Many Mansions' . . . six symbols to signify a powerful rhetoric, and here fully nine to signify a most powerful rhetoric, a level of imprecation rarely exceeded or seldom met in the extant sermon manuscripts.[10]

'A Warning to Professors' demonstrates well this predilection for repetition. In the section of the sermon which summons to self-examination Edwards employs a very pointed repetition of the phrase 'you that':

> Thus, I make no doubt some will be apt to do, in applying to

---

[6] Ibid., pp. 508-509. Emphasis added.

[7] Ibid., p. 491.

[8] Kimnach, 'Pursuit of Reality', p. 111. 'These traits are specificity, unity, and intensity.' Ibid.

[9] Kimnach discusses the question of these 'decibel ratings' in some detail. Whilst acknowledging that the meaning of the marks or signs which appear on certain sermons is 'dubious' and 'obscure', Kimnach concludes that the sign was originated by JE. He concludes further that the signs probably constituted 'a kind of "decibel rating" for imprecatory sermons.' *Works*, 10:166 n. 4.

[10] *Works*, 19:491.

themselves this use of examination, if they can be persuaded to apply it to themselves at all. Whether these things be true of you, let your own consciences speak, *you that* neglect secret prayer; *you that* live in secret, unclean, lascivious actions; *you that* indulge an inordinate appetite for strong drink; *you that* defraud or oppress others; *you that* indulge a spirit of revenge and hatred towards your neighbour.[11]

Towards the close of this same sermon Edwards again makes skilful use of repetition with the clause 'It is a wonder' as he emphasizes five times the astonishing nature of God's patience and longsuffering. It is interesting to note the acceleration in the repetition of this clause towards the close of the passage:

It is a wonder of God's patience, that he doth not break forth upon you, and strike you dead in a moment; for you profane holy things in a more dreadful manner than Uzza did, when yet God struck him dead for his error. And whereas he was struck dead for only one offence; you are guilty of the same sin from week to week, and from day to day.

It is a wonder that God suffers you to live upon earth, that he has not, with a thunderbolt of his wrath, struck you down to the bottomless pit long ago. You that are allowedly and voluntarily living in sin, who have gone on hitherto in sin, are still going on, and do not design any other than to go on yet; *it is a wonder* that the Almighty's thunder lies still, and suffers you to sit in his house, or to live upon earth. *It is a wonder* that the earth will bear you, and that hell doth not swallow you up. *It is a wonder* that fire doth not come down from heaven, or come up from hell, and devour you; that hell-flames do not enlarge themselves to reach you, and that the bottomless pit hath not swallowed you up.[12]

In the following passage, which occurs towards the close of Edwards' Application in 'Wicked Men Inconsistent with Themselves', it is the mesmerizing repetition of the construction 'why, when . . .' followed by that of the verb 'condemn' that is particularly striking:

[11] *Works* (Hickman), 2:189. Emphasis added.
[12] Ibid., p. 190. Emphasis added.

So when wicked men are enquired of *why, when* they professed to believe a future state, they took no more pains to prepare for it; *why, when* they professed to be the followers of Christ the Lamb of God, they were no more like him; *why, when* they owned him for their head, and expressed such wonderful love to him, they could turn and become his enemies; *why, when* they lived in hope of a life of such unspeakable glory in heaven, they set their affections wholly on this world; *why,* seeing they made such a show of regard to God and their duty at one time, they discovered such a total disregard at another; *why, when* they made such pretences to religion, and had such appearances of it in some things, they were so irreligious and wicked in others; what will they answer? Wicked men will appear *self-condemned* every way: their own reason and their own consciences, their own mouths and their own actions, have *condemned* them: their reason and consciences will still *condemn* them, and God will *condemn* them, and men and angels will and must *condemn* them: so that they will appear universally *condemned;* they will have nothing to say for themselves, nor will any one have any thing to say for them.[13]

It is by means of this construction 'why, when . . .' that Edwards establishes a remarkable juxtaposition between appearance and reality. Whereas the temporal clause (when) expresses the more positive, hopeful aspects of his hearers' profession, the interrogative clause (why) expresses the more negative, pessimistic reality. The sheer repetition of this construction in a subordinate clause is such that it continually anticipates the deferred arrival of the main verb in the words 'what will they answer?' J. I. Packer's observation to the effect that Edwards' preaching is at times 'almost hypnotic in its power to rivet attention on the successive folds of truth sliding out into view'[14] is well demonstrated by this passage. It contains one of the finest of his 'rhythmic devices'.[15]

In 'The Final Judgment' Edwards makes the following very pointed use of repetition as he addresses 'those who live in secret wickedness':[16]

[13] Ibid., p. 928. Emphasis added.
[14] Packer, 'Jonathan Edwards and Revival', in *A Quest for Godliness*, p. 314.
[15] *Works*, 10:237.
[16] *Works* (Hickman), 2:199.

Before human judges are brought only those things which are known; but before this judge shall be brought the most 'hidden things of darkness, and even counsels of the heart,' 1 Cor. iv. 5. *All your* secret uncleanness, all your secret fraud and injustice, *all your* lascivious desires, wishes, and designs, *all your* inward covetousness, which is idolatry, *all your* malicious, envious, and revengeful thoughts and purposes, whether brought forth into practice or not, shall then be made manifest, and you shall be judged according to them. Of these things, however secret, there will be need of no other evidence than the testimony of God and of your own consciences.[17]

In 'Christ's Agony' Edwards once again utilizes repetition for the sake of emphasis – here his emphasis falls upon the corruption and wickedness by which Christ was surrounded at his crucifixion. One of the interesting features of his use of repetition here is the element of slight variation that occurs within the reiterated phrase itself:

> *It was the corruption and wickedness of men* that contrived and effected his death; *it was the wickedness of men* that agreed with Judas, *it was the wickedness of men* that betrayed him, and that apprehended him, and bound him, and led him away like a malefactor; *it was by men's corruption and wickedness* that he was arraigned, and falsely accused, and unjustly judged. *It was by men's wickedness* that he was reproached, mocked, buffeted, and spit upon. *It was by men's wickedness* that Barabbas was preferred before him. *It was men's wickedness* that laid the cross upon him to bear, and that nailed him to it, and put him to so cruel and ignominious a death. This tended to give Christ an extraordinary sense of the greatness and hatefulness of the depravity of mankind.[18]

In the following passage from 'The Excellency of Christ' the word 'never' is reiterated for the purpose of highlighting the glory of Christ in his last sufferings. Lesser describes Edwards' use of repetition here as 'a concatenation of nevers'[19] :

---

[17] Ibid. Emphasis added.
[18] Ibid., p. 870. Emphasis added.
[19] *Works,* 19:561.

Then was Christ in the greatest degree of his humiliation, and yet by that, above all other things, his divine glory appears. Christ's humiliation was great, in being born in such a low condition, of a poor virgin, and in a stable. His humiliation was great, in being subject to Joseph the carpenter, and Mary his mother, and afterwards living in poverty, so as not to have where to lay his head; and in suffering such manifold and bitter reproaches as he suffered, while he went about preaching and working miracles. But his humiliation was *never* so great as it was in his last sufferings, beginning with his agony in the garden, till he expired on the cross. *Never* was he subject to such ignominy as then; *never* did he suffer so much pain in his body, or so much sorrow in his soul; *never* was he in so great an exercise of his condescension, humility, meekness, and patience, as he was in these last sufferings; *never* was his divine glory and majesty covered with so thick and dark a veil; *never* did he so empty himself and make himself of no reputation, as at this time. And yet, *never* was his divine glory so manifested, by any act of his, as in yielding himself up to these sufferings. When the fruit of it came to appear, and the mystery and ends of it to be unfolded in its issue, then did the glory of it appear; then did it appear as the most glorious act of Christ that ever he exercised towards the creature.[20]

'Men Naturally God's Enemies' contains a remarkably probing passage in which Edwards combines his use of the searching question with his use of repetition. It is a fine example of that 'element of attack' which Martyn Lloyd-Jones regarded as an essential aspect of true preaching:

What other account can you give of your own carriage, but only your being God's enemy? *What other account can be given* of your opposing God in your ways; walking so exceeding contrary to him, contrary to his counsels, contrary to his commands, and contrary to his glory? *What other account can be given* of your casting so much contempt upon God; your setting him so low; your acting so much against his authority, and against his kingdom and interest in the world? *What other account can be given* of your so setting your

---

[20] *Works* (Hickman), 1:684. Emphasis added.

will in opposition to God's will, and that so obstinately, for so long a time, against so many warnings as you have had? *What other account can be given* of your joining so much with Satan, in the opposition he is making to the kingdom of God in the world? And that you will join with him against God, though it be so much against your own interest, and though you expose yourself by it to everlasting misery?[21]

In the spring of 1728 Edwards preached a sermon on Daniel 4:35: 'And all the inhabitants of the earth are reputed as nothing: and he doeth according to his will in the army of heaven, and among the inhabitants of the earth: and none can stay his hand, or say unto him, What doest thou?' It is a text that emphasizes the absolute sovereignty of God – Edwards' Doctrine here is that 'God does whatever he pleases.' In the course of the sermon he makes a brilliant use of what Kimnach terms 'incremental repetition':[22]

> He created the earth *as he pleased;* he made a place for the sea *where he pleased;* he raised the mountains *where he pleased,* and sunk the valleys *where he pleased.* He created what sort of creatures to inhabit the earth and waters *he pleased,* and *when he pleased* he brought a flood of waters and covered the whole earth, and destroyed all its inhabitants.
>
> And *when he pleases,* he'll dissolve this curious frame of the world and break all to pieces and set it on fire, when the earth and all the works that are therein shall be burnt up and the heavens shall be dissolved and rolled together as a scroll; *when God pleases,* he'll roll all together as when a man takes down a tent. In such things as these relating to the material world does God manifest his sovereignty.[23]

This passage contains a remarkable fourfold shift in the use of the reiterated clause, (variously) 'as he pleased', 'where he pleased', 'when he pleased', 'and when he pleases'. Firstly, there is a shift in the *theme* of the reiterated clause; at the end of the first paragraph Edwards moves from

---

[21] Ibid., 2:135.
[22] *Works,* 10:238. Emphasis added.
[23] Cited ibid., p. 238. Emphasis added.

the theme of creation to that of judgment. Secondly, there is a shift from *place to time* in the reiterated clause – a shift from the word 'where' to the word 'when'; he moves from the sovereignty of God with regard to the place of creation in the beginning to the sovereignty of God with regard to the time of judgment at the end. This coincides with the shift in theme. Thirdly, there is a shift in the *position* of the reiterated clause; at the close of the first paragraph Edwards transfers the clause from the end of the sentence to the beginning. This coincides with the shift in theme and with the shift from place to time. Fourthly, there is a shift in the *tense* of the reiterated clause; at the outset of the second paragraph he shifts from a past reference ('and when he pleased') to a future reference ('and when he pleases'). It will be evident that there is not only a beautiful rhythm and cadence about this passage; there is also something deeply ominous and foreboding about it. The hearer is left waiting for the impending sovereign intervention of the great God in the final judgment.

With regard to 'the rhythmic devices of repetition and parallelism'[24] evident in a passage such as this, Kimnach reports that 'it has been remarked that "repetition of words and constructions is the essence of his style." His earlier sermon manuscripts indicate that a tendency to repetition was as innate in Edwards as his love of concrete images and details. But genius and toil turned what might well have been a rhetorically fatal vice into a source of formidable literary power.'[25] More significantly still, this 'tendency to repetition' became, under the tight rein of a shrewd, discriminating judgment, a source of formidable rhetorical and homiletical power. Indeed, repetition constitutes a crucial aspect of that 'movement'[26] which Dabney regarded as one of the 'cardinal requisites of the sermon'.[27] There can be little doubt but that Edwards' skilful use of repetition is a very significant aspect of that compelling, almost mesmerizing, momentum by which his finest sermons are characterized.

---

[24] Ibid., p. 237.
[25] Ibid.
[26] Dabney, *Sacred Rhetoric*, p. 121.
[27] Ibid.

14

EXCLAMATION

When Kimnach, the Yale editor, defines 'Edwards' essential rhetorical arsenal' as 'vivid imagery, vigorous statement, repetition,
parallelism, and analogy *a fortiori,*'[1] he somewhat surprisingly does
not refer explicitly to Edwards' frequent use of exclamation. It is, of
course, quite possible that Kimnach tacitly subsumes exclamation
under 'vigorous statement'. But the phenomenon of exclamation
is sufficiently prominent in Edwards' sermons to deserve separate
consideration. Indeed, he makes extensive use of all four of the different types of sentence specified by the Oxford philologist, C. T.
Onions: 'Sentences may be divided into the four following classes according to their form or the kind of meaning they express: I. Statements. II. Requests, i.e. commands, wishes, concessions. III Questions.
IV. Exclamations.'[2] Exclamation, for its part, is defined by the *Oxford
Dictionary of English Grammar* as 'a word, phrase, or clause expressing some emotion.'[3] This definition is confirmed by John Eastwood:
'An exclamation is a sentence spoken with emphasis and feeling.'[4]
Exclamations thus clearly presuppose and, indeed, express this note
of emphasis, excitement, and emotion. There can be no question but
that exclamation constitutes a significant part of 'Edwards' essential
rhetorical arsenal' and thus constitutes a significant element in that
liveliness and vigour in his sermons to which, historically, insufficient
attention has been given.

[1] *Works,* 10:294.
[2] Cited in *Oxford Dictionary of English Grammar,* 1994 ed., s.v. 'exclamation'.
[3] Ibid.
[4] John Eastwood, *Oxford Guide to English Grammar* (Oxford: The University Press, 1994),
p. 24.

Many of his sermons contain significant sections, indeed, often entire paragraphs, that are dominated by the classic exclamative words 'how' or 'what'. In the course of his doctrinal analysis of 'Guilt' in 'Christ Exalted' Edwards suddenly breaks forth into the following exclamatory lament:

> What multiplied and what aggravated sins some men are guilty of! What guilt lies on some particular persons! How much more on some particular populous cities! How much more still on this wicked world! How much does the guilt of the world transcend all account, all expression, all powers of numbers or measures! And above all, how vast is the guilt of the world, in all ages, from the beginning to the end of it! To what a pitch has guilt risen! The world being, as it were, on every side, loaded with it, as with mountains heaped on mountains, above the clouds and stars of heaven.[5]

Later in the same sermon he again makes striking use of the exclamative as he emphasizes the magnitude of Satan's rebellion against God and then demonstrates the glorious superiority of Christ over Satan and all his instruments:

> God had appointed his Son to be the heir of the world; but the devil has contested this matter with him, and has strove to set himself up as God of the world. And how exceedingly has the devil exalted himself against Christ! How did he oppose him as he dwelt among the Jews, in his tabernacle and temple! And how did he oppose him when on earth! And how has he opposed him since his ascension! What great and mighty works has Satan brought to pass in the world! How many Babels has he built up to heaven, in his opposition to the Son of God! How exceeding proud and haughty has he appeared in his opposition! How have he and his instruments, and sin, affliction, and death, of which he is the father, raged against Christ! But yet Christ, in the work of redemption, appears infinitely above them all. In this work he triumphs over them, however they have dealt proudly; and they all

---

[5] *Works* (Hickman), 2:214.

appear under his feet. In this the glory of the Son of God, in the work of redemption, remarkably appears.[6]

'Man's Natural Blindness in the Things of Religion' contains a striking passage in which Edwards' reiterated use of the construction 'How …! And yet how …!' or 'How …! But yet how …!' is skillfully utilized both for the sake of strong emphasis and powerful contrast:

> The desperate blindness that is natural to men, appears in their being so ignorant and blind in things that are so clear and *plain*. Thus if we consider how great God is, and how dreadful sin against him must be, and how much sin we are guilty of, and of what importance it is that his infinite Majesty should be vindicated; how plain is it, that man's righteousness is insufficient! And yet how greatly will men confide in it! how will they ascribe more to it, than can be ascribed to the righteousness of the sinless and glorious angels of heaven. What can be more plain in itself, than that eternal things are of infinitely greater importance than temporal things? And yet how hard is it thoroughly to convince men of it! How plain is it, that eternal misery in hell is infinitely to be dreaded! And yet how few appear to be thoroughly convinced of this! How plain is it, that life is uncertain! And yet how much otherwise do most men think! How plain is it, that it is the highest prudence in matters of infinite concern to improve the first opportunity, without trusting to another! But yet how few are convinced of this! How reasonable is it, considering that God is a wise and just being, to suppose that there shall be a future state of rewards and punishments, wherein every man shall receive according to his works! And yet, how does this seem like a dream to most men![7]

'The Justice of God in the Damnation of Sinners', unquestionably one of Edwards' greatest sermons, contains the following passage in the early stages of the Application. It demonstrates the preacher's use of exclamation in conjunction with his pointed use of the indicative in the second person:

---

[6] Ibid., pp. 216-217.
[7] Ibid., p. 252.

How *many* sorts of wickedness have you not been guilty of! How manifold have been the abominations of your life! What profaneness and contempt of God has been exercised by you! How little regard have you had to the Scriptures, to the word preached, to sabbaths, and sacraments! How profanely have you talked, many of you, about those things that are holy! After what manner have many of you kept God's holy day, not regarding the holiness of the time, nor caring what you thought of in it! Yea, you have not only spent the time in worldly, vain, and unprofitable thoughts, but immoral thoughts; pleasing yourself with the reflection on past acts of wickedness, and in contriving new acts. Have not you spent much holy time in gratifying your lusts in your imaginations; yea, not only holy time, but the very time of God's public worship, when you have appeared in God's more immediate presence? How have you not only not attended to the worship, but have in the mean time been feasting your lusts, and wallowing yourself in abominable uncleanness! How many sabbaths have you spent, one after another, in a most wretched manner! Some of you not only in worldly and wicked thoughts, but also a very wicked outward behaviour! When you on sabbath-days have got along with your wicked companions, how has holy time been treated among you! What kind of conversation has there been! Yea, how have some of you, by a very indecent carriage, openly dishonoured and cast contempt on the sacred services of God's house, and holy day! And what you have done some of you alone, what wicked practices there have been in secret, even in holy time, God and your own consciences know.

And how have you behaved yourself in the time of family prayer! And what a trade have many of you made of absenting yourselves from the worship of the families you belong to, for the sake of vain company! And how have you continued in the neglect of secret prayer! Therein wilfully living in a known sin, going abreast against as plain a command as any in the Bible! Have you not been one that has cast off fear, and restrained prayer before God?[8]

---

[8] Ibid., 1:671. It is interesting to note that the Yale edition has interpreted much of this passage as interrogatory rather than as exclamative and has therefore utilized question

If the emphasis in the passage just cited falls upon 'the exceeding sinfulness of sin', the emphasis in the following passage falls upon 'wrath to the uttermost'. 'Wrath upon the Wicked to the Uttermost' is a powerfully awakening sermon that was preached in May 1735 in the final stages of the revival in Northampton. The sermon is based upon 1 Thessalonians 2:16: 'To fill up their sins alway; for the wrath is come upon them to the uttermost.' This passage is found in the Application and it demonstrates both Edwards' skilful use of repetition and his sustained use of exclamation:

> How *dreadful* the wrath of God is, when it is executed to the uttermost. To make you in some measure sensible of that, I desire you to consider whose wrath it is. The wrath of a king is the roaring of a lion; but this is the wrath of Jehovah, the Lord God Omnipotent. Let us consider, what can we rationally think of it? How dreadful must be the wrath of such a Being, when it comes upon a person to the uttermost, without any pity, or moderation, or merciful circumstances! What must be the uttermost of his wrath, who made heaven and earth by the word of his power; who spake, and it was done, who commanded, and it stood fast! What must his wrath be, who commandeth the sun, and it rises not, and sealeth up the stars! What must his wrath be, who shaketh the earth out of its place, and causeth the pillars of heaven to tremble! What must his wrath be, who rebuketh the sea, and maketh it dry, who removeth the mountains out of their places, and overturneth them in his anger! What must his wrath be, whose majesty is so awful, that no man could live in the sight of it! What must the wrath of such a Being be, when it comes to the uttermost, when he makes his majesty appear and shine bright in the misery of wicked men! And what is a worm of the dust before the fury and under the weight of this wrath, which the stoutest devils cannot bear, but utterly sink, and are crushed under it. – Consider how dreadful

---

marks rather than exclamation marks for part of it. We believe, however, that the passage reads more naturally if it is understood as emphatic exclamation rather than as searching interrogation. See *Works*, 19:348-49. JE soon resumes this powerful expostulation against the sins of the people of Northampton with a further relentless use of the exclamative, in conjunction with a very pointed use of the second person pronoun, ibid., pp. 671-672.

the wrath of God is sometimes in this world, only in a little taste or view of it. Sometimes, when God only enlightens conscience, to have some sense of his wrath, it causes the stout-hearted to cry out; nature is ready to sink under it, when indeed it is but a little glimpse of divine wrath that is seen. This hath been observed in many cases. But if a slight taste and apprehension of wrath be so dreadful and intolerable, what must it be, when it comes upon persons to the uttermost! When a few drops or little sprinkling of wrath is so distressing and overbearing to the soul, how must it be when God opens the flood-gates, and lets the mighty deluge of his wrath come pouring down upon men's guilty heads, and brings in all his waves and billows upon their souls! How little of God's wrath will sink them! Psal. ii. 12. 'When his wrath is kindled but a little, blessed are all they that put their trust in him.'[9]

In his famous sermon 'Sinners in the Hands of an Angry God' Edwards again makes very powerful use of exclamation in order to convey great emphasis, urgency, and intensity. The following passage in the course of the Application begins with two very striking exclamatory noun phrases:

The fury of God! the fierceness of Jehovah! O how dreadful must that be! Who can utter or conceive what such expressions carry in them? But it is also 'the fierceness and wrath of *Almighty* God.' As though there would be a very great manifestation of his almighty power in what the fierceness of his wrath should inflict; as though omnipotence should be as it were enraged, and exerted, as men are wont to exert their strength in the fierceness of their wrath. Oh! then, what will be the consequence! What will become of the poor worm that shall suffer it! Whose hands can be strong? and whose heart can endure? To what a dreadful, inexpressible, inconceivable depth of misery must the poor creature be sunk who shall be the subject of this![10]

It is important to note that Edwards does not simply make use of exclamation in the context of the themes of sin and judgment.

[9] Ibid., 2:124.
[10] Ibid., p. 10.

In the following passage from 'Christian Cautions' the emphasis falls upon the beauty, the amiableness, and the desirability of holy, righteous, Christian lives:

> If we live in any way of sin, we live in a way whereby God is *dishonoured;* but the honour of God ought to be supremely regarded by all. If every one would make it his great care in all things to obey God, to live justly and holily, to walk in every thing according to christian rules; and would maintain a strict, watchful, and scrutinous eye over himself, to see if there were no wicked way in him; would give diligence to amend whatsoever is amiss; would avoid every unholy, unchristian way; and if the practice of all were universally as becometh Christians; how greatly would this be to the glory of God, and of Jesus Christ! How greatly would it be to the credit and honour of religion! How would it tend to excite a high esteem of religion in spectators, and to recommend a holy life! How would it stop the mouths of objectors and opposers! How beautiful and amiable would religion then appear, when exemplified in the lives of Christians, not maimed and mutilated, but whole and entire, as it were in its true shape, having all its parts and its proper beauty! Religion would then appear to be an amiable thing indeed.[11]

Thus Edwards' use of exclamation was not merely denunciatory; it was also doxological. This doxological use of the exclamative is perhaps supremely seen in 'Heaven is a World of Love'. The doctrinal section of this sermon closes with a beautiful description of heaven, of which we cite part:

> And all this in a garden of love, the Paradise of God, where everything has a cast of holy love, and everything conspires to promote and stir up love, and nothing to interrupt its exercises; where everything is fitted by an all-wise God for the enjoyment of love under the greatest advantages. And all this shall be without any fading of the beauty of the objects beloved, or any decaying of love in the lover, and any satiety in the faculty which enjoys love. O!

[11] Ibid., p. 174.

what tranquility may we conclude there is in such a world as this! Who can express the sweetness of this peace? What a calm is this, what a heaven of rest is here to arrive at after persons have gone through a world of storms and tempests, a world of pride, and selfishness, and envy, and malice, and scorn, and contempt, and contention and war! What a Canaan of rest, a land flowing with milk and honey to come to after one has gone through a great and terrible wilderness, full of spiteful and poisonous serpents, where no rest could be found! What joy may we conclude springs up in the hearts of the saints after they have passed their wearisome pilgrimage to be brought to such a paradise! Here is joy unspeakable indeed; here is humble, holy, divine joy in its perfection.[12]

---

[12] *Works*, 8:385. I have, in the main, utilized the Yale edition here rather than the 1852 edition. In view of the obviously exclamatory character of this passage I have replaced two question marks in the Yale edition with two exclamation marks. See earlier observation on 'The Justice of God in the Damnation of Sinners'.

15

THE USE OF SCRIPTURE

Writing in 1830, Sereno E. Dwight gave this assessment of his great-grandfather's grasp of the truth of the Scriptures: 'His knowledge of the Bible, evinced in his sermons – in the number of relevant passages which he brings to enforce every position, in his exact discernment of the true scope of each, in his familiar acquaintance with the drift of the whole Scriptures on the subject, and in the logical precision with which he derives his principles from them – is probably unrivalled.'[1] Similarly, Kimnach, writing in 1992 on the occasion of the publication of the first of the six volumes of Jonathan Edwards' *Sermons and Discourses* by Yale University Press, gave this assessment: 'His sermons, alone, prove Edwards to have been a "textuary among textuaries," one of the most imaginative and profound students of the Bible's style and substance in colonial America . . . The aptitude and penetration displayed in his use of scriptural passages are truly extraordinary. Any consideration of Edwards' literary qualities must give priority to his use of the Scripture.'[2] These assessments of Edwards' use of the Scriptures in his sermons are just. His sermons do indeed reveal a very remarkable acquaintance with and marshalling of the Scriptures. The New England divine was unquestionably, like Apollos, 'mighty in the Scriptures'.

The secret of this remarkable acquaintance with the Scriptures emerges in Edwards' 'Resolutions'. Most of the 'Resolutions' were written in 1722 during the 'New York period' when he was a young man of

[1] *Works* (Hickman), 1:clxxxix.
[2] *Works*, 10:207.

19 years of age.[3] His 28th Resolution demonstrates the pre-eminent position occupied by the study of the Scriptures:

> 28. *Resolved*, To study the Scriptures so steadily, constantly, and frequently, as that I may find, and plainly perceive, myself to grow in the knowledge of the same.[4]

With regard to the 'Resolutions' Kimnach observes that '28 establishes the Bible as the central book in Edwards' reading program.'[5] It is a valid assumption that a significant proportion of the thirteen hours each day, which Edwards himself claimed to spend habitually in study, was spent in the study of the Scriptures; and it is evident that there is the closest possible connection between his use of time, his study and knowledge of the Scriptures, and his ability in marshalling and utilizing that knowledge in his sermons.

'The Character of Paul an Example to Christians', in which the Apostle Paul is set forth as an example to all believers, contains the following passage that demonstrates the remarkable facility with which Edwards adduces particular scriptures to confirm his assertions:

> The things that grieve other men are outward crosses; losses in estates, or falling under contempt, or bodily sufferings. But these things grieved not him. He made little account of them. The things that grieved him, were those that hurt the interests of religion; and about those his tears were shed. Thus he was exceedingly grieved, and wept greatly, for the corruptions that had crept into the church of Corinth, which was the occasion of his writing his first epistle to them. 2 Cor ii. 4. 'For out of much affliction and anguish of heart, I wrote unto you, with many tears.' The things about which other men are jealous, are their worldly advantages and pleasures. If these are threatened, their jealousy is excited, since they are above all things dear to them. But the things that kindled the apostle's jealousy, were those that seemed to threaten the interests of religion, and the good of the church: 2 Cor. xi. 2, 3. 'For I am jealous over you with a godly jealous; for

---

[3] See ibid., p. 55.
[4] Ibid.
[5] Ibid.

I have espoused you to one husband, that I may present you as a chaste virgin to Christ. But I fear, lest by any means, as the serpent beguiled Eve through his subtlety, so your minds should be corrupted from the simplicity that is in Christ.' The things at which other men rejoice are their amassing earthly treasures, their being advanced to honours, their being possessed of outward pleasures and delights. But these excited not the apostle's joy; but when he saw or heard of any thing by which the interests of religion were promoted, and the church of Christ prospered, then he rejoiced: 1 Thess. i. 3. 'Remembering without ceasing your work of faith and labour of love, and patience of hope in our Lord Jesus Christ, in the sight of God and our Father.' And chapter ii. 20. 'Ye are our glory and joy.' He rejoiced at those things, however dear they cost him, how much soever he lost by them in his temporal interest, if the welfare of religion and the good of souls were promoted; Phil. ii. 16, 17. 'Holding forth the word of life, that I may rejoice in the day of Christ, that I have not run in vain, neither laboured in vain. Yea, and if I be offered upon the sacrifice and service of your faith, I joy and rejoice with you all.' He rejoiced at the stedfastness of saints: Col ii. 5. 'For though I be absent in the flesh, yet am I with you in the spirit, joying and beholding your order, and the stedfastness of your faith in Christ.' And he rejoiced at the conviction of sinners, and in whatever tended to it. He rejoiced at any good which was done, though by others, and though it was done accidentally by his enemies: Phil. i. 15, 16, 17, 18. 'Some indeed preach Christ even of envy and strife; and some also of good will. The one preach Christ of contention, not sincerely, supposing to add affliction to my bonds. But the other of love, knowing that I am set for the defence of the gospel. What then? notwithstanding, every way, whether in pretence or in truth, Christ is preached; and I therein do rejoice, yea, and will rejoice.' When the apostle heard any thing of this nature, it was good news to him: 1 Thess. iii. 6, 7. 'But now, when Timotheus came from you unto us, and brought us good tidings of your faith and charity, and that ye have good remembrance of us always, desiring greatly to see us, as we also you; therefore, brethren, we were comforted over you in all our affliction and distress by your faith.' When he heard such tidings, his heart was wont to be enlarged in the praises of God: Col. i. 3, 4. 'We give thanks to God and the Father of our Lord Jesus Christ, praying always for you, since we heard of your faith in Christ Jesus, and of the love which ye have to all the saints.' He was not only wont to praise God when he first heard such tidings, but as often as he thought of such things, they were so joyful to him, that he readily praised God. Phil. i. 3, 4, 5. 'I thank my God upon every remembrance of you, always in every prayer of mine for you all making request with joy, for your fellowship in the gospel from the first day until now.' Let us compare ourselves with such an example, and examine how far we are of such a spirit.[6]

This extended passage demonstrates the validity of Kimnach's assessment that 'Edwards' most impressive use of the Scripture is in the very fabric or verbal contexture of his sermons.'[7] The vast majority of his sermons are characterized by a very judicious selection and a very well-integrated use of the Scriptures.

His preaching is, however, also characterized by an occasional tendency to excess in Scripture citation. Kimnach is, we believe, correct when he asserts: 'There are numerous instances in his sermons where the sheer accumulation of Scripture passages obviously surpasses the requirements of scripture proof or even elucidation.'[8] The sermon 'Christ's Agony' contains a striking example of this very thing At one point in his Application Edwards cites, in succession and in full, the Parable of the Unjust Judge, the Parable of the Friend at Midnight, and Christ's encounter with the woman of Canaan.[9] Moreover he precedes these with a citation of Luke vi. 12, which demonstrates 'the engagedness of Christ's spirit in this duty'.[10] Homiletical wisdom would suggest that there is something excessive about such a compilation of Scripture. Kimnach, however, describes his excessive use of Scripture quotation in some sermons as 'a new type of rhetorical argument, incantation'.[11]

---

[6] *Works* (Hickman), 2:861.

[7] *Works*, 10:210.

[8] Ibid.

[9] See *Works* (Hickman), 2:875.

[10] Ibid.

[11] *Works*, 10:210. Kimnach appears to have been influenced in this by Perry Miller who

This Kimnach defines as 'the ritual invocation of the Word through the quotation of Scripture passages at crucial points in the sermon.'[12] It should be noted that it is one thing to contend that Edwards' use of Scripture citation is at times excessive; it is quite another thing to describe it as 'incantation'. The latter is an extravagant assertion.

This tendency to excess in citation from the Scriptures is further demonstrated in 'God Amongst His People', the manuscript of which is marked 'November 1735, Thanksgiving.' Edwards' text on this occasion was Isaiah 12:6: 'Cry out and shout, thou inhabitant of Zion: for great is the Holy One of Israel in the midst of thee.' Lesser makes the following observation on the preacher's sheer accumulation of Scripture citations:

> Though it is an uncommon practice in much of his preaching during the period, he harvests Scripture in broad swaths now, quoting the first five verses from the forty-third of Isaiah in the Doctrine, and then, one upon another, three verses from the fifty-fifth chapter, two from the twenty-ninth, three from the thirty-fifth, and three from the forty-ninth in the Application. Sometimes he reduces a lengthy text to one of more practical size, paring the middle verses of Ps. 111:3-9, for instance, while still preserving the integrity of its narrative; at other times, he all but creates a longer text by reaping a succession of shorter ones, as he does with Ps. 97:12, 22:23, 30:4, 132:9, and 145:10-12 to explain the 'work of praise' expected of saints. He transcribes in whole or in part, in particular or in paraphrase, roughly seven scriptural texts per manuscript page, nearly 150 in all, attributing only half of them. Citations from seventeen books of the Old Testament, including two from Habakkuk, crowd out those from the New Testament by more than six to one, the nearly sixty excerpts from Psalms, twice those from Isaiah, forming a rich mosaic of intricate figures

---

employs the term and the concept of 'incantation' in his intellectual biography. Indeed, in seeking to analyse JE's originality, Miller selects 'incantation' as the quintessence of that originality: 'Therefore to read him in the hope of discriminating between what is his and what is traditional, one must seize upon occasional passages, definitions by the way, the peculiar use of key words, and above all the use of words as incantation.' *Edwards*, p. 48.

[12] Ibid.

and tropes. His biblicism, always remarkable, if seldom on display like this, is nothing short of stunning here. [13]

It is important to note, however, that it is one thing to assert that Edwards' *knowledge* of the Scriptures is stunning; with this we readily concur. It is quite another thing to assert that his *use* of the Scriptures in this particular sermon is stunning; with this we do not concur. The extent to which the Scriptures should be cited in any given sermon is, of course, ultimately a matter of judgment. Moreover, it should be noted that this is essentially a matter of *homiletical*, not *literary*, judgment; and if it be deemed churlish to criticize the great American preacher at times in this respect, it should be further noted that the validity of this criticism, in principle, can be demonstrated by the kind of *reductio ad absurdum* of which Edwards himself was particularly fond. Thus if it be maintained that it is wrong to criticize this, or any other, preacher concerning the *quantity* of Scripture citation in any given sermon precisely because the Scriptures are the word of God, then that is tantamount to asserting that there is, in principle, no limit to the quantity of Scripture that might be cited in any given sermon; thus a sermon that consisted, let us say, of biblical citation to the extent of 99% would be supposedly beyond criticism and even stunning!

It is important to note, therefore, that some homileticians advise strongly (and, we believe, correctly) against the overuse of the citation of the Scriptures in the sermon. J. W. Alexander (1804-1859), for instance, specifically warns against this danger: 'Avoid heaping up of texts, like stones without mortar.'[14] The 'stones', in Alexander's mind, are obviously the particular scriptures cited and the 'mortar' is obviously the explanation or exposition of those scriptures. Alexander's point here is that it is homiletically undesirable to accumulate too many scriptures, one upon the other, without that cohesion supplied by their explication and exposition in the preacher's own words.

It is interesting to note that the passage cited above from 'The Character of Paul an Example to Christians' demonstrates another sig-

---

[13] *Works*, 19:451.
[14] James W. Alexander, *Thoughts on Preaching: Being Contributions to Homiletics* (repr., Edinburgh: Banner of Truth, 1975), p. 3.

nificant homiletical trait on Edwards' part in his adduction of parallel passages, namely, that of leading with his ideas and then confirming those ideas with the citation of appropriate scriptures. Thus whilst the sermon itself invariably leads with the text, which is then expounded, the parallel Scripture citations are often placed after the ideas and are adduced in confirmation of them, generally at the close of a paragraph. This excellent homiletical practice of leading with the ideas in the main body of the sermon is further demonstrated by the following passage from 'Living Peaceably One With Another'. This sermon was preached at Bolton, Connecticut, in December 1723. Bolton was a hamlet situated about fifteen miles southeast of Edwards' home in East Windsor. It had only recently been settled, and for the most part by people from Windsor and East Windsor itself. To his regret, his father, Timothy Edwards, had been responsible for inveigling him away from New York in order that he might assume a pastorate that was nearer to home and thus closer to the paternal eye. Thus it was on November 11 that Jonathan Edwards had signed the Bolton church-book and had officially begun his second pastorate. The young Yale graduate was to remain at Bolton until May 1724. But his experience at Bolton stood in stark contrast to that at New York. His parting from New York was clearly a 'melancholy parting'[15]; that from Bolton, in order to assume a tutorship at Yale, was clearly one of relief. The basic problem at Bolton was that of contentiousness – the theme the young preacher specifically addressed in this sermon. Minkema notes that the sermon 'contains some pointed remarks about "this town,"... suggesting that this backwoods hamlet was not a peaceable kingdom.'[16] 'They were at each others' throats',[17] comments Marsden. Edwards took as his text on this occasion Romans 12:18: 'If it be possible, as much as lieth in you, live peaceably with all men':

> We ought to our utmost to endeavour to live in peace, be at peace with those who have injured, wronged and abused us. We must

---

[15] Cited *Works*, 14:4.

[16] Ibid., p. 116.

[17] Marsden, *Edwards*, p. 97. I am indebted to Marsden's biography for much of the detail relating to Bolton in this paragraph.

not only live at peace with those that are friendly to us. It will not suffice that we don't quarrel and fall out with our good neighbors or near relations, that we let them alone that let us alone, and to be at peace with men while they do not abuse us, and those that are kind to us. But we are commanded to love those [that] hate us; we must do all the good we can to them that do what evil they can to us; to be peaceable and quiet and well-wishers to them who are full of hatred and strife towards us. Matt. 5:43-44, 'Ye have heard that it hath been said, Thou shalt love thy neighbour, and hate thine enemy. But I say unto you, Love your enemies, bless them that curse you, do good to them that hate you, and pray for them which despitefully use you, and persecute you'; and [v.] 46, 'For if ye love them that love you, what reward have ye? do not even the publicans the same?'[18]

Precisely the same pattern of statement followed by scriptural proof is also found in 'True Nobleness of Mind'. In this sermon, which was preached in February or March 1728, Edwards sets forth the example of the Bereans described in Acts 17:11: 'These were more noble than those of Thessalonica, in that they received the word with all readiness of mind, and searched the scriptures daily, whether those things were so':[19]

All wicked men do delight in filthiness; they love that which is above all things most abominable and most defiling to the soul. They greedily swallow it down, as the dog eats his own vomit, and wallow themselves in it, as the swine wallows in the mire. They make themselves like beasts by their delighting in sensual lusts, by worldlymindedness, intemperance, lasciviousness. They make themselves like the most filthy poisonous beasts in malice and spite and envy. And all sin exceedingly defiles the soul and makes it more filthy than the beasts. Job 15:16 'How much more abominable and filthy is man, that drinketh iniquity like water.' Is. 57:20, 'The wicked are like the troubled sea, whose waters cast up mire and dirt.'[20]

---

[18] *Works*, 14:123.
[19] See ibid., p. 228.
[20] Ibid., p. 235.

This common practice on Edwards' part to lead with his ideas and then to confirm those ideas with a citation from the Scriptures has perhaps contributed to an alleged conclusion by Miller concerning Edwards which must be challenged. Minkema alleges that, according to Miller, 'Edwards used Scripture merely as an embellishment, an afterthought, for his ideas.'[21] The basic problem here is that Minkema appears to have misread Miller at this point; indeed, Minkema has, on the basis of a misreading of Miller, attributed to Miller a view of Edwards' position with regard to the place of the Scriptures in his sermons that is untenable for two reasons. Firstly, Miller does not, on the page cited by Minkema, make such an assertion; and secondly, even if Miller had made such an assertion, it would have been palpably erroneous.[22] It is one thing to note that, in his adduction of parallel passages, Edwards often leads with his ideas and then confirms those ideas with the Scriptures; it is quite another thing to allege that his use of the Scriptures is merely an embellishment or an afterthought. It is surely palpably obvious that Edwards' ideas are generated, governed, and controlled by the Scriptures themselves. The fact that he frequently led with his thought and then cited the Scriptures does not mean that the Scriptures were an afterthought. Edwards demonstrates repeatedly that the Scriptures were at one and the same time both the source and the confirmation of his exposition. His frequent practice of citing collateral scriptures last is simply an aspect of his homiletical *modus operandi*.

It is interesting to note in this context that the remarkable revival of interest in the writings of Jonathan Edwards since the 1930's has, paradoxically, been characterized to some extent by a neglect of that which is unquestionably the central, governing principle of his life and thought, namely, the Bible. This neglect is seen to be all the more astonishing when it is remembered that Edwards was, above all else, a preacher of the word of God. Stephen J. Stein, the editor of the Yale

---

[21] Ibid., p. 15. The major problem here is that Minkema's reference in footnote 6 – Miller, *Jonathan Edwards* (New York, Sloan, 1949), p. 48 – does not sustain the assertion for which it is cited. If Minkema's page reference is correct, then the only explanation is that Minkema has misread Miller's reference to Stoddard as if it were a reference to Edwards.

[22] Minkema himself implies that he also regards such a view as erroneous. See *Works*, 14:15-16.

volume *Notes on Scripture,* makes the following observations in this respect:

> 'Notes on Scripture,' adds to the increasingly complex picture of Edwards as an intellectual by documenting the centrality of the Bible in his activities. Previous literature has often failed to reckon sufficiently with the scriptural principle in his thought, despite the widespread presence of biblical language, citations, and discourse throughout his writings. Early estimations overstated Edwards' scientific and philosophical precociousness and contributed to the masking of this aspect of his thought.[23]

> The negative attitude toward biblical scholarship expressed in Perry Miller's intellectual biography of Edwards . . . is even more telling . . . Miller had little interest in the biblical side of the New England preacher's thought and, correspondingly, little patience with it . . . It appears that for Miller commentary on the Bible was an unimportant, if not embarrassing, dimension of Edwards' thought.[24]

Indeed, Miller clearly regarded John Locke as the major formative influence upon the New England divine. It is important, therefore, to note the response of Vincent Tomas (1916-1995) – the William Herbert Perry Faunce Professor of Philosophy at Brown University – to Miller's influential biography of Edwards. 'How can anyone', asks Tomas, 'who has perused Edwards' works fail to mention Scripture as one of the dominating intellectual influences in his life?'[25] It is evident

---

[23] *Works,* 15:21-22.

[24] Ibid., p. 32.

[25] Vincent Tomas, 'Edwards' Master was the Bible, not Locke', in *Jonathan Edwards and the Enlightenment,* John Opie, ed. (Lexington, Massachusetts: D. C. Heath and Company, 1969), p. 37. Sweeney, '"Longing for More and More of It"?, p. 26, observes that 'we have neglected the scholarly work that he took most seriously. The lion's share of Edwards's time during every week of his adult life was spent wrestling with the words of holy writ. But though we know a great deal now about his ethics, metaphysics, epistemology and aesthetics – not to mention his pastoral ministry and his role in New England's revivals – few know much at all about Edwards's exegetical labors. Names such as Matthew Poole, for example, or Arthur Bedford, or Humphrey Prideaux, scarcely ring a bell today among Edwards scholars. But these were his interlocutors – much more than Locke, Berkeley and Newton.' 'How peculiar it is that scholars have largely neglected the biblical Edwards. Among the

that Tomas did not approve of the fact, but he contended correctly, *contra* Miller, that 'Edwards' master was the Bible, not Locke.'[26]

---

thousands of publications devoted to Edwards since his death, only a few, a tiny fraction, deal primarily with this theme.' Ibid., p. 29.

[26] Ibid., p. 36.

16

DIFFERENT CATEGORIES OF HEARERS

After the death of his grandfather, Solomon Stoddard, on February 11, 1729, Jonathan Edwards' preaching routine in Northampton basically consisted of delivering two sermons on the Lord's Day (one in the forenoon and one in the afternoon), each of which, according to Mark Valeri, 'probably took from an hour to an hour and a half to deliver'.[1] It also involved another discourse on a week-day evening. Edwards also preached on many special occasions, both at home and abroad. Fast-day sermons, election-day sermons,[2] Thanksgiving sermons, funerals, preaching invitations and preaching tours, ordination services, the Boston Lecture, the Enfield sermon, the Commencement at Yale, the Synod of New York, and the Farewell Sermon – such special occasions often elicited new sermons; and it is an interesting fact that a number of his most famous sermons, notably 'God Glorified'; 'Distinguishing Marks'; 'The Church's Marriage to her Sons and to her God'; 'Saints Absent from the Body'; 'A Strong Rod Broken and Withered'; 'The Sorrows of the Bereaved Spread before Jesus', were all specifically prepared for and preached at special occasions such as these. It is not always realized, however, that in addition to this considerable spectrum of preaching responsibility Edwards also occasionally arranged special meetings in Northampton in which he addressed special categories of hearers that differed according to age. Stout and Hatch

---

[1] *Works,* 17:16.
[2] See ibid., pp. 87-100. 'In "The Dangers of Decline" we have one of Edwards' few contributions to this genre.' The sermon was 'probably delivered on the election day of May 27, 1730.' Ibid., p. 87.

emphasize that such special meetings were especially prominent during the Great Awakening; indeed, the Yale co-editors point to 'a series of seven special meetings at which Edwards preached from July 1740 to August 1741 to specific age cohorts within his congregation: three for children (aged one to fourteen), two for young people (fifteen to twenty-five), and one each for middle-aged people (twenty-six to fifty) and elderly (over fifty).'[3] 'Edwards saw it as his ministerial duty to preach to the specific needs both of his congregation as a whole and of the individual groups within it . . . He knew that different groups among his congregation required special and specific lessons.'[4]

There is an obvious connection between Edwards' tendency to hold *special meetings* for different categories of hearers and his tendency to address *special categories of hearers* in his sermons. It is precisely because 'different groups among his congregation required special and specific lessons' that he also frequently addressed different categories of hearers in his Applications. In some sermons the different categories are based upon *age, gender,* and *position;* in other sermons they are based upon *spiritual condition.* Again, in certain sermons there is a cross-fertilization of these two broad categories. The clear, tacit supposition in his mind in such a categorization of his hearers is that every congregation is a *mixed auditory* that consists of different groups which occupy different positions and sustain different relationships. As such they were vulnerable to different temptations, susceptible to different sins, and characterized by different duties. They needed, therefore, to be addressed with different admonitions and exhortations. Edwards thus demonstrates here a theory of discriminating application which recognized and addressed these different spiritual needs.

We see here, in Edwards' frequent categorization of his hearers, the almost certain influence of William Perkins (1558-1602) upon the New England preacher. Perkins stood at the very fountainhead of the English Puritan tradition and exercised a very influential ministry in the pulpit of Great St Andrews, Cambridge. In 1592 he published

---

[3] *Works,* 22:156.
[4] Ibid., p. 168.

in Latin his *Arte of Prophecying* and in 1606 this was published posthumously in an English translation. This homiletical classic was to become part of what Kimnach has called 'the vital homiletic tradition of New England'.[5] In this seminal work Perkins advocates the addressing of different categories of hearers: 'Application is the skill by which the doctrine which has been properly drawn from Scripture is handled in ways which are appropriate to the circumstances of the place and time and to the people in the congregation.'[6] Perkins emphasizes not only 'kinds of application', but also 'the divers condition of men and people'.[7] The great value of addressing different categories of hearers lies in the fact that this particular method of Application is conducive to that 'point'[8] which Dabney regarded as one of the 'cardinal requisites of the sermon'.[9] Indeed, this particular method utilized by Edwards belongs to that type of Application which Dabney described as 'special' in contradistinction to that which is 'general':

> The application may be either general or special. The former is one which urges a principle of duty concerning all classes of hearers alike ... The special application is that which separates the hearers into classes and directs the truth to their several consciences, in the particular phase appropriate to each. The advantage of this method is, that it singles out the hearer more closely, and brings the truth into more immediate contact with his heart. Definiteness is the necessary condition of pungent effect.[10]

Kimnach describes 'specificity' as one of Edwards' 'distinguishing traits as a master of the sermon'.[11] His 'power of specification', contends Kimnach, 'is one of his most prominent traits.'[12] One of Edwards'

---

[5] *Works*, 10:9.

[6] William Perkins, *The Art of Prophesying with The Calling of the Ministry* (Edinburgh: Banner of Truth, 1996), p. 54.

[7] William Perkins, *The Arte of Prophecying*, in *The Works of that Famous and Worthy Minister of Christ in the Universitie of Cambridge*, vol. 2 (London: Printed by John Legatt, 1631), p. 665.

[8] Dabney, *Sacred Rhetoric*, p. 105.

[9] Ibid.

[10] Ibid., p. 174.

[11] Kimnach, 'Pursuit of Reality', p. 111.

[12] Ibid.

greatest sermons, 'Christian Cautions' has a very fine contextual introduction, it makes excellent use of the examples of Nehemiah and Eli,[13] it has some outstanding interrogatory sections, and it addresses different categories of hearers both according to age, gender, or position and according to different spiritual conditions. It is a sermon which demonstrates Edwards' remarkable versatility as a preacher. In the following passages he combines the use of the searching interrogative with the deliberate targeting of different categories of hearers. Firstly, he addresses 'husbands and wives':

> To *husbands and wives*. Inquire whether you do not live in some way of sin in this relation. Do you make conscience of performing all those duties which God in his word requires of persons in this relation? or do you allow yourselves in some ways which are directly opposite thereto? Do you not live in ways that are contrary to the obligations into which you entered in your marriage covenant . . . But are you not rather quick to spy faults, and ready to make the most of them? Are not very little things often the occasion of contention between you? Will not a little thing often ruffle your spirits towards your companions? and when any misunderstanding is begun, are you not guilty of exasperating one another's spirits by unkind language, until you blow up a spark into a flame?
>
> Do you endeavour to accommodate yourselves to each other's tempers? Do you study to suit each other? or do you set up your own wills, to have your own ways, in opposition to each other, in the management of your family concerns? Do you make it your study to render each other's lives comfortable? or is there not, on the contrary, very often subsisting between you a spirit of ill will, a disposition to vex and cross one another?[14]

The next category is one frequently addressed by the preacher, namely, that of 'parents and heads of families':

> I shall apply myself to *parents and heads of families*. Inquire

---

[13] *Works* (Hickman), 2:179, 183.
[14] Ibid., p. 183.

whether you do not live in some way of sin with respect to your children, or others committed to your care: and particularly inquire,

Whether you do not live in sin, by living in the *neglect of instructing* them. Do you not wholly neglect the duty of instructing your children and servants? or if you do not wholly neglect it, yet do you not afford them so little instruction, and are you not so unsteady, and do you not take so little pains in it, that you live in a sinful neglect? Do you take pains in any measure proportionate to the importance of the matter? You cannot but own that it is a matter of vast importance, that your children be fitted for death, and saved from hell; and that all possible care be taken that it be done speedily; for you know not how soon your children may die. Are you as careful about the welfare of their souls as you are of their bodies? Do you labour as much that they may have eternal life, as you do to provide estates for them to live on in this world? . . .

Do you not live in a *sinful neglect of the government* of your families? Do you not live in the sin of Eli? who indeed counselled and reproved his children, but did not exercise government over them. He reproved them very solemnly, [as 1 Sam. ii. 23, 24, 25.] But he did not restrain them; by which he greatly provoked God, and brought an everlasting curse upon his house: [1 Sam. iii. 12.] 'In that day I will perform against Eli all things which I have spoken concerning his house. When I begin, I will also make an end. I will judge his house for ever; because his sons made themselves vile, and he restrained them not.'[15]

The final category addressed in this section of the sermon is that of 'children':

I shall now apply myself to *children*. Let them examine themselves, whether they do not live in some way of sin towards their parents. Are you not guilty of some undutifulness towards them, in which you allow yourselves? Are you not guilty of despising your

---

[15] Ibid. Kimnach describes the theme of parental omission or neglect as 'one of Edwards' most persistent themes, whether preaching in Northampton or Stockbridge.' *Works*, 25:677. See 'Warring with the Devil', dated, 'St [ockbridge] Ind [ians]. April. 1754.' Ibid.

parents for infirmities which you see in them. Undutiful children are ready to contemn their parents for their infirmities. Are not you sons of Ham, who saw and made derision of his father's nakedness, whereby he entailed a curse on himself and his posterity to this day; and not the sons of Shem and Japheth, who covered the nakedness of their father? Are you not guilty of dishonouring and despising your parents for natural infirmities, or those of old age? Prov. xxiii. 22. 'Despise not thy mother when she is old.' Doth not that curse belong to you, in Deut. xxvii. 16. 'Cursed be he that setteth light by his father or his mother?'

Are you not wont to despise the counsels and reproofs of your parents? When they warn you against any sin, and reprove you for any misconduct, are you not wont to set light by it, and to be impatient under it? Do you honour your parents for it? on the contrary, do you not receive it with resentment, proudly rejecting it? Doth it not stir up corruption, and a stubborn and perverse spirit in you, and rather make you to have an ill-will to your parents, than to love and honour them? Are you not to be reckoned among the fools mentioned Prov. xv. 5. 'A fool despiseth his father's instruction?' and doth not that curse belong to you, Prov. xxx. 17. 'The eye that mocketh at his father, and despiseth to obey his mother, the ravens of the valley shall pick it out, and the young eagles shall eat it?'

Do you not allow a fretful disposition towards your parents, when they cross you in anything? Are you not apt to find fault with your parents, and to be out of temper with them?[16]

'Indicting God' was a fast-day sermon which was preached in April 1738. His text on this occasion was Jeremiah 2:5: 'Thus saith the LORD, What iniquity have your fathers found in me that they are gone far from me, and have walked after vanity, and are become vain?' This 'expostulation or challenge'[17] is, of course, a rhetorical question. 'Such an interrogation implies a strong negation',[18] observes the preacher. Thus in the sermon it is not God that is indicted ultimately, but the land and the town. The sermon is, in fact, a classic New England jeremiad

---

[16] Ibid., pp. 183-184.
[17] *Works*, 19:749.
[18] Ibid., p. 751.

in which the preacher, in Christ's name, laments and bemoans the spiritual declension of both land and town. But if the sermon is a jeremiad, it is also, as Lesser puts it, 'an anthem to America's exceptionalism and Northampton's'.[19] America is viewed in terms of the land of Israel and Northampton as 'a city set on an hill'.[20] Thus, remarkably, the Application is virtually geographical and historical as the preacher addresses both the land and the town:

I would now apply this doctrine, first, to the case of this land; and, second, to the case of this town . . .

First. I would show how that which is spoken of in the doctrine, is the case of this land. We are a covenant people. Every professing people is so, but we are so in a special manner; for God has dealt with the people of this land in many respects much as he did with the children of Israel, when he entered into covenant with them. He has brought us out and separated us from other people, among whom we were under an heavy yoke of bondage; and has brought us away over a vast ocean, as he led the people of Israel through a great wilderness; and has brought us to a great distance, that we might be a peculiar people to himself.

He has given us a good land for our possession, and to that end has taken away the land from its former inhabitants to give it to us, that we might possess it. He in a remarkable manner has cast out the heathen before us, and here has planted us and settled us, and has as it were set his tabernacle in the midst of us. He has given the free and full enjoyment of his word and ordinances, which before in our bondage, in the land from whence we came, we were denied. And here God has entered into covenant with us. Our forefathers on their first coming and settling here, did solemnly enter into covenant with God, and were often renewing their covenant. There is probably no people in the world, whose case in the manner of becoming a distinct covenant people, is so parallel with that of the church of Israel as this people. God's providences towards this land in the first settling of it were as it were its solemn espousals to Christ.[21]

[19] Ibid., p. 747.
[20] Ibid., p. 767.
[21] Ibid., p. 759.

Sermon Notebook 45 contains an interesting entry which expresses Edwards' intention to preach a sermon against the sin of theft: 'To preach a sermon against robbing fruit trees and gardens, etc. before next fruit time if I should live.'[22] This Notebook was probably begun in late 1738 or early 1739.[23] It is, therefore, highly probable that 'Dishonesty; or, The Sin of Theft and of Injustice', which was preached at Northampton in July, 1740, is the sermon thus projected. It is a very impressive treatment of the eighth commandment – 'Thou shalt not steal'; and in his Application the preacher specifically addresses *parents* and admonishes them to restrain their children from 'stealing the fruits of their neighbours' trees or fields':

> I shall hence take occasion to exhort *parents* to restrain their children from stealing, and particularly from being guilty of theft in stealing the fruits of their neighbours' trees or fields. Christian parents are obliged to bring up their children in the nurture and admonition of the Lord. But how much otherwise do they act, who bring them up in theft! And those parents are guilty of this, who – though they do not directly teach them to steal, by example and setting them about it, yet – *tolerate* them in it.
>
> Parents should take effectual care, not only to instruct their children better, and to warn them against any such thievish practices, but also thoroughly to restrain them. Children who practise stealing, make themselves vile. Stealing, by the common consent of mankind, is a very vile practice; therefore those parents that will not take thorough care to restrain their children from such a practice, will be guilty of the same sin which God so highly resented, and awfully punished, in *Eli*, of which we read, 1 Sam. iii. 13. 'For I have told him, that I will judge his house for ever, for the iniquity which he knoweth; because his sons made themselves vile, and he restrained them not.'[24]

Edwards' 'power of specification' constitutes just one element, although an important one, in the mysterious power of 'Sinners in the Hands

[22] *Works*, 10:62.
[23] I am indebted to Kimnach for the dating of this Notebook. See ibid.
[24] *Works* (Hickman), 2:226.

of an Angry God'. In the course of the Application he deliberately addresses the elderly, the young people, and the children:

> Are there not many here who have lived long in the world, and are not this day born again? and so are aliens from the commonwealth of Israel, and have done nothing ever since they have lived, but treasure up wrath against the day of wrath? Oh, Sirs, your case, in an especial manner, is extremely dangerous. Your guilt and hardness of heart is extremely great. Do not you see how generally persons of your years are passed over and left, in the present remarkable and wonderful dispensation of God's mercy? You had need to consider yourselves, and awake thoroughly out of sleep. You cannot bear the fierceness and wrath of the infinite God. – And you, young men and young women, will you neglect this precious season which you now enjoy, when so many others of your age are renouncing all youthful vanities, and flocking to Christ? You especially have now an extraordinary opportunity; but if you neglect it, it will soon be with you as with those persons who spent all the precious days of youth in sin, and are now come to such a dreadful pass in blindness and hardness. – And you, children, who are unconverted, do not you know that you are going down to hell, to bear the dreadful wrath of that God, who is now angry with you every day and every night? Will you be content to be the children of the devil, when so many other children in the land are converted, and are become the holy and happy children of the King of kings?[25]

It will be noted that this section is also interrogatory in character. Indeed, this passage is a striking example of the cross-fertilization of the use of the searching interrogative with the specific addressing of various age groups.

On September 2, 1741, exactly eight weeks after the sermon at Enfield, Edwards preached a funeral sermon at Hatfield on behalf of his deceased uncle, the Reverend William Williams. Williams had married Solomon Stoddard's daughter, Christian, the sister of Edwards' mother, Esther. Thus, in addressing the widow and the children of the deceased, Edwards was addressing his aunt and his cousins. The title

---

[25] Ibid., p. 11.

of the sermon was 'The Sorrows of the Bereaved Spread before Jesus' and the text was Matthew 14:12: 'And his disciples came and took up the body and buried it, and went and told Jesus.'[26] The sermon stands in striking contrast to the Enfield sermon. Indeed, if the Enfield sermon emphasized the *severity of God,* the Hatfield sermon emphasized the *goodness of God,* and especially the tender compassions of Christ. This very contrast demonstrates again the versatility of the Northampton preacher. The sermon is characterized by a gentle, evangelical tone. 'This is a friend, a nephew, a cousin, a fellow pastor', observe the Yale co-editors. 'This is an Edwards rarely seen in other sermons, a glimpse into a personal Edwards little seen even in his letters.'[27] The *leitmotiv* that runs throughout this simple, beautiful, and strongly consoling sermon is a variation on the theme of the exhortation, 'Therefore now go to Jesus.'[28]

In the course of his Application Edwards addresses the following parties in the congregation, of which we cite the third:

> 1) You that belong to this *church and congregation,* that are bereaved of your aged and eminent *pastor* and *father,* that has so long been a great blessing to you ...
> 2) The near relations of the deceased ...
> 3) The honoured relict, ... whom God by this awful providence has made a sorrowful widow ...
> 4) The bereaved, afflicted children ...
> 5) My honoured fathers, the sons of the deceased, that are improved in the same great work of the gospel ministry, or in other public business for the service of their generation ...[29]

---

[26] 'The preaching of this sermon at William Williams' funeral was, with modifications, actually the second preaching. The first preaching came a year earlier, upon the death of the Reverend Nehemiah Bull of Westfield, only two years older than Edwards ... Bull's death at age thirty-nine was tragic, and Edwards preached the mourning sermon to Bull's widow, his young children, and his parents.' *Works,* 22:462-463.

[27] Ibid., p. 462.

[28] *Works* (Hickman), 2:968.

[29] Miller's view that this section constitutes 'one of his sardonic touches', that 'this particularly sly passage must be read in the light of that year, 1741', and that 'Edwards deftly insulted the sons of William Williams at Hatfield' cannot be sustained. See Miller, *Edwards,* pp. 125-126. The Williams family was clearly pleased with the sermon and it was

6) The surviving pastor of this church.

7) The surviving ministers of this county.[30]

And particularly I would apply myself to the honoured relict, who stood in the nearest relation of any to the deceased, whom God by this awful providence has made a sorrowful widow. Suffer me, honoured madam, in your great affliction, to exhibit to you a compassionate Redeemer. God has now taken from you that servant of his, that was the nearest and best friend you had in this world, that was your wise and prudent guide, your affectionate and pleasant companion, who was so great a blessing while he lived, to you and your family, and, under Christ, was so much the comfort and support of your life. You see, madam, where your resort must be: your earthly friends can condole your loss, but cannot make it up to you; we must all confess ourselves to be but miserable comforters: but you may go and tell Jesus, and there you may have both support and reparation: his love and his presence is far beyond that of the nearest and most affectionate earthly friend. Now you are bereaved of your earthly consort, you may go to a spiritual husband, and seek his compassion and his company: he is the fountain of all that wisdom and prudence, that piety, that tender affection and faithful care, that you enjoyed in your departed

---

published "'at the united request of those reverend and honoured gentlemen, the sons of the deceased'". Cited Marsden, *Edwards*, p. 231. There was, moreover, a transparency about JE that Miller has clearly missed.

Almost seven years later, however, on June 26, 1748, JE preached the funeral sermon on behalf of John Stoddard, one of the sons of Solomon Stoddard, thus another of JE's uncles, and, as the sermon itself demonstrates, a very distinguished man. In this sermon he characteristically utilizes the positive example of his deceased uncle to rebuke and shame, it appears, *some* of the relatives of William Williams. See chapter on 'The Use of Example'.

It is also interesting to note that in 'The Great Concern of a Watchman for Souls', preached at the ordination of Jonathan Judd on June 8, 1743, JE made the following observation: 'There are some professors, in some of our towns, that are anti-ministerial men; they seem to have a disposition to dislike men of that order; they are apt to be prejudiced against them, and to be suspicious of them, and talk against them; and it seems to be as it were natural to 'em to be unfriendly and unkind towards their own ministers, and to make difficulty for them. But I don't believe there is a true Christian on earth that is of this character;' *Works*, 25:80-81. It is almost certain that JE had *inter alia* some of the Williams cousins in view in this observation.

[30] *Works* (Hickman), 2:968-969.

consort; in him is an infinite fountain of all these things, and of all good; in him you may have light in your darkness, comfort in your sorrow, and fulness of joy and glory in another world, in an everlasting union with your dear, deceased relative, in the glorious presence of the same *Redeemer, in whose presence is fulness of joy, and at whose right hand are pleasures for evermore.*[31]

The significance of the death of William Williams (1665-1741), just two days earlier on August 31, 1741, can scarcely be over-estimated. William Williams, the son-in-law of Solomon Stoddard, had been one of the patriarchs of New England. Stoddard had been Williams' mentor, and Williams had been Stoddard's right-hand man. In 1714 these two significant clerical figures had moved New England Congregationalism in the direction of Presbyterianism by founding the Hampshire Association which was to have oversight of ecclesiastical affairs in the region. Marsden observes that 'William Williams' influence was based on his being the most talented clerical figure in the most prominent clan among the Connecticut Valley gentry.'[32] It was Williams that had preached Edwards' ordination sermon in February 1727 and also the principal sermon at Stoddard's funeral in February 1729. In October, 1740, George Whitefield had ridden five miles from the Edwards home to preach at Hatfield and to pay his respects to the aged patriarch.[33] But if, in 1729, the mantle of Solomon Stoddard had fallen on Williams, the mantle of Williams was now, in 1741, falling on Jonathan Edwards. 'That Edwards (rather than Stephen Williams, for instance) was chosen to preach the funeral sermon for William Williams likely reflected the express wishes of the uncle and signaled his choice for leadership.'[34] The significance of this death, however, consisted not merely (and perhaps not chiefly) in Edwards' donning of the mantle of leadership, but especially in his loss of a spiritual ally, particularly on the issues of revival and opposition to Arminianism. A very significant proportion of the opposition to

---

[31] Ibid., p. 968.
[32] Marsden, *Edwards*, p. 115.
[33] I am indebted to Marsden for these details. See ibid., pp. 206-207.
[34] Ibid., p. 230.

Edwards himself that was to develop in the 1740's and 1750's was to emerge, paradoxically, from William Williams' own family.

This funeral has been described by the Yale co-editors as 'a public event with family and provincial religious, political, and military authorities in attendance';[35] and it is both fascinating and sobering to reflect that, sitting in the grieving congregation on September 2, 1741, and, indeed, specifically addressed by the preacher, were, presumably, the following members of the Williams family: Elisha Williams (1694-1755), Edwards' distinguished half-cousin, his former tutor at Yale, 'a brilliant and magnetic young man'[36] who later became the Rector of Yale and who was to be one of Edwards' most influential opponents in the communion controversy; Israel Williams (1709-1789), 'the ambitious young magistrate',[37] who for some years had conspicuously and pointedly avoided the courtesy of a visit when riding past the Edwards home; Jonathan Ashley (1712-1780), the husband of Dorothy Williams and pastor at Deerfield, who just over a year later made a dramatic attack upon the Great Awakening and who in June 1750 was a member of the ten-church council that voted in favour of Edwards' dismissal;[38] Solomon Williams (1700-1776), pastor at Lebanon, Connecticut, who in 1751 was rash enough to write against Edwards in the communion controversy and who paid the price;[39] Ephraim Williams, Sr., (1691-1754), the younger brother of the deceased patriarch, who

---

[35] *Works*, 22:461.

[36] Winslow, p. 56.

[37] Marsden, *Edwards*, p. 367.

[38] 'While the Northamptonites were waiting for Solomon Williams' published reply, they engaged Ashley to come and deliver some sermons opposing Edwards' views.' Ibid., p. 576 n. 33.

[39] Referring to *Misrepresentations Corrected* (1752), as well as to *An Humble Inquiry* (1749), Miller observes: 'For sheer destructive argumentation, they are a joy to those who like that sort of thing, and if ever a man was cut into small pieces, and each piece run through a meat grinder, it was Solomon Williams.' 'The legend is that nobody in Northampton dared let on that he had read it.' Miller, *Edwards*, p. 222. Winslow asserts that, in this work, 'Jonathan Edwards neatly decapitated his opponent.' 'This treatise . . . illustrates better than his more important works his detective quality of mind, his sureness of argumentative aim, and his ruthlessness as a controversialist. He not only felled his enemy, but bludgeoned him after he was down . . . Jonathan Edwards was expert in using a rapier, but this time he took a cudgel, and as a result the attack is not pleasant to watch.' Winslow, pp. 294, 295.

had moved to Stockbridge in 1737, had soon 'assumed the role of English squire of the village',[40] and whose land manoeuverings and machinations increasingly alienated the Indians;[41] Ephraim Williams, Jr., (1715-1755), who, in the early 1750's, told the people of Stockbridge that he would gladly spend £500 to rid the town of its minister; and Abigail Williams (1721-1791), the intelligent and attractive twenty year old daughter of Ephraim Williams, Sr., who was later to be described by Ezra Stiles as 'a woman of a most surprizing genius'[42] and who was to be a significant member of 'the powerful Williams cabal'[43] in Stockbridge. All of the aforementioned, who were specifically

[40] Marsden, *Edwards*, p. 376.

[41] 'Ephraim Williams had quickly become one of the largest landholders in town. Already by 1737 he had acquired over 11,000 acres of Mahican lands ... He and his family continued to amass great quantities of land in the area. Those lands acquired from within the township grant were often the result of shady deals and maneuverings. One technique was to sell goods an Indian resident on credit, and if they proved unable to pay, the creditor received land in return. Ephraim's undisguised motive was to amass wealth and prevent Edwards' sympathizers from gaining ground, thus solidifying his family's control of the region. The Stockbridge Indians frequently had grounds to complain that the old Colonel "molested 'em with respect to their lands and other affairs".' Wheeler, pp. 148-149.

Marsden makes this observation concerning Stockbridge's transition during the next few decades from being a predominantly Indian village to becoming an increasingly white village: 'The Williamses' road to success in fostering this transition was paved with good intentions, some genuine piety, and a desire to benefit both Indians and whites. Yet leading them down that road and eventually obscuring their original purposes were motives of self-interest and enterprise, which led the family to take for granted that they should exploit their economic opportunities. By the time Edwards arrived in Stockbridge in the 1750's, the forces of economic self-interest were, as he was especially alert to see, in control. Yet strains of piety and interest in the mission were still there as well, so that the Williamses could show some authentic righteous indignation in their efforts to keep it under their guidance.' Marsden, *Edwards*, p. 382.

[42] Cited Edmund S. Morgan, *The Gentle Puritan: A Life of Ezra Stiles, 1727-1795* (New Haven and London: Yale University Press, 1962), p. 88. Ezra Stiles, the future president of Yale (1778-1795), had made the acquaintance of Abigail Williams Sergeant, the widow of John Sergeant, in 1750. Early that year Stiles had received an invitation to come to Stockbridge to preach as a possible replacement for the deceased missionary. Stiles was clearly deeply attracted to Abigail and might well have accepted the post at Stockbridge and married Abigail, but for the fact that he was not prepared to have his orthodoxy examined and his scepticism potentially revealed. He thus declined the interview at Boston, the position at Stockbridge, and the probability of the hand of the beautiful twenty-nine year old Abigail. The position of missionary was, of course, subsequently offered to and accepted by JE himself. See Morgan's fascinating chapter 'Abigail.' Ibid., pp. 78-89.

[43] *Works*, 25:28 n. 2.

(albeit collectively) addressed by the preacher in the funeral sermon, were, in varying degrees, (some already, but most in the years to come), to be the cause of enormous trouble and grief to the preacher-theologian, not only in Northampton but also in Stockbridge, and especially over the issue of the qualifications for communion. In the eyes of his cousins, Edwards was, in the years that lay ahead, to have the temerity to depart from the position of their mutual grandfather on this issue and thus to betray the name of the Stoddard-Williams family. Indeed, although the Williams family was clearly pleased with the funeral sermon preached that day and even had the sermon published, Edwards' cousins especially were already, to some extent, it seems, harbouring in their hearts rivalries, resentments, jealousies, and ill will towards their distinguished cousin that would bear very bitter fruit during the course of the next thirteen years or so.[44] In fact, a number of them were to play a very significant part in his dismissal from Northampton and in his attempted removal from Stockbridge. Thus the gentle, compassionate, evangelical, and winsome tone of the sermon belies the storm clouds that were already gathering over the preacher's head in

---

[44] In a letter written from Stockbridge on January 30, 1753, to Sir William Pepperrell – described by Marsden, (*Edwards*, p. 402), as 'the colony's most famous New Light layman' – JE provides a detailed account of the history of the coolness of the Williams cousins towards him: 'There has for many years appeared a prejudice in the family of the Williamses against me and my family, especially ever since the great awakening in Northampton, about eighteen years ago. To inform you, Sir, of the first rise of this prejudice, and by what means and steps it was established, would be unnecessary, and would be a trespassing on your patience; only I would say, as I can say with truth, and before him who searches all hearts, that I have sought peace with them, and that their displeasure was not from any injury I offered them. It has been my care to avoid those things by which prejudices might be continued, and endeavor to live in friendship with them. However, there has been a most apparent and rooted misunderstanding, at least with some of the family, which was manifested by the frequent testimonies of their dislike and ill opinion, in what they said of me behind my back, reflecting on me and reproaching and avoiding my house. Col. Israel Williams of Hatfield, though my first cousin and lived within five miles of me and very often at Northampton riding by my house backwards and forwards continually, never set foot in my house above thrice in fourteen years before I left Northampton. Mr. [Jonathan] Ashley of Deerfield, who married into the family, though a neighbouring minister, and related to me, and very often was in the town, generally shunned the house, and very rarely came to it on any occasion. I was rarely visited by any of the rest of the family, though I very often used to visit them, endeavoring, if possible, to wear away this prejudice and strangeness. But all never availed.' *Works*, 16:554.

that very assembly. 'Everybody knew', observes Miller, 'to what lengths a feud between New England cousins could go.'[45] 'August 31, 1741', notes Marsden, 'marked a turning point in Edwards' life.'[46]

On September 10, 1741, just eight days after the funeral of William Williams, Edwards delivered the Commencement sermon at Yale in the midst of circumstances which Marsden has described as 'a cockpit of controversy'.[47] It is important to note that the Great Awakening was then at its height.[48] George Whitefield had preached at Yale the previous autumn; Gilbert Tennent (1703-1764) had preached frequently in the New Haven area in the following March; but now, in early September, James Davenport had arrived in New Haven for the week of Commencement, causing considerable consternation amongst the Yale trustees on account of his wild, sensationalist methods; and the young, intelligent, but rash David Brainerd was already demonstrating not only the intense spirituality that would later make his name legendary, but also the tendency to censoriousness that would, before long, result in his tragic expulsion from Yale.[49] 'Edwards', notes Marsden, 'arrived in New Haven in the midst of this commotion'.[50] His sermon on this momentous occasion was entitled 'The Distinguishing Marks of a Work of the Spirit of God' and was soon published under that title in expanded form in Boston.[51] 'Edwards', observes Goen, 'was attempting

---

[45] Miller, *Edwards*, p. 15. Miller also refers to 'that peculiarly New England struggle, a feud between cousins, than which nothing in the world is meaner, more bitter, or more unforgiving.' Ibid., p. 102.

[46] Marsden, *Edwards*, p. 227. I am indebted to Marsden for much of the foregoing detail concerning the Williams family.

[47] Ibid., p. 231.

[48] In a letter to Thomas Prince (1687-1758) dated December 12, 1743, JE describes the spiritual climate of this period: 'The months of August and September [1741] were the most remarkable of any this year, for appearances of conviction and conversion of sinners, and great revivings, quickenings, and comforts of professors, and for extraordinary external effects of these things. It was a very frequent thing to see an house full of outcries, faintings, convulsions and such like, both with distress, and also with admiration and joy.' *Works*, 16:118.

[49] C. C. Goen points out that Brainerd 'was expelled two months after Commencement'. *Works*, 4:57.

[50] Marsden, *Edwards*, p. 233.

[51] In terms of publications the period between July 8 and September 10, 1741, proved to be remarkably productive for JE, for it was during these two months that he preached 'Sin-

to steer between the hard Scylla of Old Light hostility, soon to turn repressive, and the swirling Charybdis of New Light enthusiasm, soon to exceed all bounds of propriety and sound religion . . . Edwards' Yale sermon was intended as an *irenicon*, but instead it marked the beginning of polarization in attitudes toward the revival. Official Yale was unmoved by his address and soon turned rigidly Old Light.'[52] 'It was the last time', notes Miller, 'that Edwards was even semi-officially honored by Yale.'[53]

There were, however, several students that were confirmed in or won over to the cause of the revival by this sermon. Amongst them were Samuel Hopkins (1721-1803), David Brainerd (1718-1747), and Samuel Buell (1716-1798), all of whom were to become protégés of the Commencement speaker. Buell had originally intended to study with Edwards, but his preaching had been so effective that he obtained a preaching license from the New Haven Association and exercised an itinerant preaching ministry for about five years before settling in a Presbyterian congregation on Long Island. In late January and early February 1742, when Edwards was absent from his own pulpit whilst on a preaching tour in the area of Leicester, Massachusetts, and Connecticut, it was the recently graduated Buell that he appointed to preach in his absence. Buell's ministry in Northampton at that time also proved to be remarkably blessed of God;[54] indeed, it was during these weeks that Sarah Edwards enjoyed those remarkable spiritual experiences that her husband himself recorded on his return and published in *Thoughts on the Revival* (1743).[55]

It was on September 19, 1746, that Samuel Buell was installed as 'pastor of the church and congregation at East Hampton on Long

---

ners in the Hands of an Angry God' at Enfield, 'The Sorrows of the Bereaved Spread before Jesus' at Hatfield, and 'The Distinguishing Marks of a Work of the Spirit of God' at New Haven. Each of these sermons was published at Boston in the same year.

[52] *Works*, 4:56-57.

[53] Miller, *Edwards*, p. 169.

[54] See *Works*, 22:509.

[55] I am indebted to Goen, editor of volume 4 in the Yale series, for much of the information in this paragraph. See also Marsden, *Edwards*, p. 240-247 for an account of these experiences and Buell's role in connection with them.

Island',[56] in which pastorate he was to remain until his death in 1798. 'Buell was a brilliant orator and itinerant evangelist', observes Kimnach. He 'did not have the learning or depth of Edwards, but he had an extraordinary evangelical presence and social graces which stood him in good stead throughout a long career.'[57] It was on this occasion that Edwards preached 'The Church's Marriage to her Sons, and to her God'. The visiting preacher took as his text Isaiah 62:4-5: 'Thy land shall be married. For as a young man marrieth a virgin, so shall thy sons marry thee: and as the bridegroom rejoiceth over the bride, so shall thy God rejoice over thee.' It was, Kimnach notes, 'Edwards' longest ordination sermon and one of his more complex homiletical efforts.'[58] In the course of the exhortations that he delivered towards the close of his sermon, he addressed pastors and people separately; indeed, with regard to the former category, he not only addressed at length 'all that are called to the work of the gospel-ministry',[59] but also more specifically 'that minister of Christ, who above all others is concerned in the solemnity of this day':[60]

> You have now heard, Reverend Sir, the great importance and high ends of the office of an evangelical pastor, and the glorious privileges of such as are faithful in this office, imperfectly repre-sented. May God grant that your union with this people, this day, as their pastor, may be such, that God's people may have the great promise God makes to his church in the text, now fulfilled unto them. May you now, as one of the precious sons of Zion, take this part of Christ's church by the hand, in the name of your great Master the glorious bridegroom, with a heart devoted unto him with true adoration and supreme affection, and for his sake knit to his people, in a spiritual and pure love, and as it were a conjugal tenderness; ardently desiring that great happiness for them, which you have now heard Christ has chosen his church unto, and has shed his blood to obtain for her; being yourself ready to spend and

---

[56] *Works* (Hickman), 2:17 n.
[57] *Works*, 25:15-16.
[58] Ibid., p. 165.
[59] *Works* (Hickman), 2:23.
[60] Ibid., p. 25.

be spent for them; remembering the great errand on which Christ sends you to them, *viz.* to woo and win their hearts, and espouse their souls to him, and to bring up his elect spouse, and to fit and adorn her for his embraces; that you may in due time present her a chaste virgin to him, for him to rejoice over, as the bridegroom rejoiceth over the bride. How honourable is this business that Christ employs you in! and how joyfully should you perform it! When Abraham's faithful servant was sent to take a wife for his master's son, how engaged was he in the business; and how joyful was he when he succeeded! With what joy did he bow his head and worship, and bless the Lord God of his master, for his mercy and his truth in making his way prosperous! And what a joyful meeting may we conclude he had with Isaac, when he met him in the field, by the well of Laharoi, and there presented his beauteous Rebekah to him, and told him all things that he had done! But this was but a shadow of that joy that you shall have, if you imitate his fidelity, in the day when you shall meet your glorious Master, and present Christ's church in this place, as a chaste and beautiful virgin unto him.[61]

Edwards concludes the sermon by addressing 'the people of this congregation, whose souls are now to be committed to the care of that minister of Christ, whom they have chosen as their pastor':[62]

Let me take occasion, dear brethren, from what has been said, to exhort you – not forgetting the respect, honour, and reverence that will ever be due from you to your former pastor, who has served you so long in that work, but by reason of age and growing infirmities, and the prospect of his place being so happily supplied by a successor, has seen meet to relinquish the burden of the pastoral charge over you – to perform the duties that belong to you, in your part of that relation and union now to be established between you and your elect pastor. Receive him as the messenger of the Lord of hosts, one that in his office represents the glorious bridegroom of the church; love and honour him, and willingly submit yourselves

---

[61] Ibid.
[62] Ibid., p. 26.

to him, as a virgin when married to a husband. Surely the feet of that messenger should be beautiful, that comes to you on such a blessed errand as that which you have heard, to espouse you to the eternal Son of God, and to fit you for and lead you to him as your bridegroom. Your chosen pastor comes to you on this errand, and he comes in the name of the bridegroom, so empowered by him, and representing him, that in receiving him, you will receive Christ, and in rejecting him, you will reject Christ.

Be exhorted to treat your pastor as the beautiful and virtuous Rebekah treated Abraham's servant. She most charitably and hospitably entertained him, provided lodging and food for him and his company, and took care that he should be comfortably entertained and supplied in all respects, while he continued in his embassy; and that was the note or mark of distinction which God himself gave him, by which he should know the true spouse of Isaac from all others of the daughters of the city. Therefore in this respect approve yourselves as the true spouse of Christ, by giving kind entertainment to your minister that comes to espouse you to the antetype of Isaac. Provide for his outward subsistence and comfort, with the like cheerfulness that Rebekah did for Abraham's servant. You have an account of her alacrity and liberality in supplying him, in Genesis xxiv. 18, &c. Say, as her brother did, ver. 31. 'Come in, thou blessed of the LORD.'[63]

It will be noted that in the sermons cited above Edwards addresses the following different categories according to *age, gender, position*, and even *locality:* children, young men and women, husbands and wives, parents and heads of families, elderly people, the different parties bereaved at a funeral, pastors in general, one pastor in particular, the congregation, and even the land and the town. The very fact that he isolates these specific groups and delivers a specific charge to each renders that charge all the more personal, pointed, and direct. It should be noted, however, that he also frequently addresses different categories of hearers according to spiritual condition. Indeed, in 'Christian Cautions', having addressed different groups according to *age, gender,* and *position*, he proceeds to address different groups according to *spiritual condition:*

---

[63] Ibid.

1. If you have been *long seeking salvation,* and have not yet succeeded, it may be this hath been the cause . . . [i.e. 'living in some way of sin']

2. If grace have not been flourishing, but, on the contrary, in *languishing circumstances in your souls,* perhaps this is the cause . . .

3. If you have been left to *fall into great sin,* perhaps this was the occasion of it . . .

4. If you live very much in *spiritual darkness,* and without the comfortable presence of God, it may be this is the cause . . .

5. If you have been long *doubting about your condition,* perhaps this is the cause . . .

6. If you have met with the *frowns of Providence,* perhaps this has been the cause . . .

7. If *death be terrible to you,* perhaps this is the foundation of it . . .[64]

It is under the sixth category, namely, the category of those that had 'met with the *frowns of Providence',* that Edwards delivers this admonition:

If you have met with the *frowns of Providence,* perhaps this has been the cause. When you have met with very sore rebukes and chastisements, that way of sin hath probably been your troubler. Sometimes God is exceedingly awful in his dealings with his own people in this world, for their sins. Moses and Aaron were not suffered to enter into Canaan, because they believed not God, and spake unadvisedly with their lips, at the waters of Meribah. And how terrible was God in his dealings with David! what affliction in his family did he send upon him! one of his sons ravishing his sister; another murdering his brother, and having expelled his father out of his kingdom, openly in the sight of all Israel, and in the sight of the sun, defiling his father's concubines on the top of the house, and at last coming to a miserable end? Immediately after this followed the rebellion of Sheba; and he had this uncomfortable circumstance attending the end of his life, that he saw another of his sons usurping the crown.

How awfully did God deal with Eli, for living in the sin of not restraining his children from wickedness! He killed his two sons

---

[64] Ibid., pp. 184-185.

in one day; brought a violent death upon Eli himself; took the ark from him, and sent it into captivity; cursed his house for ever; and sware that the iniquity of his house should not be purged with sacrifice and offering for ever; that the priesthood should be taken from him, and given to another family; and that there should never be an old man in his family.

Is not some way of sin in which you live the occasion of the frowns and rebukes of Providence which you have met with? True, it is not the proper business of your neighbours to judge you with respect to events of Providence; but you yourselves ought to inquire, wherefore God is contending with you, Job ix. 10.[65]

'Pressing into the Kingdom of God' is a sermon of particular interest precisely because of the historical context in which it was preached. Lesser gives the following information on that context: 'This four-unit sermon on salvation was delivered in February 1735, some ten weeks after the November lecture on justification and within five weeks of the onset of "the present season of the pouring out of the Spirit of God on this town".'[66] Thus, as its considerable length suggests, this sermon required four separate preaching occasions, which probably involved two successive Lord's days. In the course of his Application Edwards again directs his attention to various categories of hearers in the congregation:

> But here I would particularly direct myself to several sorts of persons.
> 1. To those sinners who are in a measure awakened, and are concerned for their salvation . . .
> 2. I would address myself to such as yet remain unawakened . . .
> 3. I would direct myself to them who are grown considerably into years, and are yet in a natural condition . . .
> 4. I would direct the advice to those that are young, and now under their first special convictions . . .[67]

---

[65] Ibid., p. 185.

[66] *Works*, 19:272. Kimnach gives the following definition of the 'preaching unit': 'The phrase "preaching unit" is a modern technical term used to identify the amount of material JE would normally preach during one session in the pulpit, since he often composed sermons requiring two or more preaching sessions to complete.' *Works*, 10:32 n. 6.

[67] *Works* (Hickman), 1:660-663.

It will be noted that, whilst the factor of age enters into these various categories, the main focus falls upon the various spiritual conditions within the congregation; and it will be further noted that in the following passage, which is directed to the second category ('such as yet remain unawakened'), the preacher cross-fertilizes the specificity of a distinct category of hearers with the use of the searching interrogative:

> When do you expect that it will be more likely that you should be awakened and wrought upon than now? You are in a Christless condition; and yet without doubt intend to go to heaven; and therefore intend to be converted some time before you die; but this is not to be expected till you are first awakened, and deeply concerned about the welfare of your soul, and brought earnestly to seek God's converting grace. And when do you intend that this shall be? How do you lay things out in your own mind, or what projection have you about this matter? Is it ever so likely that a person will be awakened, as at such a time as this? How do we see many, who before were secure, now roused out of their sleep, and crying, What shall I do to be saved? But you are yet secure! Do you flatter yourself that it will be more likely you should be awakened when it is a dull and dead time? Do you lay matters out thus in your own mind, that though you are senseless when others are generally awakened, that yet you shall be awakened when others are generally senseless? Or do you hope to see another such time of the pouring out of God's Spirit hereafter? And do you think it will be more likely that you should be wrought upon then, than now? And why do you think so? Is it because then you shall be so much older than you are now, and so that your heart will be grown softer and more tender with age? or because you will then have stood out so much longer against the calls of the gospel, and all means of grace? Do you think it more likely that God will give you the needed influences of his Spirit then, than now, because then you will have provoked him so much more, and your sin and guilt will be so much greater? And do you think it will be any benefit to you, to stand it through the present season of grace, as proof against the extraordinary means of awakening there are? Do

you think that this will be a good preparation for a saving work of the Spirit hereafter?[68]

Edwards' 'Farewell Sermon', which was delivered to the church in Northampton on July 1, 1750, just nine days after his dismissal on June 22, is justly celebrated. The tragic occasion of the sermon was, Kimnach observes, 'a long-anticipated denouement'.[69] The text chosen by the ousted minister for this supremely difficult and delicate occasion was 2 Corinthians 1:14: 'As also you have acknowledged us in part, that we are your rejoicing, even as ye also are ours in the day of the Lord Jesus.' Winslow describes the choice of this text as 'a superb choice'.[70] It was the basis of a superb sermon. Writing in 1830, eighty years after the preaching of the sermon, Edwards' great-grandson, Sereno E. Dwight, reflected the acclaim that had been accorded to the sermon thus: 'This sermon has been extensively and deservedly styled, "the best farewell sermon that was ever written."'[71] Kimnach describes it as 'one of Edwards' most carefully crafted statements and a masterpiece among his sermons . . . Relentless and methodical, the sermon seems to leave nothing to be said at its conclusion and thus achieves a sense of finality and completeness rarely found in pulpit discourse.'[72] In the course of the Application the preacher once again addresses different categories of hearers:

> But I would now proceed to address myself particularly to several sorts of persons.

---

[68] Ibid., p. 662.

[69] *Works*, 25:457.

[70] Winslow, p. 257.

[71] *Works* (Hickman), 1:cxvii.

[72] *Works*, 25:457. Kimnach makes the following observations on the manuscript of this sermon: 'The manuscript of Edwards' Farewell Sermon (1750) shows that Edwards wrote out his sermon with a care and completeness that he rarely devoted to sermons in the 1740's. The result is one of Edwards' most perfectly finished homiletical works . . .' Ibid., p. 22. 'The forty-two leaf duodecimo manuscript of the Farewell Sermon is remarkable for its length, given that twelve leaves normally constituted a single preaching unit for Edwards and it is unlikely that he preached the sermon over more than one day (morning and afternoon). The sermon is also fully written out at a time when Edwards wrote out few sermons fully, demonstrating that the more important the sermon, the more fully written out it is, even in Edwards' last years.' Ibid., p. 460.

1. Those who are *professors* of godliness amongst us . . .
2. Such among them as I leave in a *Christless*, graceless condition . . .
3. Those who are under some awakenings . . .
4. The *young* people of the congregation . . .
5. The *children* of the congregation . . .
6. All in general . . .[73]

It is under the fifth category here, namely, that of 'the *children* of the congregation', that Edwards delivers the following poignant and solemnizing appeal as he takes his farewell:

> Dear children, I leave you in an evil world, that is full of snares and temptations. God only knows what will become of you. This the Scripture has told us, that there are but few saved; and we have abundant confirmation of it from what we see. This we see, that children die as well as others. Multitudes die before they grow up; and of those that grow up, comparatively few ever give good evidence of saving conversion to God. I pray God to pity you, and take care of you, and provide for you the best means for the good of your souls; and that God himself would undertake for you, to be your heavenly Father, and the mighty Redeemer of your immortal souls. Do not neglect to pray for yourselves. Take heed you be not of the number of those who cast off fear, and restrain prayer before God. Constantly pray to God in secret; and often remember that great day when you must appear before the judgment-seat of Christ, and meet your minister there, who has so often counselled and warned you.[74]

This passage also demonstrates the validity of Kimnach's observation with regard to this sermon: 'The sermon's paradoxical assertion is that Edwards' farewell is no farewell: neither a farewell to persons nor a

---

[73] *Works* (Hickman), 1:cciv-vi.

[74] Ibid., ccvi. Miller notes the following ironical aftermath of JE's dismissal in the Northampton church itself: 'Northampton, finding to its surprise that it now had no minister, hired him Sabbath by Sabbath, at £10 the day, so that the Farewell Sermon was not technically his last . . . He delivered his last sermon on October 13, 1751; three days later he moved, with his family, to Stockbridge, to take up Seargent's mission to the Indians and the pastorate of the little church that Ephraim Williams had dominated for fourteen years.' Miller, *Edwards*, pp. 248-249.

farewell to his relationship with them, since all will be reassembled at the day of judgment before Christ.'[75]

In 1948 Miller published an article entitled 'Jonathan Edwards' Sociology of the Great Awakening' in which he specifically notes this addressing of different categories of hearers. Miller bases his thesis on an unpublished sermon, preached in late 1740, on Matthew 22:9-10: 'Go ye therefore into the highways, and as many as ye shall find, bid to the marriage. So those servants went out into the highways, and gathered together all as many as they found, both bad and good: and the wedding was furnished with guests.' 'The result is that this section of the sermon becomes in effect a sociological analysis of Northampton. It ought to modify the notion that Edwards was oblivious of social realities; if anything, it shows a highly developed sense of the groups and types that make up the community.'[76] In the third section of the article, entitled 'The Structure of Society', Miller cites extracts from this sermon under the following categories: '*Classification by age-groups:* 1. Children ... 2. The Youth ... 3. The middle-aged ... 4. The aged ... *Classification by sex:* 1. The men ... 2. The women ... *Classification by class:* 1. Those of low rank ... 2. The middle class ... *Classification by moral condition:* ... Conclusion to the whole society: ...' The Conclusion contains this marvellous peroration:

> So let all hearken to the call of Christ, by his word, and in his providence, and by his Spirit, this day: young men and maids, old men, middle aged, and little children, both male and female, both black and white, high and low, rich and poor together; great sinners, sinners against great light, against convictions of conscience, backsliders, old sinners and old seekers, self-righteous murmurers, and quarrellers with God; those that are under convictions, and those that are senseless and secure, moral and vicious, good and bad, poor, maimed, halt, and blind, prodigals eating husks with swine, vagabonds and beggars in the highways and hedges,

---

[75] *Works*, 25:457.

[76] Miller, 'Jonathan Edwards' Sociology of the Great Awakening', *New England Quarterly* 21 (March 1948): p. 62.

persons of every condition, and all parties, and every denomination whatsoever.[77]

Miller's analysis coheres to a large extent with our own. It is, however, difficult to escape the impression, in Miller's article, of 'much ado about nothing', or rather, of 'much ado about the obvious'. We concur with Miller that the Northampton pastor was not oblivious to social realities; indeed, his sermons consistently demonstrate not only an incisive knowledge of the human heart, but also an incisive knowledge of the hearts and lives of the people of Northampton. But does the fact that Edwards realized that society consisted of men and women, young people, middle-aged people, elderly people, people of different rank and of various moral or spiritual conditions and that he was able to address such categories in a judicious and discriminating manner really constitute 'a sociological analysis of Northampton'? There is, we feel, some cogency to Miller's own acknowledgement at this point: 'The danger is that I may read into him things that I imagine must be there.'[78] Edwards' addressing of different groups in his sermons according to *age, gender, and position* and according to *spiritual condition* is, in fact, a fairly common practice on his part and can be easily demonstrated from a number of his better known sermons. Such classification or categorization is, we feel, much more significant from the *homiletical* than from the *sociological* standpoint; and it demonstrates that the Northampton minister was indeed, as his epitaph declares, 'a preacher grave, solemn, discriminating'.[79]

---

[77] Ibid., pp. 62-77. We have capitalized Miller's 'his spirit' as this captures JE's Trinitarian theology better than Miller's rendering.

[78] Ibid., p. 53.

[79] These words form part of the epitaph inscribed, in Latin, on JE's tombstone in Princeton cemetery: *'Conconiator gravis, serius, discriminans . . .'* For the complete epitaph see *Works* (Hickman), 1:clxxx.

17

The Use of Instruction

One of the most common of the various categories of Application in Jonathan Edwards' sermons is that of 'Use of Instruction'. Occasionally he utilizes the alternative denomination of 'Information' or 'Inferences'. It is evident from his use of these various terms through-out his ministerial career that these are synonymous, interchangeable terms. In one his earliest sermons – a fragment entitled 'Application on Love to Christ' and composed *circa* 1722 – the New York City supply preacher begins his Application thus: 'The first use is of instruc-tion or inference'[1]; and in his last published sermon[2] – 'True Grace Distinguished from the Experience of Devils', preached before the Synod of New York in 1752 – the Stockbridge missionary begins his 'Improvement' thus: 'The first use may lie in several inferences, for our instruction.'[3] It is invariably this 'Use' that is placed first in his Application. Thus he frequently commences his Application with some phrase such as 'Hence, learn . . .', 'Hence we learn . . .', 'Hence we may learn . . .', 'Hence we may see . . .', 'Hence we may infer . . .', 'Hence we may observe . . .', 'Hence we may solve the difficulty of . . .' The clear aim of this particular category of Application is that of giving instruction, information, inferences from, or corollaries to the truth expounded in the section entitled Doctrine; it is that of providing lessons or general principles based upon the Doctrine.

This basic pattern is well exemplified by the sermon 'God's Sovereignty in the Salvation of Men', where Edwards commences his Application thus:

---

[1] *Works*, 10:608.
[2] I am indebted to Kimnach for this fact. See *Works*, 25:607.
[3] *Works* (Hickman), 2:42.

Hence we learn how absolutely we are dependent on God in this great matter of the eternal salvation of our souls. We are dependent not only on his wisdom to contrive a way to accomplish it, and on his power to bring it to pass, but we are dependent on his mere will and pleasure in the affair. We depend on the sovereign will of God for every thing belonging to it, from the foundation to the top-stone. It was of the sovereign pleasure of God, that he contrived a way to save any of mankind, and gave us Jesus Christ, his only-begotten Son, to be our Redeemer. Why did he look on us, and send us a Saviour, and not the fallen angels? It was from the sovereign pleasure of God. It was of his sovereign pleasure what means to appoint. His giving us the Bible, and the ordinances of religion, is of his sovereign grace. His giving those means to us rather than to others, his giving the awakening influences of his Spirit, and his bestowing saving grace, are all of his sovereign pleasure. When he says, 'Let there be light in the soul of such an one,' it is a word of infinite power and sovereign grace.[4]

Similarly, in 'God the Best Portion of the Christian', preached in April 1736 and based upon Psalm 73:25 ('Whom have I in heaven but thee? and there is none upon earth that I desire besides thee'), Edwards commences his Application thus:

Hence we may learn, that whatever changes a godly man passes through, he is happy; because God, who is unchangeable, is his chosen portion. Though he meet with temporal losses, and be deprived of many, yea, of all his temporal enjoyments; yet God, whom he prefers before all, still remains, and cannot be lost. While he stays in this changeable, troublesome world, he is happy; because his chosen portion, on which he builds as his main foundation for happiness, is above the world, and above all changes. And when he goes into another world, still he is happy, because that portion yet remains. Whatever he be deprived of, he cannot be deprived of his chief portion; his inheritance remains sure to him. – Could worldly-minded men find out a way to secure to themselves those earthly enjoyments on which they mainly set their

---

[4] Ibid., p. 853.

hearts, so that they could not be lost nor impaired while they live, how great would they account the privilege, though other things which they esteem in a less degree, were liable to the same uncertainty as they now are! Whereas now, those earthly enjoyments, on which men chiefly set their hearts, are often most fading. But how great is the happiness of those who have chosen the Fountain of all good, who prefer him before all things in heaven or on earth, and who can never be deprived of him to all eternity![5]

Again, in 'Men Naturally God's Enemies' the Northampton preacher gives this instructional, albeit doxological Application concerning the love of God to his enemies:

Hence we may learn,

How wonderful is the love that is manifested in giving Christ to die for us. For this is love to enemies. 'While we were enemies, we were reconciled to God by the death of his Son'. How wonderful was the love of God the Father, in giving such a gift to those who not only could not be profitable to him, but were his enemies, and to so great a degree! They had great enmity against him; yet he did so love them, that he gave his own Son to lay down his life, in order to save their lives. Though they had enmity that sought to pull God down from his throne; yet he so loved them, that he sent down Christ from heaven, from his throne there, to be in the form of a servant; and instead of a throne of glory, gave him to be nailed to the cross, and to be laid in the grave, that so we might be brought to a throne of glory.

How wonderful was the love of Christ, in thus exercising dying love towards his enemies! He loved those that hated him, with hatred that sought to take away his life, so as voluntarily to lay down his life, that they might have life through him. 'Herein is love; not that we loved him, but that he loved us, and laid down his life for us.'[6]

When, in 'The Final Judgment', Edwards commences his Application, it is, characteristically, Instruction that lies to the fore. He demonstrates

[5] Ibid., p. 106.
[6] Ibid., p. 141.

that it is the fact of the future, final, general judgment that unravels the mystery of 'the prosperity of the wicked' and 'the afflictions of the righteous' in this world:

> The *first* use proper to be made of this doctrine is of *instruction*. Hence many of the mysteries of Divine Providence may be unfolded. There are many things in the dealings of God towards the children of men, which appear very mysterious, if we view them without having an eye to this last judgment, which yet, if we consider this judgment, have no difficulty in them. As,
>
> That God suffers the wicked to live and prosper in the world. The infinitely holy and wise Creator and Governor of the world must necessarily hate wickedness; yet we see many wicked men spreading themselves as a green bay-tree; they live with impunity; things seem to go well with them, and the world smiles upon them. Many who have not been fit to live, who have held God and religion in the greatest contempt, who have been open enemies to all that is good, who by their wickedness have been the pests of mankind; many cruel tyrants, whose barbarities have been such as would even fill one with horror to hear or read of them; yet have lived in great wealth and outward glory, have reigned over great and mighty kingdoms and empires, and have been honoured as a sort of earthly gods.
>
> Now, it is very mysterious, that the holy and righteous Governor of the world, whose eye beholds all the children of men, should suffer it so to be, unless we look forward to the day of judgment; and then the mystery is unravelled. For although God for the present keeps silence, and seems to let them alone; yet then he will give suitable manifestations of his displeasure against their wickedness; they shall then receive condign punishment. The saints under the Old Testament were much stumbled at these dispensations of Providence, as you may see in Job, ch. xxi. and Psal. lxxiii. and Jer. ch. xii. The difficulty to them was so great, because then a future state and a day of judgment were not revealed with that clearness with which they are now.[7]

---

[7] Ibid., p. 198.

The sermon 'Christian Happiness', which was delivered *circa* 1720 when Edwards was aged 17, is of great significance precisely because of 'the supposition that this piece is not only the earliest extant sermon but perhaps Edwards' first formal sermon, composed for his licensure or delivered as an academic exercise.'[8] His text was Isaiah 3:10: 'Say unto the righteous, it shall be well with him: for they shall eat the fruit of their doings.' The section entitled 'Use' contains the following five Inferences, each of which is developed:

> *Inf.* I. 'Then we may infer that the godly man need not be afraid of any temporal afflictions whatsoever . . .'
> *Inf.* II. 'Hence we may see the excellent and desirable nature of true godliness . . .'
> *Inf.* III. 'We may hence learn that to walk according [to] the rules of religion and godliness is the greatest wisdom . . .'
> *Inf.* IV. 'Hence learn the great goodness of God in joining so great happiness to our duty . . .'
> *Inf.* V. 'We hence learn [what] we are to do for a remedy when we are under affliction: even embrace religion and godliness . . .'[9]

'True Grace Distinguished from the Experience of Devils' was (as a footnote in the Hickman edition explains) 'preached before the Synod of New York, convened at Newark, in New Jersey, on September 28, N. S. 1752.'[10] The Synod in question was, of course, the Presbyterian Synod of New York. 'JE's invitation to preach before the Synod of New York', surmises Kimnach, 'doubtless resulted from the influence of the Rev. Aaron Burr, then president of the College of New Jersey in Newark, who had married JE's daughter, Esther, the previous June.'[11] During the course of this journey Edwards was, in fact, able to visit his daughter

---

[8] *Works*, 10:294.

[9] Ibid., pp. 301-304.

[10] Ibid., p. 41. 'N.S.' is an abbreviation for 'New Style', or the Gregorian calendar, in contradistinction from 'Old Style', or the Julian calendar. It was in September 1752, that the new calendar was put into effect throughout the British Empire. The date was advanced by eleven days. As a result September 1752 was 'the shortest month in Anglo-American history'. Marsden, *Edwards*, p. 402. I am also indebted to George S. Claghorn, 'Transcribing a Difficult Hand: Collecting and Editing Edwards' Letters over Thirty-Five Years', in *The Legacy of Jonathan Edwards*, p. 221, for some of these details.

[11] *Works*, 25:607 n. 1.

and her husband. Moreover, it was at this Synod that he met Samuel Davies for the first time. In a letter from Stockbridge to the Reverend William McCulloch in Scotland, dated November 24, 1752, Edwards refers to his recent meeting with Samuel Davies:

> As to the state of religion in America, I have but little to write that is comfortable. But there seem to be better appearances in some other colonies, than in New England. When I was lately in New Jersey in the time of the Synod there, I was informed of some small movings and revivals in some places on Long Island and in New Jersey. I there had the comfort of a short interview with Mr. [Samuel] Davies of Virginia. From the little opportunity I had, I was much pleased with him and his conversation. He seems to be very solid and discreet, and of a very civil, genteel behavior, as well as fervent and zealous in religion . . . Mr. Davies represented to the Synod the great necessities of the people in the back parts of Virginia, where multitudes were remarkably awakened and reformed several years ago, and ever since have been thirsting after the Word and ordinances of God.[12]

It is interesting to reflect that this meeting between Edwards and Davies was not only a meeting between two of the greatest preachers that America has ever produced; it was also a meeting between the future president of the College of New Jersey and his successor. Indeed, it is a further remarkable and sobering testimony to life's uncertainty and man's frailty in this world that, before another decade had passed, these three great men of God, Aaron Burr (1716-1757), Jonathan Edwards (1703-1758), and Samuel Davies (1723-1761) – each of whom was present at the Synod and each of whom was, in turn, the president of the College of New Jersey – were to be removed from this earthly scene by a sovereign hand.

The sermon itself is an Edwardsean *tour de force* in its relentless analysis of the text, James 2:19: 'Thou believest that there is one God; thou doest well: the devils also believe, and tremble.' Kimnach makes the following observation concerning the guest preacher's selection

---

[12] *Works*, 16:544.

of this particular sermon: 'In accordance with a practice invariable from his earliest days in Northampton, he selected an old sermon for the guest appearance. In this instance he selected a sermon from 1746 ..., a seminal discourse reflecting the two most important events in his pastoral life during the 1740's: the Great Awakening and the controversy over qualifications for communion.'[13] '"True Grace, Distinguished from the Experience of Devils"(1753) is one of Edwards' more thorough analyses of the concept of grace, certainly in sermon form. It is a summary of the standards that he fought to defend in his critiques of religious experience during the Great Awakening and, later, during the controversy over qualifications for communion. His delivery of the sermon before the New York Synod can be seen as an effort to clarify his position on faith and grace before an influential audience, especially one that might not yet have taken sides on his New England controversies.'[14] It is also interesting to note that Edwards had, just a few weeks earlier, in August, commenced writing his great anti-Arminian treatise, *Freedom of the Will*.[15] He was, as Ramsey aptly expresses it, 'on the verge of the golden age in the production of his works'.[16]

The Application in this sermon is of particular interest. Kimnach notes that 'the Improvement – normally just a little longer than the Doctrine – is here five times as long.'[17] The first category in the 'Improvement' is, characteristically, that of *Instruction*, which, for its own part, consists of *eight Inferences* from the text, the third of which is demonstrated *via* the fact of the doctrinal orthodoxy of the devil:

> The *first* use may lie in several inferences, for our *instruction*.
>   1. From what has been said, it may be inferred, by parity of reason,

---

[13] *Works*, 25:605. Kimnach notes that, with the exception of ordination sermons, 'it was Edwards' invariable practice throughout his career to rework old sermons for appearances out of town, even in the case of very important guest appearances such as those at the public lecture in Boston or before the New York Presbyterian Synod.' Ibid., p. 698.

[14] Ibid., pp. 31-32.

[15] 'In August 1752 Edwards began the actual drafting of the *Inquiry*, only to be interrupted again by a high point of his continuing difficulties at Stockbridge.' *Works*, 1:7. By April 14, 1753, however, he had almost finished his first draft.

[16] Ibid., p. 8.

[17] *Works*, 25:606.

that nothing that damned men *do*, or ever will *experience*, can be any sure sign of grace . . .[18]

2. We may hence infer, that no degree of *speculative knowledge* of things of religion is any certain sign of saving grace . . .

3. It may also be inferred from what has been observed, that for persons merely to yield a *speculative assent* to the doctrines of religion as true, is no certain evidence of a state of grace. My text tells us, that the devils believe; and as they believe that there is one God, so they believe the truth of the doctrines of religion in general. The devil is orthodox in his faith; he believes the true scheme of doctrine; he is no Deist, Socinian, Arian, Pelagian, or antinomian; the articles of his faith are all sound, and in them he is thoroughly established . . .

4. It may be inferred from the doctrine which has been insisted on, that it is no certain sign of persons being savingly converted, that they have been subjects of very great *distress and terrors* of mind, through apprehensions of God's wrath, and fears of damnation . . .

5. It may be further inferred from the doctrine, That no *work of the law* on men's hearts, in conviction of guilt, and just desert of punishment, is a sure argument that a person has been savingly converted . . .

6. It follows from my text and doctrine, That it is no certain sign of grace, that persons have earnest desires and longings after salvation . . .

7. It may be inferred from what has been observed, That persons who have no grace may have a great apprehension of an external glory in things heavenly and divine, and of whatsoever is external pertaining to religion . . .

8. It may be inferred from the doctrine, That persons who have no grace may have a very great and affecting sense of many divine things on their hearts . . .[19]

---

[18] The most significant modification in the 1752 sermon, over against the original sermon, dated 'Decem. 1746', is the addition of this new head, here placed at the outset of the eight Inferences. See ibid., 607.

[19] *Works* (Hickman), 2:42-46.

It is evident from these extracts that Edwards includes in his concept of Application an *instructional, didactic, cognitive* aspect; it is evident that he believed that the truth of God should be applied not only to the heart, the conscience, and the will, but also to *the mind*. We see here once again the influence of William Perkins upon the New England preacher. In Chapter 8 of *The Art of Prophesying*, entitled 'Varieties of Application', Perkins distinguishes between two different types of Application: 'Application is of two kinds, mental and practical.'[20] 'Mental application is concerned with the mind and involves either doctrine or reproof.'[21] 'When it involves doctrine, biblical teaching is used to inform the mind to enable it to come to a right judgment about what is to be believed.'[22] Thus 'Instruction' belongs to 'mental application'. Similarly we note the influence here of *The Directory for the Publick Worship of God* (1645) when it speaks of 'the use of instruction or information' which is 'a consequence from his doctrine'.[23] It is evident from his emphasis upon the 'Use of Instruction' that Edwards stood firmly within the tradition of English Puritan homiletical practice. Indeed, this particular category of Application is sometimes virtually indistinguishable from the Doctrine.[24] There is often in his preaching an element of interweaving, of interpenetration, indeed, of interchangeability between doctrine and application. There is some validity in the claim of 'Rabbi' John Duncan (1796-1870), Professor of Hebrew and Oriental Languages in the Free Church College, Edinburgh, to the effect that Edwards' 'doctrine is all application and his application all doctrine.'[25]

[20] Perkins, p. 64.
[21] Ibid.
[22] Ibid.
[23] *The Directory for the Publick Worship of God*, in *The Westminster Confession of Faith* (Glasgow: Free Presbyterian Publications, 1997), p. 380.
[24] Minkema makes this observation in his introduction to 'None Are Saved by Their Own Righteousness': 'The Application is very analytical and, in many respects, is virtually indistinguishable from the discussion of the Doctrine.' *Works*, 14:331.
[25] Cited by Paul Helm on front flap of dust jacket in *Works* (Hickman), vol. 2.

18

CONFUTATION

It is part of the fascination of Jonathan Edwards that his entire life (1703-1758) was lived in the Age of Reason. This era, which is generally deemed to date from the Peace of Westphalia in 1648 and to have lasted until the French Revolution in 1789, is one of colossal significance in intellectual and ecclesiastical history;[1] it is also of great significance in the ministry of the New England Puritan. It is an interesting fact that Edwards was born fifty-five years after the commencement of the Age of Reason and that he was in his fifty-fifth year when he died. Thus, by the time of his death, the Age of Reason had already run one hundred and ten of its one hundred and forty-one years. Edwards lived, therefore, during the heyday of rationalism, deism, latitudinarianism, and scepticism; he lived in 'the age of Voltaire'. It was in 1734 that the French deist, Voltaire (1694-1778), published his *Lettres Philosophiques*;[2] the catastrophic Lisbon earthquake that so appalled Voltaire occurred in November 1755 when Edwards was at Stockbridge; and Voltaire's famous satirical story, *Candide*, appeared in 1759, the year after Edwards' death. It is very evident from the historical context itself that Edwards had every reason to engage in *confutation*, not only in his great anti-Enlightenment treatises of the 1750's, but also in his sermons throughout his ministry in Northampton from 1727-1750.

It is an interesting fact that the Westminster Assembly convened in the 1640's, on the very eve of the commencement of the Age of Reason.

---

[1] See Cragg.

[2] Norman L. Torrey describes Voltaire's *Lettres Philosophiques* as 'the chief inspiration for the rise of liberal thought on the Continent'. *Encyclopedia of Philosophy*, 1972 ed., s.v. 'Voltaire, François-Marie Arouet de'.

One of the major documents produced by the Westminster divines – *The Directory for the Publick Worship of God* – specifies 'confutation' as a significant aspect of Application. By 'confutation' the Westminster divines clearly intended the *polemical refutation* of false doctrine, and they gave this directive to the preacher:

> In confutation of false doctrines, he is neither to raise an old heresy from the grave, nor to mention a blasphemous opinion unnecessarily: but, if the people be in danger of an error, he is to confute it soundly, and endeavour to satisfy their judgments and consciences against all objections.[3]

It is important to note that, although Edwards does not employ the term 'Confutation' as a formal category in his Applications, yet both the concept and the practice of Confutation are significantly present in his sermons. Classically, in the Perkinsean tradition, Confutation belongs to 'mental application'; it is, therefore, not surprising to find that Edwards generally incorporates this element into the Doctrinal section of his sermons. Indeed, such Confutation constitutes a constant strand in his preaching throughout his ministerial career. Minkema makes the following observation with regard to this polemical note in Edwards' preaching:

> Always a student of current scholarly 'controversies,' Edwards preached not only on local and provincial debates regarding New England's experiment in church government. He also brought to the Northampton pulpit the issues occupying the attention of European theologians. In an era when fundamental and long-standing assumptions about religion were being questioned, Arminianism was one challenge to Calvinist orthodoxy. But anti-trinitarianism, in the forms of Arianism and Socinianism, was also spreading throughout Europe.[4]

'Man's Natural Blindness in the Things of Religion' is a very significant sermon from the standpoint of Confutation. In it Edwards refers *inter*

---

[3] *Directory for Publick Worship*, p. 380.
[4] *Works*, 14:42-43.

alia to 'the gross errors of the Arians and Deists'[5] in England as a manifestation of man's natural blindness:

> And since the *reformation,* wherein God wonderfully restored gospel light in a great part of the christian world, which was but about two hundred years ago, many are fallen away again, some to *popery,* some to gross *heresies,* and some to *atheistical* principles: so that the reformed church is greatly diminished. – And as to our nation in particular, which has been a nation favoured with light, since the reformation, above most, if not any in the world; how soon has it in great part fallen away! A great part of it to *atheism, deism,* and gross *infidelity;* and others to Arminianism, and to the Socinian and Arian heresies, to believe that Christ is a created dependent God; and to hold other foolish absurdities! And many have of late openly disputed and denied the moral evil of some of the greatest and most heinous vices . . . And in *England,* a land wherein learning flourishes as much as in any in the world, and which is perhaps the most favoured with light of any; there are many men of vast learning, and great and strong reason, who have embraced, and do at this day embrace, the gross errors of the Arians and Deists. Our nation, in all its light and learning, is full of *infidels,* and those that are *further* from Christianity than the very Mahometans themselves. Of so little avail is human strength, or human reason and learning, as a remedy against the extreme blindness of the human mind. The blindness of the mind, or an inclination to delusion in things of religion, is so strong, that it will overcome the greatest learning, and the strongest natural reason.[6]

Central amongst the doctrines on behalf of which polemical refutation was necessary in the eighteenth century was the biblical, Calvinistic doctrine of original sin. Marsden notes 'the delusive optimism regarding human nature that was sweeping the British world'[7] in the 1750's; and Holbrook makes this observation concerning the battle

---

[5] *Works* (Hickman), 2:250.
[6] Ibid., pp. 249-250.
[7] Marsden, *Edwards,* p. 449.

between the Reformation view of man and that of the Enlightenment:

> The controversy over human depravity in the eighteenth century
> was no mere intramural squabble among theologians. It was an
> important phase of a revolution that was occurring in Western
> man's estimate of his nature and potentialities. Literature, philos-
> ophy, economic and political theory, as well as theology, were to
> feel the decisive impact of this revolution. The notion of man as a
> fundamentally rational, benevolently inclined individual was emerg-
> ing as the unquestionable postulate for the expansionist mood of
> Western culture. But the doctrine of original sin marred this flatter-
> ing image. It stood for everything the spirit of the Enlightenment
> detested. Theologians and philosophers, busy developing their
> systems in the clear light of reason, were convinced that 'the idea
> of an original sin which is visited upon succeeding generations'
> was absolutely absurd and 'an insult to the first laws of logic and
> ethics.'

Thus, when Edwards entered the lists as champion of the hated
doctrine, he saw himself as not only defending a particular dogma,
but also combating an increasingly dominant drift of opinion
that had engulfed much of Europe and England and now, he
felt, was encroaching dangerously upon America.[8]

In 1740 John Taylor (1694-1761) of Norwich, England, had published *The Scripture-Doctrine of Original Sin, Proposed to Free and
Candid Examination*.[9] Initially a Presbyterian of orthodox belief, Taylor
had abandoned both his Trinitarianism and his Calvinism after study-
ing Samuel Clarke's *Scripture-Doctrine of the Trinity* (1712). 'In 1740',
notes Holbrook, 'he explicitly identified himself with the rising Pelagian and Arminian tide by his attack upon the doctrine of original sin.'[10]
Taylor wrote expansively upon 'the moral capacities of mankind' and
'the innate capacity for virtue which men untouched by the gospel

---

[8] *Works*, 3:1.

[9] There is some debate amongst scholars as to the exact date of the publication of Taylor's
book. See Clyde A. Holbrook, *Works*, 3:2 n. 5. 'H. S. Smith contends the date of Taylor's
publication is 1740 . . .; Perry Miller and Faust and Johnson hold to the traditional date of
1738.'

[10] Ibid., pp. 68-69.

enjoyed'.[11] 'Unquestionably, his mode of thought, with its emphasis on the moral aspects of Christianity and distaste for the niceties of theological disputation, reflected, if it did not pioneer, a liberal Christianity well attuned to the commonsense rationalism and moralism of the Enlightenment ... By the end of the century, his arguments in that work had become commonplace in many quarters and even had assumed a kind of orthodoxy of their own, which has lasted in liberal Christianity to the present.'[12]

The New England divine recognized immediately the tremendous danger of Taylor's work and determined to answer it in *The Great Christian Doctrine of Original Sin Defended*. Begun in the summer of 1756, this work was completed by May 26, 1757. In his Preface the Stockbridge theologian noted the influence of Taylor's book in New England itself:

> According to my observation, no one book has done so much towards rooting out of these western parts of New England, the principles and scheme of religion maintained by our pious and excellent forefathers, the divines and Christians who first settled this country, and alienating the minds of many from what I think are evidently some of the main doctrines of the gospel, as that which Dr. Taylor has published against the doctrine of original sin. The book has now for many years been spread abroad in the land, without any answer to it, as an antidote; and so has gone on to prevail with little control.[13]

It is important to note that the drift towards Arminianism and Pelagianism in England, which was accelerated by the publication of Taylor's work in 1740, coincided with a drift towards Arminianism and Pelagianism in New England subsequent to the Great Awakening. The very preaching on the exceeding sinfulness of man which, under God, had generated such profound conviction of sin during the Great Awakening, had also generated a backlash against the pivotal doctrine of original sin itself. Marsden makes the following observations:

[11] Ibid., p. 25.
[12] Ibid., p. 70.
[13] *Works*, 3:102.

The awakening, like all radical renewal movements, created a liberal backlash among those whom it had judged spiritually cold ... The Calvinist awakening thus had the ironic consequence of undermining the structures of Calvinist orthodoxy, especially around Boston ... By 1750 Boston was a vastly different place than it had been in 1740. Theologically, no one was in charge. And once the dikes of orthodoxy were breached in Boston it seemed as though there might be no stopping the flood of anti-Calvinism in the countryside.[14]

In his 'Farewell Sermon' Edwards specifically emphasizes the deteriorating situation in New England with regard to Arminianism:

Another thing that vastly concerns the future prosperity of this town, is, that you should watch against the encroachments of error; and particularly Arminianism, and doctrines of like tendency.

You were, many of you, as I well remember, much alarmed with the apprehension of the danger of the prevailing of these corrupt principles, near sixteen years ago. But the danger then was small in comparison of what appears now. These doctrines at this day are much more prevalent than they were then. The progress they have made in the land, within this seven years, seems to have been vastly greater than at any time in the like space before. And they are still prevailing and creeping into almost all parts of the land, threatening the utter ruin of the credit of those doctrines which are the peculiar glory of the gospel, and the interests of vital piety ... These principles are exceeding taking with corrupt nature, and what young people, at least such as have not their hearts established with grace, are easily led away with.

And if these principles should greatly prevail in this town, as they very lately have done in another large town I could name,

---

[14] Marsden, *Edwards*, p. 436. Holbrook describes the same backlash, albeit somewhat unsympathetically from an Edwardsean standpoint: 'As the incessant drumming upon human depravity of the Great Awakening began to die away, it was understandable that some critically minded individuals wished to give closer scrutiny to a doctrine that had helped drive distraught souls into a frenzy and cast obloquy upon human dignity. The sermons and tracts were soon flying about among clergymen in the vicinity of Boston. The Arminian battle over the doctrine of original sin was thus well launched when the full impact of Taylor's book was felt.' *Works,* 3:7-8.

formerly greatly noted for religion, for a long time, it will threaten the spiritual and eternal ruin of the people, in the present and future generations. Therefore you have need of the greatest and most diligent care and watchfulness with respect to this matter.[15]

The allusion to 'another large town I could name' is, of course, a reference to Boston. But by 1750 Edwards was clearly concerned that Arminian principles had penetrated as far as the more conservative Northampton in western New England. Indeed, as the Communion controversy gathered momentum in the late 1740's, the Northampton divine became increasingly more convinced that there was a significant connection between Arminianizing views of human nature and the Northamptonites' lax views with regard to admission to the Lord's Supper. In 1752 he sent an open letter from Stockbridge to his former congregation in Northampton, appended to the end of *Misrepresentations Corrected* – his devastating response to his cousin, Solomon Williams. In this letter Edwards specifically referred to 'the new, fashionable, lax schemes of divinity, which have so greatly prevailed in New England of late',[16] and he pointedly notes the affinity between the doctrinal position of his cousin, 'Mr W. [Williams] of Lebanon',[17] and that of 'Mr Taylor, of Norwich'.[18] Lax views on the issue of the Lord's Supper were, in Edwards' mind, symptomatic of lax views on human nature. Marsden explains thus the connection between Solomon Williams' emphasis upon 'moral sincerity' as the criterion for admission to the Lord's Supper and the eighteenth century's emphasis upon 'virtue':

> 'Virtue' was becoming the watchword of eighteenth-century thought. Modern thinkers characteristically saw virtue as a universal natural human trait that might be employed as the basis for society and cultivated as both the source and object of religion. The Northamptonites' perplexities at excluding good citizens from the church were a reflexion of such trends. The theological implic-

---

[15] *Works* (Hickman), 1:ccvii.
[16] Ibid., p. 530.
[17] Ibid., p. 529.
[18] Ibid., p. 530.

ations of such sentiments were far larger. If modern ideas of virtue became the standards by which to judge theology, as they already were in most of the British domain, Calvinism would soon disappear.[19]

It is no exaggeration to say that each new decade in the eighteenth century witnessed an intensification of the Enlightenment's onslaught upon Christianity. Indeed, by the time Edwards had moved to Stockbridge and was producing his great anti-Enlightenment treatises of the 1750's, what Cragg terms 'the high noon of rationalism'[20] had arrived in Europe. 'Its most brilliant achievement', asserts Cragg, 'was the Encyclopedia (1750-1770).'[21] Rationalism and moralism were increasingly dominating not only the intellectual but also the spiritual field. Indeed, the concept of grace was being rapidly replaced by the concept of reason, and the concept of holiness by the concept of virtue. 'The great touchstone of so much eighteenth-century thought', observes Marsden, was '"the common sense of mankind."'[22] Edwards was well aware of the intensification of the onslaught; and although New England was separated from Europe physically, intellectually, and spiritually, the ripples of European thought had been washing with the tides into Boston harbour since the beginning of the eighteenth century. The pamphlet war of the 1750's in New England gave evidence of the intensification of the battle over the doctrine of original sin and the nature of human depravity. The battle lines were already well drawn between the sons of the Enlightenment and the sons of the Reformation when the Stockbridge theologian entered the fray with his *Original Sin* (1758).

The issue of Roman Catholicism is another major recurring theme in Edwards' sermons. In 'Man's Natural Blindness in the Things of Religion' he deals in some detail with the absurdities of popery:

So it is at this day. Many nations are under *popish* darkness, and are in such gross delusions that they worship the Virgin Mary, and a

[19] Marsden, *Edwards*, p. 449.
[20] Cragg, p. 234.
[21] Ibid., p. 236.
[22] Marsden, *Edwards*, p. 437.

great multitude of dead men, whom their church has canonized for saints; some real saints, and others abominably wicked men. So they worship the *bread* in the sacrament, and account it not only the real body of Christ, but real Christ in body and soul, and divinity. They carry a *wafer,* a small piece of bread, in procession, fall down before it, *adore* it, and account it Christ himself, both in his divine and human nature; and yet believe that the body of Christ is in heaven, and in ten thousand different places on earth at the same time. They think they can do works of *supererogation;* that is, *more* good works than they are obliged to do, whereby they bring God into debt to them. They whip themselves, and put themselves to other ridiculous practices and sufferings, whereby they think they appease the anger of God for their sins. And they pay money to the priests, to *buy* the pardon of their sins; yea, they buy indulgences for *future* crimes, or pardon for sins before they commit them. They think they defend themselves from evil spirits, by sprinkling holy water. They pay money to buy the souls of their departed friends out of purgatory; they worship the *relics* of dead saints; such as pieces of their bones, their teeth, their hair, pieces of their garments, and the like. And innumerable other such foolish delusions are they under.[23]

It might conceivably be thought that, in confuting Roman Catholicism in eighteenth century New England, Edwards was 'raising an old heresy from the grave' and that he was 'mentioning a blasphemous opinion unnecessarily'. But the people of New England were, in fact, potentially in grave danger in this respect. It is important to note that the infamous Revocation of the Edict of Nantes, which had unleashed a deluge of persecution and suffering upon the Huguenots of France and which had scattered them throughout the world, had been signed into effect by Louis XIV in 1685, just eighteen years before Edwards' birth.

Moreover, when Edwards was born in 1703, Queen Anne (r. 1702-1714), a Protestant daughter of the openly Catholic James II, was upon the throne. Anne had no surviving children, and James' Catholic son,

---

[23] *Works* (Hickman), 2:249.

James III, or 'the Pretender', enjoyed the support of Louis XIV with regard to the succession to the throne of Great Britain and Ireland. Queen Anne's War with France, in which Edwards' own father, Timothy Edwards, served briefly and somewhat ingloriously in 1711 as a military chaplain, had lasted from 1702 until 1713.[24] Again, during the 'New York period' (1722-1723) the young unordained supply pastor would have encountered some of these French Huguenots. 'Such refugees were constant reminders of the dangers of coming under the rule of the Catholic Antichrist and his minions',[25] Marsden observes. Marsden also notes the political and religious circumstances that surrounded Edwards' life *in toto:* 'Edwards lived at the vortex of conflict among three civilizations – the British Protestant, the French Catholic, and the Indian. Each was fiercely struggling to control North America.'[26] 'New France was on New England's borders.'[27]

There was, therefore, a distinct precariousness to life – both physically and spiritually – in New England in the first half of the eighteenth century: 'War was no small part of the life of Edwards and

---

[24] 'Queen Anne's War (which lasted until 1713) touched the Edwards family directly and almost disastrously. In summer 1711, when Jonathan was in his eighth year, his father, the Reverend Timothy Edwards, set out from home to serve as a chaplain for a colonial military expedition against Canada. Timothy Edwards was an extraordinarily meticulous, careful man, always concerned to control every detail. He was not suited for military life. Almost immediately he fell ill with a nervous stomach. He started to keep a campaign diary, but he soon became so preoccupied with the symptoms of his illness and his spiritual well-being that he recorded little about the campaign. By the time the army reached its staging ground in Albany, he was too ill to go on and feared he might die. Eventually he was shipped by wagon back to East Windsor where he soon recovered.' Marsden, *Edwards*, p. 17.

[25] Ibid., p. 47.

[26] Ibid., p. 3. It should also be noted that in 'A Strong Rod Broken and Withered' – the funeral sermon which JE preached on behalf of his distinguished uncle, Colonel John Stoddard, on June 26, 1748 – he referred to 'Canada, the land of our enemies'. *Works* (Hickman), 2:39.

[27] Ibid., p. 12. 'The 15,000 French residents of New France would have been little threat to the far more numerous New Englanders, except for their Indian allies.' Ibid. 'New France originated in sixteenth and seventeenth-century French exploration and settlement in the New World. Between 1608 and 1763, the colony offered France a strategic foothold in North America as well as a resource base for fur, fish, and timber . . . It was not until the Seven Years' War (1756-1763) that the French colony was seriously challenged . . . With the Treaty of Paris (1763), the French colony became a possession of the British empire.' Kathryn A. Young, 'New France', in *Encyclopedia of the Enlightenment*.

his fellow New Englanders', notes Kimnach, 'for there was virtually continual war involving the English, French, and Indians in varied combinations throughout his life, if briefly intermitted from time to time. He and his fellow townsmen never knew when another Deerfield raid might occur, even if the *de facto* frontier was being pushed farther out from Northampton year by year.'[28] Thus Edwards' earliest memories were imbued with a sense of the Indian-Catholic menace. Kimnach describes the military situation and its spiritual ramifications thus:

> War with the French and their Indian allies – often characterized by New Englanders as a struggle against the Papacy and hence Antichrist – had been a virtual constant during Edwards' lifetime. Historians divide the struggle into phases, such as Queen Anne's War (1702-13), King George's War (1744-48), and The French and Indian War (1755-62), although skirmishes along the frontiers hardly ceased between the official phases. In Northampton and even more in Stockbridge, Edwards occupied a true frontier pulpit, and the affairs of war are the subject of a number of his sermons between 1745 and 1755, as well as providing a constant undercurrent of allusion that might make its appearance in any sermon during the period.[29]

Thus the potential threat of French Catholicism on the political, international, and even spiritual horizon demonstrates the distinct relevance of raising the otherwise seemingly irrelevant issue of popery in his Northampton pulpit. Moreover, the issue of Roman Catholicism was even more relevant in Stockbridge than in Northampton. The strong alliance between the French and the Indians necessarily involved the constant exposure of the Indian tribes to the wiles of Romanism. Indeed, the threat of Roman Catholicism was, as far as New England was concerned, the pre-eminent issue in the warfare which constantly loomed large on the horizon; and it was a threat to which Edwards constantly returned in the Indian sermons at Stockbridge.

'The Things that Belong to True Religion' was his introductory sermon to the Mohawk and Mahican Indians at Stockbridge in January

---

[28] *Works*, 25:127. The Deerfield massacre occurred in February 1704.
[29] Ibid., p. 12.

1751. Kimnach notes that Edwards 'made a lonely winter journey to Stockbridge in January 1751, leaving family and his beloved books and papers behind, to serve a few weeks' trial ministry.'[30] In the course of the sermon he made it abundantly clear, in simple but pointed fashion, that Roman Catholicism is not true religion:

> Now, therefore, I'll tell you what true religion is, and what that religion is that you must have if ever you are saved. True religion don't consist in praying to the Virgin Mary and to saints and angels. It don't consist in crossing themselves, in confessing sins to the priest, and worshipping images of Christ and of the saints, and other things, that the French do.
>
> Nor does true religion consist chiefly in being baptized, going to church and coming to sacraments: good Christians should do these things, but these ben't the chief things in true religion.[31]

The manuscript of the sermon 'Death and Judgment' is marked 'Mohawks Jan. 1750/51', and just below this, 'St [ockbridge] Ind [ians] March 1752'.[32] Kimnach explains the historical context in which this sermon was preached:

> Seven months before the English treaty with the Mohawks during the French and Indian wars, when in exchange for loyalty to the English cause the Mohawks were tentatively attached to the Stockbridge community, Edwards addressed an awakening sermon to them. The January 1751 sermon is at once an invitation to the fellowship of Christianity and a strict caution against all alternatives ... In the Application, Edwards instructs and exhorts the Mohawks not to trust in a second chance, such as the purgatory that the French talk about, but to undergo the radical change of heart that all men must undergo in order to placate an angry God.[33]

---

[30] Ibid., p. 25.
[31] Ibid., p. 571.
[32] Ibid., pp. 591-592.
[33] Ibid., pp. 590-591.

It is interesting to note that, for the sake of simplicity and comprehensibility, the Stockbridge missionary to the Indians identifies the heresy of purgatory not with the specific religion that teaches it (Roman Catholicism), but with the specific people that hold it (the French), with whom the Indians had had such significant contact:

> All, when they die, go directly to heaven or else to hell.
>
> The Bible tells of no such place as purgatory, which the French tell of as a place between heaven and hell where men are purified in a fire and then after a while, go to heaven.[34]

In June 1755 the Stockbridge missionary preached a sermon entitled 'In the Name of the Lord of Hosts'. 'In the summer of 1754', explains Kimnach, 'Edwards' Stockbridge parsonage had been fortified and had soldiers quartered in it against an Indian attack, and now in the summer of 1755 the inhabitants of the frontier were at the beginning of what would eventually be called the Seven Years' War.'[35] Kimnach adds that 'Edwards was not troubled by pacifistic squeamishness so long as the war was a "just war".'[36] Indeed, he was quite convinced of the colossal import of war: 'The affair of war is one of the most important of all the affairs of the universe: the state of the world of mankind principally depends upon it.'[37] But it is clearly the spiritual consequences of war that lie uppermost in his mind as he continues to warn the Indians of the spiritual dangers of the Roman Catholicism of the French:

---

[34] Ibid., p. 598.

[35] Ibid., p. 680. Kimnach explains the historical context of this sermon: 'The event represented by the sermon below was an English attack on the French Fort Saint Frederic at Crown Point on Lake Champlain. It was led by William Johnson of New York (later General Johnson) and involved a force of about 3,500 troops from New York and New England, augmented by about 400 Indians. The force departed in groups between mid-July and early August 1755, finally encountering the French and their Indian allies on September 8, south of Crown Point near Lake George. There, after a series of skirmishes that appear to have resulted in the death or wounding of most of the French and English senior officers (including Col. Ephraim Williams, Jr., of Stockbridge), the English finally claimed victory – though they suffered more casualties – after driving off the French and capturing their supplies. The nominal goal of the undertaking, the fort at Crown Point, was left for another day, which came four years later, in 1759.' Ibid.

[36] Ibid.

[37] Ibid., p. 689.

The religion of the Papists, that they are of, is contrary to God's word, and what he hates. The Pope [is an impostor; Papists] pray to images, [and] pray to [the] Virgin Mary. [They] pray to dead men. [The] Pope contrived for his people to get away money from the people [by selling them] pardon [for] sin. [They] pretend that in another world there is a fire that is on this side hell, where their people lie a great while, [until they are released by the church's intervention]. [They] won't let the people have the Bible.[38]

The frequency with which the New England preacher addresses the issue of Mahometanism is quite remarkable. That he should address the issue of Mahometanism at all from his Northampton pulpit is, at first glance, surprising precisely because both the geographical and the ideological distance between the world of New England and the Islamic world appear to make it redundant. It is surely self-evident that Mahometanism posed neither an imminent spiritual nor military threat to the people of Northampton; and yet the Northampton preacher returned repeatedly to this theme. His purpose in so doing was anthropological and soteriological. In *The History of Redemption* Edwards depicts Islam as, in effect, the Eastern Antichrist: 'The Mahometan kingdom is another of mighty power and vast extent, set up by Satan against the kingdom of Christ. He set this up in the Eastern empire, as he did that of Antichrist in the Western.'[39] Marsden explains Edwards' interest thus:

> Edwards had an intense interest in other religions, gathered all the information he could about them, and made numerous entries on them in his various notebooks ... Most fundamentally, he viewed other religions, such as Islam, as false and pernicious.[40]

This anthropological-soteriological thrust in Edwards' treatment of Mahometanism emerges in 'Man's Natural Blindness in the Things of Religion'. To illustrate – indeed, to substantiate his thesis concerning man's natural blindness in the things of religion – he

---

[38] Ibid., p. 683.
[39] *Works* (Hickman), 1:596.
[40] Marsden, *Edwards*, p. 486.

adduces the fact of 'popish darkness', 'atheism, deism, and gross infidelity', 'Arminianism', and 'the Socinian and Arian heresies'. He then proceeds to adduce the fact of Mahometanism in order to illustrate the reality that 'multitudes live and die in the most foolish and absurd notions and principles, and never seem to make any doubt of their being in the right':

> The *Mahometans* seem to make no doubt but that, when they die, they shall go to such a paradise as Mahomet has promised them; where they shall live in all manner of sensual pleasures, and shall spend their time in gratifying the lusts of the flesh. Mahomet promised them, that all who die in war for the defence of the Mahometan religion, shall go to this paradise; and they make no doubt of it. Therefore, many of them, as it were, willingly rush on upon the point of the sword.[41]

Edwards deals with Mahometanism in greater detail in 'Light in a Dark World, a Dark Heart', a quarterly lecture consisting of two units delivered in August and November 1737.[42] Once again the New England preacher focuses on the sheer foolishness and absurdity of the Mahometan religion:

> Those that first invented and preached Mahometanism were nominal Christians, and those that had enjoyed the light of the Holy Scriptures; and many of those that were drawn to embrace their religion were such. But they forsook the Scriptures, the true revelation that God gave to mankind. And the consequence is that they are become exceeding vain, childish, and ridiculous in their notions and customs. They expect an heaven of sensual pleasures and delights, that consists in gratifying their lusts, and particularly

---

[41] *Works* (Hickman), 2:250. There is a certain complexity relating to the history of this sermon. The 1834 edition of JE's works provides the following footnote: 'This Treatise is a posthumous work, collected from the author's papers. They were drawn up by him in the form of three short sermons, in his usual way of preparation for the pulpit; but were by no means finished in a manner fit for the public eye.' Ibid., n. The Yale edition reveals that in February 1740 JE preached three sermons on this very text. See 22:540. Thus 'Man's Natural Blindness in the Things of Religion' is clearly a posthumous amalgamation of those three sermons.

[42] I am indebted to Lesser for this fact. See *Works*, 19:704.

describe how, in a manner not fit to be mentioned. They hold ridiculous things about the manner in which they suppose Mahomet, their great prophet, was called, and went through seven heavens, fables almost too ridiculous to be mentioned in an assembly met for the worship of God: as how the angel Gabriel came to him with twenty pair of wings, and went with him to the first heavens, all of silver, where the stars hung on chains of gold; and saw angels, some in the shape of birds, and others of beasts; and saw among the rest a cock as white as snow, that his head reached to the second heavens, the distance of five hundred days' journey, his wings extending from east to west; that every morning God singing an hymn, the cock joins with him so loud as to set all the cocks in the world acrowing; and in the second heaven saw an angel so big that it was seventy thousand thousand days' journey between his eyes. And innumerable other such ridiculous fables, too childish to be insisted on in an assembly met for the worship of God, are the principles of their religion. To hear or read them is enough to fill one with astonishment at the blindness and sottishness of the world of mankind, when not guided by revelation, notwithstanding all that men's natural reason, or the light of nature teaches.[43]

In a recent study of Edwards' views of other religions Gerald R. McDermott criticizes the New England divine on account of the severity of his criticism of Islam. McDermott describes his denunciations of Islam as 'unusually vitriolic'[44]; and the degree of this unusual polemic against Islam he attributes to the shadow of the deistic controversy. Islam, contends McDermott, was 'the Deist stick'.[45] He points out that 'the deists ... were using Islam as a stick to shake at their orthodox opponents ... By the last decades of the century, it had become a characteristic deist move to quote Islamic sources or praise Islam in contradistinction to Christianity.'[46] McDermott explains Edwards'

---

[43] Ibid., pp. 717-718.

[44] Gerald R. McDermott, *Jonathan Edwards Confronts the Gods: Christian Theology, Enlightenment Religion, and Non-Christian Faiths* (Oxford: Oxford University Press, 2000), p. 166.

[45] Ibid., p. 171.

[46] Ibid., p. 172.

response to Islam thus: 'Islam was used by Edwards as a principal illustration for his most important arguments against the deists.'[47] McDermott's position here appears to be that the New England divine had, as it were, a vested interest in Islam precisely because, in his view, the Mahometan religion demonstrated, over against the deistic position, the insufficiency of human reason in discovering the truths of natural religion.

There is, no doubt, an important element of truth in McDermott's position here. Since the deists were, indeed, utilizing Islam as a stick with which to beat Christianity, it clearly behoved the New England divine to attack Islam. Thus, characteristically, Edwards picks the stick up and brandishes it in the face of the deists. It is important to note, however, that his theological positions were not utilitarian or pragmatic; they were a matter of conviction. McDermott fails to acknowledge the exclusiveness of Christ and the gospel in evangelical and Reformed thinking: 'That Islam deserved appreciation as a living faith seemed to be beyond his ken',[48] laments McDermott. This is a cheap criticism and it smacks of a liberal, pluralistic outlook. In repsonse one is tempted to say that it seems to be beyond McDermott's ken that, with or without deism, Edwards was, as a preacher of the gospel of Christ, necessarily bound to show opposition to a false religion such as Islam.

Deism, Arminianism, Roman Catholicism, and Mahometanism – these were the consistent, lifelong targets of Edwards' polemic, whether in his treatises or in his sermons. 'Time after time', remarks Winslow, 'he forced his definition back to the confutation of error. This is the weak point in all his writings. If only he might have felt free to tell! But no: to tell was important, but to confute was more important.'[49] Winslow is correct with regard to his predilection for confutation; and she is also correct in referring to 'his ruthlessness as a controversialist'.[50] But her observation to the effect that 'this is the weak point in all his writings' betrays the classic liberal antipathy towards the

---

[47] Ibid., p. 174.
[48] Ibid.
[49] Winslow, p. 239.
[50] Ibid., p. 295.

polemical; in fact, it betrays that *polemic against polemics* that so often characterizes the liberal theological mind. It is important to remember that, as a matter of logic, positives imply negatives. Thus 'to tell' also implies 'to confute'. It is also important to remember that the word of God itself does not shrink from utilizing these negatives; and the New England preacher-theologian, who took his cue from the word of God and not from the spirit of the age, did not shrink from utilizing them either. Indeed, we insist upon it that, far from constituting a weakness, this in fact constituted a crucial aspect of his towering intellectual and spiritual power. His colleagues and contemporaries saw the importance of this aspect of his ministry and paid tribute to it, inscribing on their late President's tombstone the words, 'a lucid controversialist, a powerful and unconquered defender of the Christian faith'.[51]

---

[51] These words again form part of JE's epitaph: '*Disputator candidus; Fidei Christianae Propugnator validus et invictus*'. See *Works* (Hickman), 1:clxxx.

19

The Use of Self-Examination

The 'Use of Self-Examination' is one of the most frequently utilized categories in Jonathan Edwards' Applications. It is under this 'Use' that he commonly unleashes one of his most powerful homiletical weapons, namely, the use of *the searching, probing interrogative;* he employed this weapon from the very commencement of his ministry. 'The Way of Holiness' belongs to the relatively obscure 'New York period' of August 1722 to April 1723 and was probably preached at some point during the winter months of this period.[1] It demonstrates that, from the very beginning of his career as a preacher, Edwards recognized that the homiletical value of the interrogative lay in its tendency, under God, to search the heart. This passage occurs under the *[Use] of Trial* – a term which he appears to have used interchangeably with the *Use of Self-Examination:*

> Is there an agreeableness between your souls and the Word of God? The Bible is the epistle of Christ that he has written to us; now, if the same epistle is also written in our hearts that is written in the Scriptures, it may be found out by comparing. Have you love to all God's commands and a respect to them in your actions? Is it your delight to obey and hearken to the will of God? Do you obey them of choice? Is it what you would choose to do if God had not threatened to punish the breach of them?
>
> Do you find by a comparison a likeness and agreeableness between your hearts and lives, and the hearts and lives of those holy

---

[1] See *Works*, 10:465 with regard to the dating of this sermon.

men that we [are] assured were such by the Word of God? Do you walk with God as Enoch did, [or] distinguish yourselves by your piety in the midst of wicked examples as Noah did? And when you read the lives of Abraham, Isaac, Jacob, Moses, and the prophets, wherein holiness is drawn to the life, you may viewing so exact a picture discover whether you have not the root of the matter in you, though it be much obscurer in you than in them. When we read the Psalms of David, we may clearly see what David's holiness was by that spirit that is breathed there; when we read the epistles of the apostles, we may know what is a truly evangelical spirit, and whether such a spirit reigns in our souls.

Do you in a measure imitate the saints and angels in heaven? They spend their duration to the glory of God; they love him above all things, are delighted with the beauties of Jesus Christ, entirely love one another, and hate sin. And those that are holy on earth have also a resemblance and imitation of them: they are of an heavenly temper, of heavenly lives and conversations.[2]

In 'A Divine and Supernatural Light' Edwards makes skilful use of a different kind of question, namely, *the rhetorical question*. The peculiar genius of the rhetorical question lies in its intrinsic persuasiveness. The *Oxford Dictionary of English Grammar* emphasizes that 'interrogative sentences . . . may also function as *statements*[3] and that 'a *rhetorical question* is . . . assertive.'[4] Similarly, in *A Comprehensive Grammar of the English Language* the rhetorical question is defined thus: 'The rhetorical question is interrogative in structure, but has the force of a strong assertion. It generally does not expect an answer.'[5] Indeed, the answer to a rhetorical question is self-evident – the question is weighted in such a way that the answer anticipated is a foregone conclusion. In each of the following passages Edwards challenges the thinking of his hearers by means of a series of such questions:

---

[2] Ibid., p. 477-478.
[3] *Oxford Dictionary of English Grammar*, 1994 ed., s.v. 'interrogative'.
[4] Ibid., s.v. 'rhetorical'.
[5] *A Comprehensive Grammar of the English Language*, 1985 ed., s.v. 'rhetorical questions'.

The Scripture also speaks plainly of such a knowledge of the word of God, as has been described, as the immediate gift of God; Ps. cxix. 18. 'Open thou mine eyes, that I may behold wondrous things out of thy law.' What could the psalmist mean, when he begged of God to open his eyes? Was he ever blind? Might he not have resort to the law and see every word and sentence in it when he pleased? And what could he mean by those wondrous things? Were they the wonderful stories of the creation, and deluge, and Israel's passing through the Red sea, and the like? Were not his eyes open to read these strange things when he would? Doubtless by wondrous things in God's law, he had respect to those distinguishing and wonderful excellencies, and marvellous manifestations of the divine perfections and glory, contained in the commands and doctrines of the word, and those works and counsels of God that were there revealed.[6]

Is it rational to suppose, that those whose minds are so full of spiritual pollution, and under the power of filthy lusts, should have any relish or sense of divine beauty or excellency; or that their minds should be susceptive of that light that is in its own nature so pure and heavenly? . . . It is rational to suppose, that this knowledge should be given immediately by God, and not be obtained by natural means. Upon what account should it seem unreasonable, that there should be any immediate communication between God and the creature? It is strange that men should make any matter of difficulty of it. Why should not he that made all things, still have something immediately to do with the things that he has made? Where lies the great difficulty, if we own the being of a God, and that he created all things out of nothing, of allowing some immediate influence of God on the creation still?[7]

'Procrastination, or, The Sin and Folly of Depending on Future Time' is a sermon based upon Proverbs 27:1: 'Boast not thyself of tomorrow; for thou knowest not what a day may bring forth.' The sermon is undated,

---

[6] *Works* (Hickman), 2:15.
[7] Ibid., p. 16.

but the Yale edition has ascribed a date of *circa* 1739-1741.[8] In the course of the sermon Edwards poses the following series of searching questions:

> Do you not set your hearts much more on this world, than you would, if you had no dependence on the morrow? Is not the language of the rich man in the gospel, the secret language of your hearts? 'Soul, thou hast much goods laid up for many years,' &c. Is not this the language of your hearts, with respect to what you have gotten already; which makes you place your happiness so much in it? And with respect to what of the world you are seeking and pursuing, is it not with a dependence on enjoying it for a great while, when you shall have obtained it? Are not your lands and other possessions which you have gotten, or are about to get, in your own imagination, yours for a great while? – Would your mind be so filled with thoughts and cares about these things, so much to the exclusion of another world; would you lay yourselves under so great disadvantages for your soul's good, by involving yourselves in worldly cares; if you had no dependence on having any thing to do with these things for more than the present day? If you did not depend on considerably more time in the world, would your inquiry be so much, What shall we eat, and what shall we drink, and wherewithal shall we be clothed? and so little, How shall we make our calling and election sure? how shall we be assured that we are upon a good foundation for another world, and that we are in such a state, that death cannot hurt us? How shall we be sure that we are ready to appear before the judgment-seat of a heart-searching God? – Would there be so much of your time spent in laying up treasure on earth – and so little in laying up treasure in heaven, that you might have store against the day of death – were it not that you put death at a distance? Would you be so much raised at your temporal prosperity, and so much sunk when you meet with crosses and disappointments in your worldly affairs, if you did not think that continuance in the world is to be depended on for more days than the present? – Let those who

---

[8] See *Works*, 22:552.

very much affect to adorn their bodies in gaudy apparel, inquire whether they would think it worth their while to spend so much time to make themselves fine, and to set themselves forth as gayer than others, if they really had no dependence that their bodies would be preserved one day longer from being clasped in the cold arms of death?[9]

There is, obviously, a particular appropriateness in the use of the searching, probing interrogative in 'Christian Cautions'. Both the text – Psalm 139:23-4 ('Search me, O God, and know my heart; try me, and know my thoughts; and see if there be any wicked way in me, and lead me in the way everlasting') – and the sub-title ('The Necessity of Self-Examination') indicate this appropriateness. Edwards' extensive use of the searching, probing interrogative here demonstrates the way in which he tends to take his cue from the text itself:

I would propose to you to examine yourselves, whether you do not live in some way of sin, – 1. In the spirit and *temper of mind* which you allow towards your neighbour.

(1.) Do you not allow and indulge a *passionate*, furious disposition? If your natural temper be hasty and passionate, do you truly strive against such a temper, and labour to govern your spirit? Do you lament it, and watch over yourselves to prevent it? or do you allow yourselves in a fiery temper? Such a disposition doth not become a *Christian*, or a *man*. It doth not become a man, because it unmans him; it turns a man from a rational creature, to be like a wild beast. When men are under the prevalency of a furious passion, they have not much of the exercise of reason. We are warned to avoid such men, as being dangerous creatures, Prov. xxii. 24, 25. 'Make no friendship with an angry man; and with a furious man thou shalt not go, lest thou learn his ways, and get a snare to thy soul.'

(2.) Do not you live in *hatred* towards some or other of your neighbours? Do you not hate him for real or supposed injuries that you have received from him? Do you not hate him, because he is not friendly towards you, and because you judge that he hath an ill spirit against you, and hates you, and because he opposes

---

[9] *Works* (Hickman), 2:240.

you, and doth not show you that respect which you think belongs to you, or doth not show himself forward to promote your interest or honour? Do you not hate him, because you think he despises you, has mean thoughts of you, and takes occasion to show it? Do you not hate him, because he is of the opposite party to that which is in your interest, and because he has considerable influence in that party.

Doubtless you will be loth to call it by so harsh a name as *hatred*; but inquire seriously and impartially, whether it be anything better. Do you not feel ill towards him? Do you not feel a prevailing disposition within you to be pleased when you hear him talked against and run down, and to be glad when you hear of any dishonour put upon him, or of any disappointments which happen to him? Would you not be glad of an opportunity to be even with him for the injuries which he hath done you? And wherein doth hatred work but in such ways as these?

(3) Inquire whether you do not live in envy towards some one at least of your neighbours. Is not his prosperity, his riches, or his advancement in honour, uncomfortable to you? Have you not, therefore, an ill will, or at least less good will to him, because you look upon him as standing in your way, you look upon yourself as depressed by his advancement? And would it not be pleasing to you now, if he should be deprived of his riches, or of his honours, not from pure respect to the public good, but because you reckon he stands in your way? Is it not merely from a selfish spirit that you are so uneasy at his prosperity?[10]

But the preacher, who was, as Kimnach emphasizes, immediately perceived by the people of Northampton to be 'a searcher',[11] has not yet completed his searching in this sermon:

I shall propose to your consideration, whether you do not live in some way of sin, and wrong in your *dealings with your neighbours*.

(1.) Inquire whether you do not from time to time *injure and defraud* those with whom you deal. Are your ways with your

---

[10] Ibid., p. 180.
[11] Kimnach, 'Pursuit of Reality', p. 105.

neighbour altogether just, such as will bear a trial by the strict rules of the word of God, or such as you can justify before God? Are you a faithful person? may your neighbours depend on your word? Are you strictly and firmly true to your trust, or any thing with which you are betrusted, and which you undertake? Or do you not by your conduct plainly show, that you are not conscientious in such things?

Do you not live in a careless sinful neglect of *paying your debts?* Do you not, to the detriment of your neighbour, sinfully withhold that which is not your own, but his? Are you not wont to oppress your neighbour? When you see another in necessity, do you not take advantage to screw upon him? When you see a person ignorant, and perceive that you have an opportunity to make your gains of it, are you not wont to take such an opportunity? Will you not deceive in buying and selling, and labour to blind the eyes of him of whom you buy, or to whom you sell, with deceitful words, hiding the faults of what you sell, and denying the good qualities of what you buy, and not strictly keeping to the truth, when you see that falsehood will be an advantage to you in your bargain?

(2.) Do you not live in *some wrong which you have formerly done* your neighbour without repairing it? Are you not conscious that you have formerly, at some time or other, wronged your neighbour, and yet you live in it, have never repaired the injury which you have done him? If so, you live in a way of sin ...

Inquire, therefore, whether you have not lived in a way of sin in this regard. Do you not see your neighbour suffer, and pinched with want, and you, although sensible of it, harden your hearts against him, and are careless about it? Do you not in such a case, neglect to inquire into his necessities, and to do something for his relief? Is it not your manner to hide your eyes in such cases, and to be so far from devising liberal things, and endeavouring to find out the proper objects and occasions of charity, that you rather contrive to avoid the knowledge of them? Are you not apt to make objections to such duties, and to excuse yourselves? And are you not sorry for such occasions, on which you are forced to give something, or expose your reputation? – Are not such things grievous to you? If these things be so, surely you live in sin, and in great sin, and have need to inquire, whether your spot be not such as is not the spot of God's children.[12]

The sermon 'Charity Inconsistent with an Envious Spirit', which is based on 1 Corinthians 13:4 ('Charity envieth not'), contains a remarkably searching passage. One of the interesting features of this particular passage is that, in moving from the first paragraph to the second, Edwards makes a significant rhetorical transition from the more inclusive first person plural pronoun *we* to the more pointed second person pronoun *you*. The searching note is thus intensified:

> And now let us inquire how these things have affected us, and how have our hearts stood, and what has been our behaviour, in these circumstances. Has there not been a great deal of uneasiness, dissatisfaction, and uncomfortable feeling, and of a desire to see those who were prosperous brought down? Have we not been glad to hear of anything to their disadvantage? and, in the forebodings we have expressed about them, have we not in reality spoken out our wishes? and, in word or deed, have we not been ready to do that which might in some respect lessen their prosperity or honour? Have we ever cherished a bitter or unkind spirit toward another because of his prosperity, or been ready on account of it to look upon him with an evil eye, or to oppose him in public affairs, or, from an envious spirit, to act with the party that might be against him? As we look back on the past, do we not see that in these, and many other kindred things, we have often exercised and allowed an envious spirit? and many times have not our hearts burned with it toward others?
>
> And turning from the past to the present, what spirit do you now find as you search your heart? Do you carry any old grudge in your heart against this or that man that you see sitting with you from Sabbath to Sabbath in the house of God, and from time to time sitting with you at the Lord's table? Is not the prosperity of one and another an eyesore to you? and does it not make your life uncomfortable, that they are higher than you? and would it not be truly a comfort to you to see them brought down, so that their

losses and depression would be a source of inward joy and gladness to your heart? And does not this same spirit lead you often to think evil, or to speak with contempt, or unkindness, or severity, of such, to those about you? And let those who are above others in prosperity, inquire whether they do not allow and exercise a spirit of opposition to the comparative happiness of those below them. Is there not a disposition in you to pride yourself on being above them, and a desire that they should not rise higher, lest they come to be equal or superior to you? and from this are you not willing to see them brought down, and even to help them down to the utmost, lest at some time they may get above you? And does not all this show that you are very much under the influence of an envious spirit?[13]

'The Spirit of Charity the Opposite of an Angry or Wrathful Spirit' is Edwards' exposition of 1 Corinthians 13:5, 'Charity . . . is not easily provoked.' The sermon contains a passage that is quite remarkable for its sustained use of the searching, probing interrogative. This passage also demonstrates the crucial connection between the use of this searching, probing interrogative and man's conscience:

> In the application of this subject, let us use it,
>
> *In the way of self-examination.* – Our own consciences, if faithfully searched and imperatively inquired of, can best tell us whether we are, or have been persons of such an angry spirit and wrathful disposition as has been described; whether we are frequently angry, or indulge in ill-will, or allow the continuance of anger. Have we not often been angry? And if so, is there not reason to think that that anger has been undue, and without just cause, and thus sinful? God does not call Christians into his kingdom that they may indulge greatly in fretfulness, and have their minds commonly stirred up and ruffled with anger. And has not most of the anger you have cherished been chiefly, if not entirely, on your own account? . . .
>
> And ask, still further, what good has been obtained by your anger, and what have you aimed at in it? or have you even thought

---

[13] *Charity*, pp. 122-123.

of these things? There has been a great deal of anger and bitterness in things passing in this town on public occasions, and many of you have been present on such occasions; and such anger has been manifest in your conduct, and I fear rested in your bosoms. Examine yourselves as to this matter, and ask what has been the nature of your anger. Has not most, if not all of it, been of that undue and unchristian kind that has been spoken of? Has it not been of the nature of ill-will, and malice, and bitterness of heart – an anger arising from proud and selfish principles, because your interest, or your opinion, or your party was touched? Has not your anger been far from that Christian zeal that does not disturb charity, or imbitter the feelings, or lead to unkindness or revenge in the conduct? And how has it been with respect to your holding anger? Has not the sun more than once gone down upon your wrath, while God and your neigbour knew it? Nay, more, has it not gone down again and again, through month after month, and year after year, while winter's cold hath not chilled the heat of your wrath, and the summer's sun hath not melted you to kindness? And are there not some here present that are sitting before God with anger laid up in their hearts, and burning there? Or, if their anger is for a time concealed from human eyes, is it not like an old sore not thoroughly healed, but so that the least touch renews the smart; or like a smothered fire in the heaps of autumn leaves, which the least breeze will kindle into a flame? And how is it in your families? Families are societies the most closely united of all; and their members are in the nearest relation, and under the greatest obligations to peace, and harmony, and love. And yet what has been your spirit in the family? Many a time have you not been fretful, and angry, and impatient, and peevish, and unkind to those whom God has made in so great a measure dependent on you, and who are so easily made happy or unhappy by what you do or say – by your kindness or unkindness? And what kind of anger have you indulged in the family? Has it not often been unreasonable and sinful, not only in its nature, but in its occasions, where those with whom you were angry were not in fault, or when the fault was trifling or unintended, or where, perhaps, you were yourself in part to blame for it? and even where there might have been just cause, has not your wrath been continued, and led you to be sullen, or severe, to an extent that your own conscience disapproved? And have you not been angry with your neighbours who live by you, and with whom you have to do daily? and on trifling occasions, and for little things, have you not allowed yourself in anger toward them? In all these points it becomes us to examine ourselves, and know what manner of spirit we are of, and wherein we come short of the spirit of Christ.[14]

Thus there appears to be a very significant, albeit tacit, connection in Edwards' mind between the use of the searching, probing interrogative in preaching and the role of the conscience in man. This connection emerges with particular prominence at the outset of the 'Improvement' in 'The Preciousness of Time':

Use 1 may be of *Self-Reflection,* to put persons upon reflections and inquiring what they have done with their time . . .

Consider therefore what you have done with your past time. You are not now beginning of time; but a great deal of your time is past and gone, and all the wit and power of the universe can't recover it. How have you spent it? Let your own consciences make answer.

There are many of you that may well conclude that half your time is gone. If you should live to the ordinary age of man, your glass is more than half run, and perhaps there may be but few sands remaining: your sun is past the meridian, and perhaps just a-setting, or going into an everlasting eclipse. Consider therefore what account can you give of your improvement of your past time. How have you let the precious golden sands of your glass run?

Every day that you have had, has been precious; yea, your moments have been precious. But have you not wasted your precious moments and precious days, yea, and precious years? If you should go to reckon up how many days you have lived, what a sum would there be? And how precious has every one of those days been, and what have you done with them? What is become of 'em all? What can you show of any improvement, or good done, or benefit

---

[14] Ibid., pp. 198-200.

obtained, answerable to all this time that you have lived? When you look back and search, don't you find this past time of your life in a great measure empty, having not been filled up with any good improvement? And if God that has given you your time, should now call you to an account, what account could you give to him?

How much may be done in a year! How much good is there opportunity for doing in such a space of time! How much service may persons do for God, and how much for their own souls, if persons do their utmost to improve it! [How much] may be done in a day! But what have you done in so many days and years that you have lived? What have you done with the whole time of your youth, you that are past your youth? What is become of all that precious season of life? What have you to show for it all? Has not all that precious season of life, even the time of youth, been in vain to you? Would it not have been as well or better for you, if you had been all that time asleep or in a state of nonexistence?

You have had a great deal of time of freedom from your worldly business. Consider what you have done with it. To what purpose have you spent it? What have you done with all the sabbath days that you have had? You han't only had ordinary time, but you have had a great deal of holy time. How have you spent it? Consider these things seriously, and let your own consciences make answer.[15]

Twice in this passage – once towards the beginning and once at the end – Edwards delivers this admonition: 'Let your own consciences make answer.' This connection between the searching interrogative and the conscience – always *implicit* in Edwards' preaching – is here much more *explicit*. The great homiletical value of the searching, probing interrogative in preaching is precisely that it searches and probes the conscience. Edwards clearly regarded conscience as a principle natural to man *qua* man; it was a crucial aspect of the image of God in man. In 'Wicked Men Inconsistent with Themselves' he describes the conscience thus: 'Conscience is a principle implanted in the heart of every man, and

[15] *Works*, 19:251-252. In the penultimate paragraph I have replaced some of the question marks in the Yale edition with exclamation marks, as I believe this reflects better the sense of some of the sentences.

is as essential to his nature as the faculty of reason, for it is a natural and necessary attendant of that faculty.'[16] Similarly, in 'A Divine and Supernatural Light' he defines the conscience thus: 'Conscience is a principle natural to men; and the work that it doth naturally, or of itself, is to give an apprehension of right and wrong, and to suggest to the mind the relation that there is between right and wrong and a retribution.'[17]

It is, however, in his treatise *The Nature of True Virtue* (1765) that he provides his most detailed analysis of the conscience. This treatise, described by Marsden as 'the most philosophical of his writings'[18] and 'an intellectual gem by any standard',[19] deals with 'the much-discussed eighteenth-century topic of "virtue".'[20] It was completed in Stockbridge in 1757 and published posthumously in 1765. One of the remarkable features of the treatise is that, in contrast to his other treatises, Edwards did not quote from the Scriptures; he did, however, appeal to their authority for what Marsden terms 'the theistic basis of his ethics'.[21] Marsden points out that, both in *Freedom of the Will* and in *The Nature of True Virtue*, the Stockbridge theologian 'signaled both that he was entering into this international conversation on moral philosophy and that he was at home with its fundamental terms'.[22] Indeed, Kimnach's observation concerning the young Jonathan Edwards is, we feel, also applicable to the Stockbridge years: 'He saw himself as a kind of Christian Philosopher before the citadel of the Enlightenment, ready to turn its lauded powers of reason and scientific inquiry back

---

[16] *Works* (Hickman), 2:919.

[17] Ibid., p. 13.

[18] Marsden, *Edwards*, p. 460.

[19] Ibid., p. 470.

[20] Ibid., p. 419.

[21] Ibid., p. 464. 'Edwards addressed *The Nature of True Virtue* to the eighteenth-century philosophers. Although he paired it with a theological treatise, he kept the theology of *Concerning the End for Which God Created the World* as broadly Christian as he could, so as to establish a wide foundation for his philosophical analysis of virtue. Unlike his other works, in *The Nature of True Virtue* Edwards did not quote Scripture, although he did appeal to its authority for the theistic basis of his ethics. His object was to establish an analysis in which, if one granted merely a few essential principles of Christian theology, one would be forced to reconsider the whole direction of eighteenth-century moral philosophy.' Ibid.

[22] Ibid., p. 467.

upon the worldly establishment in the cause of Christianity.'[23] Thus in *The Nature of True Virtue* the Stockbridge philosopher-theologian-preacher was responding to 'the late philosophers as seem to be in chief repute'. In particular, he was responding to British moralists such as the Third Earl of Shaftesbury – Anthony Ashley Cooper (1671-1713) – and the Scottish ex-Calvinist and philosopher, Francis Hutcheson (1694-1746).[24] 'Just as Edwards was writing his great treatises in the 1750's', notes Marsden, 'Scotland was emerging as the brightest intellectual center in the Western world.'[25] 'Hutcheson . . . had been arguing that *all* humankind were endowed by their Creator with a sense of moral beauty sufficient to lead them, if they followed its dictates, to a life of virtue for which they were also promised eternal rewards.'[26] Thus 'Presbyterian Scotland' was emerging as a major source and centre of 'the new corrupt thought'.[27] 'My discourse on virtue', Edwards wrote to Thomas Foxcroft from Stockbridge on February 11, 1757, 'is principally designed against that notion of virtue maintained by My Lord Shaftesbury, [Francis] Hutcheson, and [George] Turnbull; which seems to be most in vogue at this day, so far as I can perceive; which notion is calculated to show that all mankind are naturally disposed to virtue, and are without any native depravity.'[28]

Edwards' response was that the 'natural moral sense', of which Hutcheson wrote in optimistic, humanistic, and moralistic vein, was,

---

[23] *Works*, 10:201.

[24] 'Historians have long recognized Edwards's intention in this work to refute secular moralism.' William Breitenbach, 'Piety and Moralism: Edwards and the New Divinity', in *American Experience*, p. 188.

[25] Marsden, *Edwards*, p. 466.

[26] Ibid., p. 465.

[27] Ibid., p. 467.

[28] *Works*, 16:696. McClymond, pp. 50-51, makes this observation: 'Toward the end of the seventeenth century, English theology became preoccupied with ethics and the ethical implications of the Christian faith . . . Paralleling this growing stress on Christianity's ethical aspect was the emergence of "moral philosophy" as a discipline distinct from theology . . . On the western shore of the Atlantic, the moral philosophies of Samuel Clarke, Lord Shaftesbury, and Francis Hutcheson were supplanting the older Puritan theology at Harvard and Yale Colleges . . . A growing spirit of liberalism and toleration muted the shriller notes of the old-time Calvinism.'

in fact, none other than that 'natural conscience' upon which Christian theism had always insisted. 'The so-called "moral sense" of the secular philosophers', observes Gerstner, 'was simply old-fashioned conscience in a new guise.'[29] In the section entitled 'Of natural conscience, and the moral sense'[30] Edwards defines conscience thus:

> Natural conscience consists in these two things.
> 1. In that disposition to approve or disapprove the moral treatment which passes between us and others, from a determination of the mind to be easy or uneasy, in a consciousness of our being consistent or inconsistent with ourselves . . .
> 2. The other thing that belongs to the approbation or disapprobation of natural conscience, is the sense of *desert* . . . Thus has God established and ordered that this principle of *natural conscience,* which, though it implies no such thing as actual benevolence to being in general, nor in any delight in such a principle, simply considered, and so implies no truly spiritual sense or virtuous taste, yet should approve and condemn the same things that are approved and condemned by a spiritual sense or virtuous taste. And that *moral sense* which is natural to mankind, so far as it is disinterested, and not founded in association of ideas, is the *same* with this natural conscience.[31]

Thus the corollary of the 'apprehension of right and wrong' is 'the approbation or disapprobation of conscience'.[32] It is precisely because the conscience – 'God's viceregent in the soul'[33] – *disapproves* of those things that are contrary to its testimony that it begets 'unquietness', 'disturbance', 'inward trouble', and 'uneasiness of mind'.[34]

Towards the close of 'Wicked Men Inconsistent with Themselves' Edwards asks a question about the questions that he has posed: 'What will you say to such interrogations of the Judge of heaven and earth?'[35]

---

[29] Gerstner, *Rational Biblical Theology,* 1:95.
[30] *Works* (Hickman), 1:133.
[31] Ibid., p. 134.
[32] Ibid.
[33] Ibid., 2:44.
[34] Ibid., 1:133.
[35] Ibid., 2:928.

The New England preacher had himself been interrogating his hearers concerning their profession; indeed, he had been arraigning his hearers before the bar of God, pointing to that day when they would be 'called to an account by the Judge'. Again, in 'True Grace' he emphasizes that 'great convictions of conscience' constitute a 'transacting the business of the day of judgment in the conscience before-hand'.[36] 'God sits enthroned in the conscience, as at the last day he will sit enthroned in the clouds of heaven; the sinner is arraigned as it were at God's bar.'[37] Thus the interrogations of the preacher are clearly intended to *anticipate* the 'interrogations of the Judge of heaven and earth'; indeed, the interrogations of the preacher almost *merge into* the 'interrogations of the Judge of heaven and earth'. The great value of 'such interrogations' in preaching is that they promote *self-reflection* and *self-examination*.[38]

Edwards notes this remarkable capacity in man to reflect upon himself, indeed, to engage in a kind of conversation with himself, in one of his early *Miscellanies*:

> Man is as it were two, as some of the great wits of this age have observed: a sort of genius is with a man, that accompanies him and attends him wherever he goes; so that *a man has a conversation with himself*, that is, he has a conversation with his own idea.[39]

The clear homiletical and spiritual intention of Edwards' almost relentless use of the searching interrogative is that it should stimulate this 'conversation that a man has with himself'. Indeed, it is part of the homiletical and spiritual power of the searching interrogative that, under God, it not only initiates a conversation between the *preacher* and his *hearer;* it also stimulates a conversation between the *hearer* and *himself.* The questions posed demand an answer; and as the questions in the sermon die away, so the voice of conscience – often referred to in the Reformed tradition as *vox Dei* – continues to speak; thus *via* its approbation or disapprobation it yields the answers which the questions

---

[36] Ibid., p. 44.
[37] Ibid.
[38] Occasionally JE utilizes the category of 'Use of Self-Reflection' as a synonym for 'Use of Self-Examination'. See *Works*, 25:561.
[39] *Works*, 8:42.

were originally intended to elicit. Searching, probing questions are, in their tendency, intrinsically awakening; they tend, by means of the assistance of the Holy Spirit, to beget that 'unquietness', 'disturbance', 'inward trouble', and 'uneasiness of mind' which are so integral to an awakened conscience. Thus the great homiletical and spiritual value of Edwards' use of the searching question lies in the fact that it is *verbum Dei* from without addressing *vox Dei* within.

20

THE USE OF EXHORTATION

If Jonathan Edwards' emphasis upon Doctrine demonstrates his commitment to the objective aspects of the Christian faith, his emphasis upon Application demonstrates his commitment to its subjective aspects. It is important to note, that although 'Christianity begins with a triumphant indicative',[1] it does not end with the indicative mood; the indicative always moves on to the imperative in the theology and the preaching of the New Testament. It is this indicative-imperative pattern of New Testament Christianity that constitutes the tacit theological rationale for the Puritan concept of preaching as *explicatio et applicatio verbi Dei;* it constitutes the tacit theological rationale for the Puritan division of the sermon into Doctrine and Application. It has been noted, moreover, that there is, within this relationship between the indicative and the imperative moods, both an *irreversibility* and an *inseparability;* and it is the fact of inseparability that insists upon the necessity of the imperative and thus of exhortation. It is important to note that the indicatives of history do not and must not exclude the imperatives of ethics. If the indicative mood is 'assertive of objective fact', the imperative mood is 'directive'. Edwards' consistent use of the imperative mood demonstrates that his concern was not merely to *instruct the mind,* but also, through the power and blessing of the Spirit of God, to *impel the will.*

The 'Use of Exhortation' is another of Edwards' most frequently utilized categories. It is in this category that he commonly utilizes the imperative mood in the second person. 'Natural Men in a Dreadful

---

[1] Machen, p. 47.

Condition' – one of the so-called 'Occasional Sermons' on Acts 16:29-30 ('Then he called for a light, and sprang in, and came trembling, and fell down before Paul and Silas, and brought them out, and said, Sirs, what must I do to be saved?') – contains a very extended series of reiterated imperatives from the verbs *to seek* and *to labour:*

> Seek that you may be brought to lie at God's feet in a sense of your own exceeding sinfulness. Seek earnestly that you may have such a sight yourself; what an exceedingly sinful creature you are, what a wicked heart you have, and how dreadfully you have provoked God to anger; that you may see that God would be most just if he should never have any mercy upon you. Labour, that all quarrelling about God's dispensations towards sinners may be wholly subdued; that your heart may be abased and brought down to the dust before God; that you may see yourself in the hands of God; and that you can challenge nothing of God, but that God and his throne are blameless in the eternal damnation of sinners, and would be in your damnation. Seek that you may be brought off from all high opinion of your own worth, all trust in your own righteousness, and to see that all you do in religion is so polluted and defiled, that it is utterly unworthy of God's acceptance; and that you commit sin enough in your best duties to condemn you for ever. Seek that you may come to see, that God is sovereign, that he is the potter and you the clay, and that his grace is his own, and that he may bestow it on whom he will, and that he might justly refuse to show you mercy. Seek that you may be sensible, that God is sovereign as to the objects of his grace, and also as to the time and manner of bestowing it, and seek to God and wait upon him as a sovereign God. Seek that you may be sensible that God's anger is infinitely dreadful, yet, at the same time, be sensible that it is just. Labour that when you have a sense of the awfulness of the wrath of God in your mind, you may fall down before an angry God, and lie in the dust. Seek that you may see, that you are utterly undone, and that you cannot help yourself; and yet, that you do not deserve that God should help you, and that he would be perfectly just if he should refuse ever to help you.[2]

---

[2] *Works* (Hickman), 2:829.

'Pressing into the Kingdom of God' is unquestionably one of Edwards' greatest sermons. Particularly striking is the sheer length of the Application and, within this, his sustained use of the imperative in the 'Directions' that he issues:

> Be directed to sacrifice *every thing* to your soul's eternal interest. Let seeking this be so much your bent, and what you are so resolved in, that you will make every thing give place to it. Let nothing stand before your resolution of seeking the kingdom of God. Whatever it be that you used to look upon as a convenience, or comfort, or ease, or thing desirable on any account, if it stands in the way of this great concern, let it be dismissed without hesitation; and if it be of that nature that it is likely always to be a hinderance, then wholly have done with it, and never entertain any expectation from it more. If in time past you have, for the sake of worldly gain, involved yourself in more care and business than you find to be consistent with your being so thorough in the business of religion as you ought to be, then get into some other way, though you suffer in your worldly interest by it. Or if you have heretofore been conversant with company that you have reason to think have been and will be a snare to you, and a hinderance to this great design in any wise, break off from their society, however it may expose you to reproach from your old companions, or let what will be the effect of it. Whatever it be that stands in the way of your most advantageously seeking salvation – whether it be some dear sinful pleasure, or strong carnal appetite, or credit and honour, or the good-will of some persons whose friendship you desire, and whose esteem and liking you have highly valued – and though there be danger, if you do as you ought, that you shall be looked upon by them as odd and ridiculous, and become contemptible in their eyes – or if it be your ease and indolence, and aversion to continual labour; or your outward convenience in any respect, whereby you might avoid difficulties of one kind or other – *let all go;* offer all such things together, as it were, in one sacrifice, to the interest of your soul. Let nothing stand in competition with this, but make every thing to fall before it. If the flesh must be crossed, then cross it, spare it not, crucify it, and

do not be afraid of being too cruel to it. Gal. v. 24. 'They that are Christ's, have crucified the flesh, with the affections and lusts.' Have no dependence on any worldly enjoyment whatsoever. Let salvation be the one thing with you.[3]

Edwards soon resumes his use of the imperative:

Be directed to *forget the things that are behind;* that is, not to keep thinking and making much of what you have done, but let your mind be wholly intent on what you have to do. In some sense you ought to look back; you should look back on your sins. Jer. ii. 23. 'See thy way in the valley, know what thou hast done.' You should look back on the wretchedness of your religious performances, and consider how you have fallen short in them; how exceedingly polluted all your duties have been, and how justly God might reject and loathe them, and you for them. But you ought not to spend your time in looking back, as many persons do, thinking how much they have done for their salvation; what great pains they have taken, how that they have done what they can, and do not see how they can do more; how long a time they have been seeking, and how much more they have done than others, and even than such and such who have obtained mercy. They think with themselves how hardly God deals with them, that he does not extend mercy to them, but turns a deaf ear to their cries; and hence discourage themselves, and complain of God. Do not thus spend your time in looking on what is past, but look forward, and consider what is before you; consider what it is that you can do, and what it is necessary that you should do, and what God calls you still to do, in order to your own salvation.[4]

A little later in the same sermon Edwards again issues another very extended series of imperatives:

Endeavour now thoroughly to weigh in your mind the difficulty, and to *count the cost* of perseverance in seeking salvation. You that are now setting out in this business, (as there are many here who

[3] Ibid., 1:658.
[4] Ibid.

have very lately set about it; – Praised be the name of God that he has stirred you up to it!) be exhorted to attend this direction. Do not undertake in this affair with any other thought but of giving yourself wholly to it for the remaining part of your life, and going through many and great difficulties in it. Take heed that you do not engage secretly upon this condition, that you shall obtain in a little time, promising yourself that it shall be within this present season of the pouring out of God's Spirit, or with any other limitation of time whatsoever. Many, when they begin, (seeming to set out very earnestly,) do not expect that they shall need to seek very long, and so do not prepare themselves for it. And therefore, when they come to find it otherwise, and meet with unexpected difficulty, they are found unguarded, and easily overthrown. But let me advise you all who are now seeking salvation, not to entertain any self-flattering thoughts; but weigh the utmost difficulties of perseverance, and be provided for them, having your mind fixed in it to go through them, let them be what they will. Consider now beforehand, how tedious it would be, with utmost earnestness and labour, to strive after salvation for many years, in the mean time receiving no joyful or comfortable evidence of your having obtained. Consider what a great temptation to discouragement there probably would be in it; how apt you would be to yield the case; how ready to think that it is in vain for you to seek any longer, and that God never intends to show you mercy, in that he has not yet done it; how apt you would be to think with yourself, 'What an uncomfortable life do I live! How much more unpleasantly do I spend my time than others that do not perplex their minds about the things of another world, but are at ease, and take the comfort of their worldly enjoyments!' Consider what a temptation there would probably be in it, if you saw others brought in that began to seek the kingdom of heaven long after you, rejoicing in a hope and sense of God's favour, after but little pains and a short time of awakening; while you, from day to day, and from year to year, seemed to labour in vain. Prepare for such temptations now. Lay in beforehand for such trials and difficulties, that you may not think any strange thing has happened when they come.[5]

[5] Ibid., p. 659.

'Christian Knowledge' appears to have been preached at Northampton in November 1739.[6] This sermon, which has recently been republished by Yale University Press under the title 'The Importance and Advantage of a Thorough Knowledge of Divine Truth', is based upon Hebrews 5:12: 'For when for the time ye ought to be teachers, ye have need that one teach you again which be the first principles of the oracles of God; and are become such as have need of milk, and not of strong meat.' The Yale co-editors make this observation concerning the Application: 'The Application brims with practical advice ... He concludes with a list of practical directions on how to gain knowledge, including reading and searching the Scriptures and other good books, avoiding vain conversation, and seeking spiritual benefits':[7]

I shall now conclude my discourse with some *Directions* for the acquisition of this knowledge.

First. Be assiduous in reading the holy Scriptures. This is the fountain whence all knowledge in divinity must be derived. Therefore let not this treasure lie by you neglected. Every man of common understanding who can read, may, if he please, become well acquainted with the Scriptures. And what an excellent attainment would this be!

Second. Content not yourselves with only a cursory reading, without regarding the sense. This is an ill way of reading, to which, however, many accustom themselves all their days. When you read, observe what you read. Observe how things come in. Take notice of the drift of the discourse, and compare one scripture with another. For the Scripture, by the harmony of the different parts of it, casts great light upon itself. We are expressly directed by Christ, to 'search the Scriptures,' which evidently intends something more than a mere cursory reading. And use means to find out the meaning of the Scripture. When you have it explained in the preaching of the word, take notice of it; and if at any time a scripture that you did not understand be cleared up to your satisfaction, mark it, lay it up, and if possible remember it.

---

[6] 'No manuscript has been located', observe Stout and Hatch. Nevertheless, these two co-editors place the sermon in 'November 1739'. See *Works*, 22:82, 80, 539.

[7] Ibid., pp. 81-82.

Third. Procure, and diligently use other books which may help you to grow in this knowledge. There are many excellent books extant, which might greatly forward you in this knowledge, and afford you a very profitable and pleasant entertainment in your leisure hours. There is doubtless a great defect in many, that through a loathness to be at a little expense, they furnish themselves with no more helps of this nature. They have a few books indeed, which now and then on sabbath-days they read; but they have had them so long, and read them so often, that they are weary of them, and it is now become a dull story, a mere task to read them.

Fourth. Improve conversation with others to this end. How much might persons promote each other's knowledge in divine things, if they would improve conversation as they might; if men that are ignorant were not ashamed to show their ignorance, and were willing to learn of others; if those that have knowledge would communicate it, without pride and ostentation; and if all were more disposed to enter on such conversation as would be for their mutual edification and instruction.

Fifth. Seek not to grow in knowledge chiefly for the sake of applause, and to enable you to dispute with others; but seek it for the benefit of your souls, and in order to practice. If applause be your end, you will not be so likely to be led to the knowledge of the truth, but may justly, as often is the case of those who are proud of their knowledge, be led into error to your own perdition. This being your end, if you should obtain much rational knowledge, it would not be likely to be of any benefit to you, but would puff you up with pride: 1 Cor. 8.1, 'Knowledge puffeth up.'

Sixth. Seek to God, that he would direct you, and bless you, in this pursuit after knowledge. This is the apostle's direction, Jas. 1:5, 'If any man lack wisdom, let him ask it of God, who giveth to all liberally, and upbraideth not.' God is the fountain of all divine knowledge. Prov. 2:6. 'The Lord giveth wisdom; out of his mouth cometh knowledge and understanding.' Labour to be sensible of your own blindness and ignorance, and your need of the help of God, lest you be led into error, instead of true knowledge: 1 Cor. 3:18. 'If any man' would be wise, 'let him become a fool, that he may be wise.'

Seventh. Practice according to what knowledge you have. This will be the way to know more. The Psalmist warmly recommends this way of seeking knowledge in divine truth, from his own experience. Ps. 119:100. 'I understand more than the ancients, because I keep thy precepts.' Christ also recommends the same. John 7:17, 'If any man will do his will, he shall know of the doctrine, whether it be of God, or whether I speak of myself.'[8]

The category *Directions* is, in effect, a sub-section of the category *Exhortation* and generally involves, as here, a distinct specificity in the use of the imperative mood.

The series of fifteen sermons on 1 Corinthians 13 entitled *Charity and Its Fruits* was preached between April and October 1738.[9] Edwards was in his thirty-fifth year, about midway through his ministry at Northampton.[10] It was, at that point, his lengthiest series and constitutes unquestionably his finest example of consecutive exposition. The seventh sermon in the series, entitled 'The Spirit of Charity is an Humble Spirit' on 1 Corinthians 13:4-5 ('Charity vaunteth not itself, is not puffed up, doth not behave itself unseemly'), concludes with the following remarkable series of ethical imperatives:

> Let all be exhorted earnestly to seek much of an humble spirit, and to endeavour to be humble in all their behaviour toward God and men. Seek for a deep and abiding sense of your comparative meanness before God and man. Know God. Confess your nothingness and ill-desert before him. Distrust yourself. Rely only on God. Renounce all glory except from him. Yield yourself heartily to his will and service. Avoid an aspiring, ambitious, ostentatious,

---

[8] Ibid., pp. 101-102.

[9] It should be noted that *Charity and Its Fruits* consists of fifteen sermons, and not, as Tryon Edwards' edition indicates, of sixteen. The discrepancy lies in the fact that Tryon divided the fourth sermon – 'Longsuffering and Kindness' – into two Lectures. Paul Ramsey makes the following observations in this respect: 'The consecutive pagination of the fourth booklet confirms that Tryon erred in dividing the fourth sermon into two, thus producing sixteen "Lectures."' *Works*, 8:105. 'The force and meaning of this extraordinary sermon was seriously impaired when Tryon Edwards divided it into two "Lectures" – a fault repeated in all heretofore available editions which are only reprints of Tryon's publication.' Ibid., pp. 64-65. With regard to the dates for this series see *Works*, 8:105.

[10] I am indebted to Ramsey for this observation. See ibid., p. 1.

assuming, arrogant, scornful, stubborn, willful, leveling, self-justi-
fying behaviour; and strive for more and more of the humble spirit
that Christ manifested while he was on earth. Consider the many
motives to such a spirit. Humility is a most essential and distinguishing trait in all true piety. It is the attendant of every grace,
and in a peculiar manner tends to the purity of Christian feeling.
It is the ornament of the spirit; the source of some of the sweetest
exercises of Christian experience; the most acceptable sacrifice we
can offer to God; the subject of the richest of his promises; the
spirit with which he will dwell on earth, and which he will crown
with glory in heaven hereafter. Earnestly seek, then, and diligently
and prayerfully cherish an humble spirit, and God shall walk with
you here below, and when a few days shall have passed, he will
receive you in the honors bestowed on his people at Christ's right
hand.[11]

It is important to note that *Charity and Its Fruits* singlehandedly
gives the lie to the assertion made by Charles R. Brown – the Dean
of Yale Divinity School from 1910 to 1928 – with regard to Edwards'
alleged neglect of the ethical aspects of piety.[12] 'It was a perpendicular
piety he preached', Brown contended. 'It did not find adequate expression in those horizontal relations which make up the social order.'[13]
This is a wild assertion. Certainly, the horizontal dimension in Edwards'
thought is subordinated to the perpendicular dimension. But this very
subordination of the horizontal to the vertical reflects the subordination
found in the Holy Scriptures themselves. After all, is not the second

---

[11] Ibid., p. 251. With regard to the integrity of the text at this point Ramsey makes the
observation that the Andover copy ends shortly after the commencement of the first use
and thus does not include this passage, which is the second use in Tryon Edwards' edition.
Ramsey continues: 'Yet it had announced two uses of exhortation by placing a number
before 'To natural men' above. I therefore continue with TE's text (pp. 223-25), which contains a second exhortation. It should be noted, however, that TE's second exhortation is
rather indistinguishable from the first hortatory use.' Ibid., p. 250 n. 4.

[12] In 1906 Brown had given the Lyman Beecher Lectures at Yale on the topic *The Social
Message of the Modern Pulpit*. 'Denominationally', writes Roland H. Bainton, *Yale and the
Ministry* (New York: Harper Brothers, 1957), p. 205, 'he was what would today be called "an
ecumenic".' Dean Brown was clearly liberal in his theological convictions, and the gospel
that he proclaimed was clearly social in its orientation.

[13] Cited Holbrook, 'Jonathan Edwards and His Detractors', p. 387.

great commandment subordinated by the Son of God himself to the first great commandment? Moreover, it is simply not true to allege that he neglects the horizontal dimension. Turnbull makes this observation concerning the horizontal dimension in Edwards' preaching: 'In the series of sermons *Charity and Its Fruits* there is an unmistakable emphasis on man's duty to man, in the sense that the Christian man must live his life in relation to others as well as in relation to God.'[14] Ramsey, the Yale editor, describes *Charity and Its Fruits* as 'an extraordinary, systematic treatise on the Christian moral life'.[15] Indeed, Holbrook – one of the most incisive of Edwards scholars – gives this justifiable retort to 'those critics who pitch their religious views on the humanitarianism of "horizontal relations"'[16]:

> Such views . . . derive from only a partial acquaintance with the bulk of Edwards's writings and his life. The Edwards of the sermons on . . . *Charity and Its Fruits,* . . . and his countless letters has apparently been disregarded . . . But the crux of these negative views of Edwards, especially as they pertain to his thought, lies less in what is discovered in Edwards himself than in the presuppositions which the critics themselves bring to their study of the man.[17]

In the last sermon in *Charity and Its Fruits* – 'Heaven, a World of Charity or Love' – Edwards delivers the following remarkable series of imperatives in his stirring final exhortation:

> Let the consideration of what has been said of heaven stir up all earnestly to seek after it . . .
>
> Do not care much for the friendship of the world; but seek heaven, where there is no such thing as contempt, and where none are despised, but all are highly esteemed and honoured, and dearly beloved by all. You that think you have met with many abuses, and much ill-treatment from others, care not for it. Do not hate them for it, but set your heart on heaven, that world of love, and press

---

[14] Turnbull, p. 141.
[15] *Works,* 8:1.
[16] Holbrook, 'Jonathan Edwards and His Detractors', p. 388.
[17] Ibid., pp. 387-388.

toward that better country, where all is kindness and holy affection. And here for direction how to seek heaven,

First, Let not your heart go after the things of this world, as
your chief good. Indulge not yourself in the possession of earthly
things, as though they were to satisfy your soul. This is the reverse
of seeking heaven; it is to go in a way contrary to that which leads
to the world of love. If you would seek heaven, your affections
must be taken off from the pleasures of the world. You must not
allow yourself in sensuality, or worldliness, or the pursuit of the
enjoyments or honours of the world, or occupy your thoughts
or time in heaping up the dust of the earth. You must mortify
the desires of vain-glory, and become poor in spirit and lowly in
heart.

Second, You must, in your meditations and holy exercises, be
much engaged in conversing with heavenly persons, and objects,
and enjoyments. You cannot constantly be seeking heaven, without
having your thoughts much there. Turn, then, the stream of your
thoughts and affections towards that world of love, and towards
the God of love that dwells there, and towards the saints and
angels that are at Christ's right hand. Let your thoughts, also, be
much on the objects and enjoyments of the world of love. Com-
mune much with God and Christ in prayer, and think often of all
that is in heaven, of the friends who are there, and the praises and
worship there, and of all that will make up the blessedness of that
world of love. 'Let your conversation be in heaven.'

Third, Be content to pass through all difficulties in the way to
heaven. Though the path is before you, and you may walk in it if
you desire, yet it is a way that is ascending, and filled with many
difficulties and obstacles. That glorious city of light and love is, as
it were, on the top of a high hill or mountain, and there is no way
to it but by upward and arduous steps. But though the ascent be
difficult, and the way full of trials, still it is worth your while to
meet them all for the sake of coming and dwelling in such a glorious city at last. Be willing, then, to undergo the labour, and meet
the toil, and overcome the difficulty. What is it all in comparison
with the sweet rest that is at your journey's end? Be willing to
cross the natural inclination of flesh and blood, which is down-

ward, and press onward and upward to the prize. At every step it will be easier and easier to ascend; and the higher your ascent, the more will you be cheered by the glorious prospect before you, and by a nearer view of that heavenly city where in a little while you shall for ever be at rest.

Fourth, In all your way let your eye be fixed on Jesus, who has gone to heaven as your forerunner. Look to him. Behold his glory in heaven, that a sight of it may stir you up the more earnestly to desire to be there. Look to him in his example. Consider how, by patient continuance in well-doing, and by patient endurance of great suffering, he went before you to heaven. Look to him as your mediator, and trust in the atonement which he has made, entering into the holiest of all in the upper temple. Look to him as your intercessor, who for ever pleads for you before the throne of God. Look to him as your strength, that by his Spirit he may enable you to press on, and overcome every difficulty of the way. Trust in his promises of heaven to those that love and follow him, which he has confirmed by entering into heaven as the head, and representative, and Saviour of his people.[18]

It is sometimes objected that an insistence upon the use of the imperative mood in the preaching of the word of God is inconsistent with the theological principles of Calvinism. The tacit rationale for this objection is that, supposedly, exhortation implies ability; but man, it is noted, is characterized by total inability. Thus, allegedly, inability precludes exhortation. According to this view the preacher lies under no duty to utilize the imperative mood or to engage in exhortation. Such objections lie at the heart of the Hyper-Calvinistic position. But the problem with such reasoning is that it recoils upon the word of God. It is abundantly evident from the Scriptures themselves that inability does not eliminate responsibility; it is also abundantly evident from the Scriptures that exhortation does not imply ability. In the Scriptures exhortations are consistently addressed to both sinners and saints. It should be noted that the New England preacher was no Hyper-Calvinist; he was a biblical Calvinist. He did not permit the iron

---

[18] *Charity,* pp. 365-367.

logic of a flawed theological system to destroy the balance taught in Scripture. He recognized that inablity does not and must not preclude the use of the imperative and the delivery of exhortation. For Edwards there was clearly a vital connection between the imperative and what he describes in *Religious Affections* as 'the imperate acts of the will'.[19] In the latter 'something is directed and commanded by the soul to be done, and brought to pass in practice.'[20] Thus the imperative commands the will; and the will, in turn, issues its own commands. It is very important to note that the eighteenth-century New England Calvinist preacher never shrank from utilizing this imperative as he consistently addressed exhortations to sinners and saints alike.

---

[19] *Works* (Hickman), 1:325.
[20] Ibid.

21

THE USE OF THE INDICATIVE

One of the ancillary methods of Application employed by Jonathan Edwards is that of the use of the indicative mood in the second person. It is, of course, in the second person that both the interrogative and the imperative most commonly and most naturally operate; but it is interesting to note that Edwards' use of the second person pronoun also extends to the indicative mood itself.[1] This very fact reflects the forthrightness, the directness, and the boldness that characterize the sermons of the New England preacher. It is a striking fact that the transition in his sermons from Doctrine to Application is often marked by a corresponding transition from the *third* person to the *second* person in the indicative mood.[2] Kimnach has helpfully analysed

---

[1] The interrogative is, of course, strictly speaking, an aspect or sub-section of the indicative mood itself. Daniel B. Wallace distinguishes helpfully, however, between the 'declarative indicative' and the 'interrogative indicative'. *Greek Grammar Beyond the Basics: An Exegetical Syntax of the New Testament* (Grand Rapids: Zondervan, 1996), p. 449.

[2] Lesser confirms this general pattern in JE's sermons in his Introduction to 'Our Weakness, Christ's Strength' (June 1735), whilst noting an interesting exception to it in this sermon: 'Generally, Edwards writes (and preaches) his sermons in the third person, reserving the second person for uses and exhortations, the first person singular for rare pastoral, that is, personal, appeals, and the first person plural for equally rare occasions, fast days and days of thanksgiving. So, while it is not surprising to find just one sentence in the whole of a sermon in the first person plural . . . , it is unusual to find all sentences over several pages phrased so (here, every sentence under both heads of the first proposition, "We, as we are in ourselves, are utterly without any strength or power to help ourselves").' *Works,* 19:377. With regard to this particular sermon, which was '"prepared for the fast appointed on [the] occasion of uncle Hawley's death"', Lesser emphasizes the following: 'And there is a profound shift in grammatical person.' Ibid. It should be noted, however, that the text itself utilizes the first person plural: 'For when we were yet without strength, in due time Christ died for the ungodly.' Thus JE appears to have taken his cue, as often, from the text itself. It is also true that his extensive use of the first person plural in this sermon underlines

the basic patterns in Edwards' use of personal pronouns in his sermons:

> As indicated by the personal pronouns used, the point of view in
> the 'average' Edwards sermon has certain basic patterns. Thus in
> the Opening of the Text, the unity of the minister and congrega-
> tion is emphasized by references to the first person plural: 'we
> are told;' 'in this passage the apostle says (to us),' and so forth.
> In the Doctrine, and sometimes in the Application, references
> to the saved and the damned are usually in the third person,
> emphasizing their status as objects of contemplation by the group
> comprising the preacher and congregation: 'they glorify God,'
> or 'they writhe in pain,' as the case may be. In the Application,
> however, and particularly in the uses of exhortation, the point
> of view is radically altered by shifting to the second person. The
> preacher separates himself from the congregation, as if leaving
> them to stand alone under the light of the Word.[3]

This transition from the more objective third person to the more
subjective second person is demonstrated very strikingly by 'Sinners in the
Hands of an Angry God'. A comparison between the final paragraph
of the Doctrinal section and the first paragraph of the Application
(cited below) highlights the startling character of the transition under
consideration. Edwards moves from the third person ('natural men',
'they', 'them') to the second person ('you', 'every one of you that are
out of Christ', 'your'). The stark and startling nature of this transition
underlines the truth of Kimnach's observation: 'The Application . . . is
usually marked by a significant alteration in tone and rhetoric.'[4]
Edwards begins his Application in this famous sermon thus:

> The use of this awful subject may be for awakening unconverted
> persons in this congregation. This that you have heard is the case
> of every one of you that are out of Christ. – That world of misery,
> that lake of burning brimstone, is extended abroad under you.

---

the sense of collective frailty and fallibility. It was this tragic event on June 1st, 1735, that
effectively marked the *terminus ad quem* of the Northampton awakening.

[3] *Works*, 10:254.

[4] Ibid., p. 39.

There is the dreadful pit of the glowing flames of the wrath of God; there is hell's wide gaping mouth open; and you have nothing to stand upon, nor any thing to take hold of; there is nothing between you and hell but the air; it is only the power and mere pleasure of God that holds you up.

You probably are not sensible of this; you find you are kept out of hell, but do not see the hand of God in it; but look at other things, as the good state of your bodily constitution, your care of your own life, and the means you use for your own preservation. But indeed these things are nothing; if God should withdraw his hand, they would avail no more to keep you from falling, than the thin air to hold up a person that is suspended in it.

Your wickedness makes you as it were as lead, and to tend downwards with great weight and pressure towards hell; and if God should let you go, you would immediately sink and swiftly descend and plunge into the bottomless gulf; and your healthy constitution, and your own care and prudence, and best contrivance, and all your righteousness, would have no more influence to uphold you and keep you out of hell, than a spider's web would have to stop a falling rock. Were it not for the sovereign pleasure of God, the earth would not bear you one moment; for you are a burden to it: the creation groans with you; the creature is made subject to the bondage of your corruption, not willingly; the sun does not willingly shine upon you to give light to serve sin and Satan; the earth does not willingly yield her increase to satisfy your lusts; nor is it willingly a stage for your wickedness to be acted upon; the air does not willingly serve you for breath to maintain the flame of life in your vitals, while you spend your life in the service of God's enemies. God's creatures are good, and were made for men to serve God with, and do not willingly subserve to any other purpose, and groan when they are abused to purposes so directly contrary to their nature and end. And the world would spew you out, were it not for the sovereign hand of him who hath subjected it in hope. There are the black clouds of God's wrath now hanging directly over your heads, full of the dreadful storm, and big with thunder; and were it not for the restraining hand of God, it would immediately burst forth upon you. The sovereign pleasure of God, for the present, stays his rough wind; otherwise it would come with fury, and your destruction would come like a whirlwind, and you would be like the chaff of the summer thresh-ing-floor.[5]

The specific rhetorical strategies utilized by Edwards in the Enfield sermon have recently been analysed by the literary historian, J. A. Leo Lemay: 'Jonathan Edwards achieves extraordinary tension and suspense by brilliant rhetorical strategies. The increasing immediacy of person, time, and place throughout "Sinners in the Hands of an Angry God" explains much of its escalating emotional appeal.'[6] 'The personal refer-ences in the sermon gradually become more immediate', observes Lemay. 'In the Use or Application section, Edwards abruptly changes from *they* to *you* . . . The increasing immediacy of personal reference helps make the sermon a persuasive rhetorical masterpiece.'[7] It is, of course, 'the pronominal shift'[8] involving the second person, whether the subject or the object of the verb, that generates this 'increasing immediacy of person'.[9]

Earlier in the same year Edwards had preached 'Youth Is Like a Flower That Is Cut Down' to a private meeting of young people in Northampton. His text on this occasion was Job 14:2: 'He cometh forth like a flower, and is cut down.' 'This sermon was written in Feb-ruary 1741', note the Yale co-editors, 'to commemorate the death of Billy Sheldon, a young person of Northampton who had died suddenly of an illness.'[10] In a very striking, poignant passage in the Application Edwards makes pointed use of the indicative mood in the second person; at the same time he also makes pointed use of a contrast between the second person *you* and the third person *he:*

---

[5] *Works* (Hickman), 2:9.
[6] Lemay, p. 186.
[7] Ibid., pp. 186-187.
8 Ibid., 187.
[9] Ibid., p. 186.
[10] *Works*, 22:319. The Yale co-editors, Stout and Hatch, with Farley, are, in fact, not con-sistent with regard to the actual cause of Billy Sheldon's death, attributing it to 'an illness' on 22:319 and to 'drowning' on 22:30.

He was young as you are. He was in like circumstances with many of you. A little while ago he appeared as likely to live as you. When you lately saw him at meeting, when he lately stood up to make open profession of the Christian religion, when he lately sat at the Lord's table, when he lately was in company with one and another of you, what was there to show him to be nearer death than you are? What appearance was there of his being so near to eternity? He knew not of it. None of his friends knew anything of it. None of you could see any more signs of approaching death in him than in you or in others.

But yet now he is gone. This flower you lately saw flourishing in the morning and spring of life is cut down; it is not [to] be seen. And you are yet spared. You as yet have an opportunity to prepare for death.[11]

It has been noted that 'The Justice of God in the Damnation of Sinners' contains 'an application that makes up fully two-thirds of his text'.[12] Towards the close of a very lengthy 'Use of Conviction' Edwards delivers an extremely pointed charge in the second person in a manner evocative of a vigorous charge delivered by a counsel for the prosecution in a court of law:

You have not only neglected your salvation, but you have willfully taken direct courses to undo yourself. You have gone on in those

[11] Ibid., p. 326. Stout and Hatch also note the following interesting fact concerning the occasion of the next repreaching of the sermon: 'On February 21, 1748, he delivered a revised and extended version after the death of his daughter Jerusha, who only months before had nursed the dying David Brainerd.' Ibid., p. 320. JE records both occasions, in his own hand and in different inks, at the top of the first page: 'To a private meeting of young people after Billy Sheldon's death, Feb. 1740, 41.' Afterwards preached the doctrinal part with the new application at the end on occasion of the death of my daughter Jerusha, Feb. 21, 1747, 8.' Ibid., p. 321. Thus the second occasion involved certain additional material. The Yale co-editors make a fascinating observation concerning the quality of the paper utilized by JE on the two occasions: 'The differences in paper are dramatic. The paper for the 1741 preaching is of uniform size and good stock, while that from 1748 is made up of scraps of fan paper, very thin and irregularly shaped.' Ibid. The difference in the quality of the paper noted here reflects the increasing problems experienced by JE with regard to the availability of paper both in his later years at Northampton and also during the Stockbridge years. See also Marsden, *Edwards*, p. 483.

[12] *Works*, 19:337.

ways and practices that have directly tended to your damnation, and have been perverse and obstinate in it. You can't plead ignorance; you had all the light set before you that you could desire; God told you that you was undoing yourself; but yet you would do it: he told you that the path you was going in led to destruction, and counseled you to avoid it; but you would not hearken: how justly therefore may God leave you to be undone! You have obstinately persisted to travel in the way that leads to hell for a long time, contrary to God's continual counsels and commands, till it may be at length you are got almost to your journey's end, and are come near to hell's gate, and so begin to be sensible of your danger and misery; and now account it unjust and hard, if God won't deliver you! You have destroyed yourself, and destroyed yourself willfully, contrary to God's repeated counsels, yea, and destroyed yourself in fighting against God: now therefore why do you blame any but yourself, if you are destroyed? If you will undo yourself in opposing God, and while God opposes you by his calls and counsels, and, it may be too, by the convictions of his Spirit, what can you object against it, if God now leaves you to be undone?[13] You would have your own way, and did not like that God should oppose you in it, and your way was to ruin your own soul: how just therefore is it, if now at length, God ceases to oppose you, and falls in with you, and lets your soul be ruined, and as you would destroy yourself, so should put to his hand to destroy you, too! The ways you went on in had a natural tendency to your misery: if you would drink poison, in opposition to God, and in contempt of him and his advice, who can you blame but yourself

---

[13] It is disconcerting to note that in the Yale edition of 'The Justice of God in the Damnation of Sinners', Lesser twice refers to 'his spirit' [sic] when the context indicates that this is clearly a reference to the Third Person of the Godhead: 'And now God has greatly added to his mercy to you, by giving you the strivings of his spirit, whereby you have a most precious opportunity for your salvation in your hands.' Ibid., p. 355. 'If you will undo yourself in opposing God, and while God opposes you by his calls and counsels, and, it may be too, by the convictions of his spirit, what can you object against it, if God now leaves you to be undone?' Ibid., pp. 371-372. The Hickman edition (1834) twice refers, significantly, to 'his Spirit'. See Works (Hickman), 1:673, 678. I have capitalized the word 'Spirit' because this rendering surely captures JE's intention and his theology, even if it does not reproduce his actual spelling.

if you are poisoned, and so perish? If you would run into the fire against all restraints both of God's mercy and authority, you must e'en blame yourself if you are burnt.[14]

In 'Wicked Men Useful in their Destruction Only' he delivers the following remarkable passage in that section of the Application which he entitles 'Use of Conviction and Humiliation':

> How much is done for you in the course of God's *common provid-ence!* Consider how nature is continually labouring for you. The sun is, as it were, in a ferment for mankind, and spending his rays upon man to put him under advantage to be useful. The winds and clouds are continually labouring for you, and the waters are going in a con-stant circulation, ascending in the air from the seas, descending in rain, gathering in streams and rivers, returning to the sea, and again ascending and descending for you. The earth is continually labour-ing to bring forth her fruit for your support. The trees of the field, and many of the poor brute creatures, are continually labouring and spending their strength for you! How much of the fulness of the earth is spent upon you! How many of God's creatures are devoured by you! How many of the lives of the living creatures of God are destroyed for your sake, for your support and comfort! – Now, how lamentable will it be, if, after all, you be altogether useless, and live to no purpose! What mere cumberers of the ground will you be! Luke xiii. 7. Nature, which thus continually labours for you, will be burdened with you. This seems to be what the apostle means, Rom. viii. 20, 21, 22 where he tells us, that the creation is made subject to vanity, and brought into the bondage of corruption; and that the whole creation groans, and travails in pain, under this bondage ...
>
> Consider what a shame it is that you should live in vain, when all the *other creatures,* inferior to you, glorify their Creator, according to their nature. You who are so highly exalted in the world, are more useless than the brute creation; yea, than the merest worms, or things without life, as earth and stones: for they all answer their end; none of them fail of it. They are all useful in their places, all render their proper tribute of praise to their Creator: while you are mere nuisances in the

[14] Ibid., pp. 371-372.

337

creation, and burdens to the earth; as any tree of the forest is more useful than the vine, if it bear not fruit.[15]

The sermon 'Wrath upon the Wicked to the Uttermost' contains a passage remarkable not only for its use of the second person in the indicative mood, but also for its skilful use of the *leitmotiv* of 'continuing in sin':

> The use I would make of this doctrine is, of warning to natural men, to rest no longer in sin, and to make haste to flee from it . . . Here *let those who yet continue in sin*, in this town, consider particularly,
>
> Under what *great means* and advantages *you continue in sin*. God is now favouring us with very great and extraordinary means and advantages, in that we have such extraordinary tokens of the presence of God among us; his Spirit is so remarkably poured out, and multitudes of all ages, and all sorts, are converted and brought home to Christ. God appears among us in the most extraordinary manner, perhaps, that ever he did in New England. The children of Israel saw many mighty works of God, when he brought them out of Egypt; but we at this day see works more mighty, and of a more glorious nature.
>
> We who live under such light, have had loud calls; but now above all. Now is a day of salvation. The fountain hath been set open among us in an extraordinary manner, and hath stood open for an extraordinary time: *yet you continue in sin*, and the calls that you have hitherto had have not brought you to be washed in it. What extraordinary advantages have you lately enjoyed, to stir you up! . . . The chief talk in the town has of late been about the things of religion, and has been such as hath tended to promote, and not to hinder, your souls' good. Every thing all around you hath tended to stir you up; *and will you yet continue in sin?*
>
> *Some of you have continued in sin* till you are far advanced in life. You were warned when you were children; and some of you had awakenings then: however, the time went away. You became men and women; and then you were stirred up again, you had the

---

strivings of God's Spirit; and some of you have fixed the times when you would make thorough work of seeking salvation. Some of you perhaps determined to do it when you should be married and settled in the world; others when you should have finished such a business, and when your circumstances should be so and so altered. Now these times have come, and are past; *yet you continue in sin.*

Many of you have had remarkable warnings of providence. Some of you have been warned by the deaths of *near relations;* you have stood by, and seen others die and go into eternity; yet this hath not been effectual. Some of you have been near death *yourselves,* have been brought nigh the grave in sore sickness, and were full of your promises how you would behave yourselves, if it should please God to spare your lives. Some of you have very narrowly escaped death by dangerous accidents; but God was pleased to spare you, to give you a further space to repent; *yet you continue in sin.*

Some of you have seen times of remarkable outpourings of the Spirit of God, in this town, in times past. *You* had the strivings of the Spirit of God too, as well as others. God did not so pass by your door, but that he came and knocked; yet you stood it out. Now God hath come again in a more remarkable manner than ever before, and hath been pouring out his Spirit for some months, in its most gracious influence; *yet you remain in sin until now.* In the beginning of this awakening, you were warned to flee from wrath, and to forsake your sins. You were told what a wide door there was open, what an accepted time it was, and were urged to press into the kingdom of God. And many did press in; they forsook their sins, and believed in Christ; *but you, when you had seen it, repented not, that you might believe him.*

Then you were warned again, and still others have been pressing and thronging into the kingdom of God. Many have fled for refuge, and have laid hold on Christ; *yet you continue in sin and unbelief.* You have seen multitudes of all sorts, of all ages, young and old, flocking to Christ, and many of about your age and your circumstances; but you still are in the same miserable condition in which you used to be. You have seen persons daily flocking to Christ, as doves to their windows. God hath not only poured out his Spirit on this town, but also on other towns around us, and they are flocking in there, as well as here. This blessing spreads further and further; many, far and near, seem to be setting their faces Zionward: yet you who live here, where this work first began, *continue behind still;* you have no lot or portion in this matter.[16]

This passage is a fine illustration of that 'point'[17] which Dabney describes as one of the 'cardinal requisites of the sermon'[18]; it demonstrates that pointedness, thrust, and incisiveness which he regarded as integral to the sermon *qua* sermon: 'The style which best seconds this structure is that which is lucid, compact and nervous, which individualizes the hearer and addresses him in the second person, which prefers the special statement to the general and the concrete to the abstract.'[19] The great value of the use of the indicative mood in the second person is that it 'individualizes the hearer' and thus deals with him with greater pointedness and immediacy.

Kimnach notes that this transition from the third person to the second person sometimes involves a 'stylistic technique' which he terms 'the manipulated point of view'[20] or 'the manipulation of perspective'.[21] This remarkable shift of perspective is one in which 'the human point of view'[22] is suddenly transposed into 'a divine point of view'.[23] It involves the virtual luring of the unsuspecting hearer-spectator into an attitude of detached, objective contemplation of something or someone contemptible, at which point the hearer-spectator is suddenly deserted as the preacher now rounds upon him and declares that he is the despicable object of contemplation. Kimnach explains this technique thus:

> Particularly in imprecatory sermons, Edwards may at any moment alter the point of view, giving the shock of a sudden new perspective.

16 Ibid., pp. 123-124. Emphasis added.
17 Dabney, *Sacred Rhetoric*, p. 105.
18 Ibid.
19 Ibid., p. 127.
20 *Works*, 10:254.
21 Ibid., p. 236.
22 Ibid., p. 255.
23 Ibid.

Thus, he may develop an image, say, of a 'muck worm,' crawling and slithering through the barnyard, apt to be trodden under foot at any moment – all in all a contemptible object – in a third person (objective) narration. Just as the congregation has become fascinated in contemplating the despicable object from the point of view of an attentive human observer, Edwards is likely to assert, 'you are that miserable worm!' and then continue the development of the image, but from the worm's point of view, enumerating in detail the heat and stench of the worm's surroundings, the threatening hooves overhead, and so forth. In the same way, Edwards is fond of first delineating experiences and ideas from the human point of view, and then – with little or no transition – suddenly re-envisioning them from a divine point of view.[24]

'All That Natural Men Do Is Wrong' contains a striking example of this 'shift in perspective':

If a man has an adulterous wife that carries it with a seeming respectfulness to him, not from real love, but only to flatter and blind [him], that she may the more freely and with less molestation keep company with an adulterer; if he knows that her seeming respectful carriage is not from love to him, but from love to another man, will he not abhor her respectful carriage? Will not that respectful carriage of hers be provoking and abominable to him? Will he not, instead of counting himself obliged by it, look upon it as the highest injury, and that he has just cause to have his wrath provoked by it? But this is the case with you towards God. That seeming respect that you show to God in your external behavior don't proceed from the least jot of real respect in your heart; but you do but flatter God in it, and it really proceeds from respect to something else. 'Tis from respect to some idol, that you set up in the room of God, to whom you give that respect that is God's due, and that you deny to him. Thus treacherously and deceitfully do you deal with God.[25]

---

[24] Ibid.

[25] *Works*, 19:531-532. This sermon is particularly significant with regard to JE's concept of seeking.

It will be noted that this passage commences with 'a third person (objective) narration', but suddenly shifts to a second person (subjective) critique with the statement, 'But this is the case with you towards God.' Thus the objective and detached perspective suddenly shifts to a perspective that is subjective and involved. There is, as Kimnach puts it, 'the shock of a sudden new perspective'.[26] The preacher thus isolates the congregation before God. The objective observer, who has been *looking on* in tacit condemnation of the 'adulterous wife', has, in fact, suddenly *become* the 'adulterous wife', just as the injured husband has suddenly *become* the offended God. The pointed use of the indicative mood in the second person continues to the end of the paragraph: 'Thus treacherously and deceitfully do you deal with God.'

It is important to note that Edwards' sermons are generally characterized by a definite sense of movement and progress. The movement is from the more objective to the more subjective, from the more impersonal to the more personal, from the more indirect to the more direct. There is generally a distinct hastening of the homiletical tempo as the sermon progresses; and the transition from the third person to the second person in the indicative mood in the Application is a significant aspect of this hastening tempo. Indeed, his method in this respect is, we believe, superior to that advocated by Jay E. Adams. Adams contends that all too often preaching degenerates into lecturing. He draws a contrast between what he terms the 'lecture stance'[27] and the 'preaching stance'.[28] The 'lecture stance' is, he contends, characterized by the 'third person emphasis',[29] whereas the 'preaching stance' is characterized by the 'second person emphasis'.[30] The central issue here is, he contends, one of 'stance' or 'orientation'. Indeed, Adams urges that the whole sermon be cast in the second person, even the various headings. 'The preacher . . . using a genuine preaching outline, applies all along the way; indeed, in one sense the whole sermon is application.'[31]

---

[26] *Works*, 10:255.

[27] Jay E. Adams, *Preaching with Purpose: The Urgent Task of Homiletics* (Phillipsburg, N.J.: Presbyterian and Reformed, 1982), p. 43.

[28] Ibid.

[29] Ibid., p. 51.

[30] Ibid.

[31] Ibid., p. 54.

The problem with Adams' position here is that it overstates the case. We do not deny that all too often preaching degenerates into lecturing; and we do not deny the significance and value of the use of the second person. But to cast the entire sermon in the second person is, we believe, excessive and tends to be homiletically too aggressive. Indeed, the over-use of the second person will tend, in the final analysis, to undermine its own effectiveness. It is interesting to note that Edwards does not play his hand too early in this respect. He invariably waits until the Application before he shifts from the third person to the second person. His use of the second person in the indicative is ultimately all the more effective precisely because of the startling contrast established between the more comfortable third person and the more uncomfortable second person. It is what Lloyd-Jones called 'the element of attack'[32] – judiciously and strategically employed.

[32] D. M. Lloyd-Jones, *Preaching and Preachers* (London: Hodder and Stoughton, 1971), p. 71.

22

OBJECTIONS AND ANSWERS

The cover of Jonathan Edwards' notebook, 'Notes on Natural Philosophy', contains a list of rules or resolutions with regard to literary theory which includes the following entry:

> [15.] Oftentimes it suits the subject and reasoning best to explain by way of objection and answer, after the manner of dialogue, like the Earl of Shaftesbury.[1]

This entry was probably written in the early months of 1726, and these rules constitute, according to Kimnach, Edwards' 'earliest notes on style and literary strategy';[2] indeed, they constitute 'a general theory of writing which provided a foundation for Edwards' later writings, including sermons'.[3] The Third Earl of Shaftesbury, Anthony Ashley Cooper (1671-1713), was a British politician and philosopher. 'Lord Shaftesbury', writes R. G. Frey, 'was one of the shaping influences on the intellectual currents of the early and mid-eighteenth century both in Britain and abroad. His *Characteristicks of Men, Manners, Opinions, Times* (1711), a collection of writings, proved extraordinarily influential in literary and artistic circles as well as the world of philosophy and, to a lesser extent, religion.'[4] The Earl of Shaftesbury was a 'Deistic moralist';[5] but the very fact that Edwards utilized Shaftesbury's literary suggestion, in spite of his own inveterate opposition to deism and moralism, demonstrates his essential literary eclecticism. Edwards was

---

[1] *Works*, 10:184.
[2] Ibid., p. 180. See 8:704 with regard to the date of this entry.
[3] Ibid.
[4] R. G. Frey, 'Shaftesbury, Anthony Ashley Cooper', in *Encyclopedia of the Enlightenment*.
[5] *Works*, 10:185.

interested in 'the latest, most popular literary forms';[6] and the Earl's evident theological principles clearly constituted no reason in Edwards' mind why he should not learn from the deist the value of 'the dialogue technique'[7] of Objections and Answers and utilize it in the sermon.

Edwards employs this technique in 'The Eternity of Hell Torments', which was preached in April 1739 as a response to the position of the deceased, yet highly influential, Archbishop John Tillotson. In this sermon he deals with Objections to the doctrine of everlasting punishment which had been raised by the Archbishop almost fifty years earlier:

> Before I conclude this head, it may be proper for me to answer an objection or two, that may arise in the minds of some . . .
>
> Another objection may arise from God's threatening to Nineveh. He threatened, that in forty days Nineveh should be destroyed, which yet he did not fulfil. – I answer, that threatening could justly be looked upon no otherwise than as *conditional*. It was of the nature of a *warning*, and not of an absolute denunciation. Why was Jonah sent to the Ninevites, but to give them warning, that they might have opportunity to repent, reform, and avert the approaching destruction? God had no other design or end in sending the prophet to them, but that they might be warned and tried by him, as God warned the Israelites, Judah and Jerusalem, before their destruction. Therefore the prophets, together with their prophecies of approaching destruction, joined earnest exhortations to repent and reform, that it might be averted.
>
> No more could justly be understood to be certainly threatened, than that Nineveh should be destroyed in forty days, *continuing as it was*. For it was for their wickedness that that destruction was threatened, and so the Ninevites took it. Therefore, when the cause was removed, the effect ceased. It was contrary to God's known manner, to threaten punishment and destruction for sin in this world absolutely, so that it should come upon the persons threatened unavoidably, let them repent and reform and do what they

would: Jer. xviii. 7, 8. 'At what instant I shall speak concerning a nation, and concerning a kingdom, to pluck up, and to pull down, and to destroy it; if that nation against whom I have pronounced turn from their evil, I will repent of the evil that I thought to do unto them.' So that all threatenings of this nature had a *condition* implied in them, according to the known and declared manner of God's dealing. And the Ninevites did not take it as an *absolute* sentence of denunciation: if they had, they would have despaired of any benefit by fasting and reformation.

But the threatenings of eternal wrath are positive and absolute. There is nothing in the word of God from which we can gather any condition. The only opportunity of escaping is in this world; this is the only state of trial, wherein we have any offers of mercy, or place of repentance.[8]

One of the interesting and almost ironic features of this passage is that, in the course of it, Edwards utilizes the literary technique of one freethinker to refute the theological position of another freethinker; he utilizes the literary technique of Objection and Answer advocated by the Third Earl of Shaftesbury in order to refute the theological position concerning the eternity of hell torments advocated by Archbishop Tillotson. It should be noted in passing that this interesting fact demonstrates both the extent and the limits of Edwards' eclecticism. On the one hand, he was quite prepared to assimilate into his preaching the literary suggestion of the Earl of Shaftesbury; on the other hand, it was unthinkable to him that he should assimilate into his theology or his preaching the doctrinal suggestion of Archbishop Tillotson.

The sermon in which this technique of Objections and Answers is most prominent is 'Christian Charity: or, The Duty of Charity to the Poor, Explained and Enforced'. According to Mark Valeri, this sermon was 'possibly a contribution lecture'[9] – an occasion on which charitable

---

[8] *Works* (Hickman), 2:87.

[9] *Works*, 17:456. The basic problem with Valeri's editorial preface is that it reveals all too often an essentially socio-economic interpretation of JE's ministry in Northampton and even of this particular sermon. 'In The Duty of Charity to the Poor', observes Valeri, 'Edwards levels the charge of self-interestedness and avarice against members of the upper

donations would have been requested on behalf of the poor. Delivered in Northampton in January 1733, it was also 'the first sermon that Edwards dated'.[10] It appears, moreover, to be the first sermon in which he utilized this particular technique of Objections and Answers. Valeri notes that during the period from 1730 to 1733 Edwards experimented with the organization or structure of his sermons and introduced certain innovations. The issue of persuasion is, Valeri contends, integral to Edwards' use of Objections and Answers:

> As Edwards attempted to convey increasingly complex theological concepts to his congregation, he experimented with different ways of organizing his sermons . . . And in 'The Duty of Charity to the Poor', he devotes less than one unit of the sermon to doctrine and the entirety of the remaining four units to application, the third major division of which had eleven subpoints in the form of objections and answers.
>
> Such innovations reflect Edwards' attempts to make controversial theological issues intelligible. He wanted to persuade, not just to inform.[11]

Thus, remarkably, eighty percent of this sermon is devoted to Application, the principal method of which is that of objections and detailed answers.[12] The appropriateness of this particular homiletical

---

and middle social orders of society who fail to take responsibility for their neighbors of lesser means . . . Economic competition and factionalization indicated to Edwards Northampton's lack of grace.' Ibid., pp. 31-32. Valeri strains to make the (on his thesis) necessary connection between what he regards as the underlying social and economic problems in Northampton on the one hand and JE's preaching ministry on the other. Interestingly, Valeri himself makes the following observation: 'Of the seventy sermons by JE published in the eighteenth and nineteenth centuries, none dealt explicitly with public affairs. Only recently, with attention to unpublished and especially occasional sermons, have historians begun to uncover the civic dimensions of JE's thought.' Ibid., p. 17 n. 9. It is important to remember that JE was, above all else, a preacher of the word of God. In the very nature of the case the Bible comprehends all aspects and areas of life. But to focus primarily upon the social, the economic, and the civic in analysing the preaching of JE is, we believe, a mistake. The underlying issues in Northampton, as in any town, were essentially spiritual and moral, not social and economic.

[10] Ibid., p. 370.
[11] Ibid., pp. 13-14.
[12] See ibid., p. 369.

approach lies in the fact that, in this sermon, the text itself – Deuteronomy 15:7-11 – specifically warns against objections:

> Moreover, God strictly warns against objections, ver. 9. 'Beware that there be not a thought in thy wicked heart, saying, The seventh year, the year of release, is at hand; and thine eye be evil against thy poor brother, and thou give him nought, and he cry unto the Lord against thee, and it be sin unto thee'... Therefore God warns the children of Israel against making of this an objection to helping their poor neighbours, that the year of release was near at hand; and it was not likely that they would be able to refund it again before that time, and then they should lose it wholly, because then they would be obliged to release it. God foresaw that the wickedness of their hearts would be very ready to make such an objection; but very strictly warns them against it, that they should not be the more backward to supply the wants of the needy for that, but should be willing to give him: 'Thou shalt be willing to lend, expecting nothing again.'
>
> Men are exceedingly apt to make objections against such duties, which God speaks of here as a manifestation of the wickedness of their hearts: 'Beware that there be not a thought in thy wicked heart,' &c. The warning is very strict. God doth not only say, Beware that thou do not actually refuse to give him, but, Beware that thou have not one objecting thought against it, arising from a backwardness to liberality. God warns against the beginnings of uncharitableness in the heart, and against whatever tends to a forbearance to give.[13]

Thus, having explained the text, adduced parallel passages of Scripture to reinforce the Christian obligation of charity, and delivered an exhortation to his hearers to perform this duty, Edwards then announces in the final applicatory section: 'I proceed now to answer some objections, which are sometimes made against this duty.' We cite the second of these eleven objections:

---

[13] *Works* (Hickman), 2:163-64.

OBJECT. II. If I be liberal and bountiful, I shall only make a righteousness of it, and so it will do me more hurt than good. To this I say,

The same answer may be made to this, as to the former objection, *viz.* That you may as well make the same objection against doing any religious or moral duty at all. If this be a sufficient objection against deeds of charity, then it is a sufficient objection to prayer; for nothing is more common than for persons to make a righteousness of their prayers. So it is a good objection against your keeping the sabbath, or attending any public worship, or ever reading in the Bible; for of all these things you are in danger of making a righteousness. – Yea, if the objection be good against deeds of charity, then it is as good against acts of justice; and you may neglect to speak the truth, may neglect to pay your debts, may neglect acts of common humanity; for of all those things you are in danger of making a righteousness. So that if your objection be good, you may throw up all religion, and live like heathens or atheists, and may be thieves, robbers, fornicators, adulterers, murderers, and commit all the sins that you can think of, lest if you do otherwise, you should make a righteousness of your conduct.[14]

In March 1738, just three years after the revival in the town of Northampton, Edwards preached a sermon entitled 'Temptation and Deliverance; or, Joseph's Great Temptation and Gracious Deliverance'. His text was Genesis 39:12: 'And he left his garment in her hand, and fled, and got him out.' In this sermon the preacher deals with three objections against his own indictment of the 'custom of frolicking'. We cite his third answer, which, interestingly, consists, in large part, of rhetorical questions:

OBJECTION. If we avoid all such things, it will be the way for our young people to be ignorant how to behave themselves in company.
ANSWER. But consider what this objection comes to. It certainly comes to this, *viz.* That the pouring out of the Spirit of God upon a people, tends to banish all good conduct, good breeding, and

---

[14] Ibid., p. 169.

decent behaviour from among them; and to sink them down into clownishness and barbarity! The Spirit of God did actually put an end to this practice among us. – But who is not ashamed to make such an objection? Will any of our young converts talk thus? Will you, that think you were converted by the late pouring out of the Spirit of God, and are made holy persons, heirs of eternal life, talk so blasphemously of it?[15]

'Charity Disposes us Meekly to Bear the Injuries Received from Others' contains a series of three Objections and Answers, the first of which is particularly striking:

Objection 1. Some may be ready to say, *that the injuries they receive from men are intolerable;* that the one who has injured them has been so unreasonable in what he has said or done, and it is so unjust and injurious and unjustifiable, and the like, that it is more than flesh and blood can bear; that they are treated with so much injustice that it is enough to provoke a stone: or that they are treated with such contempt, that they are actually trampled on, and they cannot but resent it. But in answer to this objection, I would ask a few questions. And,

First, Do you think the injuries you have received from your fellow-man are more than you have offered to God? Has your enemy been more base, more unreasonable, more ungrateful, than you have to the High and Holy One? Have his offences been more heinous or aggravated, or more in number, than yours have been against your Creator, Benefactor, and Redeemer? Have they been more provoking and exasperating than your sinful conduct has been to him who is the author of all our mercies, and to whom you are under the highest obligations?

Second, Do you not hope that as God hitherto has, so he will still bear with you in all this, and that notwithstanding all, he will exercise toward you his infinite love and favour? Do you not hope that God will have mercy upon you, and that Christ will embrace you in his dying love, though you have been such an injurious enemy; and that, through his grace, he will blot out your trans-

---

[15] Ibid., pp. 232-233.

gressions and all your offences against him, and make you eternally his child, and an heir of his kingdom?

Third, When you think of such long-suffering on God's part, do you not approve of it, and think well of it, and that it is not only worthy and excellent, but exceeding glorious? And do you not approve of it, that Christ should have died for you, and that God, through him, should offer you pardon and salvation? Or do you disapprove of this? And would you have liked God better, if he had not borne with you, but had long since cut you off in his wrath?

Fourth, If such a course be excellent and worthy to be approved of in God, why is it not so in yourself? Why should you not imitate it? Is God too kind in forgiving injuries? Is it less heinous to offend the Lord of heaven and earth, than for a man to offend you? Is it well for you to be forgiven, and that you should pray to God for pardon, and yet that you should not extend it to your fellow-men that have injured you?

Fifth, Would you be willing, for all the future, that God should no longer bear with the injuries you may offer him, and the offences you commit against him? Are you willing to go and ask God to deal with yourself for the future, as in holding this objection, you think of dealing with your fellow-men?

Sixth, Did Christ turn again upon those who injured and insulted and trod on him, when he was here below; and was he not injured far more grievously than ever you have been? And have you not more truly trodden under foot the Son of God, than you were ever trodden on by others? And is it a more provoking thing for men to tread on and injure you, than for you to tread on and injure Christ? These questions may sufficiently answer your objection.[16]

What is so interesting here is the fact that all six of Edwards' extended answers consist in their entirety of questions. 'These questions may sufficiently answer your objection.' That questions can be assertions, and thus, paradoxically, answers is, of course, the peculiar genius of rhetorical questions. Rhetorical questions are weighted in such a way

---

[16] *Charity,* pp. 92-94.

that the answers are self-evident; they are a foregone conclusion. Thus there is an intrinsic persuasiveness about them. It should be noted that Edwards reasons cogently with his hearers here; and as he does so, he probes their consciences, compelling them, as it were, to concur with him, or else indict themselves at the bar of God.

In 'The Manner in which the Salvation of the Soul is to be Sought' Edwards raises the objection made by many with regard to the perceived unreality of hell. He demonstrates cogently that the same objection was made in the days of Noah with regard to the coming Flood:

OBJ. But here possibly it may be objected by some, that though it be true they have often been told of hell, yet they never saw anything of it, and therefore they cannot realize it that there is any such place. They have often heard of hell, and are told that wicked men, when they die, go to a most dreadful place of torment; that hereafter there will be a day of judgment, and that the world will be consumed by fire. But how do they know that it is really so? How do they know what becomes of those wicked men that die? None of them come back to tell them. They have nothing to depend on but the word which they hear. And how do they know that all is not a cunningly devised fable?

ANS. The sinners of the old world had the very same objection against what Noah told them of a flood about to drown the world. Yet the bare word of God proved to be sufficient evidence that such a thing was coming. What was the reason that none of the many millions then upon earth believed what Noah said, but this, that it was a strange thing, that no such thing had ever before been known? And what a strange story must that of Noah have appeared to them, wherein he told them of a deluge of waters above the tops of the mountains! Therefore it is said, Heb. xi. 7. that 'Noah was warned of God of things not seen as yet.' It is probable, none could conceive how it could be that the whole world should be drowned in a flood of waters; and all were ready to ask, where there was water enough for it; and by what means it should be brought upon the earth? Noah did not tell them how it should be brought to pass; he only told them that God had said that it should be: and that proved to be enough. The event showed their folly in not depending on the mere word of God, who was able, who knew how to bring it to pass, and who could not lie.[17]

In the controversy over the Lord's Supper that dominated the last two years of his pastorate in Northampton Edwards made significant use of the technique of Objections and Answers, both in his treatise, *An Humble Inquiry into the Rules of the Word of God Concerning ... Full Communion in the Visible Christian Church* (1749), and also in his *Letures on the Qualifications for Full Communion in the Church of Christ*, delivered in February and March 1750. Kimnach notes an interesting difference between the treatise and the lectures: 'Formally, treatise and lecture series are similar in beginning with positive arguments and concluding with objections. In the proportions, however, there are some notable differences. The treatise contains eleven reasons, or proofs, for Edwards' position followed by twenty objections and his answers. The lecture series, on the other hand, begins with twenty-two arguments for his position followed by ten objections and answers, reversing the proportions of rhetorical offense and defense, as it were.'[18] The fourth Objection relates to the question as to whether Judas was present at the inception of the Lord's Supper; and Edwards' Answer demonstrates unequivocally, albeit in passing, his belief in the doctrine of 'limited atonement' or 'particular redemption':

> *Obj.* IV is concerning Judas' being admitted to the Lord's Supper with the other disciples.
>
> *First Answ.* By denying that Judas was there ...
>
> And there are two things more that prove that Judas was not present at the Lord's Supper. One is that those that Christ gives the bread and wine to at the Lord's Supper, he at the same time said thus to them: 'This is my body, which is given *for you;* and this is my blood, which was shed *for you.*' Now this could not be said to Judas. Christ's blood was not shed for him, for Christ gave him his decree as one that was certainly to go to hell before his blood was shed. Christ's death was not only not designed for him in God's secret decree, but it was visibly not for him, any more than

---

[17] *Works* (Hickman), 2:55-56.
[18] *Works*, 25:350.

to those that were in hell before he died. For he had his sentence
openly declared before his death, as much as they, or as much as
the devils. Nor did he shed his blood for him, any more than for
the devils.[19]

Kimnach describes the passages in which Edwards employs 'the
traditional Objection-Answer formula' as 'the "dialogue" passages'.[20]
This dialogue technique, the value of which was reinforced in Edwards'
mind by the literary suggestion of the Third Earl of Shaftesbury, was
utilized extensively by the New England preacher. In the process, of
course, he often demonstrates his formidable logical powers. But the
homiletical value of this particular method of Application is that it introduces a dialogical, conversational element into his preaching. This
is a significant aspect in the realism and the vitality that characterize
his sermons. It is important to note that the indefatigable scholar, who
commonly spent thirteen hours a day in his study, was not divorced
from the realities of life. Indeed, he continually demonstrates in his sermons a remarkable knowledge of the human heart with all of its sinful,
subtle subterfuges. By means of this formula he answers and exposes
those subterfuges; indeed, he generally demolishes them in such a way
that the objections of men – whether from the regenerate heart, the
unregenerate heart, or the enemies of the truth – lie shattered on the
ground.

[19] Ibid., pp. 419-421.
[20] *Works*, 10:246.

23

The Use of Example

Jonathan Edwards' most incisive analysis of the biblical concept of example is found in 'The Character of Paul an Example to Christians'. The sermon contains this pivotal passage:

The greatest example of all, that is set before us in the Scripture to imitate, is the example of Jesus Christ, which he set us in his human nature, and when in his state of humiliation. This is presented to us not only as a great pattern, but as a perfect rule. And the example of no man is set forth, as our rule, but the example of Christ. We are commanded to follow the examples which God himself set us, or the acts of the divine nature. Ephes. v. 1. 'Be ye therefore followers of God, as dear children.' And Matt. v. 48. 'Be ye therefore perfect, even as your Father which is in heaven is perfect.' But the example of Christ Jesus, when on earth, is more especially our pattern. For, though the acts of the divine nature have the highest possible perfection, and though his inimitable perfection is our best example, yet God is so much above us, his nature so infinitely different from ours, that it is not possible that his acts should be so accommodated to our nature and circumstances, as to be an example of so great and general use, as the perfect example in our nature which Christ has set us. Christ, though a divine person, was man, as we are men; and not only so, but he was, in many respects, a partaker of our circumstances. He dwelt among men. He depended on food and raiment, and such outward supports of life, as we do. He was subject to the changes of time, and the afflictions and calamities of this evil world, and to abuse from men's corruptions, and to temptations from Satan, as we are;

was subject to the same law and rule that we are, used the same ordinances, and had many of our trials, and greater trials than we. So that Christ's example is the example that is chiefly offered in Scripture for our imitation. But yet the example of some that are fallen creatures, as we are, may in some respects be more accommodated to our circumstances, and more fitted for our instructions, than the example of Jesus Christ. For though he became man as we are, and was like us, and was in our circumstances in so many respects, yet in other things there was a vast difference. He was the head of the church, and we are the members. He is Lord of all, we are his subjects and disciples. And we need an example, that shall teach and direct us how to behave towards Christ our Lord and head. And this we may have better in some, that have Christ for their Lord as well as we, than in Christ himself. But the greatest difference lies in this, that Christ had no sin, and we all are sinful creatures, all carry about with us a body of sin and death. It is said that Christ was made like to us in all things, sin only excepted. But this was excepted, and therefore there were many things required of us, of which Christ could not give us an example. Such as repentance for sin, brokenness of spirit for sin, mortification of lust, warring against sin. And the excellent example of some, that are naturally as sinful as we, has this advantage; that we may regard it as the example of those, who were naturally every way in our circumstances, and laboured under the same natural difficulties, and the same opposition of heart to that which is good, as ourselves; which tends to engage us to give more heed to their example, and the more to encourage and animate us to strive to follow it. And therefore we find that the Scripture does not only recommend the example of Christ, but does also exhibit some mere men, that are of like passions with ourselves, as patterns for us to follow. So it exhibits the eminent saints of the Old Testament, of whom we read in the Scripture, that they inherit the promises. Heb. vi. 12. 'That ye be not slothful, but followers of them who through faith and patience inherit the promises.' In the eleventh chapter of Hebrews, a great number of eminent saints are mentioned as patterns for us to follow.[1]

[1] *Works* (Hickman), 2:855. *Charity and Its Fruits* contains a passage on the issue of

It is evident from this statement that Edwards noted in the biblical concept of example a *distinct gradation*. In the first place there is the supreme, perfect, transcendent, and ultimately inimitable example of God himself. In the second place there is the perfect example of the Lord Jesus Christ which he set in his state of humiliation and in circumstances which were, in many respects, akin to ours. In the third place there is the example of the saints of the Old and New Testaments who were fallen creatures and thus men of like passions and of like corruptions as ourselves. This very gradation in the concept of example demonstrated, as far as Edwards was concerned, that God has condescended in this matter of example and has accommodated himself to our circumstances and frailties by giving us not only his own perfect example, but also the perfect example of Christ, the God-Man, and even the imperfect example of 'some mere men' in order that

---

example which is somewhat reminiscent of the passage cited above. Preaching on 1 Corinthians 13:4 ('Charity suffereth long, and is kind') JE once again demonstrates the pastoral value of 'the example of the saints'. Earlier in the same sermon he adduces 'the example that Christ has set us'; but here he goes on to show the special value of the example of those who were 'men of like passions with ourselves', and adduces David in particular as an example of longsuffering:

'I would mention the examples of the saints of whom we have an account. Though the example of Christ alone might be sufficient, being the example of the person who is our Head, our Lord and Master, whose followers we all profess to be, and his example a perfect example; yet some may be ready to say with regard to the example of Christ that he had no corruption in his heart, and that it cannot be expected of them that they should do as he did. Though this be no reasonable objection, yet the examples of saints that are men of like passions with ourselves are not without their special use, and may in some respects have a peculiar influence. There have been many of these who have set bright examples of this long-suffering, which has been recommended.

'One which I shall mention is of David. With what meekness did he bear the injurious treatment which he received from Saul? – when he hunted him as a partridge in the mountain, and pursued him with a most unreasonable envy and malice, and murderous design, who had ever behaved himself dutifully towards him. And when he had opportunity put into his hands of cutting him off, and at once delivering himself from him, and others would have been ready to think it very lawful and commendable to take such an opportunity in their own defense to kill one who sought their lives; yet Saul being the Lord's anointed he chose rather to commit himself still to God, and venture his life in his hands, Saul being yet suffered to live. And when after this he saw that his goodness did not overcome Saul, but that he still pursued him, and David's life seemed to be in imminent danger, and when again he had the opportunity of destroying him, he chose rather to go out as a wanderer and an outcast, than to injure the one that would have destroyed him.' *Works*, 8:201-202. The last two-thirds of the final sentence are supplied in the Yale edition from Tryon Edwards' edition.

we might be all the more encouraged and animated to follow them.

In the same sermon Edwards naturally adduces the example of the Apostle Paul himself. He states the following as his Doctrine: 'We ought to follow the good examples of the apostle Paul . . . The Holy Ghost directed that the good examples of the apostle Paul should be noticed by other Christians, and imitated.'[2] He develops this exemplaristic use of the Apostle thus:

> If we would have right notions of Christianity, we should observe those in whom it shone, of whom we have an account in the Scriptures. For they are the examples that God himself has selected to set before us to that end, that from thence we might form our notions of religion; and especially the example of this apostle. God knows how to select examples. If therefore we would have right notions of Christianity, we ought to follow the good example of the apostle Paul.[3]

Indeed, Edwards develops his use of 'the great example of the apostle'[4] in order both to *shame* and *inspire* his hearers:

> Such an example may well make us ashamed; for how weak and uneasy is the faith of most Christians! . . . Seeing we have such a blessed example set before us in the Scriptures, let it prompt us earnestly to seek, that we may soar higher also . . . Such superior examples as we have are enough to make us for ever blush for our own attainments in the love of Christ, and rouse us earnestly to follow after those who have gone so far beyond us.[5]

Edwards demonstrates here that the biblical concept of example is intrinsically imperatival and that it can legitimately be used for the purpose of *reprehension* as well as for the purpose of *exhortation*. In other words, the positive examples of the Scriptures, such as Paul's outstanding example, can be used both to *humble* and to *elevate;* his example is such that it both *shames* and *inspires*.

---

[2] Ibid.
[3] Ibid., p. 865.
[4] Ibid., p. 860.
[5] Ibid., p. 858.

This powerfully exemplaristic strand in Edwards' preaching is demonstrated *firstly* by the fact that he preached a number of sermons which are, in their entirety, devoted to the consideration of the example of the saints of the Old or the New Testament. Thus the sermon 'Temptation and Deliverance' adduces the example of Joseph's purity in an unashamedly exemplaristic manner.[6] Edwards refers, for instance, to 'that excellent example set before us'. 'This behaviour of Joseph is doubtless recorded for the instruction of all', he insists. 'And there are many examples in Scripture, which have the force of precept; and recorded, as not only worthy, but demand our imitation. The conduct of Joseph is one.'[7] Indeed, Edwards utilizes the example of Joseph in a deliberately imperatival manner *via* his sustained use of the verb of obligation *ought:*

It is very evident that we ought to use our utmost endeavours to avoid sin; which is inconsistent with needlessly doing those things, that expose and lead to sin ... Our care and endeavour cannot be infinite, as the evil of sin is infinite; but yet it ought to be to the utmost of our power; we ought to use every method that tends to the avoiding of sin ... It is evident that we ought to avoid those things that expose and lead to sin; because a due sense of the evil of sin, and a just hatred of it, will necessarily have this effect upon us, to cause us so to do ... But certainly, we ought not to take the less care to avoid sin, or all that tends to it, for the freeness and greatness of God's mercy to us, through which there is hope of pardon; for that would be indeed a most ungrateful and vile abuse of mercy ... It is evident that we ought not only to avoid sin, but things that expose and lead to sin; because this is the way we act in things that pertain to our temporal interest ... And surely we ought to treat God as a dear friend: we ought to act towards him, as those that have a sincere love and unfeigned regard to him; and so ought to watch and be careful against all *occasions* of that which is contrary to his honour and glory ... Now this plainly shows, that we ought, in our behaviour towards God, to keep at a

---

[6] See 19:809. This sermon was published posthumously in *Sermons* (1765).
[7] *Works* (Hickman), 2:229.

great distance from sin, and from all that exposes to it . . . Seeing we are to pray we may not be led into temptation, certainly we ought not to run ourselves into it . . . There are many precepts of Scripture, which directly and positively imply, that we ought to avoid those things that tend to sin.[8]

This powerfully exemplaristic strand in Edwards' preaching is demonstrated *secondly* by the fact that he preached numerous sermons which appeal in part to the example of the saints of the Old and New Testaments. Such examples are either positive or negative. In 'Christian Cautions' he adduces the positive example of Nehemiah:

Nehemiah took great care that no burden should be borne after the beginning of the sabbath, Nehem. xiii. 19. 'And it came to pass, that when the gates of Jerusalem began to be dark before the sabbath,' *i.e.* began to be darkened by the shade of the mountains before sun-set, 'I commanded that the gates should be shut, and charged that they should not be opened till after the sabbath; and some of my servants set I at the gates, that there should be no burden brought in on the sabbath-day.'[9]

Conversely, in 'Procrastination, or, The Sin and Folly of Depending on Future Time' he adduces the negative example of Esau:[10]

Nor remembering the sad example of Esau, 'who for a morsel of meat sold his birthright; and afterwards, when he would have inherited the blessing, he was rejected, for he found no place of repentance, though he sought it carefully with tears.' Heb. xii. 16, 17.[11]

The sermon 'Charity Disposes us Meekly to Bear the Injuries Received from Others' is particularly interesting from the standpoint of example. In this sermon Edwards adduces the positive example of Joseph, to whom Mary was betrothed:

---

[8] Ibid., pp. 227-229.

[9] Ibid., p. 179.

[10] Stout and Hatch note that this sermon is undated. The approximate date which they assign to the sermon is 'c. 1739-41'. *Works*, 22:552.

[11] *Works* (Hickman), 2:241.

Another instance is that of Joseph, the betrothed husband of Mary the mother of Jesus, under a supposed injury from her, though it was no real injury, yet it was the same trial to him as if it had been real. The instance to which I have respect, is that of which we have an account in Matt. 1:18-19, 'Now the birth of Jesus Christ was on this wise: When as his mother Mary was espoused to Joseph, before they came together, she was found with child of the Holy Ghost. Then Joseph her husband, being a just man, and not willing to make her a public example, was minded to put her away privily.' Mary was espoused to Joseph, was bound to him by a solemn contract, a contract to be his wife; and after this he perceived that she was with child before they came together, and concluded she had been false and treacherous to him, and had been guilty of adultery; for a carnal commerce with another man in such a case was adultery by the law of Moses, and was to be punished with death, as you may see. This, if it had been as he supposed, would have been an injury of that sort which of all others is wont most to provoke and exasperate men . . . But Joseph being a just man, and a right man of a right spirit, it did not put him into a rage; he was inclined to spare Mary, and not to make it a day of vengeance. Though he chose to put her away and to have nothing further to do with her, yet he was careful out of good will and tenderness to her, though he did not desire she should be his, that she should not be made a public example; and therefore was contriving to keep the matter private, which was a remarkable instance of that of which I have been speaking. Most other men would not have been much concerned about keeping the matter private in such a case as Joseph supposed this to be, nor thought themselves obliged to trouble themselves about the ill consequence of it being known of her that had been so false to him; but would have been ready to have said, let her take the consequence of her own abominable treachery and lewdness.[12]

---

[12] *Works*, 8:202-203. 'Another instance of Tryon's abbreviation of Andover (or rather of the sermon booklet he edited) was his entire deletion of Edwards' use of Joseph as one of the "saints" of old who was "longsuffering" on account of the condition of Mary, his betrothed. Tryon in the nineteenth century felt that illustration to be in bad taste, as Edwards did not in the eighteenth.' Ibid., p. 110.

One of the most interesting facts relating to this particular example is that this paragraph was completely omitted by Edwards' great-grandson, Tryon Edwards, in his 1852 edition of *Charity and Its Fruits*.[13] It can only be presumed that the frankness of the great-grandfather in his treatment of the admittedly delicate matter of Mary's presumed infidelity offended somewhat the sensibilities of the great-grandson, or that, in the judgment of the latter, such a treatment would, if published, offend the sensibilities of mid-nineteenth-century Christians, or both. It should be noted, therefore, that Edwards is simply expounding, with a commendable frankness, the implications of the clear statements of the Scriptures themselves in this matter.

Conversely, in 'Temptation and Deliverance' Edwards adduces the negative example of Peter in his self-confidence as a warning to those who are confident of their own strength with regard to the danger of immorality: 'But you should consider that the most self-confident are most in danger. Peter was very confident that he should not deny Christ, but how dreadfully otherwise was the event!'[14]

On occasion Edwards presents a cluster of biblical examples in rapid succession, as in this passage from the sermon 'The Spirit of Charity is an Humble Spirit':

> Consider, too, how Pharaoh and Korah, and Haman, and Belshazzar, and Herod, were awfully punished for their pride of heart and conduct; and be admonished, by their example, to cherish an humble spirit, and to walk humbly with God and toward men.[15]

This collective negative example demonstrates his almost instinctive imperatival and hortatory use of the concept of example in his preaching.

Similarly, in 'The Spirit of Charity the Opposite of a Censorious Spirit' Edwards once again presents a cluster of biblical examples in rapid succession, although on this occasion he provides much more comment and analysis:

---

13 Compare *Charity*, p. 89, with *Works*, 8:202-203.
14 *Works* (Hickman), 2:231.
15 *Works*, 8:250-251.

How often when the truth comes fully to appear do things appear far better concerning others than persons were at first ready to judge? There are many instances in the Scripture. When the children of Reuben and children of Gad and the half tribe of Manasseh had built an altar near Jordan, the rest of their brethren heard of it and presently concluded it to be a turning away from the Lord, and resolved rashly to go to war against them. But when the truth came to light, it appeared otherwise; it then appeared that they had built that altar for a good end, as you may see in the twenty-second chapter of Joshua. Eli thought Hannah drunk, when he saw her lips move. But when the truth came to light it was quite otherwise. She was praying and pouring out her soul before God, . . . So David concluded from what Ziba told him, that Mephibosheth had manifested a rebellious, treasonable spirit against his crown; and so far concluded that he acted upon a censorious judgment, greatly to Mephibosheth's wrong. But when the truth came to appear it was quite otherwise, . . . Elijah judged ill of the state of Israel that none were true worshippers of God but himself. But when God told him the truth it proved far otherwise; *viz.* that there were seven thousand, . . . And how commonly are things so! How often have we upon thorough examination found things better of others than we have heard, and than we at first were ready to judge! And there is probably no one way in which persons are so commonly wronged as in the judgments which persons make and freely express of them and their actions.[16]

'The Most High a Prayer-Hearing God' was 'preached on a fast appointed on the account of an epidemical sickness at the eastward (of Boston)'[17] in January 1736. Edwards' text on this occasion was simply the first part of one verse – the exclamatory part of Psalm 65:2: 'O thou that hearest prayer'. 'Hence we gather this doctrine', announced the preacher, 'that it is the character of the Most High, that he is a God

[16] Ibid., pp. 290-291. I have followed the version published by Yale, although I feel that in the final sentences an exclamation mark is more appropriate to the context than a question mark.

[17] *Works* (Hickman), 2:113 n.

who hears prayer.'[18] In the course of developing the doctrinal section of the sermon, Edwards makes a very striking use of the examples of the Bible as he proceeds to substantiate his central thesis:

> That God is eminently of this character, appears by the greatness of the things which he hath often done in answer to prayer. Thus, when Esau was coming out against his brother Jacob, with four hundred men, without doubt fully resolved to cut him off, Jacob prayed and God turned the heart of Esau, so that he met Jacob in a very friendly manner; . . . So in Egypt, at the prayer of Moses, God brought those dreadful plagues, and at his prayer removed them again. When Samson was ready to perish with thirst, he prayed to God, and he brought water out of a dry jaw-bone, for his supply, . . . And when he prayed, after his strength was departed from him, God strengthened him, so as to pull down the temple of Dagon on the Philistines: so that those whom he slew at his death were more than all those whom he slew in his life. – Joshua prayed to God, and said, 'Sun, stand thou still upon Gibeon, and thou, Moon, in the valley of Ajalon;' and God heard his prayer, and caused the sun and moon to stand still accordingly. The prophet 'Elijah was a man of like passion' with us; 'and he prayed earnestly that it might not rain; and it rained not on the earth by the space of three years and six months. And he prayed again, and the heaven gave rain, and the earth brought forth her fruit;' . . . So God confounded the army of Zerah, the Ethiopian, of a thousand thousand, in answer to the prayer of Asa, . . . And God sent an angel, and slew in one night an hundred and eighty-five thousand men of Sennacherib's army, in answer to Hezekiah's prayer, . . .[19]

It should be noted that, in adducing the examples of Jacob, Moses, Samson, Joshua, Elijah, Asa, and Hezekiah, the preacher's purpose is not only *illustrative, exemplaristic,* and *implicitly imperatival,* but also *theocentric.* Once again we note Edwards' ability to adduce examples which might be deemed to possess a *prima facie* anthropocentric focus and to invest them with a significant *theocentric* focus: 'That God is

[18] Ibid., p. 113.
[19] Ibid., p. 115.

eminently of this character, appears by the greatness of the things which he hath often done in answer to prayer.'

It is interesting to note that Edwards openly encouraged his hearers to adopt such an exemplaristic approach in their own private reading of the Scriptures. In 'Christian Cautions' he counsels his hearers thus:

> When you read in the historical parts of Scripture an account of the sins of which others have been guilty, reflect on yourselves as you go along, and inquire whether you do not in some degree live in the same or like practices. When you there read accounts how God reproved the sins of others, and executed judgments upon them for their sins, examine whether you be not guilty of things of the same nature. When you read the examples of Christ, and of the saints recorded in Scripture, inquire whether you do not live in ways contrary to those examples. When you read there how God commended and rewarded any persons for their virtues and good deeds, inquire whether you perform those duties for which they were commended and rewarded, or whether you do not live in the contrary sins or vices. Let me further direct you, particularly to read the Scriptures to these ends, that you may compare and examine yourselves in the manner now mentioned.[20]

There is, interestingly, a fourth category of examples utilized by Edwards in his sermons. In addition to the examples of God, of Christ, and of the Old or New Testament saints, he occasionally adduces the example of contemporaries, acquaintances, or distinguished relatives or friends. This category is of particular interest because, unlike the first three, it is extra-biblical; it is not, however, unbiblical.[21] It includes those who, in times of revival, turn in great numbers to Christ. Thus in 'Ruth's Resolution' he refers to those who (as he puts it in *A Faithful Narrative*) 'did as it were come by flocks to Jesus Christ':[22]

> When those that we have formerly been conversant with are turning to God and to his people, their example ought to influence us.

---

[20] Ibid., p. 177.
[21] The Scriptures themselves countenance the use of the example of saints that are unnamed in the Scriptures. See, for instance, *Heb.* 13:7.
[22] *Works* (Hickman), 1:348.

Their example should be looked upon as the call of God to us, to do as they have done. God, when he changes the heart of one, calls upon another; especially does he loudly call on those that have been their friends and acquaintance. We have been influenced by their examples in evil; and shall we cease to follow them, when they make the wisest choice that ever they made, and do the best thing that ever they did? If we have been companions with them in worldliness, in vanity, in unprofitable and sinful conversation, it will be a hard case, if there must be a parting now, because we are not willing to be companions with them in holiness and true happiness. Men are greatly influenced by seeing one another's prosperity in other things. If those whom they have been much conversant with, grow rich, and obtain any great earthly advantages, it awakens their ambition, and eager desire after the like prosperity: how much more should they be influenced, and stirred up to follow them, and be like them, when they obtain that spiritual and eternal happiness, that is of infinitely more worth, than all the prosperity and glory of this world![23]

It is interesting to note that the imperatival use that Edwards makes of the example of those described here is perfectly consistent with the fifth of the nine negative signs or non-signs that he specified in his Commencement sermon at Yale on September 10, 1741, in the midst of the Great Awakening: 'It is no sign that a work is not from the Spirit of God, that example is a great means of it.'[24] The Commencement preacher goes on to to defend the validity of the concept of imitation both from history and from the Scriptures:

There never yet was a time of remarkable pouring out of the Spirit, and great revival of religion, but that example had a main hand. So it was at the reformation, and in the apostles' days, in Jerusalem and Samaria, and Ephesus, and other parts of the world, as will be most manifest to any one that attends to the accounts we have in the Acts of the Apostles.[25]

[23] Ibid., p. 665.
[24] *Works* (Hickman), 2:263.
[25] Ibid., pp. 263-264.

In 'True Saints, When Absent from the Body, Are Present with the Lord' – the sermon preached on the occasion of the funeral of David Brainerd – Edwards, having expounded his text with great thoroughness in the Doctrine, turns almost immediately in the Application to a consideration of the example of Brainerd himself. Indeed, Brainerd's example lies at the centre of the 'use of exhortation' that dominates the Application. Once again, in his Conclusion, we note the clear imperatival implications of the exemplary:

> But here, as a special enforcement of this exhortation, I would improve that dispensation of God's holy providence, which is the sorrowful occasion of our coming together at this time, *viz.* the death of that eminent servant of Jesus Christ, in the work of the gospel-ministry, whose funeral is this day to be attended; together with what was observable in him, living and dying . . .
>
> And how much is there in the consideration of such an example, and so blessed an end, to excite us, who are yet alive, with the greatest diligence and earnestness, to improve the time of life, that we also may go to be with Christ, when we forsake the body! . . .
>
> How much is there, in particular, in the things that have been observed of this eminent minsiter of Christ, to excite us, who are called to the same great work of the gospel-ministry, to earnest care and endeavours, that we may be in like manner faithful in our work; that we may be filled with the same spirit, animated with the like pure and fervent flame of love to God, and the like earnest concern to advance the kingdom and glory of our Lord and Master, and the prosperity of Zion! How amiable did these principles render this servant of Christ in his life, and how blessed in his end! The time will soon come, when we also must leave our earthly tabernacles, and go to our Lord that sent us to labour in his harvest, to render an account of ourselves to him. O how does it concern us so to run as not uncertainly; so to fight, not as those that beat the air! And should not what we have heard excite us to depend on God for his help and assistance in our great work, and to be much in seeking the influences of his Spirit, and success in our labours, by fasting and prayer; in which the person spoken of was abundant? . . . Oh that the things that were seen and heard

in this extraordinary person, his holiness, heavenliness, labour, and self-denial in life, his so remarkably devoting himself and his all, in heart and practice, to the glory of God, and the wonderful frame of mind manifested in so stedfast a manner, under the expectation of death, and the pains and agonies that brought it on, may excite in us all, both ministers and people, a due sense of the greatness of the work we have to do in the world, the excellency and amiableness of thorough religion in experience and practice, and the blessedness of the end of such a life, and the infinite value of their eternal reward, when absent from the body and present with the Lord; and effectually stir us up to endeavours that in the way of such a holy life, we may at last come to so blessed an end. – *Amen.*[26]

Eight and a half months later, on Sunday June 26, 1748, Edwards preached another very significant memorial sermon in Northampton – that of Colonel John Stoddard.[27] Colonel Stoddard was the second son of Solomon Stoddard and was thus the preacher's uncle. He had been a man of affairs, a military commander, a political leader, and a wealthy real estate merchant. Not only did he become, on his inheritance, the richest man in Northampton, but also its most influential magistrate; indeed, he was virtually the village squire. Colonel Stoddard's relationship with Edwards was clearly very close. 'John, a Harvard graduate of some learning and a man of piety', writes Marsden, 'took his young nephew under his wing and remained his most important ally and patron.'[28] 'Probably no eighteenth-century clergyman in America

[26] Ibid., pp. 32, 35-36.
[27] 'Col. John Stoddard, the political leader of Northampton during Edwards' pastorate, was also Edwards' uncle on his mother's side, and from the beginning one of Edwards' most important supporters. Stoddard had headed the selection committee that brought Edwards to Northampton as colleague of the Rev. Solomon Stoddard, and having made this commitment he supported Edwards through the building and seating of the new meetinghouse, the Bad Book affair, a salary settlement, and many other stressful episodes during Edwards' pastorate. Significantly, when Stoddard was taken with his final illness while in attendance at the General Court, Sarah Edwards went to Boston to care for him. During this period of mounting tensions within the Northampton church, the loss of Stoddard, both as an advisor and as a mediator in the community, was a great personal loss to Edwards.' *Works*, 25:312.
[28] Marsden, *Edwards*, p. 114. Again I am indebted to Marsden for these details concerning Colonel John Stoddard.

sustained a closer relationship to so powerful a regional magistrate . . . Magistrate and pastor, uncle and nephew, stood shoulder to shoulder as God's representatives for preserving the old order and promoting true religion.'[29] The Colonel's unexpected death in June 1748 at the age of sixty-six as a result of a stroke on a routine visit to Boston to serve as Northampton's representative to the General Court was, like the death of another uncle, William Williams, almost seven years earlier, a tremendous blow to the Northampton pastor.

The sermon preached on this occasion – 'God's Awful Judgment in the Breaking and Withering of the Strong Rods of a Community' on the text from Ezekiel 19:12 ('Her strong rods were broken and withered') has been described by Miller as 'one of the finest of his short pieces'.[30] It contains a remarkable eulogy to the patriarch of Northampton and New England. 'Great personal grief is not explicit in this memorial sermon', comments Kimnach, 'but the sense of loss may have contributed to the intensity suffusing Edwards' remarkable meditation upon the just ruler at the beginning of the Doctrine.'[31] Moreover, just as the Doctrinal section consists of a more general, objective delineation of 'the character of a "strong rod"',[32] so the Application consists, virtually in its entirety, of a more particular, subjective delineation of the character of 'this "strong rod"'.[33] Indeed, Edwards' eulogy is unashamedly exemplaristic. 'Every thing in him was great, and becoming a man in his public station. Perhaps never was there a man that appeared in New England to whom the denomination of *a great man* did more properly belong.'[34] He utilizes Stoddard's example, not only to *inspire*, but also to *shame*. With his eye at least in part on some of his cousins from the Williams family, the preacher unleashed this salvo:

> The greatness and honourableness of his disposition was answerable to the largeness of his understanding. He was naturally of a great mind; in this respect he was truly the son of nobles. He

---

[29] Ibid., p. 343.
[30] Miller, *Edwards*, p. 218.
[31] *Works*, 25:312.
[32] *Works* (Hickman), 2:37.
[33] Ibid., p. 40.
[34] Ibid., p. 39.

greatly abhorred things which were mean and sordid, and seemed to be incapable of a compliance with them. How far was he from trifling and impertinence in his conversation! How far from a busy meddling disposition! How far from any sly and clandestine management to fill his pockets with what was fraudulently withheld, or violently squeezed, from the labourer, soldier, or inferior officer! How far from taking advantage from his commission or authority, or any superior power he had in his hands; or the ignorance, dependence, or necessities of others; to add to his own gains with what properly belonged to them, and with what they might justly expect as a proper reward for any of their services! How far was he from secretly taking bribes offered to induce him to favour any man in his cause, or by his power or interest to promote his being advanced to any place of public trust, honour, or profit! How greatly did he abhor lying and prevarication! And how immovably stedfast was he to exact truth! His hatred of those things that were mean and sordid was so apparent and well known, that it was evident that men dreaded to appear in any thing of that nature in his presence.[35]

It is important to note that 'the heir-apparent to much of Stoddard's power'[36] was none other than Edwards' cousin, Israel Williams. The root of the estrangement between the Northampton pastor and his cousin (and indeed others from the wider Williams family) appears to lie in Edwards' uncompromising dealing with the doctrine of justification by faith in November 1734. 'Among those who opposed Mr. Edwards on this occasion', wrote Sereno E. Dwight in 1830, 'were several members of a family, in a neighbouring town, nearly connected with his own, and possessing, from its numbers, wealth, and respectability, a considerable share of influence. Their religious sentiments differed widely from his, and their opposition to him, in the course which he now pursued, became direct and violent.'[37] Edwards had good grounds for being suspicious of Israel Williams' doctrinal principles and

---

[35] Ibid., p. 39.
[36] Marsden, *Edwards*, p. 345.
[37] *Works* (Hickman), 1:xliii.

ethical practices, and in the course of the sermon pointedly depicted both Colonel Stoddard's doctrinal orthodoxy on the one hand and the lack of ethical integrity in some of the Williams family on the other:

> He was thoroughly established in those religious principles and doctrines of the first fathers of New England, usually called the *doctrines of grace*, and had a great detestation of the opposite errors of the present fashionable divinity, as very contrary to the word of God, and the experience of every true Christian. And as he was a friend to truth, so he was a friend to vital piety and the power of godliness, and ever countenanced and favoured it on all occasions.[38]

> Those that are by Divine Providence set in a place of public authority and rule, are called 'gods, and sons of the Most High,' Psalm lxxxii. 6. And therefore it is peculiarly unbecoming them to be of a mean spirit, a disposition that will admit of their doing those things that are sordid and vile; as when they are persons of a narrow, private spirit, that may be found in little tricks and intrigues to promote their private interest. Such will shamefully defile their hands to gain a few pounds, are not ashamed to grind the faces of the poor, and screw their neighbours; and will take advantage of their authority or commission to line their own pockets with what is fraudulently taken or withheld from others. When a man in authority is of such a mean spirit, it weakens his authority, and makes him justly contemptible in the eyes of men, and is utterly inconsistent with his being a strong rod.[39]

The significance of the death of Colonel John Stoddard at this juncture lay in the fact that, in the mysterious providence of God, the mantle of power was to fall from the shoulders of Edwards' greatest ally, John Stoddard, to the shoulders of perhaps his greatest enemy, Israel

---

[38] Ibid., 2:40.

[39] Ibid., p. 37. Marsden confirms the suspicion that JE had 'some of his Williams cousins' in view here, and especially Israel Williams – 'the heir-apparent to much of Stoddard's power'. Marsden, *Edwards*, p. 344-345.

Williams. Within two years of the death of the Colonel the great New England preacher-theologian would be dismissed from his church by two hundred and thirty votes to twenty-three.[40]

It will be noted that, with the exception of this fourth category, the examples adduced by Edwards are drawn entirely from the Holy Scriptures themselves. Yet even this fourth category has the general sanction of Scripture. Thus Edwards not only frequently utilized the example of the characters of the Bible in his sermons, he also cogently defended this homiletical practice, and even encouraged his hearers to measure and evaluate themselves against the examples, both positive and negative, which they found in their own study of the Scriptures. For Edwards, positive example in the Scriptures had the force of precept, negative example the force of warning. Indeed, he clearly endorsed the imperatival, hortatory, parenetic implications of the biblical concept of example. 'God knows how to select examples',[41] he insists. The writings of the New England divine contain *a theology of the concept of example*.

[40] Kimnach notes the following interesting fact concerning Colonel Stoddard and Stockbridge: 'The far-seeing Stoddard had in 1736 laid out a township in the western marches at Housatonnuck, and being in charge of the settlement he took the lead in the establishment of an Indian mission there, at a place eventually named Stockbridge, and so he had provided one last pastorate for his nephew, though it was occupied only after his death.' *Works*, 25:313. There is a certain irony in the reflection that, if the long shadow of Solomon Stoddard lay across the grandson in his tragic dismissal from the pastorate in Northampton, it is also true that the long shadow of Colonel John Stoddard lay across the nephew in a more positive vein in his being called to the mission at Stockbridge.

[41] *Works* (Hickman), 2:865.

24

MOTIVES

'I have diligently endeavoured to find out and use the most powerful motives to persuade you to take care for your own welfare and salvation.'[1] It was thus that the ousted Northampton pastor addressed the people in his 'Farewell Sermon' on July 1, 1750, as he reflected candidly upon his ministry of the previous twenty-three years. These 'most powerful motives' are obviously objective inducements presented by the preacher to the minds of his hearers. Indeed, for Edwards 'motives' and 'persuasives' are synonymous, interchangeable terms.[2] It will be immediately evident from this statement that for him there is a very important connection between the adduction of motives and the issue of persuasion in preaching. Edwards constantly reasoned with both sinner and saint; and it is evident from his sermons that the motives adduced were powerful, spiritual reasons brought to bear upon the souls of his hearers in order that the preaching of the word might, by the power of God's Spirit, induce in them a response of obedience.

The use of *motives* in his Applications is a very striking and interesting aspect of his preaching. But it is important to note that the motives or inducements he presented are essentially of two kinds: they are either general and informal or specific and formal. The general and informal motives underlie all of Edwards' preaching and lie in solution, as it were, throughout his sermons. Two such general motives are those of *fear* and *love*. In *Religious Affections* he makes this observation:

---

[1] Ibid., 1:ccv. Emphasis added.
[2] See ibid., p. 84.

No other principles will ever make men conscientious, but one of these two, *fear* or *love* . . . Hence, God has wisely ordained, that these two opposite principles of love and fear, should rise and fall, like the two opposite scales of a balance; when one rises the other sinks.[3]

There can be little doubt but that this motive of fear constitutes the rationale behind Edwards' colossal emphasis upon the doctrine of hell and upon the judgment of God. It is evident that from the very beginning of his ministry he regarded the fear of hell as being of fundamental significance in the awakening of the unconverted. In one of his earliest sermons, 'Christ's Sacrifice' – preached in New York City *circa* 1723 and based on Hebrews 9:12 ('Neither by the blood of goats and calves, but by his own blood he entered once into the holy place, having obtained eternal redemption for us'), the young supply preacher makes this assertion: 'The consideration of hell commonly is the first thing that rouses sleeping sinners.'[4]

The following extract from 'The Wisdom of God, Displayed in the Way of Salvation' demonstrates Edwards' presentation of the opposite motive of love:

Man now has greater *motives* offered him to love God than otherwise he ever would have had . . . There are greater *manifestations* of the love of God to us, than there would have been if man had not fallen; and also there are greater *motives* to love him than otherwise there would have been. There are greater *obligations* to love him, for God has done more for us to win our love. Christ hath died for us . . . – By man's having thus a more immediate, universal, and sensible dependence, God doth more entirely secure man's undivided respect. There is a greater motive for man to make God his all in all – to love him and rejoice in him as his only portion.[5]

The motive of love here is not so much the love of God for his child as the love of the child for his God, although it must be emphasized

---

[3] Ibid., p. 259.
[4] *Works*, 10:603.
[5] *Works* (Hickman), 2:151.

that these two loves are inextricably connected; indeed, the one is a response to the other. 'We love him, because he first loved us.'[6] Thus, although fear is generally the first motive that makes men conscientious, love is unquestionably the higher, nobler motive. 'Perfect love casts out fear.'[7]

A third general motive is that of the concept of *opportunity*. In 'The Portion of the Wicked' Edwards reminds his Northampton hearers that they live in 'a land of light' – a land that enjoys 'the Bible and the sabbath'.[8] Similarly, in 'The Folly of Looking Back in Fleeing out of Sodom' he reminds the congregation of the following fact:

> We, in this land of light, have long enjoyed greater advantages than most in the world ... The wonders that we have seen among us of late, have been of a more glorious nature than those that the children of Israel saw in Egypt and in the wilderness.[9]

Thus he appeals, interestingly, to both history and geography; he appeals to both time and place. Indeed, the preacher was convinced that both he and his hearers were living at a very special time in history. The revival in Northampton in 1734-35 and the Great Awakening of the early 1740's constituted, as far as Edwards was concerned, 'special seasons of mercy'.[10] At such times, when the Spirit of God was poured out, God was 'extraordinarily present'.[11] Thus Edwards emphasized that during such seasons his hearers enjoyed 'advantages' which were 'perhaps tenfold'[12] greater than they ordinarily had been; he emphasized that they enjoyed very great privileges and opportunities at such times. Thus he consistently uses the concept of spiritual opportunity as a fulcrum or a lever in his preaching.

This motive of opportunity is particularly evident in the sermon 'Sinners in Zion Tenderly Warned'. Edwards' text was Isaiah 33:14: 'The

---

[6] 1 John 4:19.
[7] 1 John 4:18.
[8] *Works* (Hickman), 2:879.
[9] Ibid., p. 67.
[10] Ibid., 1:539.
[11] Ibid., p. 393.
[12] Ibid., 2:67.

sinners in Zion are afraid; fearfulness hath surprised the hypocrites. Who among us shall dwell with the devouring fire? who among us shall dwell with everlasting burnings?' Dated December 1740, this sermon was preached about six years after the revival in Northampton of 1734-1735 and thus at the dawn of the Great Awakening of the early 1740's:

> Now, God is pleased again to pour out his Spirit upon us; and he is doing great things amongst us. God is indeed come again, the same great God who so wonderfully appeared among us some years ago, and who hath since, for our sins, departed from us, left us so long in so dull and dead a state, and hath let sinners alone in their sins; so that there have been scarcely any signs to be seen of any such work as conversion. That same God is now come again; he is really come in like manner, and begins, as he did before, gloriously to manifest his mighty power, and the riches of his grace. He brings sinners out of darkness into marvellous light. He rescues poor captive souls out of the hands of Satan; he saves persons from the devouring fire; he plucks one and another as brands out of the burnings; he opens the prison-doors, and knocks off their chains, and brings out poor prisoners; he is now working salvation among us from this very destruction of which you have now heard.[13]

It will be noted that Edwards makes deliberate use here of the concept of opportunity – an opportunity which was given in the past, which had now returned six years later, and which may well be, before long, irrevocably lost – in order to highlight the urgency of the gospel message: 'Now, now, then, is the time, now is the blessed opportunity to escape those everlasting burnings.'[14] Kimnach describes this in terms of 'the rhetoric of temporal urgency'.[15]

A fourth general motive adduced by Edwards is one that could be described as that of the *temporal-eternal axis*. Edwards very frequently reasons with his hearers concerning the relative value of time and eternity. Thus in 'Man's Natural Blindness in the Things of Religion' he

---

[13] Ibid., p. 205.
[14] Ibid.
[15] *Works*, 25:112.

demonstrates powerfully the foolishness of man in spiritual and eternal things:

> It appears, in that they are so blind in those *same things* in relig-
> ious matters, which they are sufficiently sensible of in other mat-
> ters. In temporal things they are very sensible that it is a point
> of prudence to improve the first opportunity in things of great
> importance. But in matters of religion, which are of infinitely the
> greatest importance, they have not this discernment. In temporal
> matters they are sensible that it is a great folly long to delay and
> put off, when life is in danger, and all depends upon it. But in
> the concerns of their souls, they are insensible of this truth. So
> in the concerns of this world, they are sensible it is prudence to
> improve times of special advantage, and to embrace a good offer
> when made them. They are sensible that things of long contin-
> uance are of greater importance, than those of short duration; yet
> in religious concerns, none of these things are sensibly discerned.
> In temporal things they are sufficiently sensible, that it is a point
> of prudence to lay up for hereafter, in summer to lay up for winter,
> and to lay up for their families, after they are dead; but men do
> not generally discern the prudence of making a proper provision
> for a future state. – In matters of importance in this world, they
> are sensible of the wisdom of taking thorough care to be on sure
> grounds; but in their soul's concerns they see nothing of this. Our
> Saviour observed this to be the case with the Jews when he was
> upon earth. 'Ye hypocrites, ye can discern the face of the sky, and
> of the earth: but how is it that ye do not discern this time?'[16]

This is essentially an implicit *a fortiori* construction – it is implicitly an argument from the lesser to the greater. It is *via* the *a fortiori* or 'all the more reason' construction that Edwards commonly develops analogical bridges between the seen and the unseen.[17] In other words, his argument is essentially this: If men are so wise and prudent in 'the concerns of this world', how much more wise and prudent ought they to be in 'the concerns of their souls'. Edwards employs this motive of

---

[16] *Works* (Hickman), 2:252.
[17] See *Works*, 10:250.

the temporal-eternal axis with great frequency in his sermons. It is an unanswerable argument.

What is particularly striking about Edwards' preaching, however, is that he not only utilizes general, informal motives, which lie in solution throughout his sermons, but also adduces specific, formal motives. Indeed, the use of specific motives constitutes a significant element in his Application. It is an interesting fact that his homiletical interest in the use of motives dates from the very commencement of his ministry. The earliest extant sermon that contains a formal presentation of motives is 'The Duty of Self-Examination'. Edwards' Doctrine was this: *'Tis our most important duty to consider our ways.'* In the Application the young preacher proceeds to explain the reasons why this duty of self-examination is 'miserably neglected in the world':[18] 'It is because they have reprobate minds, and have brought themselves down very near to the level of thoughtless, poor inconsiderate beasts, by their sins.'[19] It is at this point that he proceeds to present three motives, of which we cite the first:

> But that it not be so with us, let us hearken to that solemn command of the Lord of hosts to us in our text to consider our ways; and that we may be assisted so to do, let us lend our attention to the following motives and directions.
>
> [I. *Motives*]
>
> *First*. For motive, consider the great danger we are in in this world, in what danger of losing our souls and dropping into remediless misery. We are surrounded and encompassed with dangers on every side, within and without. Without us we have enemies everywhere lying in ambush for us, and within our own breasts we have enemies armed with poisoned arrows and deadly weapons. They are all conspiring our hurt, yea, our greatest hurt, our irrecoverable overthrow. The enemies within are assistants to our enemies without, and our enemies without spur on our internal enemies. The world allures and entices us; the devil, he makes the fairest show and representation of the world that possibly he can, as he did to

---

[18] Ibid., p. 489.
[19] Ibid.

our souls. The world shoots fiery darts at our souls, and the devil adds a new force to them as they come along. The devil, he is laying snares for us, and the world helps the devil; and both join in with our lusts, and betwixt them all three thus combined, thousands of inconsiderate souls are carried down into destruction as a foolish ox to the slaughter. If we will not consider in such danger as this, when will we consider? If a man will not consider in the midst of an army of enemies, we may justly look upon him as foolish to the last degree.

Wherefore, let all consider for their own safety: consider what danger they are in, and by what means they may escape this danger. Let none think themselves so free from danger as to be escaped from this duty of consideration. Every inconsiderate man is in danger of eternal ruin, for it is a thing essential to a man in Christ, and so out of danger of hell, that he be considerate. All have need of consideration. Every truly godly man accounts the danger of offending his God greater than the wicked esteem the danger of burning in hell. Wherefore, consider your ways, for you are every moment in danger of being drawn into an offence of your Maker, and so thereby of losing the light of his countenance and the manifestation of his favor, and of being deprived of your own comfort and exposing yourself to remorse of conscience.[20]

In the course of his Application in 'Living Peaceably One With Another' Edwards presents seven motives to the contentious people of Bolton as inducements to the cultivation of peace, the fifth of which we cite:

We will offer some motives to move us to to do what in us lies to live peaceably with all men . . .

Fifth. Let it be considered how much it tends to make our lives happy, to live peaceably with all men. 'Tis the contrary that makes our lives in this world unpleasant. How happy are they who live in peace and unity: it makes all troubles seem the less, and makes the world easy to us. We cannot consult our own happiness more than by endeavoring to live peaceably with all men. All happiness

---

[20] Ibid., pp. 489-490.

consists in peace. There is no happiness of no kind but what is derived in peace, either peace with our fellow creatures or peace of conscience, peace in our own minds or peace with God. All happiness on earth and all happiness in heaven consists in peace, and all evil consists in contention, either contention with ourselves, fellow creatures, or God. Even bodily pain is the result of contention, even contention and struggle of nature with the painful sensation. Therefore 'peace' is put very often in Scripture for all manner of good. It was the usual salutation, 'Peace be with you,' thereby intending their desires of their good and happiness in general. And so it is evidently intended in Scripture oftener than otherwise.[21]

'The Christian Pilgrim; or, The True Christian's Life a Journey Towards Heaven', dated September 1733, is a sermon based upon Hebrews 11:13-14: 'And confessed that they were strangers and pilgrims on the earth. For they that say such things declare plainly that they seek a country.' Towards the close of the sermon Edwards buttresses his exhortation, 'so to spend the present life, that it may be only a journey towards heaven', with the following five motives, the last of which we cite in full:

And consider further for motive,

1) How worthy is heaven that your life should be wholly spent as a journey towards it . . .

2) This is the way to have death comfortable to us . . .

3) No more of your life will be pleasant to think of when you come to die, than has been spent after this manner . . .

4) Consider that those who are willing thus to spend their lives as a journey towards heaven may have heaven . . .

5) Let it be considered, that if our lives be not a journey towards heaven, they will be a journey to hell. All mankind, after they have been here a short while, go to either of the two great receptacles of all that depart out of this world: the one is heaven; whither a small number, in comparison, travel; and the other is hell, whither

---

[21] *Works*, 14:129-130.

the bulk of mankind throng. And one or the other of these must be the issue of our course in this world.[22]

'The Nature and End of Excommunication' is 'Edwards' only extant excommunication sermon, or at least the only one identified as such.'[23] It is based on 1 Corinthians 5:11: 'But now I have written unto you not to keep company, if any man that is called a brother be a fornicator, or covetous, or an idolater, or a railer, or a drunkard, or an extortioner; with such an one no not to eat.' The sermon was, as Edwards' own hand records at the top of the sermon's first page, 'preached on the occasion of the excommunication of John Bridgman's wife, which was July 22, 1739.'[24] Mrs Bridgman had been guilty of drunkenness. She had been admonished – indeed, specifically mentioned by name – in the course of a disciplinary sermon in the July of the preceding year. But the wayward communicant member had not demonstrated that 'sorrow unto repentance' required by the Scriptures and was now, a year later, publicly excommunicated. 'The excommunication of Mrs. Bridgman', note the Yale co-editors, 'was the first to take place in Northampton since 1711.'[25] Edwards' emphasis in this sermon falls, however, not upon the individual in question and her sin, but upon the biblical principle and duty of the excommunication of 'those members of the visible christian church who are become visibly wicked'.[26] The Northampton pastor concludes the sermon with the adduction of five motives:

> I shall apply this subject in a brief use of exhortation to this church, to maintain strictly the proper discipline of the gospel in general, and particularly that part of it which consists in excommunication. To this end I shall just suggest to you the following motives.
> 1. That if you tolerate visible wickedness in your members, you will greatly *dishonour* God, our Lord Jesus Christ, the religion which you profess, the church in general, and yourselves in particular. As those members of the church who practise wickedness,

---

[22] *Works* (Hickman), 2:246.
[23] *Works*, 22:64.
[24] Cited ibid., p. 67.
[25] Ibid., p. 66.
[26] *Works* (Hickman), 2:118.

bring dishonour upon the whole body, so do those who tolerate them in it. The language of it is, that God doth not require holiness in his servants; that Christ doth not require it in his disciples; that the religion of the gospel is not a holy religion; that the church is not a body of holy servants of God; and that this church, in particular, hath no regard to holiness or true virtue.

2. Your *own good* loudly calls you to the same thing . . .

3. The good of those who are *without* should be another motive . . .

4. *Benevolence* towards your offending brethren themselves, calls upon you to maintain discipline in all its parts . . .

5. But the absolute *authority of Christ* ought to be sufficient in this case, if there were no other motive . . .[27]

Again, in 'Hypocrites Deficient in the Duty of Prayer' – a sermon preached in June 1740 on Job 27:10 ('Will he always call upon God?') – Edwards adduces the following four motives as spiritual incentives to the faithful practice of prayer, the last of which we cite in its entirety:

But here let the following things be particularly considered as motives to perseverance in this duty.

1. That perseverance in the way of duty is necessary to salvation, and is abundantly declared to be so in the Holy Scriptures . . .

2. In order to your own perseverance in the way of duty, your own care and watchfulness is necessary . . .

3. To move you to persevere in the duty of prayer, consider how much you always stand in need of the help of God . . .

4. Consider the great benefit of a constant, diligent, and persevering attendance on this duty. It is one of the greatest and most excellent means of nourishing the new nature, and of causing the soul to flourish and prosper. It is an excellent mean of keeping up

---

[27] Ibid., p. 121. It is important to note that these motives are found in the Hickman, but not in the Yale edition. The Yale co-editors make this observation with regard to the extant manuscript: 'The sermon consists of an Exposition and Doctrine, with no Application; since the manuscript gives no indication that there was once an Application (the Doctrine leaves off in mid-page), it is possible that the service of excommunication did not call for one. This sermon first appeared in *Practical Sermons, Never Before Published* (Edinburgh, 1788).' *Works*, 22:67.

an acquaintance with, and of growing in the knowledge of, God. It is the way to a life of communion with God. It is an excellent mean of taking off the heart from the vanities of the world, and of causing the mind to be conversant in heaven. It is an excellent preservative from sin and the wiles of the devil, and a powerful antidote against the poison of the old serpent. It is a duty whereby strength is derived from God against the lusts and corruptions of the heart, and the snares of the world.

It hath a great tendency to keep the soul in a wakeful frame, and to lead us to a strict walk with God, and to a life that shall be fruitful in such good works, as tend to adorn the doctrine of Christ, and to cause our light so to shine before others, that they seeing our good works shall glorify our Father who is in heaven. And if the duty be constantly and diligently attended, it will be a very pleasant duty. Slack and slothful attendance upon it, and unsteadiness in it, are the causes which make it so great a burden as it is to some persons. Their slothfulness in it hath naturally the effect to beget a dislike of the duty, and a great indisposition to it. But if it be constantly and diligently attended, it is one of the best means of leading not only a christian and amiable, but also a pleasant life; a life of much sweet fellowship with Christ, and of the abundant enjoyment of the light of his countenance

Besides, the great power which prayer, when duly attended, hath with God, is worthy of your notice. By it men become like Jacob, who as a prince had power with God, and prevailed, when he wrestled for the blessing. See the power of prayer represented in James v. 16-18. By these things you may be sensible how much you will lose, if you shall be negligent in this great duty of calling upon God; and how ill you will consult your own interest by such a neglect.[28]

Edwards' great intellectual *tour de force* – *Freedom of the Will* (1754) – is of particular significance with regard to the issue of motives. In this treatise motives are discussed, not from a homiletical, but from a philosophical and psychological standpoint. The section entitled 'Con-

---

[28] Ibid., pp. 75-77.

cerning the Determination of the Will' consists of an incisive analysis of the relationship between the will and motives:

> It is that motive, which, as it stands in the view of the mind, is the strongest, that determines the Will . . .
>
> By *motive*, I mean the whole of that which moves, excites, or invites the mind to volition, whether that be one thing singly, or many things conjunctly. Many particular things may concur, and unite their strength, to induce the mind; and when it is so, all together are as one complex motive. And when I speak of the *strongest* motive, I have respect to the strength of the whole that operates to induce a particular act of volition, whether that be the strength of one thing alone, or of many together.
>
> Whatever is objectively a motive, in this sense, must be something that is *extant in the view or apprehension of the understanding*, or perceiving faculty. Nothing can induce or invite the mind to will or act any thing, any further than it is perceived, or is in some way or other in the mind's view; for what is wholly unperceived and perfectly out of the mind's view, cannot affect the mind at all. It is most evident, that nothing is in the mind, or reaches it, or takes any hold of it, any otherwise than as it is perceived or thought of.
>
> And I think it must also be allowed by all, that every thing that is properly called a motive, excitement, or inducement to a perceiving, willing agent, has some sort and degree of *tendency*, or *advantage* to move or excite the Will, previous to the effect, or the act of the Will excited. This previous tendency of the motive is what I call the *strength* of the motive. That motive which has a less degree of previous advantage, or tendency to move the Will, or which appears less inviting, as it stands in the view of the mind, is what I call a *weaker* motive. On the contrary, that which appears most inviting, and has, by what appears concerning it to the understanding or apprehension, the greatest degree of previous tendency to excite and induce the choice, is what I call the *strongest* motive. And in this sense, I suppose the Will is always determined by the strongest motive.[29]

[29] Ibid., 1:5-6.

Edwards' fundamental definition of the will in terms of motives demonstrates that he has, at this point, *subjective motives* in view. He defines the will in terms of 'the strongest motive',[30] 'the greatest apparent good',[31] and 'the last dictate of the understanding'.[32] 'It is that motive, which, as it stands in the view of the mind, is the strongest, that determines the Will.'[33] His fundamental definition of moral agency in the same treatise, however, demonstrates that he has, at that point, *objective motives* in view: 'To moral Agency belongs ... a capacity which an Agent has of being influenced in his actions by moral inducements or motives, exhibited to the view of understanding and reason, ...'[34] Thus there is some legitimacy in the charge that in *Freedom of the Will* the Stockbridge philosopher-theologian fails to distinguish adequately between subjective motives and objective motives. 'We do not regard President Edwards as infallible', remarks Dabney. 'The essential structure of his argument is indestructible, but it has some excrescences and blemishes ... He sometimes seems to confound objective inducement with subjective motive.'[35] Dabney points out that, in the context of *Freedom of the Will*, 'the real "motive" is not the thing "addressed *to* the mind", but the subjective appetency determined by the "state of the mind" to which the object is addressed.'[36] We might add that in Edwards' sermons the motives presented are indeed 'addressed *to* the mind'; they are objective inducements. Yet there is an important connection between subjective motives and objective inducements. The subjective motive is 'the greatest apparent good'; and the objective inducement is the greatest objective good. Thus 'the thing "addressed *to* the mind"' (the objective inducement) may, by the power of the Spirit of God, so influence the mind that it becomes 'the subjective appetency' of the mind (the subjective motive). When so embraced the objective motive becomes, in effect, one with the subjective motive.

[30] Ibid., p. 6.
[31] Ibid.
[32] Ibid., p. 7.
[33] Ibid., p. 5.
[34] Ibid., p. 12.
[35] Robert L. Dabney, *Discussions*, vol. 3 (1892; reprint, Vallecito, California: Ross House Books, 1980), p. 239.
[36] Ibid., p. 219.

Edwards is, of course, clearly *not* suggesting here, in moralistic or humanistic vein, that in the proclamation of God's word motives excite or influence the unregenerate will independently of the Spirit of God. Rather, his position is clearly that motives constitute means in the hands of the Spirit of God. He notes that 'motives dispose the mind to action.'[37] Thus the *fear of hell* constitutes potentially a very powerful motive in the minds of men, as a result of which men may be induced, by the influence of God's Spirit, to flee to Christ for salvation. What is so interesting about Edwards' sermons in this respect is the way in which he incorporates these philosophical and psychological principles concerning motives and the will into his preaching. Indeed, it is precisely because motives and the will are so intimately related in Edwards' thought that he commonly places his list of motives in close proximity to his exhortations. *Imperatives* command the will; *motives* provide inducements to the will to obey.

It is important to note that there is, in Edwards' mind, an inextricable connection between *motives, moral agency,* and *the image of God in man.* He constantly emphasizes that man *qua* man is a noble, intelligent, rational creature. The reason for this is, of course, that man is made in the image of God. But *moral agency* is also a crucial aspect of the image of God. 'And herein does very much consist that image of God wherein he made man, . . . by which God distinguished man from the beasts, *viz.* in those faculties and principles of nature, whereby he is capable of moral Agency. Herein very much consists the *natural* image of God.'[38] 'The brute creatures are not moral Agents.'[39] The Stockbridge theologian defines *moral agency* thus:

A *moral Agent* is a being that is capable of those actions that have a *moral* quality, and which can properly be denominated good or evil in a moral sense, virtuous or vicious, commendable or faulty. To moral Agency belongs a *moral faculty,* or sense of moral good and evil, or of such a thing as desert or worthiness, of praise or blame, reward or punishments; and a capacity which an Agent

---

[37] *Works* (Hickman), 1:30.
[38] Ibid., p. 12.
[39] Ibid.

has of being influenced in his actions by moral inducements or motives, exhibited to the view of understanding and reason, to engage to a conduct agreeable to the moral faculty.[40]

Thus it is precisely because man is a moral agent that he is capable of being influenced by motives. Such motives are 'moral inducements'; they are spiritual allurements, incentives, and enticements. They are integral to that 'moral suasion' to which man is constantly susceptible and which, by definition, belongs to the very essence of the preaching of the word of God.

It is also evident that Edwards saw an inextricable connection between the *significance of motives* and the *principle of self-love*. He emphasizes this connection in 'Charity Contrary to a Selfish Spirit':

> That to love ourselves is not unlawful is evident from that, that the law of God makes it a rule and measure by which our love to others should be regulated. Thus God commands, 'Thou shalt love thy neighbor as thyself' [Matt. 19:19]; which command certainly supposes that we may and must love ourselves. And it also appears from this, that the Scripture from one end of the Bible to the other is full of things which are there held forth to work upon a principle of self-love. Such are all the promises and threatenings of the word of God, and all its calls and invitations; its counsels to seek our own good, and its warnings to beware of misery. Which things can have influence upon us in no other way than as they tend to work upon our hope or fear ... But I apprehend that as self-love in this sense is no fruit of the Fall, but is necessary and what belongs to that nature of all intelligent beings which the Creator hath made, that it is alike in all. And that saints and sinners and all love happiness alike, and have the same unalterable propensity to seek and desire happiness.[41]

---

[40] Ibid.

[41] *Works*, 8:254-55. A comparison of the Andover copy with the Tryon Edwards edition demonstrates that the latter edition employs the phrase 'full of motives' rather than the phrase 'full of things'. See *Charity*, p. 160. The meaning is, of course, the same in either case.

This is a passage of great significance with regard to Edwards' philosophy of motivation. It is precisely because man, whether regenerate or unregenerate, is an intelligent, rational being, made in the image of God, that he loves his own happiness. Such love for his own happiness is, according to Edwards, 'not unlawful';[42] it is 'unalterable and instinctive'.[43]

Similarly, in 'Degrees of Glory' Edwards specifically defends the concept of self-love implicit in his exhortation 'to seek high degrees of glory in heaven'. Utilizing the Objection and Answer technique that he employs so frequently, he answers the potential objection: 'It will show a selfish spirit for me to seek high degrees of glory':

> *Ans.* 1. Self-love is a good principle, if well-regulated. 'Tis no irregular thing for us to love our own happiness: 'tis not this that is what is properly called selfishness; but 'tis the inordinancy of self-love: it's being ungoverned that denominates a selfish person.
>
> Self-love, when directed and regulated by the will and word of God, is a good principle. Many things are proposed in the word of God to work upon self-love in the saints. Yea, happiness was offered to Adam in innocency to influence his self-love, and the angels and saints in heaven love themselves, yea, and the man Christ Jesus. He therefore prayed for his own happiness and glory. John 17:5, 'And now, O Father, glorify me with thine own self with the glory which I had with thee before the world was.'[44]

It will be noted that Edwards makes a very important distinction here between *self-love* and *selfishness*. *Selfishness* is sinful; it is the result of the fall of man. *Self-love* is natural and necessary; it is an aspect of the image of God in man. It is precisely because of Edwards' vigorous and cogent defence of the legitimacy of the principle of self-love that we dissent from Gerstner's assertion that, in his sermons, 'Edwards makes an evangelistic appeal to an unworthy motive',[45] namely, that of

---

[42] *Charity*, p. 160.
[43] Ibid., p. 161.
[44] *Works*, 19:622.
[45] Gerstner, *Evangelist*, p. 63.

'self-interest'.[46] Edwards does indeed appeal to self-interest; but why is self-interest an unworthy motive? Self-interest is, after all, synonymous with self-love; and Edwards has demonstrated that 'self-love in this sense is no fruit of the Fall, but is necessary and what belongs to that nature of all intelligent beings which the Creator hath made, that it is alike in all.'[47] Thus if the principle of self-love or self-interest is natural and necessary, it cannot possibly be unworthy. Dabney confirms the truth of this position:

> The attempt to propagate suitable emotions is, then, lawful for the speaker; yea, there is no argument which does not implicitly do it. You will reason with men: 'This conduct is for your interest.' You may profess to have restricted yourself to simple evidence; but just in the degree in which your argument is conclusive, you make a virtual appeal to self-love. You demonstrate: 'This course is for the good of our neighbour.' You have made an appeal to benevolence. You show: 'This act is dangerous.' You resort to your hearer's fear. Again, every man practices this rhetoric of persuasion upon himself . . .
>
> Since the legitimacy of the art of persuasion depends upon our resorting to the appropriate feelings, the first question to be answered is: To what class of emotions may the preacher appeal? I reply, only to the moral and spiritual . . . Now, moral motive alone leads to moral volition.[48]

An analysis of the formal, specific, objective, moral motives or inducements presented by Edwards in his sermons reveals the following distinct patterns: in the first place, he commonly appeals to the *self-love* or *self-interest* of his hearers; he appeals to man's love of his own happiness, both in this life and in the life to come. In the second place, he commonly appeals to the *benevolence* of his hearers; he appeals to the principle of concern for the happiness of others. In the third place, he commonly appeals to the *concept of the glory of God;* he appeals to the duty of man to promote that glory and

---

[46] Ibid.
[47] *Works*, 8:255.
[48] Dabney, *Sacred Rhetoric*, pp. 237-238.

the kingdom in which that glory is manifested. Indeed, the appeal to the concept of the glory of God and the appeal to benevolence are not unconnected with the appeal to man's self-love, since the two great commandments, with which they cohere, are themselves conducive to (and not destructive of) man's happiness in both this world and the world to come. Thus the concept and the use of motives on Edwards' part is consistent with his biblical, Calvinistic anthropology. The New England preacher was a remarkable 'fisher of men'; and it is his vision of the *imago Dei* that constrains him regularly to bait the hook of the truth of God with specific, objective inducements. That the adduction and presentation of motives plays such a significant role in his preaching demonstrates powerfully his essential intellectual consistency; it demonstrates the essential consistency that pertains between the theological, philosophical, psychological, and homiletical aspects of the thought of 'the Sage of Northampton'.[49]

[49] *Works*, 22:26.

25

STYLE

The only collection of sermons that Jonathan Edwards personally saw through the press was that of *Five Discourses on Important Subjects,* published in 1738. The five discourses in question were 'Justification by Faith Alone', 'Pressing into the Kingdom of God', 'Ruth's Resolution', 'The Justice of God in the Damnation of Sinners', and 'The Excellency of Christ', all of which (with the exception of the last sermon) were 'delivered in the time of the late wonderful work of God's power and grace'[1] in Northampton in 1734-1735. Lesser observes that the Preface affixed to the *Five Discourses* 'constitutes his most sustained discussion of practical homiletics'.[2] It is of particular significance with regard to the issue of style:

> The practical discourses that follow have but little added to them, and now appear in *that very plain and unpolished dress* in which they were first prepared and delivered; which was mostly at a time when the circumstances of the auditory they were preached to, were enough to make a minister neglect, forget, and despise *such ornaments as politeness and modishness of style and method,* when coming as a messenger of God to souls deeply impressed with a sense of their danger of God's everlasting wrath, to treat with them about their eternal salvation. – *However unable I am to preach or write politely,* if I would, yet I have this to comfort me under such a defect, that God has showed us he does not need such talents in men to carry on his own work, and that he has been pleased to *smile upon and bless a very plain unfashionable way of preaching.*

[1] *Works* (Hickman), 1:620.
[2] *Works,* 19:xi.

And have we not reason to think, that it ever has been, and ever will be, God's manner, to bless the foolishness of preaching to save them that believe, *let the elegance of language and excellency of style* be carried to never so great a height, by the learning and wit of the present and future ages?[3]

The concept of 'politeness', from which Edwards deliberately distances himself in this Preface, was a concept that emerged with great prominence during the Enlightenment. 'Although a concept with an old pedigree', writes Lawrence E. Klein, 'politeness was transformed in the later seventeenth century and the early eighteenth, receiving new meanings that proved distinctive for Enlightenment usage.'[4] Emanating from the French salons and the English coffeehouses of that period, the concept of *politesse* or *politeness* was one that was associated with a certain courtesy, civility, gentlemanliness, and sophistication in discourse and discussion; it was associated with a certain moderation or restraint. 'In the eighteenth century', notes Klein, 'the French tradition of *politesse* merged with Addisonian and Shaftesburian ideas.'[5] But the culture of politeness was, by the second decade of the eighteenth century, beginning to infiltrate New England. Peter J. Thuesen notes, in this context, the significance of the Dummer gift of books to Yale College in 1713 (the books were not accessible until *circa* 1718) in introducing Edwards to 'the polite "republic of letters" of the European Enlightenment'.[6] Thuesen identifies this 'polite' literature as 'Anglican, latitudinarian, or Enlightenment':[7]

As recent scholarship has shown, this republic of letters was an informal network of learned individuals who eschewed the dogmatism of the medieval and Reformation eras and instead adopted a moderate, latitudinarian, worldly sensibility. Members of this imagined community, in theory at least, ignored distinctions

---

[3] *Works* (Hickman), 1:621. Emphasis added.
[4] Lawrence E. Klein, 'Politeness', in *Encyclopedia of the Enlightenment*.
[5] Ibid.
[6] Peter J. Thuesen, 'Edwards' Intellectual Background', in *The Princeton Companion to Jonathan Edwards*, Sang Hyun Lee, ed. (Princeton and Oxford: Princeton University Press, 2005), p. 19.
[7] Ibid., p. 26.

of nationality and religion and willingly assisted each other in cultivating an ecumenical spirit of dispassionate inquiry. In England, this new attitude of polite learning was associated especially with John Locke, but its proponents also included the Cambridge Platonists Ralph Cudworth and Henry More, the Anglican bishop Edward Stillingfleet and archbishop of Canterbury John Tillotson, the essayists Joseph Addison and Sir Richard Steele, and the philosophers Samuel Clarke and Anthony Ashley Cooper, the third earl of Shaftesbury. These and other figures, writing between the late seventeenth and early eighteenth centuries, espoused a version of Christianity that emphasized morality and reason over strict doctrinal formulations. By the early eighteenth century, this 'polite' style was so pervasive in the Church of England that the once-triumphant Calvinism of the Puritan revolution had virtually disappeared as an effective force in English life.[8]

Edwards' interest in this international 'republic of letters' is incontestable; and whilst it must be insisted upon that this interest reflects primarily his essential literary eclecticism, there is also evidence that suggests that, at least during the period of his tutorship at Yale, he himself felt the powerful lure of this international 'republic of letters'. It is very interesting to note that his earliest notes on style and literary strategy, written on the cover of the notebook 'Notes on Natural Philosophy', contain the following literary, stylistic rules, the first two of which were drawn up in 1723 and the last by 1726:

[4. [Let much] modesty be seen in the style.

6. *The world will expect more modesty because of my circumstances – in America, young, etc. Let there then be a superabundance of modesty, and though perhaps 'twill otherwise be needless, it will wonderfully make way for its repetition in the world. Mankind are by nature proud and exceeding envious, and ever jealous of such upstarts; and it exceedingly irritates and affronts 'em to see 'em appear in print. Yet the modesty ought not to be affected and foolish, but decent and natural.*[9]

---

[8] Ibid., pp. 19-20.
[9] *Works*, 10:181.

17. Before I venture to publish in London, to make some experiment in my own country; to play at small games first, that I may gain some experience in writing. First to write letters to some in England, and to try my [hand at] lesser matters before I venture in great.[10]

There can be no doubt that there is, at first glance, something surprising about these Notes; and it is important that their significance should not be suppressed in the misguided interests of hagiography. Minkema notes 'his expansive private aspirations';[11] and Kimnach observes 'more than a hint of sheer personal ambition'.[12] Indeed, Kimnach draws the following conclusion:

> Thus, at this early stage of his career, Edwards was planning to stake out a claim in the world of letters; he had not yet published anything, but he was thinking of the conditions necessary for the favorable acceptance of successive future writings. The extent of his ambition and the tenor of his self-confidence are further adumbrated in number 17, where he identifies London as the center of his cultural world and lays plans for a methodical, prudent siege. Even Boston was no more than a playground for this unknown backwoods upstart! Well might he caution himself about allowing immodesty to show; these entries prove him to have been supremely ambitious and coolly, though not foolishly, self-confident.[13]

Kimnach contends that 'the reiterated insistence upon modesty',[14] whilst not divorced from the humility of true spirituality, was in large part

---

[10] Ibid., p. 185. 'A number of the rules are in JE's shorthand', explains Kimnach, 'indicated in the text by italics.' Ibid., p. 181 n. 1.

[11] *Works*, 14:6.

[12] *Works*, 10:186.

[13] Ibid., pp. 186-187. Marsden makes this observation: 'Amid both the exhilarations of New York and the tensions of the summer back at East Windsor, the nineteen-year-old Jonathan was laying out a monumental design . . . The pastorate was his calling, yet he was resolved that his life's work would not be just local. He was determined to be an international figure. This was part ambition – of which he had a lot – yet he also saw it as his larger calling, if God granted him the grace, to play a role in promoting God's earthly kingdom at a crucial moment in the history of redemption.' Marsden, *Edwards*, p. 59.

[14] Ibid., p. 186.

'a stylistic strategy'.[15] He detects here a 'superficial stylistic self-efface-ment'[16] on the part of the Yale tutor.

There is a clear tension here between Edwards' considerable literary ambition on the one hand and his concern, doubtless partly spiritual and partly strategic, for modesty on the other. Indeed, it is not inconceivable that, at this stage in his career, the Yale tutor was experiencing a consid-erable internal struggle between the lure of academic and literary fame on the one hand and the call of Christ to preach the offence of the cross on the other. The evidence of a certain ambivalence on Edwards' part with regard to the issue of style coheres with this tension; his attitude towards this issue reveals elements of both attraction and repulsion. Indeed, Thuesen posits 'an Edwards caught between two worlds'.[17] He contends that 'Edwards himself, throughout his subsequent career, seemed torn between two philosophical worlds: the tradition of Protest-ant scholasticism and the new republic of Enlightenment letters.'[18] There is, doubtless, some truth in Thuesen's position. But it should be noted that the Preface of 1738, written some twelve years after the last of these notes on style and literary strategy, reveals a very forthright rejection of the claims of politeness and modishness in preaching. If Edwards was at one stage caught between opposing worlds, there can be little doubt as to which world, in the final analysis, held the upper hand.[19]

Thus if the negative emphasis of the 1738 Preface is *contra* polite-ness, the positive emphasis is on behalf of plainness. The emphasis falls, albeit somewhat defensively, upon 'a very plain unfashionable way of preaching' – upon 'that very plain and unpolished dress' in which

---

[15] Ibid.

[16] Ibid., p. 180.

[17] Thuesen, p. 26.

[18] Ibid., p. 21.

[19] We believe that Thuesen exaggerates JE's interest in polite literature. See ibid., pp. 26-27. Certainly, as his 'Catalogue' demonstrates, JE sought out and read avidly books that belonged to this category. But this simply proves his essential literary eclecticism. He was, moreover, constantly concerned to stay abreast of the latest and subtlest deviations from the truth of the gospel of Christ. Thuesen fails to consider JE's 'Catalogue' in the context of the entire corpus of his works. In particular, he fails to note the significance of the Preface to the *Five Discourses*.

these sermons were first prepared and delivered. This is an emphasis that recurs in other sermons. In 'The Church's Marriage to her Sons, and to her God' – the sermon preached on the occasion of the installation of Samuel Buell – Edwards speaks disapprovingly of those who are 'gratified by a florid eloquence, and the excellency of speech and man's wisdom'.[20] Conversely, in 'Man's Natural Blindness in the Things of Religion' he speaks approvingly of 'the plain preaching of the gospel of his Son'.[21] The 'plain style' is clearly set in antithesis to 'a florid eloquence'; it is set in antithesis to that cult of polish, politeness, modishness, and elegance of style that was so highly esteemed in the Age of the Enlightenment. It is evident from these phrases that, as far as Edwards was concerned, the style of preaching, upon which the blessing of God had fallen in the past and upon which the church might expect it to fall in the future, was a style that was characterized by *plainness*.

We note here the clear influence of the Puritan homiletical tradition upon the New England preacher. That tradition is articulated in *The Directory for the Publick Worship of God*. In the section entitled 'Of the Preaching of the Word' the Westminster divines make this assertion:

> The doctrine is to be expressed in *plain* terms; . . . But the servant of Christ, whatever his method be, is to perform his whole ministry: . . . *Plainly, that the meanest may understand;* delivering the truth not in the enticing words of man's wisdom, but in demonstration of the Spirit and of power, lest the cross of Christ should be made of none effect; abstaining also from an unprofitable use of unknown tongues, strange phrases, and cadences of sounds and words; sparingly citing sentences of ecclesiastical or other human writers, ancient or modern, be they never so elegant.[22]

[20] *Works* (Hickman), 2:20.

[21] Ibid., p. 254.

[22] *Directory for Publick Worship*, pp. 379, 381. Emphasis added. It is evident that JE was both familiar with and in substantial agreement with the *Westminster Standards*. In 'Christ's Agony' he refers approvingly to 'the Assembly's Catechism'. Ibid., p. 873. Again, in a letter 'To the Rev. Mr. Erskine', dated July 5, 1750, in which the ousted Northampton pastor is clearly contemplating the possibility of a ministry in Scotland, he asserts that 'as to my

Thus the Puritan 'plain style' insisted upon simplicity, clarity, directness, and comprehensibility. It deliberately eschewed any striving after artistic elegance or magnificent oratory; it was essentially an unassuming, unadorned style. J. I. Packer has summarized the Puritans' philosophy of style thus: 'They systematically eschewed any rhetorical display that might divert attention from God to themselves, and talked to their congregations in plain, straightforward, homely English . . . Dignified simplicity – "studied plainness", as one of their number once put it – was their ideal.'[23]

The Northampton preacher clearly shared this commitment to 'studied plainness'. His homiletical style is not florid, witty, or metaphysical. There is nothing pretentious about his style; it is not theatrical, ostentatious, or deliberately entertaining. His sermons are characterized by simplicity, sobriety, modesty, and clarity. This fact is evidenced by the kind of vocabulary, phrases, and sentences that are found throughout his sermons. It should be noted that his sentences are essentially simple, not complex. He does not employ long, complex, latinized sentences, replete with subordinate clauses. His sermons are not prolix; indeed, his style is much simpler than that of John Owen. The essential simplicity of Edwards' sentences is reflected in his frequent use of the fundamental verbs *to be* and *to have*. The Yale historian, Edmund S. Morgan, highlights 'that incredible simplicity of language which no one else could quite approach.'[24] It is a very striking fact that the author of *Freedom of the Will*, with all of its intellectual brilliance, was also the preacher of plain, simple, sober, unadorned sermons on the great truths of the word of God.

It is interesting, however, to note the negative reaction that the obvious plainness of Edwards' style has sometimes elicited, especially

---

subscribing to the substance of the Westminster Confession, there would be no difficulty.' *Works* (Hickman), 1:cxxi. Again, in the Conclusion to *Original Sin* JE makes the following ironic and sardonic observation: 'and no wonder then, if the superficial observation of vulgar Christians, or indeed of the herd of common divines, such as the Westminster Assembly, &c. falls vastly short of the apostle's reach, and frequently does not enter into the true spirit and design of his epistles.' Ibid., p. 233.

[23] Packer, *Puritan Preaching*, pp. 285-286.

[24] Morgan, *Gentle Puritan*, pp. 33-34.

in the past. Kimnach reports the following extreme reaction to the New England preacher-theologian: 'A writer who professed indifference to "modishness" and "politeness", Edwards has been mistaken occasionally for an American primitive who was oblivious to the subtleties of literary style and the traditions of *genre*.'[25] Similarly, Lesser reports the nineteenth-century assessment of Edwards' style: 'So pervasive was the nineteenth-century view that his was one of "the most remarkable specimens of bad writing" of his time that an editor of *Religious Affections* abridged the text to reduce "its monstrous profusion of words", and another rendered the whole of "Sinners in the Hands of an Angry God" in "other language".'[26] It is important, therefore, to note the more balanced assessment of his style by Samuel Finley (1715-1766). Finley was to become the fifth president of the College of New Jersey from 1761-1766, following the deaths of both Edwards and Samuel Davies; and when Edwards' *The Great Christian Doctrine of Original Sin Defended* was published in 1758, not long after the author's death, Finley affixed to this work 'A Brief Account of the Book and Its Author', in which he provided the following judicious analysis of President Edwards' style: 'His language was with propriety and purity, but with a noble negligence; nothing ornamented. Florid diction was not the beauty he preferred. His talents were of a superior kind. He regarded thoughts, rather than words. Precision of sentiment and clearness of expression are the principal characteristics of his pulpit style.'[27] President Finley's description of Edwards' style contains a significant element of truth. It recognizes the fact that his writings are sometimes characterized by a certain inattention to style – indeed, that there are, at times, certain stylistic inelegancies which are probably partly provincial in origin.

Nevertheless, it is very important to note that Edwards' writings, and especially his sermons, are also characterized by a definite attention to style – indeed, that there is, at times, a brilliance about his style. Thus the paradox here is that there is, at the same time, both a certain

[25] *Works*, 10:168.
[26] *Works*, 19:34.
[27] *Works* (Hickman), 1:144.

denigration and a certain *cultivation* of style on his part. Twentieth-century literary critics have, interestingly, demonstrated a much greater appreciation for the literary qualities of his style than their nineteenth-century counterparts. Cady describes Edwards as 'so careful a stylist';[28] Lemay refers to him as 'such a verbal genius';[29] 'Edwards' style has been condemned as awkward, prolix, and redundant', notes Kimnach, 'but it can also be dynamic and powerful, one of impressive density and oceanic rhythms';[30] and Philip F. Gura observes that 'Edwards craft-ed a prose style hypnotic in its cadence and seductive in its persuasive power.'[31]

There is, therefore, a lingering complexity about the issue of Edwards' style. On the one hand, there is on his part an avowed cult of plainness; on the other hand, there are unquestionably many passages, both in these *Five Discourses* and in other sermons and discourses, which are rhetorically quite brilliant. 'Edwards seemed to scorn rhetoric', observes Turnbull incisively, 'yet used it.'[32] Kimnach contends that 'Edwards frequently manifests great sensitivity to the merest turn of phrase.'[33] He notes 'the meticulous prose of his earlier sermons'[34] and 'the great sentences and greater paragraphs that characterize his homiletics.'[35] 'The Nakedness of Job', one of Edwards' earliest sermons, demonstrates these rhetorical skills. 'The sermon is characterized', notes Kimnach, 'by memorably fine passages.'[36] The following passage is one of the finest examples of Edwards' cultivation of rhythm and cadence:

> Death serves all alike; as he deals with the poor, so he deals with the rich: is not awed at the appearance of a proud palace, a numerous attendance, or a majestic countenance; pulls a king out of his throne, and summons him before the judgment seat of God, with as few

[28] Cady, p. 63.

[29] Lemay, p. 189.

[30] Wilson H. Kimnach, 'The Literary Techniques of Jonathan Edwards' (Ph.D. diss., University of Pennsylvania, 1971), pp. 379-380.

[31] Gura, p. 93.

[32] Turnbull, p. 63.

[33] *Works*, 10:168.

[34] *Works*, 25:6.

[35] Ibid.

[36] *Works*, 10:401.

compliments and as little ceremony as he takes the poor man out
of his cottage. Death is as rude with emperors as with beggars,
and handles one with as much gentleness as the other.[37]

Kimnach notes the significance of this early sermon in Edwards'
development as a preacher: 'Calling attention to the reality within
accepted truths, or discovering a rhetoric that would make truth real
to his audience, was to become the central mission for Edwards as a
preacher, and in this sermon that mission is fairly launched.'[38] From
the very beginning of his preaching ministry he clearly sought, like the
Preacher in Ecclesiastes, 'to find out acceptable words'.[39]

Moreover, the *Five Discourses* themselves, to which the aforementioned Preface is affixed, contain some remarkable passages. In
'The Justice of God in the Damnation of Sinners' the thirty-one year
old preacher delivers a brilliant analysis of 'the exceeding sinfulness of
sin':

> That it is just with God eternally to cast off wicked men, may
> more abundantly appear, if we consider how much sin they are
> guilty of. From what has been already said, it appears, that if men
> were guilty of sin but in one particular, that is sufficient ground of
> their eternal rejection and condemnation. If they are *sinners,* that
> is enough. Merely this, might be sufficient to keep them from ever
> lifting up their heads, and cause them to smite on their breasts,
> with the publican that cried, 'God be merciful to me a sinner.' But
> sinful men are full of sin; principles and acts of sin: their guilt
> is like great mountains, heaped one upon another, till the pile is
> grown up to heaven. They are totally corrupt, in every part, in all
> their faculties; in all the principles of their nature, their under-
> standings, and wills; and in all their dispositions and affections.
> Their heads, their hearts, are totally depraved; all the members of
> their bodies are only instruments of sin; and all their senses, see-
> ing, hearing, tasting, &c. are only inlets and outlets of sin, channels
> of corruption. There is nothing but sin, no good at all. Rom. vii.

[37] Ibid., p. 406.
[38] Ibid., p. 400.
[39] Ecclesiastes 12:10

18. 'In me, that is, in my flesh, dwells no good thing.' There is all manner of wickedness. There are seeds of the greatest and blackest crimes. There are principles of all sorts of wickedness against men; and there is all wickedness against God. There is pride; there is enmity; there is contempt; there is quarrelling; there is atheism; there is blasphemy. There are these things in exceeding strength; the heart is under the power of them, is sold under sin, and a perfect slave to it. There is hard-heartedness, hardness greater than that of a rock, or an adamant-stone. There is obstinacy and perverseness, incorrigibleness and inflexibleness in sin, that will not be overcome by threatenings or promises, by awakenings or encouragements, by judgments or mercies, neither by that which is terrifying nor that which is winning. The very blood of God our Saviour will not win the heart of a wicked man.

And there are actual wickednesses without number or measure. There are breaches of every command, in thought, word, and deed: a life full of sin; days and nights filled up with sin; mercies abused and frowns despised; mercy and justice, and all the divine perfections, trampled on; and the honour of each person in the Trinity trod in the dirt. Now if one sinful word or thought has so much evil in it, as to deserve eternal destruction, how do they deserve to be eternally cast off and destroyed, that are guilty of so much sin![40]

The sheer rhetorical and spiritual power of this passage lies in the tremendous simplicity and intensity with which the scriptural truth of man's total depravity and corruption is portrayed. The urgency and the cogency of the message of the plight of man are reflected in the preacher's dramatic, nervous reiteration of the verb *to be*. 'There is pride; there is enmity; there is contempt; there is quarrelling; there is atheism; there is blasphemy.' The passage is, moreover, a striking example of that 'movement'[41] which, according to Dabney, is one of the 'cardinal requisites of the sermon'.[42] 'In style', Dabney contends, 'movement

---

[40] *Works* (Hickman), 1:670.
[41] Dabney, *Sacred Rhetoric*, pp. 105, 121-126.
[42] Ibid., p. 105.

requires a certain economy of words.'[43] 'The language of the orator must possess, in all its flow, a nervous brevity and a certain well-ordered haste, like that of the racer pressing to his goal.'[44] It is not unfair to contend that Edwards' sermons reveal at times an intriguing tension between what might be described as 'the *de jure* plain' and 'the *de facto* brilliant'.

It is important to note that, in the context of early eighteenth century New England, the very concept of style bore certain connotations and was viewed, at least by the Puritan tradition, with some suspicion. Kimnach explains the situation thus:

> Of course, part of the problem is also that, as in the seventeenth century, preaching styles were associated with theological poitions. In Edwards' day many of the most eloquent preachers of the East were suspect in his eyes of being rationalist, Arminian, or just theologically jejune. He would therefore rather deny excellence in his carefully wrought sermons than be thought – perhaps even by himself – to be a creature of wit and style. He was too serious, too full of thought, and too honest for *style*.[45]

Thus a false dichotomy appears to have developed to some extent in Puritan New England between the concept of style and the concept of orthodoxy, as if the former were somehow antithetical or inimical to the latter. This situation thus accounts in large part for the paradox that, on the one hand, the Northampton preacher appears to have no pretensions to style, whilst, on the other hand, he appears to attain to it. It must be noted, however, that the style to which he attains is not a style characterized by 'artificiality and ornateness'[46] – but rather a style characterized by the concept of 'the nakedness of ideas'. The seventh in Edwards' list of rules is very significant in this respect and reads as follows:

> 7. When I would prove anything, to take special care that the matter be so stated that it shall be seen most clearly and distinctly by everyone just how much I would prove; and to extricate all

---

[43] Ibid., p. 123.
[44] Ibid., p. 124.
[45] *Works*, 10:24.
[46] Ibid., p. 23 n. 2.

questions from the least confusion or ambiguity of words, so that the ideas shall be left naked.[47]

Kimnach explains thus the paradox of Edwards' renunciation of style on the one hand and his actual achievement of it on the other: 'Since he was consciously developing a heart-piercing manner of writing that would be as spare and efficient as an arrow, he assumed that "style", being an adventitious decoration, would have to be left out. It would not have struck Edwards that that efficacious verbal expression for which he constantly strove and "style" might be the same thing.'[48]

It will be immediately evident that Miller's description of Edwards' style as 'cryptic' stands in blatant contradiction to Edwards' own description of his style as 'plain'. It is in his influential biography *Jonathan Edwards* (1949) that Miller emphasizes what he regards as 'the cryptic element in Edwards' writing'.[49] 'Edwards' writing is an immense cryptogram, the passionate oratory of the revival no less than the hard reasoning of the treatise on the will. The way he delivered his sermons is enough to confirm the suspicion that there was an occult secret in them: no display, no inflection, no consideration of the audience ... His writings are almost a hoax, not to be read but to be seen through.'[50] Thus, as far as Miller is concerned, Edwards' writings – his sermons included – require an esoteric deciphering; and the double key that unlocks this cipher is, according to the Harvard scholar, that of John Locke and Sir Isaac Newton. 'Consequently', Miller insists, 'when we go behind Edwards' early publications to find the hidden meanings, we discover in the "Notes" not one key but two, a dual series of reflections, often intermingled but not yet synthesized. The one proceeds out of Locke and becomes what posterity has called his "idealism"; the

---

[47] Ibid., p. 181.

[48] Ibid., pp. 23-24.

[49] Miller, *Edwards*, p. 50.

[50] Ibid., p. 51. Miller further insists: '*The Freedom of the Will* is an immense cipher.' Ibid., p. 262. In what McClymond, p. 7, describes as 'a minor academic skirmish', Vincent Tomas (1916-1995) – the William Herbert Perry Faunce Professor of Philosophy at Brown University – vigorously rejected Miller's thesis. Miller had adduced the 'immense cryptogram' hypothesis in support of his view that JE was an essentially modern thinker. See 'The Modernity of Jonathan Edwards', *New England Quarterly* 25 (1952): pp. 66-69.

other begins with Newton and becomes what has been less widely appreciated, his naturalism.'[51] It should be noted, however, *contra* Miller, that it is one thing to assert that Edwards was, as a young man, significantly influenced by 'the new philosophy' and 'the new science' which were introduced into the curriculum at Yale *circa* 1718 as a result of the Dummer gift of books;[52] it is quite another thing to suggest that John Locke and Sir Isaac Newton constitute the keys that unlock the 'immense cryptogram' of his writings. Indeed, it is difficult to avoid the conclusion that Miller was almost obsessed with the idea that the major formative influences upon Jonathan Edwards were Locke and Newton. This fact is demonstrated by specific reference to both the philosopher and the scientist on page after page of Miller's intellectual biography. Edwards' finest biographer, George M. Marsden, offers the following justifiable criticisms of Miller's biography: 'Miller's portrait is ... a triumph of the imagination.'[53] 'Miller ... let his creativity get the best of him in his biography of Edwards.'[54] Marsden describes the biography as 'influential, brilliant, and often misleading'.[55] It must, therefore, be insisted upon, *contra* Miller, that Edwards' style was not cryptic, but plain; it was not esoteric, but transparent.[56] The principal influences upon Edwards were, moreover, not Newton and Locke, but the Bible and the great heritage of the Reformers and the Puritans; and the 'occult secret' that, according to Miller, lay behind the sermons and

[51] Ibid., pp. 71-72.

[52] 'Amounting to nearly five hundred titles amassed by Jeremiah Dummer through donations in England (Richard Steele and Isaac Newton were among the donors), the collection constituted a massive updating of Yale's then meager resources.' *Fiering*, p. 22. Dummer was a colonial agent whose gift of books to the new library at Yale introduced both Locke and Newton for the first time, not only to Yale, but also, it seems, to American college life in general. Wallace E. Anderson makes this observation: 'Up to this time neither Locke nor Newton had been taught in any American college.' *Works*, 6:15.

[53] Marsden, *Edwards*, p. 61.

[54] Ibid., pp. 60-61.

[55] Ibid., xvii. We do not deny that there are flashes of brilliance in Miller's biography. Particularly impressive is Miller's ability to evoke something of the atmosphere of eighteenth-century New England. The problem lies in his central thesis, which interprets JE almost exclusively in terms of the influence of Locke and Newton. This thesis is, we believe, massively flawed.

[56] Kimnach deals with Miller's eccentric, although influential, views in this respect. 'Edwards did not preach "esoteric cryptograms" over the heads of his people'. 25:45.

their undramatic delivery was none other than the invisible power of the sovereign Spirit of God.

26

DELIVERY

Delivery is to the pulpit what style is to paper. Thus, whereas the issue of style presupposes a reading of the sermon, the issue of delivery presupposes a hearing of the preaching itself. Indeed, delivery is essentially pulpit style. But if the issue of Jonathan Edwards' style is controverted, the issue of his delivery is even more controverted. The traditional notion, at least until recently, has been that 'Edwards preached from a manuscript in a monotone.'[1] Kimnach, editor of both the first and the last volumes of Edwards' *Sermons and Discourses* in the Yale series, tends to perpetuate this traditional notion when he refers to 'Edwards, the undramatic preacher with the unimpressive voice.'[2] Even Gerstner, who is second to none in his admiration of Edwards as a preacher, alleges considerable mediocrity in the area of delivery:

> Jonathan Edwards was, in my opinion, the greatest preacher, from the standpoint of content of his messages, who has appeared in history since apostolic times. From the standpoint of delivery, he possibly was one of the most mediocre the Church has ever known. He had none of the grand eloquence of George Whitefield or that powerful or sonorous voice. Apparently there were no real gestures, just a solemn reading of the manuscript most of the time, much to the chagrin of his senior pastor, Solomon Stoddard.[3]

---

[1] Jim Ehrhard, 'A Critical Analysis of the Tradition of Jonathan Edwards as a Manuscript Preacher', *Westminster Theological Journal* 60 (1998): p. 74.

[2] *Works*, 10:114.

[3] Gerstner, *Rational Biblical Theology*, 1:480. Gerstner goes on to make this assertion: 'But from the standpoint of deep and solid exegesis, clear and profound articulation of doctrine, searching, thorough, and fervent evangelistic application, I have never found Edwards' equal ... My verdict is that this is a preacher extraordinary of the Word of God.' Ibid.

His preaching went on without ceasing and one understands why he could never accept Stoddard's advice not to read his own sermons from the pulpit. Even Edwards could never have produced this volume of sermonic and other literary output if he had been required even materially to memorize it for pulpit presentation. Being confined to the manuscript even in the outline sermons which were very full he had none of the freedom of utterance displayed by others.[4]

But one of the problems with Gerstner's assessment is that it ignores the very important homiletical principle that *writing and reading* on the one hand and *writing and memorizing* on the other are not the only possibilities with regard to the preparation and delivery of sermons; indeed, that they are not, in fact, the ideal method. There is a third possibility with regard to delivery – that advocated by Dabney, and utilized by many great preachers – namely, that of *diligent preparation and extemporaneous delivery* (possibly from an outline) in which the preacher is, in effect, thinking on his feet and in which a process of invention or reinvention is actually occurring in the pulpit. Moreover, Gerstner's assessment of Edwards in this regard surprisingly ignores the overwhelming evidence from Edwards' own manuscripts to the effect that, increasingly, he did in fact move in this very direction in his preparation and delivery. It is simply incorrect to make the sweeping assertion that 'he could never accept Stoddard's advice not to read his own sermons from the pulpit.' A much more nuanced assessment of the issue is required. Gerstner appears to have merely perpetuated a stereotypical caricature of Edwards' delivery which ignores the development that clearly occurred in his preaching over the years.

It is important to note that one of the major homiletical influences upon the Northampton pastor, alongside that of his own father, Timothy Edwards, was that of his maternal grandfather, Solomon Stoddard, whose assistant and successor he became in Northampton in 1727 and 1729 respectively. This influence must inevitably have extended, to some degree, to the issue of delivery. It is significant that

---

[4] Ibid., 3:82.

Stoddard 'preached in the grand manner'.[5] Moreover, it is significant not only that he preached extemporaneously, but also that he was highly critical of those who did not. In 1723 he had preached his famous sermon, 'The Defects of Preachers Reproved', in which he strongly condemned the practice of reading sermons. It is interesting to note the connection in his mind between *extemporaneousness* and *affection* in preaching:

> *The reading of sermons is a dull way of preaching.* Sermons when read are not delivered with authority and in an affecting way . . . When sermons are delivered without notes, the looks and the gesture of the minister, is a great means to command attention and stir up affection. Men are apt to be drowsy in hearing the word, and the liveliness of the preacher is a means to stir up the attention of the hearers, and beget suitable affection in them. Sermons that are read are not delivered with authority, they savor the sermons of the scribes, Matthew 7:29. Experience shows that sermons read are not so profitable as others.[6]

It is reasonable to suppose that Stoddard's obvious opposition to the 'essay-sermon' and to 'reading preachers' cannot but have influenced his grandson. Kimnach makes the following observation: '"Rational Christianity" and the essay-sermon may have been flowing with the tides into Boston harbor at the beginning of the eighteenth century, but they would not progress to the Connecticut valley if Solomon Stoddard could help it.'[7] In the light of this very significant influence upon him it was surely antecedently improbable that Edwards would not seek to move, at least to some extent, in the direction of extemporaneousness in his preaching.

It should be noted that recent scholarship has exploded once and for all the traditional, stereotypical concept of Edwards' delivery. Kimnach, the Yale editor who has engaged in the most detailed analysis of Edwards' sermons, notes that 'the extant sermon manuscripts, probably at least

[5] *Works*, 10:12.
[6] Cited Ehrhard, p. 77.
[7] *Works*, 10:14.

four-fifths of the original sermon corpus, number roughly 1,200[8] and makes the following significant observations on the basis of this crucial manuscript evidence:

> This mass of sermons can be roughly divided among the three chronological periods ... 1722-27, 1727-42, 1742-58. In the first period, there are about 65 sermons, all fully written out. The second period comprises about 645 sermons, the vast majority of which are fully written out, although significant outlining appears here and there in the last 140 or so. The final period, 1742-58, includes about 510 sermons, the majority of which are more or less in outline. Moreover, within this last period, the 'Indian sermons,' most of which are the barest outlines, represent all but a handful of the 200 sermons written after the move to Stockbridge.[9]

There are suspicious blanks in Edwards' generally tightly crowded sermon manuscripts as early as 1722 or 1723 (in Job 1:21, for instance), but in themselves they do not count for much, being so few and far apart. As Edwards gained mastery of the pulpit, however, and as his time was increasingly taken up by study and pastoral duties, he gradually began outlining sections of his sermons. Now some of this outlining is apt to be found in any part of a sermon, and Edwards presumably outlined those parts that were simplest or easiest for him to remember. But by 1729 a pattern begins to emerge: the conclusions of the Doctrine and Application divisions of the sermon are most apt to be left in outline. Moreover, these outlines are not 'pure' outlines, that is, the outline itself does not fill up the page. Rather, a series of heads is scattered over several pages where they might be expected to come in a fully developed text. Some of them have additional material beneath them and some do not; in these passages there is every degree of development or non-development. The conclusion is inescapable that by 1729 Edwards was not writing out his sermons in first drafts, but rather blocking them out, perhaps with

---

[8] Ibid., p. 130.
[9] Ibid., p. 131.

the aid of outlines ... and developing them as the difficulty of the subject required and time permitted.[10]

Minkema confirms the untenable nature of the traditional view:

Contrary to time-honored descriptions of Edwards as a statue-like, inflectionless speaker, his sermon manuscripts indicate that he varied his delivery, sought eye contact with his listeners, and extemporized on occasion. Having succeeded the master preacher Stoddard, who had condemned the common practice of reading sermons from the pulpit, Edwards experimented with ways to free himself from total reliance on his manuscripts. Increasingly he employed special marks or cues, which allowed him to look up from his notes and then easily locate where he had left off. One such mark was the 'pick-up' line, which was merely a curved line drawn to separate key points. He even began to compose portions of his sermons in outline, underdeveloped introductory state-ments, and fragmentary phrases for extemporaneous delivery.[11]

'The Threefold Work of the Holy Ghost' – preached *circa* April 1729 and based upon John 16:8 ('And when he is come, he will reprove the world of sin, of righteousness, and of judgment') – provides an excellent illustration of the 'fragmentary phrases' to which Minkema refers:

'Tis the work of the Holy Ghost to convince [men of sin in order to their salvation]. So dull and stupid are the souls of men naturally, so under the power of that blinding, stupefying thing sin, that even natural conscience is lulled asleep and the natural reason is

---

[10] Ibid., p. 102. Kimnach traces the evolution in JE's actual composition and delivery of sermons thus: 'For Edwards the preacher, techniques of abbreviation and consolidation were nothing new. In 1727 he had shifted from a larger octavo sermon booklet to a smaller duodecimo, probably so that his booklet would not be so obvious in his hand. At the same time he had started expanding the page count of his sermon booklets to accommodate two preaching units in one booklet rather than shuffle between two booklets of a fixed number of pages. Around 1730 Edwards began the heavy use of 'pick up lines,' visual devices that enabled him to pick up where he had left off, after looking up from his booklet, more easily than searching through his tiny writing. Although Edwards had experimented with various kinds of outline and textual abbreviation even in his early sermons, around 1740 he began outlining or abbreviating his syntax much more heavily, and this practice would increase, generally, for the remainder of his career.' *Works*, 25:5.

[11] *Works*, 14:12.

kept from a free exercise by it, so that they will not be sensible, etc. Experience. Instances in Scripture manifest it. Peter's sermon [Acts 2]. Jailor [Acts 16:27-34].[12]

The Holy Ghost convinces [men of their] helplessness in any way of their own contriving. There are many ways that sinners under awakenings hope to help themselves, to escape their danger.

When they see the danger they are in, the souls in the next place naturally bend themselves to seek help.

Help in friends.

[They] lay obligation upon God, upon his justice, upon his honor. By his Word. Declarations of mercy. Promises. Providence. Showing mercy to others.

By righteousness. By prayers. Pitiful cries, etc. They think to help themselves by strength. Converting themselves.[13]

Minkema notes 'the sketchy nature that sections of some of his sermons assumed'[14] and emphasizes the significance of this particular sermon in Edwards' development as a preacher:

The style of the sermon marks a transition for Edwards. Perhaps due to the demanding and lengthy nature of the discourse, he used abbreviations more than ever before. While parts of the discourse are fully written out, others are written in a sometimes terse, sometimes fragmentary manner. Scattered sections amount to nothing more than lists of points contained in mere words or phrases meant to be expounded extemporaneously. The uneven nature of the sermon's composition may reflect Edwards' increasingly poor health, which resulted in a debilitation in June. Taken as a whole, however, this composition suggests that Edwards was also experimenting, not so much with changing the formal structure of the sermon itself, but with his own powers of memory and association, as well as with how to produce sermons more efficiently.[15]

---

12 Ibid., p. 381.
13 Ibid., p. 383.
14 Ibid., p. 13.
15 Ibid., p. 374.

It would appear that, for about two years after Edwards' installation in the Northampton church in 1727, Solomon Stoddard had preached 'half of every Sabbath', whilst Edwards himself had delivered 'two discourses weekly', one on the Lord's Day and the other on a weekday evening.[16] That the year 1729 should constitute a significant homiletical turning-point for him is not surprising, as it was on February 11 of that year that his grandfather died, leaving him the sole minister of the church. Lesser has noted the practical significance of this event in terms of the increased responsibilities and pressures that now devolved upon him:

> At Northampton a far heavier pulpit load, unmet by the work of New York, Bolton, and New Haven, forced change in his habits of composition, especially after his grandfather's death, when the demand almost doubled. His sermon manuscripts now take on all the writerly quirks found in the later ones: a hurried march of abbreviations, cropped words, closed vowels, dashes and fragments, transpositions and interlineations.[17]

In a recent article entitled 'A Critical Analysis of the Tradition of Jonathan Edwards as a Manuscript Preacher', Jim Ehrhard has challenged the 'caricatures of him as a boring manuscript preacher'[18] and the widely accepted notion that he was 'lamely dependent on his manuscript'.[19] Ehrhard contends that the evidence points to 'an increasing tendency toward a more extemporaneous style':[20]

> Everything in the Yale collection indicates that Edwards preached extemporaneously, although not completely without notes. His pulpit notes even include devices to help him emphasize various points, and his outlines often clearly indicate that he intended to speak completely extemporaneously at certain points.
>
> In light of this evidence, there appears to be no reason for continuing to hold to the idea of Edwards as a manuscript preacher.[21]

---

[16] *Works*, 19:7.
[17] Ibid.
[18] Ehrhard, p. 71.
[19] Ibid.
[20] Ibid., p. 78.
[21] Ibid., pp. 83-84.

In particular, Ehrhard highlights 'Edwards' shift, around 1741, away from writing out his manuscripts in full to simply outlining the main/important thoughts. While the Yale collection does include full manuscripts for some sermons following that period, the majority are sermons preached on special occasions. Some scholars have suggested that this change in Edwards' delivery occurred after Whitefield's visit to his church in October, 1740.'[22]

This view of the significance of Whitefield's visit has recently been reaffirmed by Stout and Hatch, the co-editors of the Yale volume of *Sermons and Discourses* 1739-1742: 'By December 1740 unmistakable evidence appears in Edwards' manuscript sermons that he had begun to experiment with and perfect his own revival rhetoric in Whitefieldian directions ... For his part, Edwards increasingly outlined his sermons in order to achieve the appearance of Whitefield's extemporaneity.'[23] Indeed, Stout and Hatch assert that he 'was obsessed with Whitefield, and in his own way he began to imitate him.'[24] But the question that must be asked is this: What is the evidence for this alleged obsession with Whitefield? Edwards surely had the wisdom to realize immediately that there was, ultimately, something profoundly inimitable about George Whitefield's preaching. It is interesting to note that Kimnach gives this notion of Edwards' imitation of Whitefield fairly short shrift:

> But even this notion is open to serious question, for Edwards was always his own man, and though he laboriously copied pages of other men's books into his own notebooks, he invariably picked just those ideas that passed his own rigorous tests for a place in his own system of thought and rejected their less sound neighbors out of hand. So, it seems, he (who had experimented with extensive outlining before he saw Whitefield) would have taken the measure of Whitefield's delivery and used what he could use, and rejected the rest.[25]

---

[22] Ibid., p. 81. In the course of this visit Whitefield 'preached four sermons in the Northampton meetinghouse and one in the Edwards home'. *Works*, 22:203.

[23] *Works*, 22:31.

[24] Ibid.

[25] *Works*, 10:122. Kimnach returns to this issue in his later Yale volume: 'A prevalent representation of JE's later preaching is summarized by Ola E. Winslow: "After Whitefield

Thus the *occasion* should not be confused with the *cause*. The fact that Edwards moved significantly in the direction of extemporaneousness not long after Whitefield's visit to Northampton does not, in and of itself, prove that Whitefield's example lay behind this development. It is well to remember that crucial principle of logic: *Post hoc non ergo propter hoc.*[26] It is, surely, far more reasonable to suppose that the Great Awakening, which, under God, was triggered in New England by Whitefield's seraphic itinerant preaching and in which Edwards was himself very soon to play such a colossal role, introduced a dramatic interruption into the normal routines of the Northampton preacher and compelled him to adapt rapidly to a method of preaching in which the actual time required for preparation was significantly reduced.

It is a very interesting fact, and one that has scarcely been noticed until recently, that at the end of the handwritten notes of 'Sinners in the Hands of an Angry God' there is a brief, two-page outline or synopsis of the sermon. Stout and Hatch make the following observation: 'A rare two-leaf outline or synopsis of the sermon, accompanying the booklet, strongly suggests that Edwards preached this sermon many more than three times and that he did so extemporaneously.'[27] This fragment reads as follows:

1. [Sinners] always exposed to fall.
2. Suddenly fall.
3. By their own weight.
4. Nothing but God that holds 'em up.
   (1) No want of power in G.

---

came, Jonathan Edwards, like most other American preachers who had been in sympathy with the new evangelism, spoke extemporaneously, aided only by a brief outline. He continued this practice until the end of his life" (*Jonathan Edwards* [New York, Macmillan, 1940], 137. The sermon texts printed below disprove the assertion, even in the case of more abbreviated texts. Furthermore, if Solomon Stoddard had not frightened Edwards into *memoriter* delivery early in his career when he declared in print that reading sermons "is not to be allowed" ('The Defects of Preachers Reproved' [Boston, 1724], 23), it is unlikely that the transit of Whitefield would have worked a late revolution.' *Works*, 25:7 n. 6.

[26] *The fact that something occurs after this does not mean that it occurs on account of this.*

[27] *Works*, 22:403. Kimnach, whilst conceding the problematic nature of this fragment, concludes that both ink and hand indicate July-August, 1756 and that it was probably preached to the white congregation, since it is not marked 'St. Ind.', the invariable label on the sermons preached to the Indians. *Works*, 10:145 n. 3.

(2) They deserve it.

(3) They are condemned to it. 'Tis the place they belong to.

(4) God is angry enough with them.

(5) The devil if not restrained would immediately fly upon them and seize them as his own.

(6) They have those hellish principles in them, that if God should take off his restraints.

(7) 'Tis no security that there are no visible means of death at hand.

(8) Their own care and prudence to preserve their own lives.

(9) The schemes they lay out for escaping damnation.

(10) There is no promise.[28]

Application

Use of awakening.

This is the case with you.

You are, as it were, heavy with sin and those things are as spiders' webs.

The black clouds of wrath hang over you.

The bow is bent.

The wrath of God is like a rapid stream that is damned up.

Your damnation don't slumber.

You hang over the pit by a slender thread and the flames of wrath flashing about it.

God holds the thread in his hand.

You are held over just as one holds a spider or some hateful insect over a furnace.

There is no other reason to be given why you did not go to hell last night.

1. Whose wrath this is.

2. 'Tis misery that shall be inflicted to that end: to show what the wrath of Jehovah is.

3. 'Tis the fierceness of his wrath, especially on gospel sinners.

4. 'Tis certain unavoidable wrath.

5. 'Tis speed of wrath. You know not how soon.

6. 'Tis everlasting wrath.

---

[28] Ibid., p. 35.

7. 'Tis certain unavoidable wrath, Job 21:19-20.[29]

On January 15, 1758, Edwards bade farewell to his Indians in Stockbridge. The sermon delivered on that occasion was 'Watch and Pray Always'. One week earlier he had, in fact, preached a farewell sermon to the Mahican Indians – 'now but a small remnant of his original mission congregation though perhaps a devoted group of Christian converts'.[30] 'Watch and Pray Always' 'was probably his "stirrup sermon" as he left Stockbridge'.[31] It is, Kimnach contends, 'a good example of a late outline':[32]

Luke 21:36. Watch ye, and pray always.

I. Many dreadful things are coming upon this wicked world.

II. The righteous, and they only, shall be thought fit to escape those things that shall come.

III. All at last must be called to appear before Christ.

Christ will come.

All must see him.

All must [be] brought before him.

IV. The righteous shall be thought worthy to stand before Christ and no others.

1. The righteous worthy.

2. Wicked not worthy.

V. We should watch and pray always that we may be thought worthy {to stand before Christ}.

1. Watch

2. Pray

3. Always

Application

What must watch against.

---

[29] *Works*, 10:144-145.

[30] *Works*, 25:711.

[31] Ibid.

[32] *Works*, 10:128. 'As for the white congregation at Stockbridge', notes Kimnach, 'for the most part they heard the written-out sermons from the early Northampton days, usually in somewhat abbreviated form. On a few rare occasions Edwards seems to have written a sermon for the white congregation . . . But such sermons . . . are exceedingly rare . . . and one can generalize that Edwards did not regularly compose sermons for the whites at Stockbridge.' Ibid., p. 127.

How watch.
What need of watching.
Always.
Prayer.
> What pray for.
> How pray.[33]

Thus the manuscript evidence alone proves incontrovertibly that Edwards developed significantly as a preacher in terms of his delivery; indeed, it indicates that there were two significant turning-points in his development in this respect: a minor turning-point in 1729 and a major turning-point in 1740-1741. As 'The Threefold Work of the Holy Ghost' demonstrates, he began to experiment very early in his ministry with a somewhat more extemporaneous method of delivery. Again, the catalyst of the Great Awakening in the early 1740's appears to have generated an even more radical shift in his homiletical practice. The manuscript evidence is irrefutable that he did not always read a full manuscript, that he clearly extemporized in his preaching to some extent after 1729, that he often preached from an outline after 1740-1741, and that the traditional notion concerning his delivery must, therefore, be regarded as, to some extent at least, a caricature of the truth.

Edwards' reputation as a preacher may well have suffered, at least until recently, from a rather interesting *literary vicious circle* which has been drawn along these lines: it is a well-established fact that Edwards read many of his sermons *verbatim* in the pulpit. Moreover, virtually the only sermons of his that were published prior to the 1990's were those that were 'complete'; it is only very recently that 'incomplete' or 'fragmentary' sermons have been published.[34] It is evident from these latter sermons that their very incompleteness constitutes an obvious reason why they would have been passed over for publication in favour of complete sermons. It has, therefore, been tacitly assumed by many that

---

[33] Ibid., pp. 128-129. See also 25:716.

[34] I am indebted to Minkema for confirming that a few outlines were published prior to those included in the Yale edition, such as those in Alexander Grosart's *Selections from the Unpublished Writings* (1865), but this work has been difficult to obtain.

Edwards always wrote out his sermons in full and that he always read them *verbatim* in the pulpit. It is this literary vicious circle that has probably contributed significantly to his reputation for mediocrity in delivery.

More recently, however, an opposite tendency has arisen within Edwards scholarship, namely, that of concluding, on the basis of the very evidence that has exploded the old, stereotypical caricature of Edwards as 'a boring manuscript preacher', that the sermon underwent in the 1740's a significant *marginalization*. Kimnach contends that 'the sermon manuscripts of the 1740's and 1750's suggest that the sermon was becoming marginalized within the cycle of Edwards' literary activities.'[35] He alleges an increasing 'indifference'[36] on Edwards' part, 'the notable decline in sermon composition in the 1740's and 1750's,'[37] and 'the virtual end of sustained effort in the composition of sermons'[38] during this period. Indeed, Kimnach discerns what he regards as the ultimate *deterioration, fragmentation,* and *disintegration* of the sermon form in Edwards' hands:[39]

[35] *Works*, 25:38.

[36] *Works*, 10:124. Again, in a symposium held as part of the Leverton Lecture Series on April 18, 1973, Kimnach made this observation: 'His later sermons are really beyond discussion because they degenerate into outlines. He may have filled in these outlines in the pulpit. I suspect he wasn't too successful at it, however, simply because, when an important occasion arose in the later years, he wrote out his sermon just as completely as he did earlier, which would indicate that when the chips were down he needed the written manuscript. I have pondered this for a long time, but I don't see how I can get around saying that Edwards paid less and less attention to the sermon and took his preaching less and less seriously, even several years before he left Northampton.' Wilson H. Kimnach, 'Symposium', in *Jonathan Edwards: His Life and Influence*, pp. 51-52.

The problem with this line of argument, however, is that it does not establish the point for which it is adduced. It simply does not follow that, because on significant occasions such as the 'Farewell Sermon' in July 1750 or the sermon preached before the Synod of New York in September 1752 JE reverted back to the full manuscript, he was necessarily unsuccessful in preaching more extemporaneously. After all, it is not in the least surprising that on an occasion as difficult and as delicate as that of delivering a farewell sermon to a church that had just dismissed him, and that unjustly, he should wish to exclude all spontaneous utterances of the moment.

Moreover, it is surely obvious that JE must have 'filled in these outlines in the pulpit' precisely because, if he did not, the sermons would have been massively reduced in length.

[37] Ibid., p. 73.

[38] Ibid., p. 115.

[39] See ibid., p. 36.

The evidence of the sermon manuscripts of the forties indicates that, even before 1744, Edwards was giving several things priority over the sermons, whether in materials or effort in production. As the decade wears on, not only do the sermon booklets look more and more like bundles of waste paper and the outlines grow more and more like bare lists, but the very nature of the notation in the booklets changes. Whereas Edwards had always written in his booklets the words that he expected to speak to the congregation, and even in the outline form preserved the decorum of the oration, he now began to write notes *on* sermons. Besides the brief notes for heads, or in place of a head, one is likely to encounter such statements as 'Conclude with some consideration to enforce the whole' (Luke 12:35-36), and often there is no hint of what that consideration might be.[40]

Thus in his last years Edwards seems to have continued to concern himself primarily with his studies, his publications, his role in the international clerical and intellectual community, and with such important practical matters as preserving his mission and defending his hapless Indians against the vicious depredations of frontier entrepreneurs. As a result, his career as a preacher faded away into a few scrawled lines on old notebook leaves.[41]

Moreover, Kimnach engages in the speculation that this alleged 'indifference' reflects an emotional disengagement from Northampton in the 1740's. 'Gradually, subtly, and perhaps even subconsciously, but nevertheless unquestionably, Edwards was withdrawing from Northampton.'[42] Indeed, Kimnach alleges that the period 1743-1758 is characterized by 'a long diminuendo in homiletical emphasis'.[43]

It should be noted that the major line of evidence for Kimnach's conclusion here is Edwards' undeniable shift away from the full manu-

---

[40] Ibid., pp. 123-124.
[41] Ibid., p. 127. 'During the 1740's Edwards exerted ever wider circles of influence through his publications, his ordination sermons, and his correspondence. He was becoming more of a public thinker and leader'. *Works*, 25:17.
[42] Ibid., p. 125.
[43] *Works*, 25:46.

script to the outline. This transition has now been irrefutably established by the Yale series. The transition itself is, of course, inextricably connected with a movement towards extemporaneousness in delivery. But does the evidence adduced by Kimnach support his conclusion? It is, surely, a *non sequitur* to assume, on the basis of an otherwise increasingly skeletal approach to sermon preparation, that Edwards' attitude to his preaching was necessarily perfunctory and his performance necessarily disappointing. The basic problem with Kimnach's position is that it fails to distinguish between the *sermon form* and the *act of preaching*. It is surely quite wrong to regard the sermon as some sort of unalterable, inviolable art form. Preachers develop; and as they develop, so the sermon form itself evolves. Indeed, both homiletical wisdom and homiletical experience indicate that (to use an Edwardsean mode of expression) 'these two opposite principles' of meticulous writing and reading on the one hand and extemporaneous utterance on the other 'should rise and fall, like the two opposite scales of a balance; when one rises the other sinks.'[44] Thus it is absolutely certain that, as Edwards wrote less, so he extemporized more; but it is also theoretically quite possible that the diminution in writing and the increase in extemporizing indicate, not a fading, but a flowering of his career as a preacher. It is theoretically quite possible that what Edwards gained by extemporizing surpassed, or at least balanced, what he lost.

Kimnach notes that, whilst the Indian sermon manuscripts are 'generally skimpy to skeletal',[45] there is, in Stockbridge, 'a strange Indian Summer of the sermon for three brief weeks'[46] in January 1751. But the very fact that Kimnach adverts to this 'strange Indian Summer of the sermon' demonstrates that the Yale editor thinks instinctively in terms of the full manuscript. His tacit assumption here appears to be that the full manuscript betokens maximal care and performance, whereas the brief outline betokens less than maximal care and performance. But this is a gratuitous assumption and it tends to confuse *methodology* on the one hand with both *motivation* and *performance* on the other. Kimnach

[44] The allusion here is to a mode of expression utilized in *Works* (Hickman), 1:259.
[45] *Works*, 25:29 n. 4.
[46] *Works*, 10:125.

might be correct in his hypothesis, at least to some extent and in some respects; but the evidence he adduces does not establish his conclusion. In extemporaneous preaching so much depends on the degree of reflection, meditation, indeed rumination upon the sermon matter. Mere outlines can be very deceptive.

Moreover, the tenuousness of Kimnach's line of reasoning at this point can be easily demonstrated by means of an historical analogy. It is a fact that during the first ten years of his ministry, in South Wales (1927-1938), Lloyd-Jones wrote out one sermon each week. He did this, as he himself informs us, not in order to read the sermon from the pulpit, but essentially as a homiletical discipline.[47] It is also a fact that he did not continue this particular discipline subsequent to his becoming the minister of Westminster Chapel in London. His practice throughout his ministry in London (1938-1968) was that of preaching extemporaneously from an outline, sometimes written out on the back of an envelope. A superficial comparison of his method in Wales with that in London might lead one to conclude that there was a deterioration or disintegration of the sermon form in Lloyd-Jones' hands. But this were fatally to confuse the sermon form with the act of preaching. It is utterly impossible to glean from one of Lloyd-Jones' sermon outlines either the richness of the content or the drama of the delivery. The sermon outline represents but the bare bones; it was

---

[47] With regard to his first ten years in the ministry Lloyd-Jones reports the following: 'I tried to write one sermon a week; I never tried to write two. But I did try to write one for the first ten years. I felt that writing was good discipline, good for producing ordered thought and arrangement and sequence and development of the argument and so on . . . Then as time went on, and as with many others, I wrote less and less, and by now I cannot remember when I last wrote a sermon.' Lloyd-Jones, *Preaching and Preachers*, pp. 215-216. Murray casts further light on this matter in his biography of Lloyd-Jones: 'The reason for the full manuscript was not a concern for a literary form, still less for something to read in the pulpit, it was rather to be sure that he was clear in the substance of his message. He believed that a preacher should know what he was going to say from the beginning to the end. Within weeks, however, he found it impossible to write two sermons in full and thus his settled habit for many years became to write one sermon fully, and the other – though he thought it out in detail – only to record in outline. At first the full sermon manuscript went with him into the pulpit, but he soon found that practice inhibiting, and his custom became to read the fully-written sermon through some three times, and then to have no more than an outline of it with him when he was preaching.' Murray, *D. Martyn Lloyd-Jones: The First Forty Years*, pp. 154-155.

only in the preaching of the sermon that those bare bones came to life with such energy and power. We do not pretend that the New England minister was a preacher of the calibre of the minister of Westminster Chapel. Lloyd-Jones was an orator; Edwards was not. But the analogy demonstrates the need for caution. It should never be forgotten that there is a mysterious, elusive, intangible, spiritual element in preaching that can never fully be captured merely by the scholarly examination of manuscripts.

Inextricably intertwined with this issue of delivery is not only the issue of *extemporaneousness*, but also that of *affection*. This issue is very important precisely because the caricature that has prevailed historically with regard to Edwards' sermon delivery is one that has tended to suppress the notion of affection on his part. It is, therefore, important to note that he clearly believed very strongly in a correlation of *matter* and *manner* in the preaching of the word of God; he clearly believed in a correlation of *light* and *heat*. This emphasis emerges very clearly in 'The True Excellency of a Gospel Minister'. This sermon was preached on August 30, 1744, at the ordination of the Scots-born Presbyterian, Robert Abercrombie (1712-1780), to the work of the gospel ministry in Pelham, Massachusetts.[48] Edwards took as his text on this occasion John 5:35: 'He was a burning and a shining light.' It is an interesting fact that Edwards never wrote at length on the subject of preaching. 'For all of his influence on the pulpit', observes Stout, 'Edwards never prepared a formal preaching manual in the tradition of William Ames, Solomon Stoddard, or Cotton Mather. His most systematic statements on the role of a minister appeared in his frequently printed ordination sermons – virtually the only occasional sermons he published.'[49] Thus his treatment of the subject of preaching occurred in essentially *ad hoc* contexts such as this. There is, however, sufficient material in the corpus of his sermons and treatises to enable us to synthesize from

---

[48] Abercrombie was a 'fellow New Light supporter of the Great Awakening'. *Works*, 25:82. Kimnach also notes the following interesting fact: 'Just six years after the delivery of this sermon, the Rev. Robert Abercrombie would sit on the council that voted for a separation between Jonathan Edwards and his congregation, certifying Edwards' ministry in Northampton a failure. Abercrombie voted in the negative.' Ibid., p. 83.

[49] Stout, *New England Soul*, p. 228.

these observations a basic philosophy of preaching. In the course of this ordination sermon he lays down this significant homiletical manifesto:

> If a minister has light without heat, and entertains his auditory with learned discourses, without a savour of the power of godliness, or any appearance of fervency of spirit, and zeal for God and the good of souls, he may gratify itching ears, and fill the heads of his people with empty notions; but it will not be very likely to reach their hearts, or save their souls. And if, on the other hand, he be driven on with a fierce and intemperate zeal, and vehement heat, without light, he will be likely to kindle the like unhallowed flame in his people, and to fire their corrupt passions and affections; but will make them never the better, nor lead them a step towards heaven, but drive them apace the other way.[50]

For Edwards the preaching of the word of God was no more *light without heat* than it was *heat without light*; the *manner* must be correlated to the *matter*.

The following passage is an extract from 'True Saints, When Absent from the Body, Are Present with the Lord' – the sermon preached on the occasion of the funeral of David Brainerd. Edwards' assessment of Brainerd's gifts and qualities as a preacher inevitably reveals his own ideals in this area:

> He had extraordinary gifts for the pulpit. I never had an opportunity to hear him preach, but have often heard him pray ... And his manner of preaching, by what I have often heard of it from good judges, was no less excellent; being clear and instructive, natural, nervous, forcible, moving, and very searching and convincing. – He rejected with disgust an affected noisiness, and violent boisterousness in the pulpit; and yet much disrelished a flat, cold delivery, when the subject of discourse, and matter delivered, required affection and earnestness.[51]

This same emphasis upon 'affection and earnestness' in preaching again emerges strongly in the following extracts from *Thoughts on the Revival*:

[50] *Works* (Hickman), 2:958.
[51] Ibid., p. 33.

I think an exceeding affectionate way of preaching about the great things of religion, has in itself no tendency to beget false apprehensions of them; but on the contrary, a much greater tendency to beget true apprehensions of them, than a moderate, dull, indifferent way of speaking of them. An appearance of affection and earnestness in the manner of delivery, though very great indeed, if it be agreeable to the nature of the subject . . . has so much the greater tendency to beget true ideas or apprehension in the minds of the hearers concerning the subject spoken of, and so to enlighten the understanding: and that for this reason, That such a way or manner of speaking of these things does, in fact, more truly represent them, than a more cold and indifferent way of speaking of them.[52]

The New England divine then goes on to criticize that depreciation of affection which had become fashionable in certain circles:

I should think myself in the way of my duty, to raise the affections of my hearers as high as I possibly can, provided that they are affected with nothing but truth, and with affections that are not disagreeable to the nature of the subject. I know it has long been fashionable to despise a very earnest and pathetical way of preaching; and they only have been valued as preachers, who have shown the greatest extent of learning, strength of reason, and correctness of method and language. But I humbly conceive it has been for want of understanding or duly considering human nature, that such preaching has been thought to have the greatest tendency to answer the ends of preaching; and the experience of the present and past ages abundantly confirms the same. Though, as I said before, clearness of distinction and illustration, and strength of reason, and a good method, in the doctrinal handling of the truths of religion, is many ways needful and profitable, and not to be neglected; yet an increase in speculative knowledge in divinity is not what is so much needed by our people as something else. Men may abound in this sort of light, and have no heat. How much has there been of this sort of knowledge, in the christian world, in this age! Was there ever an age, wherein strength and penetration

---

[52] Ibid., 1:391.

of reason, extent of learning, exactness of distinction, correctness of style, and clearness of expression, did so abound? And yet, was there ever an age, wherein there has been so little sense of the evil of sin, so little love to God, heavenly-mindedness, and holiness of life, among the professors of the true religion? Our people do not so much need to have their heads stored, as to have their hearts touched; and they stand in the greatest need of that sort of preaching, which has the greatest tendency to do this.[53]

In the light of Edwards' considerable emphasis upon 'affection and earnestness' in preaching, the fundamental question that arises with regard to his own preaching is this: Is it intrinsically likely that he should not only *defend* and *admire*, but also actually *promote* 'an exceeding affectionate way of preaching', 'an appearance of affection and earnestness in the manner of delivery', 'a very earnest and pathetical way of preaching', 'a most affectionate and earnest manner of delivery', 'a great degree of *pathos*, and manifestation of zeal and fervency in preaching the word of God' if, in fact, his own preaching was a living contradiction of this stated homiletical philosophy? For it must be evident that, if the traditional notion of Edwards' delivery is correct, then there is indeed the most palpable contradiction between his homiletical philosophy on the one hand and his practice on the other.

It must surely be evident, moreover, that the testimony of ear- and eye-witnesses of Edwards' preaching is of paramount importance in any assessment of his delivery. It is significant, however, that this crucial line of evidence has been somewhat neglected by the Yale editors. The testimony of Samuel Finley is again of great importance in this respect:

> In his youth he appeared healthy, and with a good degree of vivacity; but was never robust. In middle life, he appeared very much emaciated (I had almost said, mortified) by severe studies, and intense applications of thought. Hence his voice was a little languid, and too low for a large assembly; though much relieved and advantaged by a proper emphasis, just cadence, well-placed pauses,

[53] Ibid.

and great distinctness in pronunciation . . . Neither quick nor slow of speech, there was always a certain *pathos* in his utterance, and such skill of address, as seldom failed to draw the attention, warm the hearts, and stimulate the consciences of the auditory.[54]

The testimony of Dr West of Stockbridge is also very significant in this respect. In response to a question posed by Sereno E. Dwight as to whether Edwards was an eloquent preacher, Dr West gave this reply:

> If you mean, by eloquence, what is usually intended by it in our cities; he had no pretensions to it. He had no studied varieties of the voice, and no strong emphasis. He scarcely gestured, or even moved; and he made no attempt, by the elegance of his style, or the beauty of his pictures, to gratify the taste, and fascinate the imagination. But, if you mean by eloquence, the power of presenting an important truth before an audience, with overwhelming weight of argument, and with such intenseness of feeling, that the whole soul of the speaker is thrown into every part of the conception and delivery; so that the solemn attention of the whole audience is rivetted, from the beginning to the close, and impressions are left that cannot be effaced; Mr Edwards was the most eloquent man I ever heard speak.[55]

It is evident, then, that a much more nuanced assessment of Edwards' delivery is required than that which has often been given. It is one thing to say – as indeed it must be said – that he did not possess the marvellous voice, the powerful delivery, the brilliant extemporaneousness, and the natural dramatism of George Whitefield; it is quite another thing to say that he 'preached from a manuscript in a monotone'. There has been, historically, a neglect of the significance of his obvious earnestness, solemnity, intensity, and affection as a preacher. These qualities in his preaching are, however, now being increasingly recognized. 'Whatever the subject', contends Marsden, 'the personal intensity of Edwards's otherwise undramatic preaching style reflected his deep commitment to all that he was saying and was therefore often deeply

---

[54] Ibid., p. 144.
[55] Ibid., cxc.

affecting to his hearers.'[56] Marsden goes on to provide this judicious assessment of Edwards' delivery:

> Although Edwards had none of the dramatic gestures of a White-field or a Tennent and was said to preach as though he were staring at the bell-rope in the back of the meetinghouse, he could be remarkably compelling. An admirer described his delivery as 'easy, natural and very solemn. He had not a strong, loud voice; but appeared with such gravity and solemnity, and spake with such distinctness, clearness and precision; his words were so full of ideas, set in such a plain and striking light, that few speakers have been so able to demand the attention of an audience as he.' Through sheer intensity he generated emotion. 'His words often discovered a great degree of inward fervor, without much noise or external emotion, and fell with great weight on the minds of his hearers. He made but little motion of his head or hands in the desk, but spake so as to discover the motion of his own heart, which tended in the most natural and effectual manner to move and affect others.' The combination of controlled but transparent emotion, heartfelt sincerity both in admonition and compassion, inexorable logic, and biblical themes could draw people into sensing the reality of ideas long familiar.[57]

---

[56] Marsden, 'Foreword', in *The Salvation of Souls*, p. 13.
[57] Marsden, *Edwards*, p. 220.

27

THE SPIRIT OF GOD

On August 8, 1751, the ousted Northampton minister was installed both as missionary to the Stockbridge Indians and as pastor of the hamlet's church. For the fast that preceded this occasion he preached a sermon to the Mohicans and the Mohawks which was based upon Acts 16:9: 'And a vision appeared to Paul in the night; There stood a man of Macedonia, and prayed him, saying, Come over into Macedonia, and help us.' In this sermon the Stockbridge missionary emphasizes the absolute necessity of the preaching of the gospel of Christ. But he then proceeds to emphasize also the absolute necessity of God's blessing upon that gospel preaching; he makes it clear that that blessing is inextricably connected with the operation of the Spirit of God: 'Unless God gives his Spirit, all will be in vain.'[1] There can be no question but that this simple statement represents Jonathan Edwards' lifelong conviction with regard to preaching; and any analysis of his preaching would be inexcusably deficient if it were to neglect this element which he clearly regarded as absolutely pivotal.

Edwards' interest in the person and work of the Spirit is, of course, inextricably connected with his Trinitarianism, and in his *Personal Narrative* (written *circa* 1740 and first published by Samuel Hopkins in 1765)[2] he reveals the crucial importance of the Third Person of the Godhead in his own Christian experience:

> I have, many times, had a sense of the glory of the Third Person in the Trinity, and his office as Sanctifier; in his holy operations, com-

[1] 'The Salvation of Souls', p. 154. The manuscript contains this notation: 'Fast before installment. Stock[bridge] Ind[ians] and Mohawks Aug[ust] 1751.'
[2] See *Works*, 16:747.

municating divine light and life to the soul. God in the communications of his Holy Spirit, has appeared as an infinite fountain of
divine glory and sweetness; being full, and sufficient to fill and satisfy
the soul; pouring forth itself in sweet communications; like the sun
in its glory, sweetly and pleasantly diffusing light and life.[3]

But alongside of (and, indeed, inseparably linked with) Edwards'
practical and experimental interest in the Spirit of God is his dogmatic
and polemical interest. This latter interest has essentially two *foci*, namely,
his controversy with Arminianism and his defence and advocacy
of the phenomenon of revival. It is an interesting fact that a very
significant proportion of his published material focuses upon these
two issues. If the bulk of his earlier treatises relates to his defence of
revival – *A Faithful Narrative* (1737), *The Distinguishing Marks of a
Work of the Spirit of God* (1741), *Some Thoughts on the Revival* (1743),
and *Religious Affections* (1746) – the bulk of his later treatises relates to
his controversy with Arminianism – *Freedom of the Will* (1754), *Original
Sin* (1758), and *The Nature of True Virtue* (posthumously in 1765).
It is interesting to note that the latter, described by Ramsey as 'his
great, late works',[4] resume and develop the anti-Arminian thrust of his
first publication, *God Glorified in Man's Dependence* (1731). Indeed, in
Edwards' mind the controversy with Arminianism on the one hand and
the defence of revival on the other hand were intimately related; and it
was the role of the sovereign Spirit of God both in the phenomenon of
conversion and in that of revival that related them.

It was on Thursday July 8, 1731, in Boston that Edwards delivered
his first major salvo against Arminianism. The hub of New England,
Boston was to emerge, by the time of the waning of the Great Awakening in the mid 1740's, as the hub of Arminianism also; but when
Edwards delivered 'God Glorified in Man's Dependence', Boston's
tendencies towards Arminianism were little more than straws in the
wind from Harvard. Miller describes the scene in his characteristically
imaginative and evocative manner:

---

[3] *Works* (Hickman), 1:xlvii.
[4] *Works*, 8:9.

The first week in July was Commencement at Harvard College, when degree-holders held reunion, and to give the lecture at that time was a special honour, a chance to address the largest available concentration of New England scholarship and influence. But when Jonathan Edwards came out of the Connecticut Valley, we may indeed be certain that all ministers not bedridden or in their dotage, together with the President, professors, and tutors of Harvard College, as well as many substantial citizens, were on hand.[5]

Thus, when the tall, soft-spoken member of the Yale class of 1720 came before his Boston audience, he confronted an initial distrust born of Harvard's apprehensions. But there was a still more pressing reason why the Boston leaders were anxious about his performance: Edwards was not only a son of the Valley and of Yale, he was the grandson and heir of Solomon Stoddard, of the 'Pope' who for over half a century had ruled Northampton and from it built an empire, like some Biblical Pharaoh, along both banks of a river, from Deerfield to the Sound. He had detached Hadley, Hatfield, Springfield, Westfield, Longmeadow, Suffield, Deerfield from the dominion of Boston, and made them into a new principality with Northampton their capital.[6]

In his lecture the twenty-seven year old Northampton preacher referred to 'those doctrines and schemes of divinity that are in any respect opposite to such an absolute and universal dependence on God'.[7] He clearly had Arminianism and its correlates in view and insisted that the scheme of the Arminians is one that derogates from the glory of the Holy Spirit in particular:

> However they may allow of a dependence of the redeemed on God, yet they deny a dependence that is *so absolute* and universal. They own an entire dependence on God for *some* things, but not for others; they own that we depend on God for the gift and accept-

[5] Miller, *Edwards*, pp. 4-5.
[6] Ibid., p. 9.
[7] *Works* (Hickman), 2:6.

ance of a Redeemer, but deny so absolute a dependence on him for the obtaining of an *interest* in the Redeemer. They own an absolute dependence on the Father for giving his Son, and on the Son for working out redemption, but not so entire a dependence on the Holy Ghost for *conversion,* and a being in Christ, and so coming to a title to his benefits. They own a dependence on God for *means* of grace, but not absolutely for the benefit and success of those means.[8]

Edwards argues here that, although Arminians posit 'an absolute dependence' upon the Father and the Son in the matter of man's salvation, yet by positing only 'a partial dependence' on the Holy Spirit in the matter of 'the obtaining of an *interest* in the Redeemer', they put the creature in God's stead and thus rob the Spirit of the glory due to his work and to his name.

Mark Valeri notes the logical connection, in the Boston lecture, between Calvinism and Trinitarianism on the one hand and between Arminianism and anti-trinitarianism on the other hand:

The central theme of 'God Glorified' is the dependence of fallen humanity on all three persons of the Trinity for salvation ... Those who judge human beings to be not completely depraved grant them independence from God, deny the need for either the Son or the Spirit, and therefore, by implication, reject the Godhead. Any concession to human ability, such as is made by Arminians, amounts to unbelief. Conversely, a doctrine of sin in Calvinist fashion affirms humanity's need for all persons of the Trinity and therefore glorifies God.[9]

Edwards defends the Calvinist view of human nature by linking it to the doctrine of the Trinity ... By implication, Arminian views on human nature, which deny humanity's complete dependence on God, effectively contradict the logic of the Trinity.[10]

---

[8] Ibid., pp. 6-7.
[9] *Works,* 17:35-36.
[10] Ibid., p. 196.

Thus his reasoning in 'God Glorified' is essentially that a high view of man coheres with a low view of the Spirit; thus Pelagianism coheres with Unitarianism. Conversely, a low view of man coheres with a high view of the Spirit; thus Calvinism coheres with Trinitarianism.[11] It is for this reason that we find throughout the whole corpus of his writings a colossal emphasis both upon original sin and upon the supernatural influences of the Spirit of God. Thus, in the final analysis, Arminianism (which is Semi-Pelagianism) is subversive of the doctrine of the Trinity. It is precisely because Arminianism subverts the role and thus the absolute sovereignty of the Spirit that it is corrosive of the doctrine of the deity of the Spirit of God. As far as Edwards was concerned, the tendency of Arminianism was essentially anti-trinitarian and thus essentially deistic; conversely, Calvinism was in its very nature and tendency powerfully trinitarian and thus powerfully anti-deistic.

It was in 1712, just nineteen years prior to Edwards' Boston lecture, that Samuel Clarke (1675-1729), a prominent clergyman-theologian in the Church of England, had published *The Scripture Doctrine of the Trinity*. This work constituted a significant landmark in the Trinitarian Controversy which had broken out in England in the 1690's. 'In this seminal work', observes Minkema, 'Clarke renounced the Athanasian Creed's formulation of three co-equal and co-eternal persons as unscriptural and treated the trinitarian question as non-essential to the faith.'[12] Indeed, the Boyle lecturer on 'The Being and Attributes of God' (1704-1705) is described by G. R. Cragg as 'perhaps the greatest exponent'[13] of the latitudinarian position. Clarke was essentially deistic in tendency – a rationalist whose exaltation of man's innate powers went hand in hand with a derogation of the deity and the glory of the Spirit of God. Indeed, Clarke was a classic contemporary demonstration of the fact that Pelagianism cohered with anti-Trinitarianism. Edwards was well aware of the significance of Clarke – in *Freedom of the Will* (1754) he specifically mentions 'Dr Samuel Clark' [*sic*] as one

---

[11] We are dealing here with the issue of *man as a sinner*, not with the issue of *man made in the image of God*.

[12] *Works*, 14:43 n. 3.

[13] Cragg, p. 158.

of 'the chief of the Arminian writers'.[14]

Thus it is the person and work of the Spirit of God that constitutes the connecting link in Edwards' mind between his inveterate opposition to Arminianism and his lifelong interest in revival. The very fact that he has been described as *the* theologian of revival'[15] is, moreover, sufficient, in and of itself, to establish the fact of the crucial importance of the Spirit of God in his thinking. He experienced the phenomenon of revival in Northampton and the Connecticut River Valley in 1734-1735 and also in the Great Awakening in New England in the early 1740's. Moreover, he recorded and analysed the first, more localized movement of God's Spirit in *A Faithful Narrative of the Surprising Work of God* (1737) and he analysed and defended the second, more extensive movement of God's Spirit in *Some Thoughts concerning the Present Revival of Religion in New England* (1743). These very facts are powerful testimony both to the role assigned by Edwards to the Spirit of God in the advancement of the kingdom of God and also to his unashamed Trinitarianism.

Edwards' classic definition of revival is found in *A History of the Work of Redemption*. This series of sermons was delivered in 1739, approximately four years after the Connecticut Valley revival and on the eve of the Great Awakening. The treatise constitutes, as Goen emphasizes, Edwards' 'theology of history':[16]

> It may here be observed, that from the fall of man, to our day, the work of redemption in its effect has mainly been carried on by remarkable communications of the Spirit of God. Though there be a more constant influence of God's Spirit always in some degree attending his ordinances; yet the way in which the greatest things have been done towards carrying on this work, always have been by remarkable effusions, at special seasons of mercy . . . And this in the days of *Enos*, was the first remarkable pouring out of the Spirit of God that ever was. There had been a saving work of God on the hearts of some before; but now God was pleased to bring

---

[14] *Works* (Hickman), 1:25.
[15] J. I. Packer, front flap of dust jacket, *Works* (Hickman) vol. 1.
[16] *Works*, 4:71.

in a harvest of souls to Christ.[17]

Edwards contrasts here 'a more constant influence of God's Spirit always in some degree attending his ordinances' with 'remarkable communications of the Spirit of God' or 'remarkable effusions, at special seasons of mercy'. It is evident from this *apologia* for revival that he saw the Spirit of God as operating essentially on two different levels – that of the ordinary and that of the extraordinary. Pivotal to this concept of the operations of the Spirit of God is the concept of degree. In times of revival the Spirit of God is communicated or poured out in remarkable measure and to a remarkable degree. Pivotal also to this understanding of the operations of the Spirit of God is the concept of periodicity. 'The days of Enos' constituted such a period; during those days 'a harvest of souls' was brought in to Christ. Indeed, this concept of harvest is one which Edwards' grandfather, Solomon Stoddard, utilized. In his *Faithful Narrative* Edwards reports that Stoddard had enjoyed, during the course of his long and influential ministry in Northampton, 'five harvests, as he called them',[18] namely, in 1679, 1683, 1696, 1712, and 1718.[19] In *An Humble Attempt*, which was published in Boston in 1748 and which was essentially a plea for an international concert of prayer, Edwards links the phenomenon of revival with the seeking of God's face in prayer: 'God has also his days of mercy, accepted times, chosen seasons, wherein it is his pleasure to show mercy, and nothing shall hinder it; times appointed for the magnifying of the Redeemer and his merits, and for the triumphs of his grace.'[20]

Such 'days of mercy, accepted times, chosen seasons' were, of course, a manifestation of that 'absolute sovereignty' of God upon which Edwards so much insisted. The very concepts of degree and periodicity, which are so integral to his theology of revival, demonstrate the sovereignty of the Spirit of God in this matter. The sovereignty of the Spirit is analogous to that of the wind; each enjoys a sovereignty with regard to the time and place of his operations. The Spirit's sovereignty is

---

[17] *Works* (Hickman), 1:539.
[18] Ibid., p. 347.
[19] See C. C. Goen, *Works*, 4:5.
[20] *Works* (Hickman), 2:294.

manifested *inter alia* by differing responses to the same sermon. Why was it that, when Edwards preached 'Sinners in the Hands of an Angry God' to his own congregation in Northampton in June 1741, no extraordinary effects were reported, and yet, when the same sermon was preached to the people of Enfield a few weeks later on July 8, the effects were astonishing? The people of Enfield were, at the time, reputed to be hardened towards the gospel. This disparity in the respective effects on the two occasions demonstrates powerfully that the blessing of God does not fall *ex opere operato* upon any sermon, however great. The only valid, scriptural answer to the question as to why the effects at Enfield were incomparably greater than those at Northampton is one which ascribes that disparity to the sovereignty of the Third Person of the Trinity: 'The wind bloweth where it listeth.'[21]

It is important to note the way in which Edwards' insistence upon the sovereignty of the Spirit of God in revival is either misunderstood or ignored. The Yale editor, Mark Valeri, for instance, offers the following tentative suggestion with regard to Edwards' interest in revival: 'It is tempting to suggest that he eventually turned to revival – the collective manifestation of the conversion of individuals – as an avenue of escape from the political and economic affairs, even the pastoral encounters, that occasioned his denunciations of human nature.'[22] This suggestion betrays an astonishing misunderstanding of Edwards' whole concept of revival, not to mention his doctrine of man. Revival was not something to which he 'turned'; it was not some kind of last-ditch tactic to which he resorted when all else failed; it was not a phenomenon that lay within his own power; 'the collective manifestation of the conversion of individuals' was not something that he could produce at will; it was not 'an avenue of escape', but rather the very thing for which he consistently longed, prayed, and looked from the hand of a sovereign God. The problem with this observation by Valeri is that, at best, it seriously confuses *revival* with *revivalism;* it also seriously neglects the sovereignty and the power of the Spirit of God. For Edwards revival was nothing less than an outpouring of the Spirit, a special season of

[21] John 3:8
[22] *Works,* 17:44.

mercy, a remarkable effusion or communication of the Third Person of the Triune God.

With regard to the first revival in 1734-1735 it is important to note that in *A Faithful Narrative* Edwards specifically mentions his preaching on the doctrine of justification as being, if not the cause, at least the occasion, of that time of blessing. In his characteristically self-effacing manner he states: 'There were some things said *publicly* on that occasion, concerning justification by faith alone.'[23] He goes on to make the following observation:

> Although great *fault* was found with *meddling* with the *controversy* in the pulpit, by such a person, and at such a time – and though it was ridiculed by many *elsewhere* – yet it proved a word spoken in season here; and was most evidently attended with a very remarkable *blessing* of heaven to the souls of the people in this town. They received thence a general satisfaction, with respect to the main thing in question, which they had been in trembling doubts and concern about; and their minds were engaged the more earnestly to seek that they might come to be accepted of God, and saved in the way of the gospel, which had been made evident to them to be the true and only way. And *then* it was, in the latter part of *December, that the Spirit of God* began extraordinarily to set in, and *wonderfully* to work amongst us; and there were, very *suddenly*, one after another, five or six persons, who were to all appearance savingly converted, and some of them wrought upon in a very remarkable manner.[24]

'The surprising work of God'[25] in Northampton in 1734-1735 lasted approximately six months and resulted, according to Edwards' estimate, in the conversion of about three hundred people in a town of some two hundred families. The *terminus a quo* for the Northampton revival was December 1734 and the *terminus ad quem* May 1735. 'In the latter part of May', Edwards recorded, 'it began to be very sensible that the Spirit of God was gradually withdrawing from us, and after this time Satan

---

[23] *Works* (Hickman), 1:347.
[24] Ibid., pp. 347-348.
[25] Ibid., p. 344.

seemed to be more let loose, and raged in a dreadful manner.'[26] 'This remarkable pouring out of the Spirit of God',[27] as Edwards described it, had come to an end. He did not deny that the passage of time might possibly reveal some admixture of corruption in the fruits of the revival. 'But in the main', he insisted, 'there has been a great and marvellous work of conversion and sanctification among the people here.'[28] The remarkable events of this six-month period demonstrate the crucial connection in his mind between the truth of God, the preaching of that truth, the Spirit of God, and the phenomenon of revival. It should be noted that some of his greatest sermons were preached at this time, namely, 'Justification by Faith Alone', 'The Preciousness of Time', 'Pressing into the Kingdom of God', 'Ruth's Resolution', 'The Folly of Looking Back in Fleeing out of Sodom', 'The Justice of God in the Damnation of Sinners', and 'Wrath upon the Wicked to the Uttermost'.

It is very evident from Edwards' writings on the Great Awakening (1740-1742) that he regarded 'Arminian principles' as the theological basis of anti-revivalism.[29] Indeed, he regarded this 'standing at a distance' as essentially *deistic* in tendency. 'Can any good medium be found', he asks in *Thoughts on the Revival* (1743), 'where a man can rest with any stability, between owning this work, and being a deist? ... Now is a good time for Arminians to change their principles.'[30] Edwards' reasoning here is essentially as follows: to deny the reality and the power of such a palpable work of the Spirit is, in effect, to deny the reality and the power of the Spirit himself, and thus to move very subtly, but inevitably, away from a Trinitarian and towards a Unitarian position. 'With remarkable prescience', remarks Goen, 'Edwards foresaw that the Great Awakening was to become a decisive watershed in American religious thought. As history would eventually reveal, many of the rationalistic opposers of the revival were really pre-Unitarians who

[26] Ibid., p. 363.
[27] Ibid., p. 349.
[28] Ibid., p. 364.
[29] See *Works*, 4:77.
[30] *Works* (Hickman), 1:422.

would develop an ever more self-conscious antithesis to evangelicalism until the result could fairly be called Deism.'[31]

'The shaping of the culture of the Boston élite in the direction of Arminianism', observes Conrad Wright, 'seems to have depended very much on the leadership of Charles Chauncy at the First Church and Jonathan Mayhew at the West Church.'[32] Chauncy (1705-1787), a graduate of Harvard, ministered in Boston for sixty years. In 1727 he was installed as junior pastor to Thomas Foxcroft at First Church in Boston. Initially orthodox, Chauncy's views became increasingly liberal after the Great Awakening. 'Dull, liberal, Arminian, and a profound scholar', notes Clifford K. Shipton, 'Dr Chauncy was a ready made Old Light.'[33] It is an interesting fact that Chauncy criticized George Whitefield for the fact that he 'was sometimes observed to speak of the affairs of salvation, with a smile in his countenance.'[34] It is a further interesting fact that Chauncy's cousin was Chauncy Whittelsey, the tutor at Yale whom David Brainerd rashly accused of having 'no more grace than this chair'.[35] During the Great Awakening Chauncy began to collect information concerning the alleged excesses of the revival from newspapers, *via* correspondence with friends, and by means of a grand tour of New England, New York, and New Jersey. There can be no doubt that James Davenport's wild excesses strengthened the hands of this champion of decorum and good order and thus facilitated Chauncy's attack on the Great Awakening. In 1743 he published his *Seasonable Thoughts on the State of Religion in New England*. Marsden summarizes the respective attitudes of Chauncy and Edwards towards the revival thus: 'Unlike Edwards, who was defending

---

[31] *Works*, 4:78. 'This conflict over the nature of man, expressed during the Great Awakening as an issue of religious address and response, was to stand as a 'continental divide' between evangelicals and rationalists. The latter would remain an intellectual élite, flowering in New England and a few other select *athenae*, while the former would garner the multitudes into popular churches seeking by means of revivals "to reform the continent and to spread scriptural holiness over these lands".' Ibid., p. 83.

[32] Conrad Wright, *The Beginnings of Unitarianism in America* (Hamden, Conn.: Archon Books, 1976), p. 8.

[33] Cited C. C. Goen, *Works*, 4:62.

[34] Cited Wright, p. 51.

[35] This incident and the events surrounding it are narrated by Marsden, *Edwards*, p. 324.

these as peripheral excesses connected with an essentially good work, Chauncy saw the excesses as overwhelming any good that the revival might have done. Such extremes could result only in damage to true religion and irreparable damage to the standing order.'[36] Thus Chauncy epitomized the connection in Edwards' mind between Arminianism and opposition to revival; in each there lurked a significant resistance to the Spirit of God.

Indeed, Edwards warns those such as Chauncy that, if they continue in their opposition to this work of the Spirit of God, they will put themselves in the position of Michal in the Old Testament:

> But we read of one of *David's* wives, even *Michal, Saul's* daughter, whose heart was not engaged in the affair, and did not appear with others to rejoice and praise God on this occasion, but kept away, and stood at a distance, as disaffected, and disliking the management. She despised and ridiculed the transports and extraordinary manifestations of joy; and the curse that she brought upon herself by it was that of being barren to the day of her death. Let this be a warning to us: let us take heed, in this day of the bringing up of the ark of God, that, while we are in visibility and profession the spouse of the spiritual *David*, we do not show ourselves to be indeed the children of falsehearted and rebellious *Saul*, by our standing aloof, and our not joining in the joy and praises of the day, disliking and despising the joys and affections of God's people because they are so high in degree, and so bring the curse of perpetual barrenness upon our souls.[37]

When the young Jonathan Mayhew (Harvard 1744) was ordained in Boston in June 1747 to 'the well-to-do and relatively new West Church, already known for progressive views',[38] he was understood to lean towards a rationalist and moralist position. In spite of the distance and isolation of Stockbridge from Boston, Edwards remained in the 1750's remarkably well abreast of the rapidly developing theological situation in New England's hub. Indeed, so alarmed was he at

---

[36] Ibid., p. 269.
[37] *Works* (Hickman), 1:385.
[38] Marsden, *Edwards*, p. 433.

the significance of a footnote in one of Mayhew's published sermons that he took the extraordinary expedient of writing in February 1757 to Dr Edward Wigglesworth (*circa* 1693-1765), Hollis Professor of Divinity at Harvard, requesting that Dr Wigglesworth intervene with his pen on behalf of the cause of Christ: 'I only write as a subject and friend of the same Lord, and a follower and fellow-disciple of the same Jesus. A regard to his interests has made me uneasy ever since I read Dr [Jonathan] Mayhew's late book, sometime the last year, and saw the marginal note of his, wherein he ridicules the doctrine of the Trinity.'[39] It is fascinating to note the vindication in the late 1740's and 1750's of Edwards' Boston discourse 'God Glorified in Man's Dependence' (1731), the essential position of which was that Arminianism involves a derogation of the Spirit of God and is thus ultimately anti-Trinitarian in its tendency. As far as the Stockbridge theologian was concerned, the writings of men such as Mayhew and Chauncy demonstrated historically that the tendency of Arminianism, moralism, and rationalism was incontrovertibly towards Unitarianism. 'Thus, the Stockbridge seer', remarks George S. Claghorn in the context of this very letter to Dr Wigglesworth, 'anticipated consequences that affected New England churches for the next century.'[40]

Samuel Clarke, Daniel Whitby, Thomas Emlyn, John Taylor – these were 'the staple diet of the liberals after 1745'.[41] 'But New England did not discover them until after the Awakening, and the suddenness with which they then began to be cited in sermons and other polemical literature makes their absence before 1745 all the more striking.'[42] 'The awakening', observes Marsden, '. . . created a liberal backlash among those whom it had judged spiritually cold . . . The Calvinist awakening thus had the ironic consequence of undermining the structures of Calvinist orthodoxy, especially around Boston . . . By 1750 Boston was a vastly different place than it had been in 1740. Theologically no one was in charge. And once the dikes of orthodoxy were breached in

---

[39] *Works*, 16:698.
[40] Ibid.
[41] Wright, p. 57.
[42] Ibid.

Boston it seemed as though there might be no stopping the flood of anti-Calvinism in the countryside.'[43] Thus Edwards' essential position in 'God Glorified in Man's Dependence' was powerfully demonstrated and vindicated in Boston itself in the 1740's and 1750's by Chauncy and Mayhew. During Edwards' own lifetime Boston orthodoxy had degenerated rapidly into Boston Arminianism, and Boston Arminianism was now degenerating rapidly into Boston Unitarianism; and remarkably the Great Awakening, by way of reaction, proved to be a colossal watershed in this astonishing decline.

But the same tendency to interpret the Great Awakening along rationalistic or anti-supernaturalistic lines is found in some of the modern intellectual heirs of Jonathan Edwards. Certainly, it is important to acknowledge that the editors of the Yale series have contributed much that is both scholarly and valuable in their definitive and critical edition of Edwards' *Works*. The very existence of the Yale series is not only a tribute to Edwards himself, but also a testimony to the significant re-evaluation of the New England philosopher-theologian-preacher that has gathered momentum in the last seventy-five years. But the basic problem with the approach of the Yale editors of the *Sermons and Discourses* is that they tend to view Edwards' preaching almost entirely from a *literary* rather than from a *spiritual* and *homiletical* standpoint. Miller, the first general editor of the Yale series, set the trend in this respect in his influential *Jonathan Edwards* (1949). 'The truth is', Miller insisted, 'Edwards was infinitely more than a theologian. He was one of America's five or six major artists, who happened to work with ideas instead of with poems or novels.'[44] This tendency to view him as an artist re-emerges repeatedly in Kimnach's 'General Introduction to the Sermons: Jonathan Edwards' Art of Prophesying.' Edwards is viewed by Kimnach essentially as 'a homiletical author'[45] or as 'a homiletical artist',[46] whilst the sermon itself is viewed essentially as a literary art-form:

---

[43] Marsden, *Edwards*, p. 436.

[44] Miller, *Edwards*, p. xxxi. 'It is this Edwards, the artist and the writer, that my volume seeks to expound.' Ibid., p. xxxiii.

[45] Wilson H. Kimnach, 'Note to the Reader', *Works*, 14:xii.

[46] *Works*, 10:258.

An essay, a play, a poem, indeed any work of literature, is ultimately the product of that mysterious mental activity known as the 'creative process.' The making of a sermon is likewise a truly artistic process, requiring of an effective preacher a degree of imaginative power and artistic discipline at least comparable to that of a poet.[47]

We do not deny that there is an element of truth in Miller's and Kimnach's position here. There is indeed a 'creative process' involved in the preparation of sermons and there is indeed a certain artistry. In the very nature of the case this process involves significant mental activity. Indeed, we lament the lack of artistry and the rhetorical impoverishment characteristic of much modern preaching. The problem with Kimnach's assertion, however, is that, characteristically, it emphasizes the *literary* aspects of sermon preparation rather than the *spiritual*. It must be insisted upon that there is something quite unique about the sermon that sets it apart from 'an essay, a play, a poem, indeed any work of literature'. It is essentially a spiritual *genre;* and, as such, it is essentially different in kind.

The same tendency to view Edwards' preaching almost entirely from a literary rather than from a spiritual and homiletical standpoint also emerges in Kimnach's analysis of the source of the power of 'Sinners in the Hands of an Angry God': 'Probably it was the striking amalgam of colloquial immediacy and archetypal authority in the organic texture of "Sinners", rather than a single category of tropes, that "burned into the minds" of the people of Enfield.'[48] Speaking more generally of the power of Edwards' preaching, Kimnach makes this observation:

If the proof comes from authority, whence the power? Again, it seems that the logical structure is peripheral to the source of literary power in Edwards' sermons. Though the subtle persuasion which results from a carefully structured argument is important, the prime source of power lies in Edwards' use of certain literary devices such as imagery, metaphor, repetition, and allusion.[49]

[47] Ibid., p. 42.
[48] Ibid., pp. 210-211.
[49] Ibid., p. 197.

It will be noted that, whilst lip-service is paid here to the authority of the Scriptures, no acknowledgement whatsoever is made of the Spirit of God. Kimnach insists that 'the prime source of power lies in Edwards' use of certain literary devices such as imagery, metaphor, repetition, and allusion.' It must surely be obvious to the Yale editors themselves that no-one would have disagreed more with this assessment than the New England preacher himself. Certainly he would have acknowledged that such 'literary devices' and 'stylistic techniques' are not unimportant in the preaching of God's word. It is crucial to note that Edwards did not neglect language; he did not, as a preacher, despise rhetoric or neglect the use of means. Indeed, his use of means is very considerable and his rhetorical skills have been, historically, much neglected. But the crucial question is this: can 'imagery, metaphor, repetition, and allusion' raise sinners from the dead? Can such things sanctify the people of God? Can they revive God's work in the midst of the years? Are 'literary devices', 'stylistic techniques', and 'colloquial immediacy' sufficient to accomplish such things? The very posing of the question reveals the answer. Thus the Yale editors often betray a distinctly naturalistic interpretation of the phenomena witnessed under Edwards' preaching ministry. McClymond is, we believe, correct when he alleges that modern Edwardsean scholarship is often characterized by a decontextualizing and a detheologizing of Edwards' ideas: 'Following Miller's lead, much of the recent scholarship on Edwards tends toward a secularizing and naturalizing interpretation of his ideas.'[50] Thus Edwards' preaching is often reduced, McClymond contends, to 'rhetorical theory'.[51]

The problem is that rhetorical theory is utterly unable to account for Enfield; and it always will be unable to account for it. More precisely, the basic problem with the evaluations of Kimnach, Cady, Lemay, Stout, and Hatch is that, in a manner that is regrettably characteristic of this school of thought, there is, on their part, little or no overt recognition of the Spirit of God; there is little or no overt recognition either of his existence, his sovereignty, or his power.

[50] McClymond, p. 4.
[51] Ibid.

Such recognition is intrinsically Trinitarian; and non-recognition is, as Edwards himself insisted, intrinsically deistic. It must not be forgotten that, as Douglas J. Elwood insists, 'his whole theology stands out against all forms of deism.'[52] It is, therefore, one of the ironies of modern Edwardsean scholarship that the great anti-deistic American theologian of the eighteenth century should, in the twentieth and twenty-first centuries, have been subjected to an interpretation that, itself, smacks of what Marsden has termed 'quasi-Deism'.[53] Indeed, the consistent interpretation of the phenomenon of Jonathan Edwards himself and of the phenomenon of revival in the Great Awakening along essentially naturalistic, indeed reductionistic, lines is yet another example of what D. A. Carson has recently called 'the gagging of God'.[54] It is another example of that virtual elimination of the Spirit of God by which, regrettably, modern, academic literary critics and church historians are all too often characterized.

It is, therefore, of the utmost importance to note that Jonathan Edwards himself would have undoubtedly insisted that 'the prime source of power' was none other than the sovereign Spirit of God. Thus in focusing almost exclusively upon what Bebbington has aptly described as 'Edwards as a *littérateur*, a master of rhetoric and imagery',[55] the Yale editors have, we believe, seriously misdiagnosed

---

[52] Elwood, p. 9.

[53] Marsden, *Jonathan Edwards in the Twenty-First Century*, p. 155. 'In contrast to Edwards's view, quasi-Deism has prevailed in the modern world, once again even among many Christian believers. Our tendency is to think of the physical world as an independent entity run by the laws known by natural science.' Ibid. Marsden's focus here is not overtly upon the issue of the neglect of the Spirit of God, but his concept of 'quasi-Deism' can, we believe, be legitimately extended to the field of literary criticism in much modern Edwardsean scholarship.

[54] See D. A. Carson, *The Gagging of God: Christianity Confronts Pluralism* (Grand Rapids: Zondervan, 1996). In the course of this book Carson laments what he terms 'the loss of biblical outlook among Christian intellectuals' (Ibid., p. 483). 'In the main, they think like secularists.' Ibid. Carson refers specifically to Stout, Hatch, and Noll and contends that they have 'sold out to the regnant paradigms' (Ibid., p. 487). With regard to Stout's recent study of George Whitefield – *The Divine Dramatist: George Whitefield and the Rise of Modern Evangelicalism* (Grand Rapids: Eerdmans, 1991) – Carson notes 'its reductionistic stance' and observes that 'there is certainly no place for the Spirit of God . . . In short, the work is profoundly secular' (Ibid., p. 485).

[55] Bebbington, p. 193.

and mislocated the ultimate source of Edwards' power; they have thus seriously misinterpreted his methodology as a preacher. They have, whether wittingly or unwittingly, aligned themselves to some extent with the deistic tendencies of the very men that Edwards himself spent so much time and energy in the 1740's and 1750's opposing. It is, surely, manifestly obvious from the entire corpus of his writings that, whilst he did not for one moment eschew rhetoric and the valid use of means, his fundamental methodology in preaching was none other than the old Puritan methodology of the word *and* the Spirit. The *authority* was that of the word of God; the *power* was that of the Third Person of the Godhead.

28

JONATHAN EDWARDS TODAY

'President Edwards', observed Samuel Hopkins in 1765, 'was one of those men of whom it is not easy to speak with justice without seeming, at least, to border on the marvelous, and to incur the guilt of adulation.'[1] This assessment is understandable. The very tributes to Edwards' intellectual powers which this phenomenon of pioneer America has continued to elicit in the last two and a half centuries demonstrate the validity of the observation. Daniel Webster (1782–1852), the American lawyer, statesman, and orator, made this claim: '*The Freedom of the Will* by Mr Edwards is the greatest achievement of the human intellect.'[2] John ('Rabbi') Duncan (1796-1870), Professor of Hebrew and Oriental Languages in the Free Church College, Edinburgh, described Edwards as 'the greatest intellect since Aristotle.'[3] Kimnach has recently conjectured that if, instead of entering the ministry, Edwards had followed his early aspirations of writing a great treatise that would '"put every man clean out of conceit with his imagination"', he might well have enjoyed 'an academic career and perhaps an international eminence comparable to that of Locke or Newton'.[4]

Justice does indeed require that due tribute be paid to the extraordinary gifts of the New England preacher. But justice also requires

---

[1] Cited *Works*, 1:1.

[2] Cited A. E. Winship, *Jukes-Edwards: A Study in Education and Heredity* (Harrisburg, Pa.: R. L. Myers & Co., 1900), p. 17.

[3] David Brown, *The Life of Rabbi Duncan* (1872; reprint, Glasgow: Free Presbyterian Publications, 1986), p. 276.

[4] *Works*, 25:42.

that any faults or flaws in 'this great and good man',[5] as Archibald Alexander described him, be exposed. The problem here is that the very brilliance of his gifts is liable to blind us to the presence of certain faults and flaws, or at least to tempt us to turn a blind eye to them. We thus excuse them or even ignore them precisely on the grounds of his unquestionable greatness. Edwards is such a towering figure in both ecclesiastical and intellectual history that there is a temptation to isolate him from his own immediate context, namely, that of pastor to the people of Northampton; indeed, his sermons and his treatises are so impressive and have been such a blessing to the church since his times that we are inclined to forget, as perhaps he did, his wider pastoral responsibilities to the people of that town.

'We do not regard President Edwards as infallible',[6] remarked Dabney wisely in the context of a certain controversy; nor (we might add) should we regard President Edwards as flawless. Obviously, any *overt* ascription to him of either infallibility or perfection would clearly be utterly unscriptural and totally contrary to 'the great Christian doctrine of original sin' which he so brilliantly defended. But any *tacit* ascription to him of either infallibility or perfection would surely be equally unscriptural. The danger of the latter is particularly subtle and is liable to occur by default. President Edwards is a figure of such colossal stature intellectually, theologically, philosophically, spiritually, and homiletically that there is a perhaps natural tendency in his admirers to shrink from sounding any note of criticism. In his Introduction to *Genius, Grief and Grace* (2001) Gaius Davies makes this general observation with regard to such reticence: 'We may find it upsetting that such heroic figures were flawed. We may be willing to admit privately that our leading characters have feet of clay. It is another thing for it to be made public, discussed freely, and for the larger-than-life figures thus, somehow, to be diminished.'[7] The danger inherent in such reticence or diffidence is, however, that of over-idealization and

---

[5] Archibald Alexander, *Thoughts on Religious Experience* (1844; reprint, Edinburgh: Banner of Truth, 1978), p. 67.

[6] Dabney, *Discussions*, 3:239.

[7] Gaius Davies, *Genius, Grief and Grace: A Doctor Looks at Suffering and Success* (Fearn, Ross-shire: Christian Focus Publications, 2001), p. 9.

romanticization, the inevitable tendency of which is hagiographical. But this tendency must be resisted. Biographical perfectionism is surely particularly incongruous when it is presented in Reformed dress.

'Edwards had some tragic flaws that contributed to his undoing in Northampton,'[8] contends Marsden. Certainly, it must be insisted upon that, in the primary cause of his dismissal in 1750, namely, his stance with regard to the Lord's Supper, the Northampton minister was correct and that he was shabbily treated by both church and council in that controversy. Marsden acknowledges the centrality of this issue in his dismissal:

> Further, we must be reminded that Edwards' conflict with Northampton was . . . over the terms of admission to the sacraments. Without his clumsily managed reversal of direction on that subject, he would have remained pastor in Northampton. True, there were pent-up resentments that came pouring out when the occasion arose. Nonetheless, the question of admission to the sacraments was in itself a momentous issue, with potential to disrupt even a harmonious relationship between a pastor and a town.[9]

But were there not also secondary issues and secondary causes involved in his dismissal? Kimnach speculates that 'the issue of his adequacy in the pulpit during the last few years'[10] might have been a significant factor in his ultimate dismissal. We regard this as highly improbable. The problem with this hypothesis is that it is tantamount to suggesting that the preacher of the incomparable *Farewell Sermon* delivered in Northampton on July 1, 1750, was being dismissed from his pulpit *inter alia* for the poor quality of his somewhat more extemporaneous sermons of the previous eight or nine years! We suggest, however, that the issue of his adequacy *out of* the pulpit during his pastorate of twenty-three years might have been a significant factor in his ultimate dismissal. Samuel Hopkins makes the following observation: 'He did not make it his custom to visit his people in their own houses, unless he was sent for by the sick, or he heard that they were

---

[8] Marsden, *Edwards*, p. 370.
[9] Ibid.
[10] *Works*, 10:124 n.

under some special affliction.'[11] We recognize most readily that there is no radical disjunction between the homiletical and the pastoral. As Christ himself shows Peter, 'feeding his sheep' is not only powerfully pastoral, but the supreme manifestation of the pastoral. Yet the category of the pastoral clearly goes beyond the category of the homiletical. It involves, on the part of the pastor, a caring for the sheep that takes him outside of and beyond the confines of the study and of the pulpit and into the homes and lives of his people. Certainly, he was, as the awakening in 1734-1735 demonstrates, pastorally available; but he was not pastorally proactive. He did not, in general, visit the people in their homes; they had to visit him in his. This would inevitably tend to create the impression of a certain aloofness, a certain remoteness, and even a certain inaccessibility on his part. Herein lies, perhaps, the Achilles' heel of Edwards' ministry in Northampton: virtually the only time the people saw their minister was when he was in the pulpit.

Marsden highlights in particular Edwards' 'personal skills'. He notes that Edwards was 'much loved by those closest to him,'[12] that is, by his immediate family and a close circle of friends; but Marsden also notes that, earlier, at Yale, 'Jonathan appears to have had miserable relationships with his fellow students.'[13] He also draws attention to the fact that, at Northampton, Edwards demonstrates at times a certain tactlessness, a certain perfectionism, and an over-confidence in the power of logic to settle disputes.[14] Marsden further observes that 'his brittle, unsociable personality contributed to the breakdown of the once-warm relationship with the townspeople ... He was not able to build up the reserve of personal goodwill that more pastoral ministers enjoyed. Edwards was keenly aware of these failings, and as the disaster developed he suggested a number of times that he might not be suited for anything but writing.'[15] Paul Helm has expressed his concern over Edwards' personal skills even more pointedly: 'There is another plausible explan-

---

[11] Cited Iain H. Murray, *Jonathan Edwards: A New Biography* (Edinburgh: Banner of Truth, 1987), p. 183.

[12] Marsden, *Edwards*, p. 6.

[13] Ibid., p. 38.

[14] See ibid., pp. 344, 370, 349.

[15] Ibid., p. 349.

ation of Edwards' dismissal, that the people had by 1750 had more than enough of their pastor's aloof and austere ways and were glad to see the back of him.'[16]

Central in this matter of a perceived aloofness or remoteness on his part is the issue of his prodigious capacity for study. Edwards was, throughout his life, an indefatigable scholar. 'Edwards usually rose at four or five in the morning,' observes Marsden, 'in order to spend thirteen hours in his study.'[17] There can be no doubt that the major factor in this was his concern to redeem the time.[18] He was, by nature, an intellectual and a contemplative.[19] He was constantly reading, meditating, and writing. It is, however, common in evangelical and Reformed circles to regard this phenomenon of thirteen hours a day spent in study as an unmitigated virtue. Certainly this ministerial work ethic is a standing rebuke to the slothfulness with which the ministry is always potentially and often historically beset. But the question that must be considered is this: Was this healthy? Was it healthy for him personally? Was it healthy for his family? Was it healthy for the church in Northampton? Is Niebuhr's description of Edwards as 'this Protestant monastic'[20] entirely to his credit? Moreover, does this relentless, indefatigable pursuit of study perhaps reflect traits in his personality which have their origin in areas other than those which are purely intellectual and spiritual? Are there in this undeniably brilliant and godly man certain tendencies which are, perhaps, psychological

---

[16] Paul Helm, review of *Jonathan Edwards: A New Biography*, by Iain H. Murray, *Scottish Bulletin of Evangelical Theology* 6 (Spring 1988): 58.

[17] Marsden, *Edwards*, p. 133.

[18] In *The Preciousness of Time, and the Importance of Redeeming It*, preached in December 1734, the Northampton minister made this observation: 'Time is a talent given us by God; he hath set us our day; and it is not for nothing, our day was appointed for some work; therefore he will, at the day's end, call us to an account. We must give account to him of the improvement of all our time. We are God's servants; as a servant is accountable to his master, how he spends his time when he is sent forth to work, so are we accountable to God.' *Works* (Hickman), 2:235.

[19] Marsden points out that JE 'is sometimes most admired as a contemplative'. Marsden, *Edwards*, p. 1.

[20] Niebuhr, *Kingdom of God*, p. 136. 'No medieval monk or seeker of utopia kept the goal more constantly before his eyes or sought to advance toward it more strenuously than did this Protestant monastic.'

in nature? Edwards' finest biographer, Marsden, does not shrink from asserting that he was 'unsociable and sometimes depressive'[21] – that he was 'reclusive and somewhat obsessive.'[22] We are not suggesting that the phenomenon of Edwards' colossal work ethic is to be explained purely in terms of psychological tendencies or traits; the main factors in this were clearly intellectual and spiritual. But we are suggesting that, running parallel with and, indeed, coalescing and converging with these factors, are elements which are perhaps psychological in origin. Was there perhaps an element of escapism in the phenomenon of thirteen hours a day spent in study? It is evident that Edwards did not feel particularly comfortable in society; it is also evident that he felt very comfortable in the study.[23]

Let us suppose, for the sake of argument, that, for just two days in the week, he had spent eleven hours per day in study and two hours in visiting his flock – what might have been the result? What might have been the result for his physical and mental welfare and what might have been the result in terms of his relationships with the people of Northampton? It is conceivable that his voluminous *Miscellanies* might have suffered a little; but there is no reason why his sermons should have been adversely affected. Moreover, it is highly probable that he would have thus laid those foundations of mutual affection and good-will which are so essential in the ministry and which might conceivably have tipped the scale in his favour in the day of trouble. It is highly probable that his ministry as a whole would have been greatly enhanced and quite possible that the crisis of 1750 would have been averted. The problem is that the thirteen hours spent in study per day and its inevitable corollary – a lack of pastoral contact with the people – create

---

[21] Marsden, 'The Quest for the Historical Edwards: The Challenge of Biography,' in *Jonathan Edwards at Home and Abroad*, p. 5.

[22] Ibid.

[23] J. W. Alexander makes this observation concerning President Edwards' study habits: 'His stores of knowledge were treasured while he was at Northampton and Stockbridge; where, as a descendant related to me, he did not know his own cows, and was so stingy of his time, as to wait in his study till the very instant when dinner was served in the adjoining room, and always retired to his books the moment he had finished his sparing meal; a practice to be condemned without hesitation.' Alexander, p. 147.

what Marsden describes as 'the image of the withdrawn intellectual.'[24] Herein lies, surely, the Achilles' heel of his ministry. Indeed, we suggest that it was not his mind, nor his character, nor even his body, but perhaps his personality that constitutes his Achilles' heel. His mind was that of a genius; his character was saintly; his body was certainly frail; but his personality reveals certain traits and tendencies which need to be probed a little more searchingly than has sometimes been the case on the part of his admirers.

There is, admittedly, as Marsden alleges, a certain elusiveness about Edwards' personality. 'Complicating the search for his personality is the fact that one of his religious principles was that personality should not be important.'[25] Character was, for him, all-important; personality was unimportant. But is personality of no significance or relevance in the ministry? Edwards' letter to the trustees of the College of New Jersey, written from Stockbridge on October 19, 1757, is very significant with regard to this issue of his personality. In the course of the letter he explains his diffidence about accepting the position of president:

> The chief difficulty in my mind, in the way of accepting this important and arduous office, are these two: first my own defects, unfitting me for such an undertaking, many of which are generally known; besides other, which my own heart is conscious to. I have a constitution in many respects peculiar unhappy, attended with flaccid solids, vapid, sizy and scarce fluids, and a low tide of spirits; often occasioning a kind of childish weakness and contemptibleness of speech, presence, and demeanor; with a disagreeable dullness and stiffness, much unfitting me for conversation, but more especially for the government of a college.[26]

It is important to note that his obvious diffidence with regard to accepting the presidency may perhaps have led him to exaggerate somewhat his own defects in this letter; and his humility may well have reinforced this. Nevertheless, we should note here his obvious awareness of certain defects and also his frank acknowledgement of them. His

[24] Marsden, *Edwards*, p. 254.
[25] Marsden, 'Quest for the Historical Edwards', p. 4.
[26] *Works*, 16:726.

focus in these poignant, almost pathetic words is upon his constitution, by which he clearly means not merely his physical constitution, but
also his temperament and his personality.[27] We note here the marks of a
man who was clearly introverted rather than extraverted, clearly solitary
rather than gregarious, and clearly more suited to private than public
activity. He himself pinpoints here a tendency to depression, an unfit-
ness for conversation, a certain lack of presence, in short, a deficiency
in what we might call the area of social graces and general personable-
ness. Moreover, the question cannot be avoided: did he perhaps, at the
outset of his ministry, capitulate rather too readily and too easily to
what he perceived as his defects in this area? Might not his uneasiness
in conversation have been gradually overcome by dint of practice and
experience? Was he perhaps too reclusive, too solitary, too unsociable,
too much the withdrawn intellectual to be a good pastor? Whilst in
the 1740's he was, *via* his correspondence and his treatises, developing
his links with the transatlantic intellectual and clerical community, was
he perhaps at the same time failing to develop his links with his own
community in Northampton? It is doubtless the case that the traits
mentioned in the letter to the trustees were, in his mind, the *cause* of his
not mingling with his congregation during the week; but might they
not well have also been the *effect?* 'Much study is a weariness of the
flesh,' notes the Preacher in Ecclesiastes; and doubtless this preacher
experienced that weariness also, even though study was clearly his
delight. But what must be the toll of thirteen hours of intensive, isolated
study day after day upon the spirits of any man over the course of more
than forty years?

The phenomenon of thirteen hours spent in study every day exemplifies a trait in the Northampton divine to which Edwards scholars have

---

[27] Somewhat surprisingly Marsden limits the significance of these words to JE's health:
'The first was the matter of his physical health. He described his "peculiar unhappy" constitution in a way that suggests chronic poor digestion resulting in low spirits, "childish weakness
and contemptibleness of speech, presence, and demeanor; with a disagreeable dullness and
stiffness, much unfitting me for conversation, but more especially for the government of a
college."' Marsden, *Edwards*, p. 430. We feel that, whilst JE's words clearly relate to some
extent to his physical health, they also clearly relate to aspects of his personality.

often drawn attention, namely, his relentlessness.[28] There is a relentless quality to his study habits, treatises, and sermons. This very relentlessness reflects, of course, certain traits which are very much to his credit, namely, his voracious intellectual and spiritual appetite, his astonishing self-discipline, his unquestionable zeal, his rapier-like polemical skills, and his remarkable thoroughness in both exposition and application. But is there perhaps something excessive about this relentlessness? Kimnach has identified a quality in Edwards' *oeuvre* which he describes as 'pursuit':

> A quality of the spirit as much as the intellect, 'pursuit' is not a matter of brilliance, originality, or inspiration, though it obviously involves a considerable degree of highly disciplined imagination. Essentially, it is the tendency to explore an idea or experience, in all of its ramifications, through a process of extrapolation much more sustained than is usually appealing – or even bearable – to mere men.[29]

Indeed, this quality of 'pursuit' in his sermons could be defined not merely as 'the pursuit of an idea in all of its ramifications', but also as 'the pursuit of the hearer into all the recesses of his heart'. If the former is often found in his Doctrine, the latter is frequently found in his Application. This quality of pursuit is unquestionably a crucial aspect of his titanic strength – but sometimes a man's strength is also his weakness.

It is for this reason that the temptation to slavish imitation of Edwards must be resisted. This temptation is a particular danger with young, inexperienced ministers. The Reformed heritage is a glorious heritage and it has its own heroes of the faith. Edwards is is one of those heroes; indeed, he is one of the mightiest. Thus the danger exists that men entering the ministry might feel it incumbent upon them to spend thirteen hours (or some such figure) in the study each day. As a seminary professor I have, over the years, often warned students not to imitate Edwards slavishly in this respect; indeed, I have expressed

---

[28] See, for instance, McClymond, p. 109.
[29] Kimnach, 'Brazen Trumpet', p. 39.

the view that, if they do, they will almost certainly run into trouble, both with their wives and with their churches! Nevertheless, I have at the same time generally expressed the view that they ought to spend approximately half of that amount of time in study each day. Sometimes it will be less than half and sometimes it may be more. It is essential that ministers of the gospel give themselves to study if they are to sustain an edifying, profitable ministry. Moreover, in an age in which the study is being replaced by the office, it is essential that ministers spend this time, not just in the study, but in study!

Similarly, I have often advised students not to follow Edwards in the matter of visitation. It is essential that pastors visit their people in their homes. Pastoral availability and accessibility, although very important, are not, in themselves, sufficient. The sick, the dying, and the bereaved need to be visited; those in trouble of any kind need to be visited; and the rest of the flock need to receive occasional visits even when there is no obvious immediate need. Moreover, if this duty is undertaken wisely and strategically there is no reason why it should undermine the priority of the pulpit; indeed, it ought to complement, reinforce, and enhance the ministry of the pulpit. The recluse does not generally make a good pastor.

Thus it should never be forgotten that both the word of God and the history of the church of Christ demonstrate that the greatest and the godliest of men have their faults and flaws. Edwards is no exception in this matter – he has his feet of clay. Yet that, significantly, is precisely the point that the Apostle is concerned to make with regard to God's servants in general: 'But we have this treasure in earthen vessels, that the excellency of the power may be of God, and not of us.' It was the manner of men in former times to place the most priceless treasure in jars of clay that were flawed and marred. Similarly, it is God's manner to place the priceless treasure of the gospel in fragile, brittle human vessels. God's purpose in this is that 'the excellency of the power', or (as the original literally suggests) that 'the hyperbole of the dynamic', might be manifestly evidenced to be of God. This great evangelical principle is powerfully demonstrated by the life and ministry of the great eighteenth-century New England preacher-theologian. The dynamic operating here is particularly fascinating. It is a dynamic that involves not only the power of God and the weakness of man; it also involves within the man himself tremendous powers and remarkable weaknesses. Within a frail, fragile body and a somewhat brittle personality lay the treasure of the gospel of Christ – a gospel that was, in his case, filtered through a mind and a soul of stratospheric proportions. There is in this great servant of God a striking contrast, in certain respects, between the vessel and the treasure – a striking juxtaposition of physical and personal frailty on the one hand and intellectual and spiritual power on the other. It is surely incontrovertible, however, that, although there is, in certain areas, evidence of frailty and imbalance in the eighteenth-century New England divine, Edwards was mightily used by God, and that, in the sovereign compensations of God, his very frailty and imbalance in these areas were not only significantly overruled, but even utilized for the greater good of the church at large, both then and since.

It is equally incontrovertible that there is a quite extraordinary power about Edwards' greatest sermons. His essential textual fidelity; his measured contextual Introductions; the judicious, nuanced, incremental development of his thought; the rich instructiveness of his sermons; their strong doctrinal and theological content; his powerful theocentricity and Christocentricity; his ability to convey a sense of the magnificence of God and a sense of the beauty of Christ; his remarkable knowledge of and marshalling of the Scriptures; his formidable logical powers; his excellent use of contrast; his striking use of imagery; his moderate, suitable use of illustration; the cogent polemical element in his preaching; his compelling, masterly Applications; their searching, awakening character; his power of specification; the winsome, wooing note in his evangelistic appeals; his powerful hortatory Conclusions; the balance between the doctrinal, the experimental, and the practical; the movement and point in his sermons; his sometimes mesmerizing use of language; the sheer persuasiveness of his preaching; the striking unity of his sermons; his ability to combine great profundity of thought with great simplicity of expression; his versatility and adaptability as a preacher; the spiritual, heavenly tone of his sermons; the blazing holiness of the preacher himself; and the blessing of the Spirit of God upon him – these constitute the complex of factors which, conjointly, contribute to the power of his sermons and to his unquestionable greatness as a preacher.

Once every few centuries there appears in the celestial sphere the phenomenon of a *supernova*. The lesser phenomenon of a *nova* is, of course, itself spectacular. The *nova* – the very term suggests that which is new – is a star, previously invisible on account of distance, which suddenly and dramatically flares and blazes into brilliance. It involves a tremendous explosion of light that results in a 70,000- or 80,000-fold increase in luminosity. Such *novae* are not uncommon. But the much rarer phenomenon of the *supernova* is even more spectacular. The distinguished British astronomer, Patrick Moore, notes that 'at maximum a supernova may shine as brightly as all the other stars in its system put together. In our own galaxy, the most famous supernova on record is that of 1572. It lay in Cassiopeia, and at its brightest was more brilliant than Venus, so that it remained visible in broad daylight.'[30] The astronomical sphere is analogous here to the ecclesiastical sphere. Once every few centuries the great God of heaven raises up in the church of Christ a man, the sheer brilliance of whose gifts appears to surpass all the light of all his immediate predecessors, contemporaries, and successors combined. Augustine, Martin Luther, John Calvin, John Owen, Daniel Rowlands, George Whitefield, C. H. Spurgeon, Martyn Lloyd-Jones – these men were *supernovae* in the theological or homiletical realm. But there is another man, who, in contrast to all of these, hails not from Europe or the Mediterranean Basin, but, astonishingly, from pioneer America, and whose gifts, both in the theological and homiletical realm, place him in the same galaxy of great men. It is, therefore, we feel, no exaggeration to say that, by the endowment of God in creation, in providence, and in redemption, Jonathan Edwards was an intellectual, theological, philosophical, spiritual, and homiletical *supernova*, the brilliance of whose light still continues to illuminate and bless those that will sit at his feet two and a half centuries later.

---

[30] Patrick Moore, *The Amateur Astronomer* (Guildford and London: Lutterworth Press, 1978), p. 189.

INDEX OF SCRIPTURE
REFERENCES

OLD TESTAMENT

An idealized impression of Northampton below Meetinghouse Hill.